Flattop Fighting
in World War II

Flattop Fighting in World War II

The Battles Between American and Japanese Aircraft Carriers

by PATRICK DEGAN

McFarland & Company, Inc., Publishers
Jefferson, North Carolina, and London

LIBRARY OF CONGRESS CATALOGUING-IN-PUBLICATION DATA

Degan, Patrick.
    Flattop fighting in World War II : the battles between
American and Japanese aircraft carriers / by Patrick Degan.
        p.   cm.
    Includes bibliographical references and index.

    ISBN 0-7864-1451-0 (softcover : 50# alkaline paper)

    1. World War, 1939–1945 — Campaigns— Pacific Area.
    2. World War, 1939–1945 — Naval operations, American.
    3. World War, 1939–1945 — Naval operations, Japanese.
    4. Aircraft carriers— United States— History — 20th century.
    5. Aircraft carriers— Japan — History — 20th century.
    6. World War, 1939–1945 — Aerial operations, American.
    7. World War, 1939–1945 — Aerial operations, Japanese.
    I. Title.
    D773.D44   2003
    940.54'25 — dc21   2003001318

British Library cataloguing data are available

Cover photographs: Aircraft from the Third Fleet, September 1945
(National Archives 80-G-421130); Task Group 38.3 at sea, December
1944 (Corbis Images)

Manufactured in the United States of America

McFarland & Company, Inc., Publishers
  Box 611, Jefferson, North Carolina 28640
  www.mcfarlandpub.com

Contents

Preface

After the end of the American Civil War Private Sam Watkins, late of Company H of the Confederate Army of Tennessee, undertook, in 1866, to write his own history of the great conflict on the claim that he was every bit as qualified to write a history as the generals and scholars. His was not a claim of ego or an attempt to dismiss the works of professional scholars and military experts but merely an observation that the common man is capable of observation, discernment, and the capacity to report honestly and accurately the events which helped shape the destinies of men and nations. In large measure, that is the essence of what it means to be an historian. And in one area, both share one quality that binds all historians—amateur and professional—and that is a passion for the past in general and of that particular aspect of the human legacy which is their own special object of study (or obsession, depending upon your point of view).

Nearly two and a half years after wrapping the manuscript to this book, my editors asked me to draft a preface for it; an explanation as to how I arrived at the point of tackling this project in the first place and how my particular approach was decided. It is, perhaps, an inevitable and necessary requirement if the reader turning these pages is to accept the fidelity to the truth of the work he is being asked to devote his time and mental energy to in the reading.

This project was the end product of a particular lifelong passion. For a first book, I had undertaken quite a challenge. However, the first work any new author undertakes is always the inevitable product of personal obsession, more than any subsequent project that writer will ever embark upon, and as such it is the one book which demands to be written first, before any other work is ever attempted.

Having been a child of the postwar baby boom, naturally, I grew up with family who were veterans of the Second World War, including a father and an uncle who were destroyer crewmen in the Pacific Theatre. Stories of their experiences, documentaries of the conflict, and books of the war, including a yellowing copy of the U.S. Navy's Bluejackets' Manual for 1944 issued to my father upon his entry into basic training, would fill my young head in lieu of traditional childrens' stories and literature (though not completely, of course).

Growing up, I always checked out library books about the war, particularly of the war against Japan; my understanding gradually maturing along with my own developing intellect. And from that beginning there also spawned a general interest in American and naval history, as well as interests in aviation and war which blossomed into that lifelong obsession with the past and the struggles of Americans to define what America stood for as a nation, both in terms of its ideals and in its determination to survive the challenges of its various enemies over two hundred years. During the course of my life, I gradually collected war histories and books on military subjects touching upon the weapons of war, tactics and battles, and the generals and admirals who led men into the field. But if I had to pick two authors who had the greatest influence upon shaping my understanding of history, then without hesitation I would have to name Bruce Catton and James Jones. Catton's ability to render the Civil War as a living story defined for me the ideal approach to making history a living thing in the mind and not just a dry recitation of fact. James Jones, best known for his World War II novel *From Here to Eternity*, brought the novelist's sensibility to the telling of history by rendering the perspective of the common soldier and thus made the war a personal thing for me as I read his words and absorbed them into memory.

When the Ken Burns documentary series *The Civil War* premiered on PBS back in 1989, it quickly and unexpectedly became the single highest-rated documentary ever aired on public television. It drew in an audience of millions of people who hadn't opened a history book since leaving high school. Reflecting upon the sudden popularity of the Civil War, it struck me then that so many people watching the series had, before that point, probably never had any interest in history to speak of, and I thought of friends and acquaintances who had little interest if not actually an active dislike of the subject. It occurred to me that a large part of this attitude stems from the approach that is taken to historical education in schools; of rote memorization of facts, dates, battles, politicians, and generals. History is not made to live in the minds of most people in this culture. Instead, it is drilled. This is destructive to anyone's passion for learning in any subject, but when it comes to historical education, rote drilling is especially corrosive. History is, after all, in its essence a story. The true story of man on this planet, the creation of this civilization out of struggle and trial and blood; an agonizing crawl through six thousand years groping for certain truths upon which justice, culture, and human freedom are built. Just as no individual can ever be truly complete without memory, no society can be complete without a sense of its own past.

The concept of living history determined the approach I took in writing *Flattop Fighting in World War II*. It was also the culmination of a lifelong obssession which expressed itself in the amassing of a large personal library and a driving urge that commanded my every attention and energies for the whole of the year spent at the keyboard of my personal computer. If this book succeeds in making the story of the war in the Pacific more than just a dry recitation of fact, of making the war came alive for the reader, then it has fulfilled its purpose. Whether it has indeed done so is for you, the reader, to judge.

— Patrick Degan
New Orleans
March 2003

Introduction

The subject of this book is the naval war against Japan, 1941–1945. It does not cover every detail of the campaign across the Pacific or every battle fought on every island, or any of the fighting which took place in China, Burma or on the Indian frontier. The entire focus is on the clash between the U.S. Pacific Fleet and the Imperial Japanese Navy in the course of four years of warfare. Only where the land and sea fighting were inextricably intertwined, such as in the Guadalcanal campaign, does this narrative detail combat between ground forces. It is the story of the clash between great fleets, of struggle against lopsided odds, of the introduction of new technologies and the evolution of a whole new paradigm of at-sea warfare and the horrendous cost imposed by admirals who failed to make the conceptual leap soon enough and sent seamen to their deaths by the hundreds and even thousands as a result.

This was a war in which the battleship became obsolete — when gunpower ceased to be the measure of naval strength as it had been for nearly four centuries. It was the first war in which two battlefleets clashed entirely with aircraft, without ever once seeing each other. It was a war whose entire course was decided by one key battle, in which the fleet with overwhelming numerical superiority was forced to turn back because its airpower had been destroyed. It was a war in which, in its single greatest battle between two roughly equivalent fleets, the victory came to the side which had virtually annihilated the other's aircraft. And it was a war in which, at the end, one navy barely 150 years old had grown to proportions never before seen on the oceans of the world, while the other was obliterated.

The Pacific War is the definitive conflict of the modern naval era, much as the Napoleonic Wars were the hallmark struggle of the Age of Sail. This war was defined by the aircraft carrier, the single most offensive platform ever devised by man. The idea of a ship which would bring armed aircraft into battle, striking at fleets and ground targets hundreds of miles away, represented a conceptual leap as profound as the ironclad warship

5

or even the steam engine. Yet at the outset of the war there were admirals in most of the world's navies who still placed their faith in the power of the dreadnought battleship. The Pacific War brutally ended that illusion in only two years and forever altered the character of naval warfare, as not even the ironclad or the steam engine had. The United States' status as a superpower is due in part to the incredible ability to project offensive striking power for hundreds of miles, which only the aircraft carrier can provide for a fleet.

It was also, in large measure, a war which fit perfectly the military character of this nation. The United States was bound to base its own protection on sea power from the earliest days of the republic. The United States definitively established its right to exist by wielding sea power to maximum effectiveness—even in a time when its fledgling navy was heavily outmatched by the superpowers of the day, Britain and France. The navy has always been the key to America's defense, given that our continent's natural protection against invasion is the oceans that surround it. When President Theodore Roosevelt sought to signal to the world the arrival of the United States upon the international stage as a power in its own right, he did so by sending a newly built fleet of battleships on a world cruise. The voyage of the Great White Fleet was the ultimate result of a book by Captain Alfred Thayer Mahan, in which he outlined basic but undeniable observations of how nations became regional and ultimately international powers by wielding a strong and effective navy. The rise of the United States as a superpower is attributable, far more than the atomic bomb, to the evolution of her navy and its effective deployment in two world wars and a cold war which has only recently ended. The bulwark of that force, the aircraft carrier, established itself in the ultimate test of fire, a world war.

The admirals of both the United States and Japan contested on a chessboard of some thirty million square miles. Men of the caliber of Chester Nimitz, Isoroku Yamamoto, Marc Mitscher and Raizo Tanaka are rightly counted among the ranks of history's most brilliant military commanders for having applied themselves upon such a vast field, with its constantly changing and often unpredictable conditions. A naval war is the most difficult to prosecute, particularly over the stretch of oceans, and a fleet commander finds himself battling not only his immediate enemy but nature itself. A World War II admiral had no more control over his battlefield than any admiral under Nelson ever enjoyed. And the advent of the airplane, the submarine, radar, and codebreaking brought such fundamental alterations in the character of naval warfare that victory or defeat turned on the ability to adapt to changing circumstances faster than one's enemy. In the battle for control of the Pacific Ocean, tactical talent, adaptability and detailed information-gathering, far more than raw air or gunpower, proved the determiners of victory in a war where battles were won or lost before a single ship in either fleet weighed anchor.

The story of the Pacific War is also that of a contest between two industrial machines racing to outproduce the other, not only to replace combat losses but to build and supply the larger warfleet. In this, the United States proved the vastly superior power. But without the capability to exploit its navy to maximum effect, the United States would have faced a longer and bloodier war than the one it fought. In no other war did the outcome so completely depend on both strategic ability and technology over and above sheer brute force. Therefore, the Pacific War is a study not only of tactics and firepower, but of the men who wielded the weapons of war at their command, where they succeeded and failed, and how they met this ultimate challenge of their lives, in the vast and unforgiving arena of the sea.

Finally, a word about the style of this narrative.

From our perspective, it is easy to determine with a half-century's worth of hindsight that the Japanese really could not have won the war. Their dearth of resources, the rampant disorganization in their highest command levels, and the logistical nightmares of attempting to fight a war on five fronts simultaneously would have rendered the Imperial military incapable, for example, of successfully prosecuting a conquest of Midway Island, much less Hawaii. Even if we had lost at Midway, they would not have succeeded in holding the island in the long term and eventually the weight of American industrial superiority would have crushed the Imperial Navy and taken us right to Japan's front doorstep. However, it certainly did not seem that way to Imperial officers who planned the war against the United States perfectly convinced that a crushing enough victory would compel America to accept peace on Japanese terms. And it certainly did not seem that way to American officers who faced a very bleak war and, from their perspective, the very real possibility of defeat. Pearl Harbor was a massively demoralizing event at the time it occurred; we had no Pacific Fleet after December 7 and Hawaiian civilian and military personnel braced themselves for an inevitable invasion. Guadalcanal, to both sides, became a black hole in which men were tossed to their deaths in an interminable struggle which seemed to have no end. And soldiers, seamen, and Marines who had survived four years of battlefield horrors were, upon being assigned to the invasion of Japan, reckoning themselves as dead men right up to the moment Hiroshima disappeared in a blinding flash. This narrative takes its perspective in that spirit.

Nomenclature

During the Second World War, vessels of the United States Navy used a ship nomenclature system which was solidly observed, with few exceptions, in the commissioning of warships.

Aircraft Carriers, both Heavy Fleet type (CV) and Light (CVL), were named for historical naval vessels (e.g., *Enterprise, Lexington, Essex, Intrepid*) or battles in U.S. history (*Saratoga, Bunker Hill, Ticonderoga, Princeton, Cowpens, Monterey*), while Escort Carriers (CVE) were invariably named for bays, sounds, and islands (*Long Island, Guadalcanal, Savo, Commencement Bay, Leyte, Kalinin Bay*). Battleships (BB) were named for states of the union (e.g., *Arizona, Missouri, South Dakota*), while Battlecruisers (CB) were named for then-territories (e.g., *Alaska*). Cruisers, both Heavy (CA) and Light (CL) were named for cities (*Baltimore, Cleveland, San Francisco, Helena, Raleigh, Juneau, New Orleans, Nashville*). Destroyers (DD), Destroyer Escorts (DE) and Destroyer Minesweepers (DMS — being essentially destroyers fitted for minesweeping duties) honored previous members of the armed services (*Fletcher, Balch, Hamman, Meade, Gridley, Aaron Ward*). Submarines (SS), except pre-war boats which were simply given alpha-numeric designations (the S-class), were all named for fish and marine creatures (e.g., *Tench, Gato, Nautilus, Archerfish, Skate, Seadragon*).

As for other ship types, Minesweepers and Submarine Rescue Vessels were named for birds, Submarine Tenders for pioneers in submarine development, Oilers after rivers, Cargo and Stores ships after stars, and Ammunition Ships after volcanoes and explosive chemicals. Seaplane Tenders were also named for sounds and bays. Attack Cargo vessels and Attack Transport ships were named for counties, Destroyer Tenders after natural geographical features (such as mountains), Transports after flag officers of the Navy and Marine Corps, Coastal Minesweepers after abstract qualities, Ocean-going Tugs after Indian tribes and Harbor Tugs after Indian words.

In the Imperial Japanese Navy, the ship nomenclature system was reflective of their culture.

Aircraft Carriers of all types were named for dragons and birds (e.g., *Akagi*, *Shokaku*—which translated as "Flying Crane"). Battleships were named for ancient provinces (*Yamato*, *Nagato*, *Fuso*, *Yamashiro*). First Class Cruisers were named for mountains (*Atago*, *Haguro*, *Sendai*), while Second Class Cruisers were named for rivers (e.g., *Yubari*, *Tenryu*, *Isuzu*). First Class Destroyers were named for poetic meteorological terms (*Kamikaze* ["divine wind"], *Yukaze* ["evening breeze"]) or poetically rendered months of the year (*Yayoi* [January], *Minaduki* [April]), while Second Class Destroyers were named for trees, flowers, and fruits, and Torpedo Boats for birds. Submarines had only alpha-numeric designations attached to them, regardless of type or class.

CHAPTER 1

Overture

Pacific

It is the greatest of the world's oceans. First discovered by Vasco de Balboa in 1510 during his exploration of the Isthmus of Panama, he named it upon first sight for the spirit of peace. It occupies an area of over fifty million square miles, contains within its vast expanse numerous island archipelagos, eight time zones, a continent, and tropical and arctic zones, and is bounded by the extreme frontiers of two different worlds. Within its space lies the demarcation known as the International Date Line, where one day is separated by another, but its expanse would come to represent a demarcation between two wholly separate and alien cultures. Across the ocean, the conception of East and West blurs, and within that uncertainty would lay the ground upon which these alien cultures would ultimately and tragically clash in a war to decide whether the principle of freedom or the principle of militarism would rule. The Chinese philosopher Lao-Tse observed that the journey of a thousand miles begins with a single step. That step would be taken some 340 years after Balboa's discovery, when the explorers of a brash new nation crossed the distance in space and time to encounter the people of an old nation and a very different world from any they had ever known.

The year was 1853. For slightly over two hundred years, the ancient kingdom of Japan had existed in virtually total isolation from the rest of the world. Catholic missionaries from Spain and Portugal had first established settlements in the Land of the Yamato in the sixteenth century, during the period of Japan's civil wars, in which rival daimÿo fought one another to claim the Shogunate, the supreme authority of the land. Ultimately, after years of bitter and bloody warfare, Ieyasu Tokugawa crushed his rivals and established his dynasty in 1603. His successors in the next thirty years would steadily and inexorably drive Christianity from the land (in part due to the fact that Catholic samurai had fought for Tokugawa's rivals in the wars) as an unwanted alien influence, until the policy culminated in a wholesale pogrom and the promulgation of the *sakoku*—the closing of the country to the outside world. Western outsiders—*gaijin*—were forbidden to live within the territory of the Home Islands, save for a single trading enclave administered by the Dutch which would be located in the port city of Nagasaki, on the southernmost Home Island of Kyushu. Any *gaijin* found at liberty in the land thereafter would be put to death. Christianity was forbidden and its practitioners forced upon pain of death to renounce the alien faith or leave the country. The types and amounts of outside trade goods were severely restricted and no Japanese was allowed to venture outside the country or have contact with *gaijin*, save for those at Nagasaki. Western technology was forbidden, particularly gunpowder. Tradition and the religions of Buddhism, Confucianism, and Shinto would be rigidly enforced, as would the feudal system on which Japanese culture had been based for centuries. Power would rest with the samurai class and the noble houses as always, and in such a state would Japan rest, peacefully and blissfully ignorant of what was happening in the outside world. In the intervening years, the Tokugawas would transform Japan into a perfect little bubble-world in which time would stand still and Order, that supreme imperative of Oriental culture, would endure. It was a state of existence which would inevitably fall. And fall it did, in very dramatic fashion.

The fisher-folk of Edo prepared their boats and tended their nets as they had always done when, on the morning of what the rest of the world reckoned as July 8, 1853, several large, black shapes entered the bay. Two of the shapes very evidently were ships of some sort but were far larger than even the largest of the Emperor's war junks—and rising from them were great columns of thick, black smoke. Hundreds lined up at the shore to watch in amazement as the "burning ships" paraded around the bay in line formation and eventually anchored themselves in the late afternoon hours to run out their guns. The black ships, which flew a flag of thirteen red-and-white stripes and a blue field with 31 stars, were the vessels of a brash young nation which had been independent for only a mere seventy years and yet had already extended itself from ocean to ocean and was now sowing its oats upon the world stage. The United States of America.

The U.S. Naval flotilla was formally designated as the Japan Expedition and consisted of two state-of-the-art sidewheel steam frigates, the USS *Susquehanna* and USS *Mississippi*, and two sail sloops-of-war, the USS *Plymouth* and USS *Saratoga*. Commanding the force was the 59 year old Matthew Calbraith Perry. Brother of the famous Oliver Hazard Perry, the Great Lakes Hero of the War of 1812, Perry's mission was to open diplomatic relations with the Empire of Japan, secure a treaty port and coaling

station to facilitate the young nation's budding Far East trade and its growing steam-powered fleet, and to secure the rights of shipwrecked seamen
who, heretofore, had been treated as felons and often mercilessly put to
death by torture. The British Empire and other European powers had
already established several trading ports in China. The United States, which
had also reached a trade agreement with China only a few years earlier,
was determined to be first in opening Japan to wider commerce. Perry
held the rank of Commodore, then the U.S. Navy's highest rank below that
of Flag Officer, and had been thoroughly briefed in his meetings with President Millard Fillmore and his diplomatic advisers of the sort of culture
he would be dealing with.

For six days, the ships held station under the shadow of Mt. Fuji, and
various sampans crewed by archers approached the *Susquehannah* with
peremptory orders for Perry's flotilla to remove itself to Nagasaki. The
self-styled "Commander-in-Chief, United States Naval Forces Stationed
in the East India, China, and Japan Seas" replied that he would blow out
of the water any war junk which approached his ships in a hostile posture
and demanded an audience with the Mikado himself.

News of the force of alien warships in the bay reached the Royal Court
in Edo. The nobles already knew of the Perry Expedition, having been
informed by the Dutch Consul as early as a year previous that the United
States had intended to send its own mission to Japan. But they were at a
loss as to what to do; they certainly did not have the military force to expel
them. Indeed, on that score, they may as well have been faced by invaders
from Mars. Offers to meet with a score of minor provincial officials were
promptly returned with rejections and reiterated that the commodore
would only meet with someone of high royal rank, as was befitting his station. This impressed the nobles in Edo sufficiently for them to offer a meeting with the Prince of Izu, the Emperor's chief councillor, protesting that
the Emperor could not meet with an outsider without risking a revolution. Perry agreed to the compromise and settled the terms for the audience. They would meet at a pavilion to be specially erected on the shore
at Kurihama, a village thirty miles south of Edo.

On July 16, Izu and an array of 5,000 soldiers and samurai were assembled to greet the landing of the American commodore. With a thirteen-gun
salute booming in the bay, fifteen boatloads of U.S. Marines, seamen, and
a Navy band escorted the barge carrying Commodore Perry. In full pomp
and majesty, Perry stepped upon the shore with his honor guard to the strains
of "Hail, Columbia" and with great formality presented to Izu a mahogany
casket bearing a letter from President Fillmore to the Emperor, conveying
the intentions of the Expedition to establish trade and full diplomatic

relations. Through interpreters, Perry announced his departure and intention to return the next year with a larger naval force behind him to open the negotiations, whereupon he and his landing party reassembled themselves on the boats and returned to the flotilla, which then weighed anchor and sailed away.

True to Perry's word, a far larger squadron of twenty-four vessels, again headed by the *Susquehanna* and with more steamers in formation, arrived in Edo Bay in February 1854. The Shogunate finally concluded that the only way to ensure peace was to concede to Perry's demands, or at least make the appearance of doing so to the commodore's satisfaction. Once again, the two sides would meet in a specially constructed pavilion, this time in Kanagawa, and assurances were granted that Perry would indeed be meeting with personages of royal rank with full authority to conduct the negotiations.

The Japanese thought to employ their traditional diplomacy of evasion, but Perry was more than equal to their game. Patiently, he rebuffed each of their "concessions" which failed to satisfy American aims but was never anything less than gracious toward his hosts. During the negotiations there followed an exchange of gifts. The Japanese envoys offered Perry a fine collection of lacquered furniture, bronze ornaments, and seashells— a gift which especially appealed to Perry as a conchologist. The commodore offered 100 guns, barrels of whisky, farm implements, clocks, stoves, a telegraph apparatus, and a miniature steam train complete with tender and track which were promptly assembled and displayed for the nobles. For the next six weeks, Perry and the Japanese slowly crafted the Treaty of Kanagawa, by which the Americans would have two ports opened to her shipping and diplomatic exchanges leading to full relations. Finally, the princes were unable to resist asking to ride on the miniature steam train. Courtiers found themselves whizzing around the circular track at a dizzying twenty miles per hour. Perry's dignity and the display of advanced American technology had won the day, and the Treaty was signed on March 31. Over the next six years, other European powers would negotiate for treaty ports and relations with Edo, and the United States pressed its case for full commercial relations, which the Shogunate finally agreed to in 1860.

Shortly thereafter, the American Civil War markedly reduced America's presence in the Far East. But the effects of Perry's mission had begun to work changes in the fabric of Japanese society which could not be reversed, though the Shogunate would try their level best to restrict these changes which would follow in the wake of the growing intercourse with the outside world. This resulted in some reactionary episodes by shoguns determined to drive the barbarian *gaijin* out. When America became embroiled in its internal troubles, the British moved in and forged treaties establishing a Japanese-British silk trade on very unequal terms. The princes of Choshu and Kagoshima initiated a rebellion against the treaties, refusing to enforce rights granted to British, French, and Dutch missions, and used their tiny naval forces to blockade ports and attack merchant vessels. On June 25, 1863, an American steamer, the *Pembroke*, anchored for the night in the Shimonoseki Strait, whereupon she was attacked by what appeared to be a European bark but flying a square flag "with a white ground with a red ball in the center."

Captain David McDougal, in command of the six-gun steam sloop USS *Wyoming*, was in hot pursuit of the Confederate commerce-raiding cruiser CSS *Alabama* and had stopped in Yokohama to top-off her coal bunkers to keep up the chase when news of the incident reached American Minister to Japan Robert S. Pruyn. Determined to punish the outrage against an American vessel and American citizens, Pruyn wired McDougal with full details of the incident and charged him with the responsibility to enforce the safety of American nationals and to execute prompt retaliation against the outlaw shogun.

McDougal weighed anchor on July 10 and set off for the island of Hare Shima, where he anchored until he had a favorable tide to begin his sortie. Six days later, at dawn with the sun rising behind him, McDougal set his ship steaming at maximum headway, 7 knots, and entered the Shimonoseki Strait. Running the powerful shore batteries, McDougal returned fire in full measure with the enemy until he rounded the headlands and sighted the village of Shimonoseki. Anchored there was a motley flotilla which represented Choshu's entire navy, the two-gun steam sloop *Sancfield*, the six-gun bark *Daniel Webster*, and the eight-gun brig *Lanrick*. The three vessels sported the rising sun banner and Choshu's personal standard, a blue flag with three white circles and a white bar above.

It was an uneven contest. Though McDougal's enemies outgunned him more than two-to-one, they were tactically inept. Choshu's ships offered a wide, inviting gap which the *Wyoming* sailed right through, closing to effective range with two ships in line while staying out of the range of the other on the opposing side of the gap. In so doing, while taking damage from 32-pound shot and at one point risking a grounding on the shallow sandbar in the harbor, which would have doomed her, the *Wyoming* shot up each "warship" in turn. The *Sancfield* slipped her mooring and charged out to challenge McDougal, but she was already damaged and the *Wyoming* simply waited for her to come forward, whereupon she fired a devastating four-gun broadside which included two smoothbore 11-inch.

Dahlgren naval rifles on pivot-mounts, the most advanced guns in service, and put several shots through the boiler. The burning and powerless *Sancfield* drifted into a line of junks anchored near the shore and exploded. On her way out of the harbor the *Wyoming* put more shot into the sinking *Lanrick* and pounded the *Daniel Webster* until she too began to take on water and settle. Choshu's fleet was completely destroyed and McDougal sailed past the burning shore batteries and back out into the China Sea, having won America's first naval engagement against the Empire of Japan in only an hour and ten minutes.

The Shogunate proved reluctant to enforce the treaties to the full and to challenge the local princes until British and French naval forces shelled Shimonoseki and Kagoshima in 1864. The resulting loss of face suffered by the Shogun inevitably led to his downfall, upon which there followed a full-scale civil war in 1867. The outcome of the War of the Restoration spelled the demise of the reactionary anti–Western Shogunate and the rise to power of one of the most significant figures in Japanese history, the Emperor Meiji. Meiji was a forward-looking monarch who was determined that Japan should enter the modern world and become like the "enlightened nations" of the West. Supported by the Genro Council, a cabal of loyalists and far-thinking reformers, the Shogunate was displaced in favor of a restoration of the authority of the Emperor. Over the succeeding years, this government gradually transformed itself into that of a constitutional monarchy on the British model, which included a full, democratically elected parliament, or Diet. As a concession to the traditionalists, the Emperor's status as a living god was codified into law even though his actual power in the government was purely formal, as according to the Western-style constitution the nation adopted for itself. The power of the samurai was greatly curtailed and a more formally structured army and navy were established. Finally, and most importantly, vastly increased trade and industrialization were encouraged and a Bank of Japan established in order to make Japan a commercial power. Japan also determined to make herself a modern military power, and began to purchase weapons and warships from Britain and invited the British to help organize and train her navy. Inevitably, this also would lead to aspirations of a colonial empire, as was the norm for the Enlightened West. Following in the 1880s and '90s, Meiji's expanding empire would add the Ryukyu and Bonin Islands, Hokkaido, and Formosa while winning the Kurile Islands through diplomacy with Imperial Russia. By the time Korea was fully annexed into the Japanese Empire in 1910, the Meiji Reforms had totally transformed a feudal state into a modern industrial and military power with a strong democratic government.

The cusp of the 20th century would prove an increasingly volatile time in which the established world order, forged so long ago by Prince Metternich after the destruction of Napoleon, would crumble until it collapsed completely into a maelstrom of violence which twice would engulf the entire world, and Japan was situated in one of the hottest spots imaginable. Her immediate next-door neighbor, China, was in a state of virtual anarchy. The Empress-Dowager sat on an increasingly rickety throne as the country divided up among rival warlords, anarchists, anti–Western reactionaries, and the competing claims of the European powers, and was riven with grinding poverty, ignorance, and desperation. The new Germany, which had forged itself out of the disparate kingdoms which had once comprised the old Holy Roman Empire, was also vigorously expanding her military and overseas empire to keep up with its rivals, the British — who in their own Houses of Parliament were debating whether maintaining a global empire was worth the expense. Imperial Russia was still clinging to its vast Eurasian empire and semifeudal social order, but was already suffering the initial strains of revolution. And in the United States, a single naval officer, Captain Alfred Thayer Mahan, noticed the degree to which neglect and a hidebound, top-heavy officer corps had virtually rotted the United States Navy to the point where America was no longer a significant player on the world stage.

Captain Mahan secured his appointment as head of the newly established Naval War College in 1884 and proceeded to both codify his observations of how a nation acquired and maintained international power and to train his students in his views. Mahan was one of the first voices in the United States to advocate a global Manifest Destiny, a view which was at that point rather unpopular in the traditionally isolationist nation, but as he would constantly reiterate to Congressional hearings in advocating more funding for the Navy, a strong fleet was "the midwife to commerce" — and that was a language they could understand. Ultimately, Mahan would assemble his observations into a coherent theory of how nations rose to global power status by maintaining and exercising warfleets upon the seas. This was a direct means of wielding military and diplomatic power thousands of miles from the homeland, expanding not only political but commercial power by the ability to protect seaborne trade and, when necessary, to wage and win wars. The theory also asserted that naval wars were won not by commerce raiding or blockading the enemy nation's ports, but only through the destruction of the enemy's warfleet.

Mahan's book, *The Influence of Sea Power Upon History*, touched off a revolution when first published in 1896 which reversed three decades of neglect in naval preparedness and development. The book came out at a time when American expansionists increasingly made their views public, appealing both to Americans' greed for more profit and their missionary sensibilities which compelled them to spread Christianity to every corner of the Earth. One of the most avid and enthusiastic readers of Captain Mahan's tome was the future Assistant Secretary of the Navy under President William McKinley, a robust, athletic, quick-tempered but intellectually gifted man who fully believed in the dream of an American empire, Theodore Roosevelt. Two years into McKinley's administration, Roosevelt would on his own authority dispatch the Asiatic Squadron to the Philippine Islands, then a possession of the decaying Spanish Empire, to stand by in the event of hostilities, a situation which was being brought about by deteriorating relations and the increasingly hysterical jingoism of the "yellow press"— most egregiously led by William Randolph Hearst. When the U.S. battleship *Maine*, visiting Havana harbor on February 18, 1898, suffered a mysterious explosion (which decades later was revealed by forensic examination of the wreck to have been a coal dust blast), the Hearst papers immediately declared that the Spaniards had sunk her with a mine. Public opinion ratcheted to fever pitch and the Congress declared war. Roosevelt's move had placed an American naval force in position to seize the Philippines before the Germans could, and now that war had broken out, the Asiatic Squadron charged right on in.

Commanding the somewhat modest force of five armored cruisers and four armored gunboats was Commodore George Dewey. He flew his flag on the *Olympia*, and was followed in the van by the *Baltimore*, *Boston*, *Raleigh*, *Concord*, *Petrel* and, bringing up the rear, the revenue cutter *McCulloch*. All in all, he had 33 guns at his disposal. Against him would be a roughly equal force in numbers but woefully inadequate quality. The only modern Spanish vessel in Manila Bay was an unseaworthy armored cruiser which was Spanish Admiral Patricio Montojo y Pasaron's flagship, the *Reina Cristina*. The rest of his force was a pathetic collection of 1100 ton cruisers and one wooden-hulled cruiser, the *Castilla*, along with a trio of tiny gunboats. They had only a third the firepower of Dewey's force.

Dewey's squadron entered Manila Bay at dawn on May 1. Coolly standing on the flying bridge and wearing his golfing cap, he turned to *Olympia*'s captain, George Gridley, and simply said, "You may fire when you are ready, Mr. Gridley."

The accuracy of the American fire was dreadful, which was why the battle took as long as it did, otherwise it would have been over in minutes. By the time Commodore Dewey's squadron had made its run through Manila Bay, the Spanish "fleet" had been annihilated utterly. Aware of the coming approach of one of the Kaiser's squadrons, Dewey landed his

Marines, promptly seized the Spanish colonial government in Manila, and waited until he could be reinforced by 11,000 additional troops preparing to debark from California. Victories on land and at sea in Cuba and the diplomatic backing of Britain and Japan secured America's incipient claim to the Philippines even after Vice Admiral Otto von Diederichs arrived on the scene several months later. The Kaiser would have to content himself with purchasing a Pacific colonial empire by buying the Caroline, Marshall, Mariana, and Palau Islands from a bankrupt and defeated Spain, which all but surrendered to the United States in the settlement of the Treaty of Paris of 1898, in which she also lost Cuba and Guam and thus one of the world's first colonial empires was no more. But the Philippines were the prize jewel in what became an undeclared American Empire. They offered American control of the Pacific trade routes and security to her shipping lanes to China and Japan, and a base from which to check Japanese power, which was already growing in the region. Dewey had won America's first Pacific War, and laid a stone on the pathway to another one in the future.

In that same year, the McKinley administration formally annexed the Hawaiian Islands. At one time an independent native kingdom, her rulers were overthrown in a coup d'état engineered by American mercenaries led by Sanford Dole back in 1893, but then President Grover Cleveland, uninterested in imperial ventures, refused petition after petition to name Hawaii as a protectorate, even going so far as to quash a bill to do so before it reached the floor of Congress. Five years later, with imperial sentiments rising, Hawaii became an American territory. It would prove a strategically useful addition to the American domains, because the central island in the archipelago, Oahu, featured a fan-shaped bay with a depth of forty feet and which was dominated by a central islet; ideal for a naval base. By 1905, construction began on facilities for Pearl Harbor.

In 1904, Czarist Russia, beginning to undergo the first stages of its collapse, made a move to expand its dominions through Manchuria by extending the Trans-Siberian Railway to Port Arthur, which had long been a Russian treaty port. The Japanese saw this as a direct threat to their own Manchurian and Korean interests. Backed by a naval alliance with Britain through which Japan was purchasing modern battleships and training her officers, and financial support by Wall Street bankers, Japan proceeded to expel the Russians from the region altogether. On February 4 of that year, she assembled a warfleet which without warning attacked and destroyed the Russian fleet at anchor in Port Arthur. Troops landed and seized the city, then proceeded to march up the Darien Peninsula to take Mukden in a very swift campaign which matched the new professionalism of Japan's modern-style army against the Russian forces, who were quickly routed. Seeking revenge, and with her imperial prestige on the line, Russia promptly dispatched the 46-ship Baltic Fleet on a cruise halfway around the world to destroy the Japanese fleet and retake Port Arthur. British intelligence kept the Japanese well informed of the enemy movements, and the Imperial Navy assembled every available heavy battleship and armored cruiser to meet the oncoming threat. It was a slowly oncoming threat, since the progress of Admiral Zinovi Rozhestvensky's battle force was hampered by first a shortage of coal which caused his fleet to linger for weeks in a Madagascar port until he simply bought several German colliers outright, and then by the insistence of High Command to attach to his force a squadron of obsolescent, underpowered gunboats. It took seven whole months for the Baltic Fleet to finally achieve a rendezvous in Cam Ranh Bay in French Indochina, allowed to them by their French allies. In all that time, the Japanese commander, Admiral Heihachiro Togo, a 58 year old veteran of the Sino-Japanese War of 1898 and honor graduate of Britain's Royal Naval College, was able to complete his preparations and the training of his crews to peak condition. He had overseen the building of a modern Imperial Navy with up-to-date warships incorporating the latest technology. Now, he deployed armed merchantmen equipped with wireless sets to alert him to the approach of the enemy. When their advance was sighted at last, Togo picked his battleground, the Strait of Tsushima, the passage between Japan and Korea.

Rozhestvensky made his approach to Tsushima through thick mists, while Togo's force cruised across the strait. The Russian admiral had an opportunity to bring his broadside to bear on Togo's fleet but seemed, at the moment of battle, to have been struck with a mental paralysis. The battle itself was a savage mêlée, in which both sides blazed away in a great display of firepower but to little effect, since accuracy on both sides was horrendous at long ranges. When the fleets closed to less than 5,000 yards, the Japanese employed high explosive shells, inflicting heavy casualties before switching to armor-piercing ordnance. The Russian fleet was simply cut to pieces, and an unconscious Rozhestvensky, injured early when his flagship *Suvoroff* was hulled and suffered the destruction of her steering control, was captured by the Japanese while being transferred by launch to another vessel. The *Oryol* was the only battleship still left afloat and the disorganized survivors broke off and made for neutral ports. The war was ultimately concluded by a peace treaty negotiated by President Theodore Roosevelt, for which he would be awarded the Nobel Peace Prize in 1905.

But the Japanese victory in the Russo-Japanese War marked a sea-change in American attitudes towards that nation. Viewed in 1904 as a protégé, her swift rise to empire was now viewed as a threat to American Pacific interests and her own Open Door policy in China. The swiftness by which her navy had built itself up was particularly alarming — especially with Japanese possessions in the Ryukyu and Bonin Islands and Formosa, which were proximate to the Philippines, logically the next object of imperial design. Roosevelt would thereupon do two things: lobby Congress for increased funding for the Navy, and cut orders for a grand review of the fleet's sixteen battleships, which would then set forth on a global cruise to signal to the world the arrival of the United States as a modern power.

The Great White Fleet — so named because the ships were intentionally painted white to signal that the cruise was primarily a diplomatic one (though President Roosevelt unsubtly hinted that should the sortie turn out otherwise, the officers would "know their responsibility") — set out from Hampton Roads, Virginia, on December 16, 1907, under the command of Admiral Robley D. Evans, a veteran of the Civil War. The fleet steamed out in a standard van formation led by the flagship *Connecticut* and proceeded southward to round the tip of South America (the Panama Canal had not yet been built) before heading northward to San Francisco, then west — for Tokyo (formerly Edo). The fleet finally arrived outside Tokyo Bay, was obliged to ride out a typhoon, and then sailed in on October 18, 1908. Admiral Evans and his officers were the honored guests of a reception given by the Emperor Meiji himself, which also included the already legendary Admiral Togo, who even participated in a blanket-tossing ritual with the Americans. Among the younger officers present at the reception were several ensigns named William Halsey, Ernest King, Raymond Spruance, and Chester Nimitz.

The Great White Fleet returned in triumph to Hampton Roads a month later. The entire world took note of the feat accomplished by the United States, which only two decades earlier had been utterly incapable of such an exercise. It was a startling display of American technology and the final shedding of isolationist thinking within the Navy, which that year officially struck the term "coastal defense battleship" from the lexicon. America's new, modern fleet was referred to as the Steel Navy. Yet, a month later, her brand new battleships, and every other battleship in the world, were instantly rendered obsolete by the commissioning of Britain's newest powerhouse, HMS *Dreadnought* — a larger, faster, more heavily armored and armed warship than had ever existed and the brainchild of Sir John Fisher. *Dreadnought* heralded a new phase in the evolution of the warship, so much so that her name became a synonym of the word battleship itself. All other warships would be judged by her standard. And yet, even as the *Dreadnought* was making her impact, and all other navies scrambled to build dreadnoughts of their own, her obsolesce and that of her descendants had already been written by two other individuals, though no one could have foreseen that in 1910. One was an inventor named John Holland, who in 1900 developed the first practical gasoline-electric propelled submarine, the USS *Holland*. The other was a civilian aviator named Eugene Ely. Ely, flying in a Curtiss biplane, did something which no one thought possible. His effort was at first dismissed as a stunt but would eventually rewrite all the rules of naval warfare, though even fewer people realized what his feats would represent than those who understood the implications of Holland's submarine. Ely gave a demonstration of flying his Curtiss off a short wooden deck erected on the stern of the armored cruiser *Birmingham*, and then gave an even more spectacular demonstration by landing on a wooden deck built onto the armored cruiser *Pennsylvania*, using a hook to snag wires across the deck to stop his flight. Nearly a decade would pass, however, before a British naval designer would make the conceptual leap and invent the aircraft carrier.

By 1920, the old world order was in total ruins. The Great War had demolished Europe and in the process destroyed eleven million lives to no purpose whatsoever. The victorious Allies took their revenge by dismembering the Austro-Hungarian Empire and stripping Germany of nearly everything she had, even virtually the means to live, by a peace so punitive that it guaranteed another war down the line. Japan, which had joined the war on the side of her ally Britain, enjoyed the spoils of victory by being granted a Mandate over the former German Pacific possessions of the Carolines, the Marshalls, the Marianas, and the Palaus, which doubled her own empire and cemented her place on the world stage. With the collapse of the Manchu Dynasty in China and the resultant state of anarchy and civil war, Japan would loom large in Asia — so much so that her militarists would increasingly vie for power over the more liberal elements in the government. Increasingly, she would be seen as a menace by the West.

The United States, under the presidency of Woodrow Wilson, had entered the Great War following the publication of the infamous Zimmerman Note, by which the Kaiser's government offered to support a Mexican reconquest of the southwestern United States — in order to ensure America being too preoccupied to intervene in Europe. The brash Yankee

Opposite: The Pacific Basin, 1931 — Control of the Pacific and Asia was divided amongst a host of colonial powers, including the United States and Japan, whose own holdings had been added to by grabbing German's former possessions in the Central Pacific and the conquest of Manchuria in 1931. The sun still never set on the British Empire, but she and the others powers were to be very soon eclipsed, violently, by the Rising Sun.

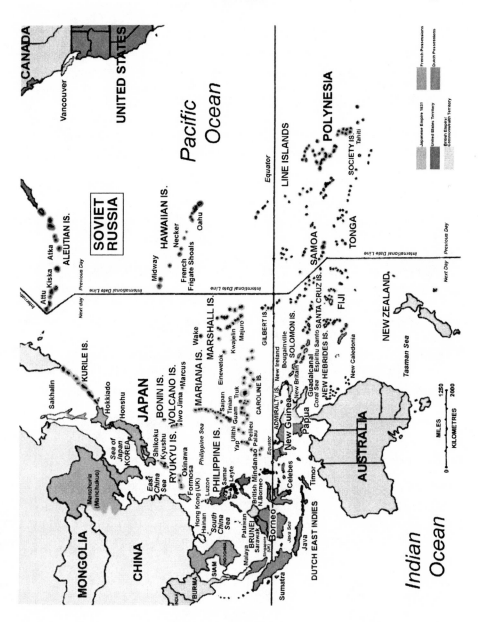

democracy had gone in eager for the fight under the banner of lofty ideals; of ending colonialism and creating a new world order based on democracy, self-determinism, and international law. The troops from America turned the tide for the Allies, who were on the edge of defeat in 1917 following the collapse of Imperial Russia into revolutionary chaos and consequent withdrawal from the war. But at Versailles, this was not enough to give President Wilson the high card at the peace table. The British and French perverted his Fourteen Points into the Versailles Treaty. In the wake of that, Wilson's effort to lobby for the treaty was doomed and his efforts to liken the result to his ideals seemed an exercise in lunacy. The United States Senate rejected the Versailles Treaty outright and in the end concluded a separate peace with Germany in 1919. Wilson collapsed with a stroke and lost the Presidency in 1920, and Congress rejected any participation in the world's first international body, the League of Nations. America would retreat back into isolationism for the next twenty years until dragged out of it by the degeneration of an unstable world into another and far more horrendous war.

As early as 1909, Theodore Roosevelt and Alfred Thayer Mahan foresaw an eventual war with the Empire of Japan. By the '20s, a cabal of naval planners conceived a strategic formulation known as War Plan Orange. Plan Orange assumed a war which began with a Japanese surprise attack, as they had done to the Russians at Port Arthur, and envisioned a long campaign across the Pacific Ocean in which the Pacific Fleet, setting out from its forward base at Pearl Harbor, would strike at the time and place of her choosing and spearhead a drive through the center of the Japanese domains. But increasingly, the aircraft carrier would bring a new element to the equation of Pacific strategy on both sides.

At the reception in Yokohama celebrating the negotiation of the Treaty of Kanagawa in 1854, one of the Emperor's court secretaries, having liberally sampled the sake, suddenly threw his arms around Commodore Perry and cried out joyously, "Nippon and America, all the same heart!"

As the ramshackle peace of the inter-war years deteriorated, that was no longer true. Especially as the calendar turned the page to the year 1941.

CHAPTER 2

Niitaka

The war between Japan and the United States began within the tranquil surroundings of a private tea garden in the precincts of a medium-sized port city on the southern tip of the Japanese home island of Honshu, a place known as Hiroshima. By one of the most savage ironies of history, it would end there, horribly, in a blast of atomic hellfire which ushered in a new and terrifying era undreamed of by all but a very few only five years earlier. It was certainly undreamed of in the mind of the man who conceived the opening gambit of that war; one-time engineering student who was also an avid baseball fan, a demon poker player, and one of the sharpest military minds of the 20th century almost without peer.

The star of Admiral Isoroku Yamamoto, 56, had risen far and fast in the hierarchy of the tradition-bound Imperial Japanese Navy. When he was appointed to the post of Commander-in-Chief of the Combined Fleet in 1939, he inherited the charge of a navy which, while a fine instrument, was not yet the rival for supremacy of the Pacific over the European powers and the United States. Under the restrictions of the Washington Naval Treaty, Japan was limited in her building of capital ships to a fixed ratio of five-five-three, which would put Japan at a perpetual disadvantage against both the United States and Great Britain in big-gun battleships and cruisers. Not covered in the Treaty, however, was the construction of aircraft carriers, since so few of them existed in 1923. This suited Yamamoto fine; he had long been a proponent of naval airpower since his days at Harvard University in the United States when he majored in the study of the oil industry, though which he first became attracted to the possibilities of aviation. He eagerly absorbed every lesson derived from experimental air operations in the world's fledgling air forces and had the opportunity to implement these lessons as the first captain of the aircraft carrier *Akagi*, commissioned in 1927. Just twelve years later, he was his fleet's supreme commander, and it was not long before his influence began to alter completely its direction from the Big Gun navy envisioned by his predecessors and contemporaries to that of a modern strike force with airpower as its

Fleet Admiral Isoroku Yamamoto, Commander-in-Chief of the Imperial Combined Fleet and mastermind of the Empire's early triumphs in the pacific. National Archives (captured Japanese archival photo) NH63430.

chief component. To those who opposed his ideas in favor of the traditional power of the Big Gun, Yamamoto dismissed the battleship as obsolete (even while the monster *Yamato*-class battleships were being built) and
propounded his theories that surface ships could be easily destroyed by
torpedo-carrying aircraft, quoting an ancient proverb: "The finest serpent
may be overcome by a swarm of ants." As his influence in the C-in-C's
post grew, he was able to bring about the design and construction of two
modern aircraft carriers, the 30,000 ton, 34-knot sisters *Shokaku* and
Zuikaku, each capable of carrying up to 80 planes. More were to follow.
He spearheaded the development of long-range flying boats capable of carrying 2,000-pound bombloads at distances up to 800 miles from home
base, and also under his command initiated the design program for a new
class of carrier-based fighter aircraft which would result in the Mitsubishi
A6M, known in history as the Zeke or, more famously, the Zero. Air training took first priority, with the object of creating a highly disciplined, com-
bat-ready corps of professional fliers. He would reorganize the Navy,
broken into various divisions, into a true Combined Fleet, and the cumu-
lative effects of his many reforms would transform the Imperial Navy from
what was a deterrent force protecting the China Seas and the Home Islands
into a far-ranging blue water fleet capable of projecting power across the
Pacific Ocean and challenging even the formidable United States Pacific
Fleet on an equal or even eventually a superior footing.

In one respect, however, he and his contemporaries in the Navy were
in agreement. They were becoming increasingly concerned with the ever-
rising aggressiveness of the ruling militarist clique which had mired the
Japanese nation in what was becoming a seemingly endless war in China.
Nor were they in favor of the recently signed pact with Nazi Germany and
Mussolini's Italy. And they did not want a war with the United States.
Admiral Yamamoto had particular reason for not desiring such a conflict.
He had seen, first hand, the material potential of the United States, a nation
rich in resources unlike Japan, which had to seek out and seize those
resources or import them at tremendous expense. He had seen American
industry up close. As an engineering student, he knew those assets formed
an inescapable equation: that such a country could, in war, put those
resources to the fullest advantage and translate that material strength into
a war machine so vast and powerful that it could crush any enemy out of
existence. Effortlessly. He feared that the new Axis Pact would end up
dragging Japan into a war it could not hope to survive, much less win. Nor
did he have any particular enmity toward the American people, and had
become sufficiently well-versed in its history to know how Americans met
the challenge of war. For these views, Yamamoto had long been the target

Harold Stark, the prewar Chief of Naval Operations. National Archives
NH49976.

of harassment by fanatical nationalist zealots, jingoists, and his political rivals in the Kodo (Army) Party, who had at times denounced him as a pro–American traitor. He had even been twice threatened with assassination.

A far-seeing thinker, Yamamoto was also a hard realist. Wishful thinking had no place in his perception. In September of 1940, Prince Fumimaro Konoye, then Premier and a strong proponent of the concept of the Greater East Asia Co-Prosperity Sphere, an all–Asian dominion of the Far East over which Japan would be at the head, summoned Yamamoto to Tokyo and asked him about the prospects of a Japanese victory in a possible conflict with the United States. The Admiral told Konoye point-blank that he "could raise havoc with them for one year or at the most eighteen months. After that, I can give no guarantees." When pressed on this matter by Admiral Ryunsuke Kusaka, Yamamoto was more precise in his assessment: "If it is necessary to fight, in the first six months to a year of war against the United States and England I will run wild. I will show you an uninterrupted succession of victories. But I must also tell you that if the war be prolonged for two or three years I have no confidence in our ultimate victory." However, as events seemed to spiral further out of control, Japanese militarism —fueled by a belief in Heavenly Destiny, the tradition of Bushido, and tinged with racism to boot— pushed the Empire even further toward the increasingly inevitable clash with the West. It was flood tide even the exalted Emperor Hirohito was powerless to stem. One year later, October 1941, General Hideki Tojo, a veteran of the China War, became the new Premier and the government was now fully in the hands of the war party.

War with the United States was, barring a miracle, inevitable. War with the British Empire and Holland certainly was, as the Japanese war machine extended the reach of the Co-Prosperity Sphere closer to the Dutch East Indies and Australia in pursuit of oil and mineral resources needed to feed Japan's insatiable diet of raw materials and energy for her industries. In response to the ongoing Japanese aggression, the Roosevelt administration had placed an embargo on scrap iron and steel in October of 1940. America would also embargo oil and other materials and take steps to freeze Japanese assets in the United States.

By the time this had occurred, Yamamoto already had prepared an operational plan to destroy the United States Pacific Fleet with one devastating blow and had set the preparations for the execution of that plan in motion. As early as the winter of 1939, Yamamoto had begun formulating in his mind the initial idea of what would ultimately evolve into the Hawaii Operation. Its inspiration, by another irony of history, came from an American naval experiment planned and executed by Admiral Harry E. Yarnell, who in 1938 staged a mock attack on the Pacific Fleet's westernmost American base in the Hawaiian Islands, Pearl Harbor, utilizing the attack wings of the aircraft carriers *Lexington* and *Saratoga*. The squadrons were launched in the early morning hours on a Sunday, using the weather as cover for the task force's approach. The 150 planes came in undetected and unopposed, achieving complete surprise and sweeping over the base at will, theoretically destroying every capital ship in the anchorage. The exercise had failed to impress the Navy and the Roosevelt administration sufficiently. But it had impressed Yamamoto greatly.

Yamamoto figured that a swift attack upon the U.S. Pacific Fleet would, in one stroke, paralyze American military power long enough for Japan to move on its true objectives in the Dutch East Indies without interference. Similar moves against British and Dutch military assets were also planned in what would develop into a month long campaign to neutralize any potential threat, but the Americans would have to be dealt with first since they posed the far greater long-range threat to Japan's immediate objectives and its long-term survival. A decisive enough strike would leave the United States without any capacity to intervene in Japanese military action for months. By the time America recovered from the attack, Japan would have secured the territorial reach of the Co-Prosperity Sphere as well as an outer defensive perimeter extending far into the Pacific, obliging the weakened American navy to charge forward into what essentially would be a Japanese lake where it could be caught and destroyed. Alternatively, if the United States became embroiled in a war with Nazi Germany, particularly in rushing to the defense of the other Western allies, the Roosevelt government might be amenable to settling for peace in the Pacific so as to relieve it from the burden of attempting to fight a war on two fronts. In his poker-player's judgment, Yamamoto had the high card, and the United States would be playing the weakened hand and be forced to move cautiously, either negotiating a peace settlement according to the new status quo in the Pacific or pursuing a strategy so conservative that it could not be effective against Japan or Germany, which would mean no effective intervention against Japan.

The Admiral didn't quite have the full concurrence of his hand-picked planning staff in his concept, however. While Rear Admiral Takijiro Onishi and Air Operations Commander Minoru Genda were positive toward the possibilities of success in this bold gambit, Yamamoto's own chief of staff, Admiral Shigeru Fukudome, gave the plan only a forty percent chance of success after a preliminary study into the project. And Onishi, generally supportive of the scheme, had his own reservations and went no further than a success projection of sixty percent. Yamamoto, however, was convinced absolutely that it would work. His conviction in this was massively reinforced when in November of 1940, the British Royal Navy launched a surprise carrier-based air attack against the Italian fleet anchored in the Mediterranean port of Taranto, whose harbor had a depth of only 80 feet. The British used obsolescent Fairey Swordfish biplanes with torpedoes specially adapted to run in the shallows of Taranto and succeeded in sinking three battleships, fully half the Italian Fleet's capital strength. The Italians never recovered from the strike and Britain commanded naval supremacy in the Mediterranean from that point forward. Confident that Japanese engineers could adapt torpedoes to operate in the even shallower forty foot depth of the bay at Pearl, Yamamoto pressed forward. Taranto had effectively erased any argument against.

The C-in-C himself personally scouted the Japanese coast for the perfect place to stage rehearsals of the attack. The area chosen was Kagoshima Bay, on the coast of the southern island of Kyushu, which bore a considerable resemblance to Pearl Harbor: a narrow channel inlet, a bay with an island in the middle, with surrounding hills on three sides. It was as close to perfect as he could get. The mock attacks staged for the rehearsals were merely an extension of the training program instituted by Yamamoto which specialized in perfecting techniques of bombing targets in confined valleys; originally designed to provide naval air support for Army operations in China and now perfectly adaptable for the proposed Pearl Harbor raid. For the next several months, the local fisher-folk were to get used to the daily appearance of torpedo and dive bombers over their skies, steadily coming to enjoy the show put on by the Navy's "flying circus." While the air rehearsals proceeded, Yamamoto cut the orders for the assemblage of the task force to venture forth into the Pacific toward the end of the year. Flagship for the battle group would be Yamamoto's old command, the *Akagi*. Joining her would be the *Kaga*, the sister ships *Shokaku* and *Zuikaku*, and two smaller carriers, the 17,300 ton *Hiryu* and the 15,900 ton *Soryu*. This represented half the available carrier strength of the Japanese fleet, boarding a total of 423 Zeke fighters, Nakijima B5N Kate torpedo bombers, and the older, fixed-landing gear Aichi D3A Val dive bombers. In Genda's judgment, six was the minimum number needed to ensure the success of the operation, factoring potential losses from enemy resistance and the need to have sufficient reserve of aircraft to deal with any retaliatory threat which might come from the base or any units of the Pacific Fleet which might escape and attempt pursuit. Accompanying the flattops would be a screening and support force consisting of two battleships, two heavy cruisers, a light cruiser, and nine destroyers. Additionally, three submarines would take the point in advance patrol and the task force would be covered by eight tankers for mid-ocean refueling. These various ships would wait at scattered ports until they received their final orders to assemble at a rendezvous at Tankan Bay, in the Kurile Islands north of the Japanese mainland. In addition to this armada, a further advance force of twenty-seven submarines would be waiting at Kwajelin in the southern Pacific to proceed to the rendezvous in the Hawaiian waters. Five would be carrying special three-man midget submarines whose task was to slip into the harbor and lie in wait to sink any American ships which might escape the air attack.

But while Yamamoto and his operations officers were set upon their plan, the Imperial General Staff was not. Their own war game projections showed a loss of at least two carriers, which generated a list of five major objections to the plan. Meanwhile, the Cabinet had decided upon the date of September 6 1941, as the day after which, "when necessary," Japan would go to war against the United States. This last minute opposition was squashed by Yamamoto himself with a blunt threat to resign his commission and retire from the Imperial Navy unless his plan was accepted. Deadline for the resignation was November 3 and the General Staff, unwilling to lose so illustrious and capable an officer on the eve of a major war, caved in and gave full assent to the Hawaii Operation.

As 1941 wound toward the end of the year, and peace negotiations between America and Japan dragged on, Yamamoto finally issued Operational Order Number One, spelling out the objectives of the strike at Pearl Harbor as well as the general campaign in the Western Pacific: the destruction of the American fleet; the cutting of American supply lines to the Orient; the interception and annihilation of any enemy forces; victories in succession to break the enemy's will to fight. X-Day would occur on Sunday, December 7, to take advantage of the American slackness on weekends, particularly on Sundays, and to catch them shortly after dawn when they would be at their most disorganized. The fanatical Kodo Party wanted a date of December 1 but Yamamoto overrode their resistance on the grounds of needing full time to ensure his preparations. As they were to make simultaneous moves against the Philippines and Malaya to throw America, Britain, and Holland into full confusion and take maximum military advantage of the destruction of the American Pacific Fleet, the General Staff acceded. While preparations for war were underway, diplomatic negotiations were continuing in Washington between the two governments. The peace talks were mainly to provide cover for the sailing of the task force, but also by Imperial "request," to legitimately explore an outside possibility of peacefully settling the differences between the United

States and Japan. Nobody in Yamamoto's staff, in the Imperial Government, aboard the ships of the fleet, and not particularly the C-in-C himself, expected any result other than war. The fleet had to be on station on time to strike and the final orders to proceed were transmitted.

Through the month of November, the 31 vessels of the task force slipped from their various ports and made their way under radio silence and full secrecy toward the Tankan Bay. November in the Kuriles is a time of bitterly cold weather, thick grey fog and seemingly perpetual dusk. But when the men of the fleet finally learned of their orders and objective, jubilation reigned in this otherwise depressing atmosphere. Cries of "Banzai!" (ten-thousand years) sounded out in the lower decks and hangars of the fleet while fuel, ammunition, and provisions were loaded aboard the ships, and each man looked forward to the opportunity to die gloriously in the service of the Emperor, the best destiny of any Japanese fighting man.

Standing on the bridge of the *Akagi* was Chuichi Nagumo, a dour traditionalist officer who wound up in command of the mighty armada at anchorage mainly due to being next on the promotion list and the fact that he was an expert navigator. Given the voyage ahead, this one asset outweighed every other strike against him. He was generally unimaginative, did not share the enthusiasm for the coming war and had no faith in the risky plan dreamed up by Yamamoto and his staff, or in the efficacy of naval air power in general, being a devoted believer in the power of the Big Gun. Yet here he was, in command of the force which was about to set the United States and Japan at each other's throats for four years, change forever the face of naval warfare, doom the battleship which he so loved to second-class status and eventual oblivion, and, though he could not know it then, be the instrument to bring about his nation's near-destruction. But Nagumo had his orders and would carry them out to perfection. As the appointed hour struck, flags went up on the *Akagi*'s mast. The ships of the armada weighed anchor and, one by one, proceeded out of the Tankan Bay on the bleak morning of November 26, 1941, sailing forth on the first leg of a 3,000 mile voyage across the Pacific Ocean to the Hawaiian Islands, and destiny.

Following upon the successful British attack at Taranto, Frank Knox, the Secretary of the Navy, had sent a memorandum to Secretary of War Henry L. Stimson which advised, in no uncertain terms, that "precautionary measures be taken immediately to protect Pearl Harbor against a surprise attack in the event of war between the United States and Japan. The greatest danger will come from the aerial torpedo." But it was the judgment of the C-in-C of the United States Pacific Fleet, Husband E. Kimmel, that stringing torpedo nets within the confines of the harbor

Vice Admiral Chuichi Nagumo, Commander of the First Air Fleet and the reluctant warrior who led the attack against Pearl Harbor. National Archives (captured Japanese archival photo) NH63423.

would prove too restrictive to ship traffic. In any case, common wisdom held that the Japanese would be too engaged with their main targets in the Dutch East Indies, which was always accepted as the primary objective of their conquests, to also attempt a strike so far eastward. Additionally, it was taken as an article of faith that although the British had managed to modify torpedoes to run in the shallows of Taranto, it would be virtually impossible for any engineers from any navy in the world to modify a torpedo to run in the far shallower depths of Pearl.

In large measure, the halcyon atmosphere of Honolulu, a tropical paradise which was much more a country club than a military base and therefore a plum location for both shore leave and permanent posting, contributed mightily to the complacency of the Army and Navy personnel stationed at Pearl. But not all minds were completely dulled to the possibilities of an aerial assault on the Pacific Fleet. As early as March of 1941, Rear Admiral Patrick Bellinger, air defense operations officer, and Army Air Force commanding General Frederick Martin, predicted the possibility of a Japanese attack employing up to six aircraft carriers and their attack wings, coming on a weekend in the early morning to achieve maximum surprise, and to forestall that occurrence recommended upgrading of the island's defenses, including the addition of up to 180 B-17D long-range bombers and other four-engined aircraft with similar ranges, the institution of continuous air patrols sweeping out to 300 miles in all directions, and the installation of radar sets. Their view was that if any Japanese force could not achieve surprise, they would in all likelihood withdraw without attempting to launch a single plane. But few of these measures would be acted upon, though one radar set would be shipped to Oahu and a squadron of B-17s — twelve — would be assigned to Oahu's air defenses. Kimmel and General Walter Short, the overall Army commander at Pearl, would focus their preparations to guard against saboteurs. Short in particular was convinced that Oahu had become a nest for spies and saboteurs who blended in with the island's Japanese-American population. As a result, Short would order planes, previously spread out in wide areas on the airfields as standard precaution against air attack, to be parked together for greater security against enemy agents attempting to blow them up, while Kimmel would have his ships, previously spread throughout the Harbor, draw in toward the docks at Ford Island as well as on the banks of the bay; a plan conceived in part to provide cluster-defense for all the main capital ships in the event of air attack but also to keep the Harbor clear for ship and boat traffic. Unfortunately, these two defense measures would bunch all the targets together just perfectly for the Japanese when they came.

Husband E. Kimmel, the C-in-C of the U.S. Pacific Fleet, who found himself a helpless witness to the destruction of his fleet on December 7. National Archives NH82800.

Kimmel and Short might have reversed these measures if they had been privy to the Japanese code traffic which was being read on a regular basis in Washington, thanks to the breaking of the "Purple" ciphers by Army and Navy decryption experts with the aid of "Magic," the most advanced codebreaking device of the time. As 1941 wore on, and the last fleeting months of peace counted down, the increased interest in Hawaii in the Japanese intercepts was noted by the Pentagon and Secretary of War Stimson. However, Washington was as obsessed with security against espionage as General Short in Pearl was—the codebreaking project was a secret so precious that for a time even President Roosevelt was not given access to the decrypts. The security of this project was considered to be of paramount importance. Plus, a certain complacency had entered into Pentagon thinking as well because they could read the Japanese code traffic and were confident that they would know the second the Japanese would attempt anything. It was also expected that the Imperial Government would follow the letter of the Hague Convention, of which both nations were signatories, and provide formal declaration of war before actually initiating hostilities. For this and other reasons, both Kimmel and Short were kept totally in the dark about the Purple intercepts and would be right up to the moment the first bombs fell on the morning of December 7.

For five days, Nagumo's armada ploughed through seas so rough that his largest aircraft carriers were bobbing like corks in a washing machine. His course took him in an arc across the Northern Pacific to avoid the shipping lanes and detection. All the while, his pilots drilled below decks with their ship-recognition and combat timing. When they were three days away from the strike, they were able to listen in on the broadcast radio from Hawaii as the ships moved closer to their objective. But during the whole transit, Nagumo was a troubled man. He feared constantly that his force would be spotted either by a patrolling submarine or even, though he seemed too far away from the shipping lanes for it, by a passing commercial vessel. He had every intention of turning back if his ships were spotted, because the potential for disaster being caught so far from home oppressed him from the time the Hawaii Operation was being planned. His operational orders in fact permitted him the option to abort the mission in the event of detection, stressing the necessity to preserve his battleforce and bring it back intact. Privately, he prayed for a message from home which said that peace negotiations had succeeded and that his mission would be unnecessary.

The task force had successfully refueled at sea on November 28, though several seamen had been lost because of the rough seas. The ships could not stop to attempt rescue and had increased speed to 24 knots to make the X-point, the area where they would turn for the final leg of the voyage. The force arrived there on December 2, and the *Akagi* then received a fleet signal from Admiral Yamamoto, aboard his flagship *Nagato* in Hiroshima Bay. It was simple, three-word message: *Niitaka Yama Nabore*. Climb Mount Niitaka. The signal that the operation was to be carried out. Nagumo had his ships veer south to complete their journey to start a war.

By December 4, the task force emerged from the worst of the weather they had slogged their way through since departing the Kuriles, and encountered improving conditions as they proceeded south. On the 6th, they were in clear seas at last and would encounter ideal conditions for launching the strike when they reached the attack point 275 miles north of Pearl Harbor. At noon that day, officers and men gathered on the flight deck of the *Akagi* for a special ceremony of high significance as a tattered, battleworn flag was unfurled and raised up the lines. It was the Rising Sun banner which had flown from the masthead of the *Mikawa*, Heihachiro Togo's flagship at Tsushima. The ceremony was carried on ship's PA and all crew stood to attention as Admiral Nagumo spoke, reading out first the Emperor's formal war decree followed by a message from Admiral Yamamoto, a statement which echoed the words of Togo and Lord Nelson, his personal hero: "The rise and fall of the Empire depends upon this battle. Everyone will do his duty to the utmost." Banzais rang throughout the great carrier as well as the singing of "Kimigayo," the Imperial anthem.

But bad news would reach Nagumo, who had not slept, in the very early morning hours of the 7th. A late intelligence report radioed to the task force indicated that the American aircraft carriers, the main targets of the strike, were not at port. Of the expected four which were known to be attached to the Pacific Fleet, only two had been in Pearl Harbor in the days the task force had been at sea. The *Yorktown* along with her newly commissioned sister ship *Hornet* had been transferred to the Atlantic to counter German U-boat activity. The *Saratoga* was long known to have been sent to the West Coast for overhaul. This left the *Lexington* and the *Enterprise*, which had been in port as late as November 28 and would still have been there if not for the latest memorandum from George C. Marshall, the Chief-of-Staff in Washington, which amounted to a war warning. It indicated that the Japanese were expected to move against the Dutch East Indies, the Philippines, and possibly even the Solomons any day. As a result, Kimmel dispatched the *Lexington*, under Rear Admiral J.H. Newland, to deliver Vindicator bombers to Midway to reinforce that island's air defenses on November 28, while Rear Admiral William F. Halsey shipped out on December 4 aboard the *Enterprise* with a squadron of Grumman F4F Wildcat fighters for Wake Island. Both carriers went forth

The nucleus of the First Air Fleet: the carriers *Akagi* (top), *Kaga* (middle), and *Soryu* (bottom), boarding 480 strike aircraft. National Archives (captured Japanese archival photo) NH73058, NH73060, NH73061.

Above: The nucleus of the First Air Fleet: the carriers *Hiryu* (top), *Shokaku* (middle), and *Zuikaku* (bottom), boarding 480 strike aircraft. National Archives (captured Japanese archival photo) NH73063, NH73066, NH73067. *Opposite:* 6 December 1941 — The last fleeting days of peace were marked by desperate fleet movements in the Pacific by the United States, while Chuichi Nagumo's First Air Fleet stealthily moved in its course to start a war.

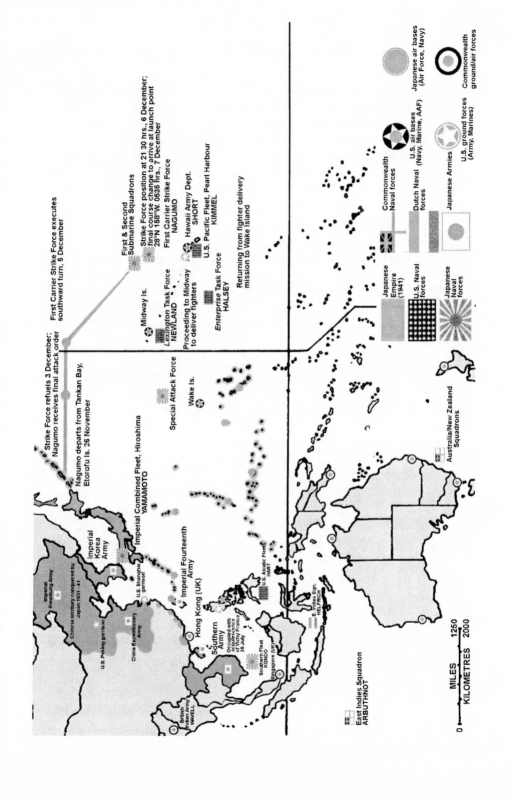

Strike Force refuels 3 December; Nagumo receives final attack order

First Carrier Strike Force executes southward turn, 5 December

Nagumo departs from Tankan Bay, Etorofu Is. 26 November

First & Second Submarine Squadrons

Strike Force position at 21 30 hrs., 6 December; final course change to arrive at launch point 26°N 158°W. 0635 hrs., 7 December

First Carrier Strike Force NAGUMO

Hawaii Army Dept. SHORT

U.S. Pacific Fleet, Pearl Harbour KIMMEL

Midway Is.

Lexington Task Force NEWLAND

Proceeding to Midway to deliver fighters

Enterprise Task Force HALSEY

Returning from fighter delivery mission to Wake Island

Imperial Combined Fleet, Hiroshima YAMAMOTO

Special Attack Force

Wake Is.

Imperial Korea Army

Chinese territory conquered by Japan 1931–41

Imperial Kwantung Army

U.S. Peking garrison

China Expeditionary Army

U.S. Shanghai garrison

Imperial Fourteenth Army

U.S. Asiatic Fleet HART

Hong Kong (UK)

Southern Army

Occupation with acquiescence of Vichy France, 26 July

E. Indies Sqn. HELFRICH

Southern Fleet KONDO

Singapore (UK)

British Indian Army WAVELL

East Indies Squadron ARBUTHNOT

Australia/New Zealand Squadrons

MILES
0   1250

KILOMETRES
0   2000

Japanese Empire (1941)

U.S. Naval forces

Japanese Naval forces

Commonwealth Naval forces

Dutch Naval forces

Japanese air bases (Air Force, Navy)

U.S. air bases (Navy, Marine, AAF)

Japanese Armies

U.S. ground forces (Army, Marines)

Commonwealth ground/air forces

with cruiser-destroyer screening forces; the two admirals rejected having any of the battleships accompany the carrier groups because they were too slow. The *Enterprise* had completed her mission quickly and had started back, expecting to be in port Saturday night. But a rain squall had forced her and the escorts to slow headway and as a result would not be in until the next afternoon. Halsey, before going out, declared that he would "blow out of the water" any Japanese ship he ran into. He also had urged Kimmel to rotate some of the fleet out to sea but the senior officer rejected this because the carriers would be gone and he did not want to send out battleships without air cover. It was a prudent decision, as far as it went. But in making it, Kimmel had unknowingly doomed his fleet to destruction.

But while Nagumo was disappointed that the prize targets were not in port, he gave it only passing notice in his calculations; he knew the main portion of the Pacific Fleet's strength would still be in his grasp. Three thousand miles away in his flagship, Isoroku Yamamoto, who had received the same report, was inwardly distressed, though he revealed nothing of the thoughts churning in his mind to his staff. The absence of the carriers from Pearl Harbor had implications which only he could fully appreciate and would cause him tension throughout the day on the 7th (the 8th in Japan, being on the other side of the International Date Line). It meant that the Americans would still have a primary instrument of retaliation even after the battleships had been destroyed. And because of that, an old proverb floated before the Admiral's consciousness: the seeds of tragedy are implanted in the blossom of victory. It was a bad omen.

Dawn rose on the morning of December 7 and found Nagumo's carriers at the launch point at latitude 28°N, longitude 158°W. Planes were gathered on the flight decks of the six carriers, and two floatplanes from the cruisers *Tone* and *Chikuma* had already been launched to scout ahead for signs at Pearl Harbor that the Americans might be suspicious or have defensive preparations underway. Air Commander Mitsuo Fuchida, one of the planners of the raid with Minoru Genda, briefed his pilots one last time on the conditions expected at Pearl, the targets to be found there, and the timing for each wave of the strike. The torpedo bombers would go in first, followed by the dive bombers. Fighters would strafe ground targets and ships, concentrating in particular on Hickam and Wheeler Fields—the two main Army Air Force bases at Pearl—to destroy planes on the ground, as well as deal with resistance, if any, from remaining enemy fighters. Finally, he told the assembled fliers that, if surprise had been achieved, he would fire one flare from his plane, which would signal the torpedo planes to go in first. But if surprise was lost, he would fire two flares, which would indicate that the Vals should strike first to create max-

A Kate torpedo bomber roars off the deck of the *Akagi*. National Archives (captured Japanese archival photo) NH50603.

imum confusion with the base defenses so the Kates could concentrate on their torpedo runs after which the squadrons would get out quickly.

At 0600 hours, Fuchida and his pilots and aircrews clambered into their planes, already idling and awaiting the signal for takeoff as the six carriers turned into the wind. A green light on the deck flashed, and Fuchida's Kate was the first to roar off the deck of the *Akagi*. He circled until the rest of his force, 183 planes in all, were airborne and assembled in formation. They climbed to ten thousand feet and headed southward. Above the clouds, the fliers were greeted by the sight of the rising sun.

It was a beautiful morning that Sunday, typical for a tropical paradise. The civilian and military populations of Oahu were awakening slowly to a day of church services, light duties, yard work, picnics, and recreation. General Short was having breakfast and dressing for his 8 a.m. golf date with Admiral Kimmel. It had been a harrying two weeks during which the men were put on one alert after another and most of them, as well as their officers, were looking forward to a trouble-free Sunday to wind down, particularly after last week's warning of a Japanese attack which had failed to materialize. Up on a high hill at the northern end of Oahu, the Army radar station manned by Privates George Elliot and Joseph Lockhard had picked up a blip in the early dawn hours, but it was assumed that it had to be a student pilot up for an early morning buzz, which was typical on such a glorious morning. At 0700 hours, however, the two operators picked up two very large pulses on the screen and phoned it in to the duty office at Fort Shafter. Lieutenant Kermit Tyler, on watch that morning, assured the two privates that the big blip had to belong to an expected flight of B-17s coming in from California and scheduled to arrive at Hickam at 0800. Either that or they were planes from the *Enterprise* returning from Wake. With that, the radar set was shut down — it had been three hours and the manual stipulated no more than three hours' operation to avoid overheating and burning out tubes — and Elliot and Lockhard left to get what remained of breakfast back at Shafter. The only other bit of undue excitement was an unconfirmed report from the destroyer USS *Ward*, which had signaled that they were depth charging a submarine which had attempted to infiltrate the harbor by following behind the minesweeper *Antares*, which was towing a target for morning gunnery drills.

The Japanese formation was flying over Oahu Bay at 0749, Pearl Harbor time. Fuchida scanned the base before him. The ships below were lying placidly at their anchorages and both airfields were quiet. He clearly sighted the juicy targets before him — eight battleships all in a row, moored two together. It was almost too good to be true, but there was the whole U.S. Pacific Fleet bunched in close. And there was not so much as a single sign that any defensive preparations had been undertaken. Surprise was theirs. Fuchida opened his cockpit, raised his flare gun, and fired the signal. The Vals climbed to 15,000 feet. while the Kates headed down to the deck. But for some odd reason, the Zekes were not breaking their formation. Frustrated, Fuchida fired a second flare and now things became confused. The Val pilots saw the second flare, assumed that the base was alerted, and began their attack run while the Kates were heading in on the ships. Despite this, Fuchida had his radio operator signal to the *Akagi* the code transmission *Tora, Tora, Tora* (tiger, tiger, tiger) to inform Admiral Nagumo that surprise had been achieved and the attack was underway. By a freak of atmospherics, the signal was picked up by the radio receivers of the *Nagato* at Hiroshima, and thus Yamamoto knew the exact moment war had begun.

Fuchida's was not the only blunder at that moment. An infinitely more serious one, which would shape the whole war to come, was occurring back in Washington. Ambassadors Kichisaburo Nomura and Saburo Kurusu had been notified that diplomatic relations were at an end, and the formal Imperial decree of war between the United States and Japan was to be delivered in the form of a fourteen part note, which had to be transmitted in separate sections in code and decrypted as the sections came in.

The two ambassadors were scheduled to meet with Secretary of State Cordell Hull to formally deliver the note at 1 p.m. exactly, Washington time. By insistence of the Emperor, if war was to happen, Japan would abide by the strictures of the Hague Convention and issue formal notice before the opening of actual hostilities. The timing was fixed to deliver the declaration of war at least a full half hour before the attack against Pearl Harbor. This was as much time as Yamamoto and the General Staff agreed was sufficient warning without compromising the mission. But the fourteenth part of the note had somehow gotten delayed in transmission, and the ambassadors had no choice but to wait until it came through and was decrypted. Unaware of the operation taking place four thousand miles away, they informed the office of Secretary Hull that their one o'clock appointment would have to be put back at least a whole hour.

Back at Pearl Harbor, color ceremonies were in progress. The navy band played the national anthem as the Stars and Stripes was run up the mast of the Pacific Fleet flagship USS *Nevada*. As navy officers on the dock stood to attention, a plane roared overhead. One noted that the number should be taken down to alert the flight operations desk of the safety violation by the pilot. Then, the first bomb fell on Wheeler Field. Fighters then appeared and began strafing the ground and the ships. Seamen and soldiers dived for cover as alarm klaxons began sounding.

The screams of dive bombers and men, the thunderclap of explosions, and bursts of machine gun shells on the ground shattered forever the tranquil atmosphere of Pearl Harbor as more and more planes with the now all-too clear Rising Sun on the wingtips roared over the base. The Vals broke formation and dived on Wheeler and Hickam fields and various other installations on Ford Island, while Kates started their final runs on the moored battleships, all of which were helpless before the Japanese. Inichi Goto, flying his Kate, led the formation and had sighted on the *Arizona*. He released his fish, causing his plane to bob up when freed of its weight, and roared overhead as the telltale wake streaked closer to the battlewagon. Goto was ecstatic when a geyser of water suddenly erupted at the side of the hull and the great ship shuddered with the blast. But machine gun and antiaircraft fire was already coming up at him, and Goto had to peel off quickly.

The Japanese were shocked that defensive fire was coming up at them so quickly; the Americans were reacting faster than they had anticipated. But the shock and confusion of the attack prevented any sort of coordinated resistance, and what antiaircraft was coming at them was sporadic at best. Many on the ground simply could not comprehend what was happening to them. More than a few were paralyzed with shock and even fear.

An attackers' eye view of Pearl Harbor during the first-wave strike. National Archives (captured Japanese archival photo) NH50931.

Men cried as buddies they had known for up to ten years or ships they had called home were being blasted apart before their eyes. It was as if the end of the world had come and they were utterly helpless to do anything but watch it happen. From his home on a hill overlooking the base, Admiral Kimmel was in a state of total shock. It took him some moments to recover his wits sufficiently to order up his car to take him to the base.

More and more Kates, and two of the midget submarines launched in advance of the attack, came in on Battleship Row and hammered the ships before them. Most didn't have steam up and were running off power supplied from the dock and which had been cut off by the bomb damage and shocks when lines were snapped. As a result, watertight doors couldn't be closed and ships flooded freely. The *California* began to list to port and showed signs that she might capsize, but her engineers rushed to open the seacocks on the starboard side to counterflood. Because of their quick action, the battleship settled on an even keel in the soft mud below, sinking down to her main deck. The *West Virginia, Tennessee*, and *Maryland* were also beginning to settle as well. Fires broke out on all battleships as bombs struck; not a single one of the capital ships was spared. Vals and

Zekes swarmed over Wheeler and Hickam Fields, Schofield Army Barracks, the Marine Corps airfield at Ewa, over Bellows Field east of Honolulu, and Kaneohe Naval Air Station on the eastern end of Oahu and demolished P-40s, B-17s, B-18s, A-20s, Wildcats, Vindicators, and PBY Catalina flying boats. Hangars were blown up, as were avgas depots and repair and supply shacks. The Japanese had a field day blasting apart fighters which were parked in the nice, neat rows General Short had ordered for protection against saboteurs. Pilots scrambled to take off against the attackers or just to get their planes under cover. P-40s which tried to taxi out to the runway were simply shot up, blowing apart as fuel tanks were ruptured by machine gun shells. They never stood a chance of getting off the ground. In the middle of this holocaust, the flight of factory-fresh B-17D bombers from California, all unarmed, came under attack as they attempted to make their landing at Hickam. Some were shot down as they made the approach while others managed to rev up and take off again, scattering to wherever they could make safe haven.

More Vals roared over the hapless battleships while Fuchida continued to circle over the Pacific Fleet, making strafing runs and otherwise assessing the effectiveness of the attack. As he flew, one of his Vals sighted on the *Arizona* and released a single bomb. The lone object plunged down and punched through the deck behind the number two main turret. Just a few seconds afterward, there erupted a colossal blast which seemed to engulf the whole ship. The shock wave buffeted Fuchida's plane and swept men off the decks of nearby ships, tossing them into the oily waters of the bay. Shells and ammunition from the stricken battlewagon fired off at random. The one bomb had penetrated all the way to the ship's magazines, detonating powder, shells, and boilers, and the USS *Arizona* disappeared in a huge fireball and a thick column of angry black smoke. Her twisted and burned remains settled to the bottom of the bay. Gone were 1,103 of her crew of 1,400, including Captain Franklin Van Valkenburgh and Rear Admiral Isaac Kidd, both of whom were on the bridge. Heavily damaged in the blast was the supply ship *Vestal* which was moored next to the *Arizona*. Bombs then fell on the *Maryland* and the *Oklahoma*. The latter vessel took such serious damage that she heeled over and capsized with additional heavy loss of life.

During the first wave attack, there was one battleship which was not helpless. The *Nevada* had her engineering crew aboard and actually had steam up and was running on her own power. The ranking officers aboard decided to get her underway and began to make a run for the channel to get into the open sea. The moving warship was greeted with cheers from everyone who could spare a look — the only vessel which was underway

The USS *Arizona* lies burning and sunken at her moorings. National Archives NH97379.

and fighting back. The Japanese bombers sighted on the all-too tempting target below them and worked out where she was going. If that ship could be sunk in the harbor entrance, Pearl would be cut off for months and the base would be useless to the Americans. Kates and Vals pounced on the battlewagon. Her course took her past Battleship Row just as the *Arizona* was exploding, and it took quick maneuvering by her pilot to port around the stricken warship and avoid destruction herself. The blast set off fires on the *Nevada*'s starboard side. Bombs and torpedoes struck and she began to go down by the head. There was no hope of escaping, and aware that the Japanese were almost certainly trying to sink her in the harbor mouth, the pilot then made for the banks of the bay to beach the *Nevada*, which he succeeded in doing. The battlewagon settled in shallow water and the crew abandoned ship quickly.

Kimmel arrived at his headquarters just prior to the destruction of the *Arizona*, where he listened morosely to the reports of the damage to his ships and destruction of his airfields. When the *Arizona* exploded, something shot right through the window and bounced off his dress whites.

A staff officer picked it up and showed what turned out to be a bent machine gun shell to the Admiral. Kimmel looked at it for long seconds and simply said, "It would have been more merciful if it had killed me." As his staff officers milled in confusion, desperately trying to coordinate countermeasures and deal with the flood of telephone calls from concerned families of the men, it was left to Commander Logan Ramsey to transmit to the world the now famous message: "Air raid, Pearl Harbor. THIS IS NO DRILL."

The first-wave attack withdrew at around 0830 hours and headed back to the carriers. Fuchida remained behind circling in his Kate high above the clouds while on the ground makeshift defenses were prepared. They didn't have long, because twenty-four minutes later the second wave attack arrived: 170 planes led by Shegekazu Shimazaki from the *Soryu* with a force of 54 Kates, 80 Vals, and 36 Zekes in all. Fuchida directed them to further attacks on Battleship Row, on the ships moored at the docks on the shores of the bay, and more bombing runs on Hickam, Kaneohe, Schofield Barracks, and Ford Island. Smoke from the earlier strike obscured the targets, so the new attack was not as accurate, though it inflicted additional damage and added to the casualties on the ground.

Despite the very thorough destruction of planes on the ground, the Japanese ended up facing some fighter resistance. General Martin, days ago, had some P-40 Warhawks as well as some obsolescent P-36s of the 47th Pursuit Squadron sent out to Haleiwa, a small training field which was little more than a dirt runway and a few huts located in the northwestern corner of Oahu. Its obscurity left it virtually unnoticed by the Japanese, and several pilots scrambled to the waiting planes, which had been revved up by the mechanics. Without orders, Lieutenants George Welch, John Webster, Harry Brown, Kenneth Taylor, and John Dains took off against the raiders. The latter was shot down by friendly fire over Schofield Barracks, but the others were able to get into combat against the enemy. Despite being outnumbered and outclassed by the Zekes, which at the time were some of the most advanced combat fighters in the world, the Americans managed to score some kills. George Welch himself downed four planes before the Japanese second wave broke off and withdrew. Welch would win the Distinguished Flying Cross for his heroic action but was denied the Congressional Medal of Honor for having flown without any authorization.

Mitsuo Fuchida waited until the second-wave planes were finished with their runs and, when the last of them had pulled out, he put his Kate about and headed back to the fleet at 0945 hours. He left in his wake a scene of devastation out of the Book of Apocalypse. In less than two hours,

The destroyer USS *Shaw* explodes in drydock. National Archives NH86118.

for the paltry loss of 29 aircraft and 54 pilots and aircrew, the Japanese had sunk or damaged every battleship in Pearl Harbor. The *Arizona* and *Oklahoma* were both destroyed, and the *Maryland, Tennessee, West Virginia, California,* and *Nevada* were all resting on the bottom of the harbor, sunk at their docks except for the latter vessel, which was beached. An additional battleship, the *Pennsylvania,* had taken bomb damage in the drydock while two destroyers ahead of her, the *Cassin* and the *Downes,* had been reduced to scrap metal. Another obsolete battleship (though the Japanese did not know that), the target ship *Utah,* had been sunk. The cruisers *Helena, Honolulu,* and *Raleigh* had been heavily damaged, as had the seaplane tender *Curtiss* and the supply ship *Vestal.* A minelayer, the *Oglala,* had capsized at her dock, while the destroyer *Shaw* had suffered a spectacular explosion of her ammunition magazines in drydock. For all intents and purposes, there was no longer a United States Pacific Fleet. Fully half the island's air strength, 188 planes, had been destroyed on the ground. The total dead stood at 2,403, nearly half of them casualties from the *Arizona* and *Oklahoma.* Added to the human toll were 1,178 wounded and 68 civilian dead.

Fuchida finally returned to the *Akagi* around 1040 hours and reported to his admiral. Nagumo was most pleased with the assessment of the strike; the mission objectives had been accomplished. But when Fuchida suggested a third attack to deal with targets which might have been obscured by smoke and fire, and Rear Admiral Tamon Yamaguchi aboard the *Hiryu* signaled that he had a strike wing ready to launch, Nagumo rejected it outright. In his view, they had achieved what they had set out to achieve, despite the absence of the American aircraft carriers. Now, his priority was to return his task force to Japan intact. It would be vital for the campaigns immediately following, and the longer they tarried in Hawaiian waters, the longer they risked detection and possible retaliation. More importantly, their fuel reserves were very limited and every drop would be needed for the voyage home. The pilots and staff officers were eager for the third strike, but Nagumo was resolved on his course of action and had signal flags run up the *Akagi*'s mast ordering the armada to put about and make a return course to Japan.

The Japanese attack on Pearl Harbor had been planned down to the last detail and had been very expertly executed. Nagumo's estimation of the tactical and strategic success of the raid had been correct as far as it went. But it also turned out to be completely wrong in several very important aspects. For a start, the battleships which had been sunk at Pearl, with the exception of the *Arizona* and *Oklahoma* (as well as the obsolete *Utah*), were perfectly salvageable for having sunk in shallow waters. In the coming months they would be raised, their damage patched over, and would proceed under their own steam to the United States for thorough reconstruction and modernization. Most of the other ships which had been heavily damaged were also repairable. Eventually, most of the ships which had been damaged and sunk in the Japanese attack would return to frontline service. On that basis alone, the Japanese attack had been a tactical failure.

The attack would also prove to be a strategic error of the first magnitude. The objective of the raid had been to paralyze American retaliatory power so as to end the threat of any interference with their coming conquests of the Dutch East Indies. But because of the U-boat threat in the Atlantic, the Americans had cut their striking power in the Pacific in half even before Nagumo's armada set forth from the Tankan Bay and what was left was already no threat to Japanese expansionist plans. The war plans the United States had formulated for the Pacific had already conceded Japanese advances in the early phase of any potential conflict. Quite contrary to the Japanese fears which had spurred the attack, the United States had neither the intention nor, at the time, the strength to interfere in any Japanese drive in the Western Pacific. In addition, the Japanese had failed to catch and destroy the main instrument of retaliation, the aircraft carriers. Despite the cant of the Big Gun lobbies in both the American and Japanese navies, the battleship had, by 1941, become obsolete. Seaborne airpower was now the measure of a navy's striking power. Taranto had proved it. Pearl Harbor had proved it. The loss of the battleships had forced the United States, by practicalities, to scrap all plans based around the illusory power of the Big Gun and to enshrine the aircraft carrier as the primary asset of naval strike capability. The United States was still building modern battleships and would rebuild the ones damaged at Pearl Harbor, but the focus would shift permanently to the ever-accelerating development of naval air power as well as the submarine. American naval power in the Pacific was paralyzed for a few weeks, but in real terms the raid had accomplished very little of actual military significance — even though at the time it may have appeared otherwise.

Additionally, the attack fell short of its purposes because the raiders had completely failed to destroy the base. They had left the airfields largely intact, and the far more important repair facilities and oil storage untouched. Indeed, it was one of the miracles of the day that the fuel tanker *Neosho*, loaded with high octane avgas and moored in the middle of Battleship Row, had been left untouched; its destruction might have set off an inferno which would have engulfed the battleships and set the oil storage tanks on Ford Island ablaze. Leaving behind a fully operational naval base with intact drydocks, machine shops, and thousands of gallons of fuel oil after bombing the fleet was the single worst mistake any nation could make in launching a war.

But of greater significance, the raid on Pearl Harbor had proved a political blunder beyond any magnitude conceivable. Because of the critical delay in the receipt and decoding of the last portion of the fourteen-part note which was the official declaration of war, Japan was now in the position of having launched a totally unprovoked sneak attack upon a peaceful United States. This touched off a rage among the Americans which was almost without precedent in history. Secretary of State Hull received the news that the attack at Pearl Harbor was underway while Ambassadors Nomura and Kurusu waited his convenience. When they were finally received and handed over their copy of the note, Hull, who already knew the sense of the message, read through the catalogue of Japan's grievances and justifications for her actions and afterward simply said, "In all my fifty years of public service, I have never seen a document so crowded with infamous falsehoods and distortions so huge I never before believed any government on this planet was capable of uttering them." The ambassadors were perfunctorily dismissed from Hull's presence.

The next day, December 8, President Franklin Roosevelt appeared before the Joint Session of Congress and made the most historically famous speech of American record:

"Yesterday, December 7th, a day which will live in infamy, the United States was suddenly and deliberately attacked by the naval and air forces

President Franklin Roosevelt signs the formal declaration of war against Japan, 8 December 1941. National Archives 70-AR-82.

of the Empire of Japan." From that beginning, the President went on to catalogue the devastation wreaked by the raiders, adding that because of the distance between Hawaii and Japan, "it is obvious that the attack was planned many days or even weeks ago. During the intervening time the Japanese Government has deliberately sought to deceive the United States by false statements of hope for continued peace." Roosevelt then listed the attacks of the Pearl Harbor raid, which brought the assembled Congress to utter silence.

"Always will our whole nation remember the character of the onslaught against us. No matter how long it may take us to overcome this premeditated invasion, the American people in their righteous might will win through to absolute victory. We will not only defend ourselves to the uttermost but will make it very certain that this form of treachery shall never endanger us again. We will gain the inevitable triumph, so help us God. I ask that the Congress declare that since the unprovoked and dastardly attaack by Janan on Sunday, December 7, a state of war has existed between the United States and the Japanese Empire."

He got approval from a unanimous Senate and with only one vote dissenting from the House of Representatives. Three days after the declaration of war against Japan, Nazi Germany and Mussolini's Italy, according to the terms of the Tripartite Pact, would declare war upon the United States, which responded in kind, and America found itself embroiled in what had become the Second World War, the greatest and bloodiest conflict in human history. And though Americans would have as powerful a determination to crush Nazi Germany, it would not match the hatred directed toward the Japanese. Racism on both sides, and rage for Pearl Harbor on the American side, had combined to produce a blood feud — fought with modern weapons in a global war. Nobody in 1941 could conceive what the ultimate end of such a war would be and the terrible price it would exact.

But of all minds in Japan, Isoroku Yamamoto's was the only one which comprehended the implications of what had happened. As Radio Tokyo broadcast the jubilant announcement of the successful destruction of the American fleet at Pearl Harbor, Yamamoto had been informed that the American government had not received the formal Imperial war decree until after the attack had had been in progress for almost an hour. With his characteristic bluntness, he spoke to his staff officers in the crowded wardroom aboard the *Nagato* and told them of this disastrous turn of fate.

"I cannot imagine anything that will infuriate the Americans more," he said to the men listening in silence. "I fear that all we have done is to awaken a sleeping giant, and to fill him with a terrible resolve."

CHAPTER 3

Defensive

During the afternoon of December 8, a single large ship, flying battle flags and with escorts trailing behind her, sailed through the entrance to Pearl Harbor and into clear sight of the still smoldering ships of the United States Pacific Fleet. On the bridge of the *Enterprise*, Rear Admiral William Halsey, his staff officers, and ship's captain George Murray took in the scene of devastation before them in grim, mute silence. Halsey's blood pressure came near to the boiling point until he growled, "Before we're through with 'em, the Japanese language will be spoken only in Hell."

Halsey had his flagship dock after having spent the previous day on a wild-goose chase for the ships of Chuichi Nagumo's First Carrier Strike Force. His pursuit had placed him well south of the enemy thanks to a stream of false sightings, which was just as well, since the *Enterprise* would never have stood a chance against six enemy flattops. He would also have to replace some of his planes. Several Wildcat fighters launched ahead had the bad luck to arrive just after the last of Fuchida's raiders were departing and were shot down by nervous gunners on the ground who were firing at anything in the air. Anything at all. Understandably, wild panic was in the air all over the island of Oahu, which had been placed under martial law by General Short just after the attack had ended. Midget submarines had been found and depth-charged, and everyone was expecting an invasion to follow. The invasion fear would persist for weeks afterward.

Six days after Congress formally declared war upon Japan, Admiral Kimmel and General Short were both relieved of their commands. William Pye was appointed to replace Kimmel on a temporary basis until the new Commander-in-Chief arrived to take charge. Salvage crews, as soon as the fires were put out, set to work on the ruined ships. Teams of divers with arc-welders either patched up torpedo damage to seal the hulls prior to pumping them out or proceeded to cut through debris and hull sections in an effort to free trapped crewmen aboard the *Oklahoma* and *Arizona* who might still be alive. Cleanup and repairs began at the airfields as well. Panic gave way to ordered chaos which in turn gave way to organized salvage as

Top: USS *Enterprise*, one of only three prewar American carriers to survive to the end of the Second World War. National Archives 80-G-66121. *Bottom*: The Grumman F4F Wildcat, a fighter which managed to hold its own with, and against, more advanced fighter planes throughout the war. National Arachives 80-G-07026.

the military machine kicked into gear to restore the base. The U.S. Navy set itself to lick its wounds and slowly, eventually, to prepare to fight another day. But until that day would arrive, the Japanese were, as Yamamoto had phrased it, running wild in the Pacific.

Starting the same day that the United States declared war, the Japanese military struck Hong Kong, Malaya, and Bangkok. In the weeks that followed, a relentless campaign began to unfold in the Western Pacific. The Philippines were bombed and attacked just prior to the full-scale invasions which ensued between December 12 and 24. The Gilbert Islands, Wake Island, Brunei, Hong Kong, and Canton all fell. Japanese carrier strike forces continued to prove in no uncertain terms that the day of the Big Gun had passed when, on December 10, the British battleship HMS *Prince Of Wales* and the battlecruiser HMS *Repulse*—both of which had participated in the destruction of the German battleship *Bismarck* in the Atlantic in May—were hit by carrier-based torpedo planes and sent to the bottom of the South China Sea off the coast of Malaya. Without air cover, neither ship stood a chance. And before the military might of Japan, it seemed that no force could stand against them. The Americans were paralyzed. The

Zeke fighters prepare to launch against targets during the opening campaign, which covered the Philippines, Singapore, Hong Kong, Rangoon, Malaya, Wake Island, Guam, and Ceylon. National Archives (captured Japanese archival photo) 80-G-176150.

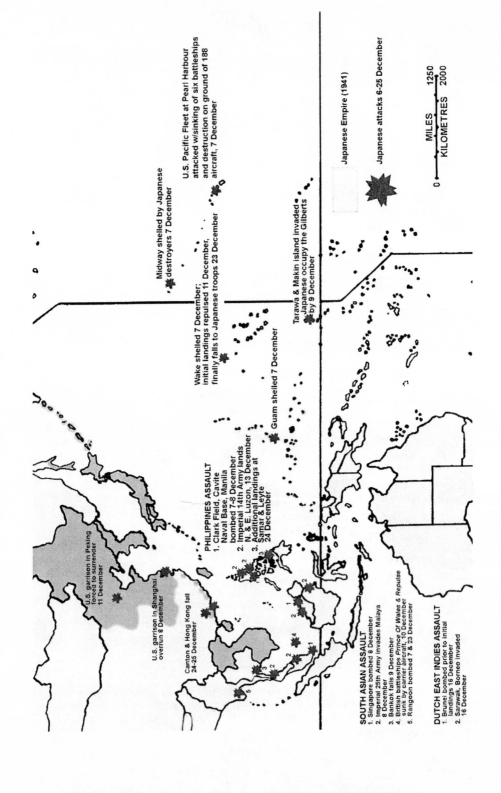

Midway shelled by Japanese
destroyers 7 December

U.S. Pacific Fleet at Pearl Harbour
attacked w/sinking of six battleships
and destruction on ground of 188
aircraft, 7 December

Wake shelled 7 December;
initial landings repulsed 11 December,
finally falls to Japanese troops 23 December

Tarawa & Makin island invaded
Japanese occupy the Gilberts
by 9 December

Guam shelled 7 December

PHILIPPINES ASSAULT
1. Clark Field, Cavite
   Naval Base, Manila
   bombed 7-8 December
2. Imperial 14th Army lands
   N. & E. Luzon, 13 December
3. Additional landings at
   Samar & Leyte
   24 December

U.S. garrison in Peking
forced to surrender
11 December

U.S. garrison in Shanghai
overrun 8 December

Canton & Hong Kong fall
24-25 December

SOUTH ASIAN ASSAULT
1. Singapore bombed 8 December
2. Imperial 25th Army invades Malaya
   8 December
3. Bangkok falls 9 December
4. British battleships *Prince Of Wales & Repulse*
   sunk by carrier aircraft, 10 December
5. Rangoon bombed 7 & 23 December

DUTCH EAST INDIES ASSAULT
1. Brunei bombed 16 December
   landings prior to initial
2. Sarawak, Borneo invaded
   16 December

Japanese Empire (1941)

Japanese attacks 6-25 December

MILES   1250
0   KILOMETRES   2000

French had already capitulated to the Axis months before and the Vichy Government virtually invited the Japanese to occupy Indochina. And the British and Dutch were forced into retreat from Asia. Beyond the wildest dreams of Hideki Tojo and the Kodo Party, beyond the hopes of Isoroku Yamamoto, the Imperial war machine was running rampant over the East, and the Western allies were powerless to stop them. Victory followed upon victory upon victory in a seemingly endless string of triumphs which fired the military onward and boosted the morale of the Japanese populace, who began to believe that Destiny really was on their side. Ultimately, this belief took on the characteristics of a faith rooted in a complacent, almost arrogant certainty which led the Japanese to convince themselves of their invincibility. War fever had mutated into a far more serious psychic ailment which gripped both the people and the officer corps right to the very top of the Japanese leadership: Victory Disease.

In the United States, President Roosevelt and Secretary Knox in the days following Pearl proceeded to reorganize the command of the U.S. Navy to restore morale and streamline operations. Ernest King, who had been serving as commander of the Atlantic Fleet and already was conducting offensive operations against the German U-boat menace while running convoys to Britain, was appointed to the newly created post of Commander-in-Chief of the United States Fleet, and the duties of Chief of Naval Operations—a post held by Admiral Harold Stark at the time of the raid—were folded into this new office. King, 63, had graduated from Annapolis in 1901 and had developed a reputation as a hard, humorless man who was more respected than loved. In his favor was a clear vision of the requirements for victory combined with a genius rooted in his broad experience with all phases of naval service: he had been an aviator, a submarine commander, staff officer, bureau chief, and member of the Naval Board. He knew both combat and administration inside-out. As a result, he brought to the position assets absolutely vital for conducting sea operations in a global war.

To replace Husband Kimmel, Chester W. Nimitz, 56, was chosen over twenty eight senior officers to be commissioned as the new Commander-in-Chief of the Pacific Fleet. In every way, he was the opposite of King in temperament—accessible, warm, outgoing. He was also a top-notch strategist, a gambler, calm in the face of impossible odds, and a man of considerable practicality who would know the quickest and most effective means to accomplish a task. He was a man who could inspire confidence

Opposite: Japan's Blitzkrieg — Pearl Harbor was merely the opening of a swift and vicious nineteen-day blitzkrieg which encompassed Southeast Asia, the Philippines, and the Dutch East Indies, and swept far into the Central Pacific.

The new leaders of the Navy after Pearl Harbor: COMINCH Admiral Ernest J. King (left) and CINCPAC Admiral Chester W. Nimitz (right). National Archives 80-G-23712 and 80-G-427844.

in the men of the Fleet, and that was perhaps a more pressing need than any other in the weeks following the sneak attack. Nimitz and King were seemingly incompatible but their personalities ended up complementing one another, and a good working balance between King in Washington and Nimitz at Pearl evolved. Together, the two men would develop the grand strategy which would ultimately bring Japan to her knees.

But for the moment, Nimitz had few assets to mount any sort of counterattack, and so he proceeded to do the only thing he could for the time being, getting his sunken battleships sufficiently repaired to undertake transit to the United States for more extensive reconstruction, repairing and restoring to operation what ships he could, and strengthening Pearl's defenses as well as rebuilding the few facilities which were destroyed or damaged in the raid. Nimitz reorganized the CINCPAC command structure. Discipline was tightened and Nimitz sought to instill confidence and a spit-and-polish demeanor in the men under his command. Gradually, the shell shocked personnel of Pearl Harbor grew back into a professional fighting force. In all these actions, Nimitz was laying the groundwork for a new fleet which would eventually strike forth into the waters of the Pacific to face the might of the Imperial Navy. But that day was still in the future, and for the time being, the prevailing tide across the ocean was Japanese.

Because American policy committed it to a "Europe First" strategy, and with the time it would take to restore the damaged ships at Pearl to service and build new warships, the paltry naval strike forces left were little better than targets for the enemy. When the Philippines came under invasion, Thomas C. Hart's United States Asiatic Fleet was compelled to retreat southward toward Java, though this was part of the strategies devised under the prewar Plan Orange. Hart's warships were to assist in the defense of the Dutch East Indies, which with their oil and mineral treasures were the capital object of the entire Japanese war effort. Admiral Hart had been kept on several years past retirement because of his experience in the Far East and subsequently was appointed to the command of a combined Allied naval force composed of battlegroups committed by the Americans, British, Dutch, and Australians. The ABDA fleet, as it became known, was the first attempt of this war at assembling a multinational battle force under a unified command, and fielded a seemingly impressive array of nine cruisers, twenty-six destroyers, and thirty-nine submarines. The fleet was to have been further augmented by the *Prince of Wales* and *Repulse*, but they were gone now. Furthermore, the one carrier which could be spared for attachment to the ABDA force, the HMS *Indomitable*, had run aground in the shoals off Bermuda weeks earlier and was thus unavailable. The fleet did have the U.S. Navy's first aircraft carrier, the USS *Langley*, but it had been converted to a seaplane tender and was no longer an operational flattop. ABDA would have no air cover going out to challenge the Japanese. In short, Hart and his Allied admirals knew ABDA's mission was doomed. The best they could hope for was to harass the enemy and inflict as much damage as possible before they were inevitably sunk.

Nevertheless, for the impossibility of their position, ABDA acquitted itself well in battle. Setting out from their bases at Batavia and Soerabaja, elements of the force engaged in raiding sorties. A squadron of American World War I–era destroyers, "four-pipers" as they were known because of their stacks, hit the Borneo port of Balikpapan on the night of January 24, 1942. The Dutch had finished blowing up oil storage and dock facilities as they retreated from the port, and the fires illuminated a Japanese convoy in the harbor. The *John D. Ford*, *Pope*, *Parrott*, and *Paul Jones* charged in, firing torpedoes and 5-inch guns. On heading back out into the open sea, they left behind three transports and a patrol boat sinking. It was the first surface battle fought by the U.S. Navy since Manila Bay in 1898 and provided an immediate morale boost. But the Japanese advance through Borneo was not slowed in the slightest, and only days later Allied airfields on

Java were hit hard by Japanese air forces, which destroyed most of the planes on the ground. This left no air cover whatsoever for the ABDA force to call upon and only hastened their demise. On February 4, four cruisers, led by the USS *Houston* and the USS *Marblehead*, and seven destroyers attempted another attack on a convoy in the Makassar Strait but were met by bombers overhead. In the ensuing action, the *Marblehead* was so heavily damaged that she barely survived to return to the States, and the *Houston*'s aft 8-inch turret was knocked out with heavy casualties. With the *Boise* having been put out of action days earlier by striking a reef, this left only one American cruiser to accompany the now much weakened ABDA fleet. A week after Singapore fell, Dutch Admiral Karel Doorman assumed command of what was left of the force. This included the battered *Houston*, the HMS *Exeter*, which had won distinction in 1939 for the pursuit of the German pocket-battleship *Graf Spee*, the HMAS *Perth*, Doorman's flagship HNMS *DeRuyter*, HNMS *Java*, and a screening group of nine destroyers which included four four-pipers, whose obsolete engines forced Doorman's formation to proceed slower than desired as they set forth, escaping from the Soerabaja base which was under heavy aerial bombardment, to attack an enemy convoy of forty-one transports. Unfortunately, the formation was escorted by a force of two heavy cruisers, two light cruisers, and fourteen destroyers. Furthermore, the enemy had control of the air and the escort force was composed of ships at peak readiness with fresh officers and crews, whereas the ABDA force was battered in both materiel and men. On the night of February 27, the two forces met in the Java Sea.

The Japanese heavies first opened fire at maximum gun range, 30,000 yards. The *Houston* and *Exeter* responded, and a shell from one of the *Houston*'s 8-inch guns struck one of the Japanese heavy cruisers below and forward of the bridge, forcing her to withdraw. But from that point on, the battle turned against the gallant but doomed ABDA fleet. The *Exeter* suffered a shell hit which penetrated to one of her fire rooms, cutting steam lines and reducing her speed to seven knots, forcing her to drop out of battle. A torpedo salvo cut down one of the Dutch destroyers in the formation. Still, Doorman pressed onward, determined to attack the convoy when reconnaissance planes found his ship and dropped flares which illuminated his whole formation. Shortly after midnight, the *Java* was struck and suffered a large explosion; she also dropped out of the battle line. The *DeRuyter* attempted a course change when an enemy salvo found the mark. The ABDA flagship sank quickly, and Doorman's last order was for the *Houston* and *Perth* to escape and not risk destruction themselves by hanging around to rescue survivors. As a result, Doorman and 344 of his officers and men went down with the ship.

The escaping ships found the main Japanese invasion force the next night, and though low on ammunition and badly damaged, the *Houston* and *Perth* charged forward into Banten Bay. In the confusion and surprise of the attack, the Japanese fired torpedoes wildly and several of their own ships were hit as a result. The two cruisers managed to sink one transport and damage three others so badly that the captains were forced to beach them. But it would prove a very short-lived triumph. A torpedo hit on the *Perth* killed her engines and she lay helpless until Japanese destroyers finished her off. Then, the *Houston* was caught in the searchlights of the convoy and suffered hit after hit after hit. The cruiser, which had been declared sunk so many times she had been nicknamed "The Galloping Ghost of the Java Coast," was now finished herself. There would be no last gallop out of this battle, and slowly, under continuing gunfire, the *Houston* settled — her own guns continuing to fire for as long as they were able. Six hundred ninety-six officers and men, including Captain Albert Rooks, met their deaths in battle against impossible odds. The next day, the *Exeter* was caught and sunk by four Japanese heavy cruisers which also took down the *Pope* and another escorting destroyer. The remaining ships which escaped were eventually found by planes from Nagumo's carriers, which sank most of the surviving vessels including two more American destroyers. At the last was the old *Langley*, one of the first aircraft carriers ever built in the world. She was ferrying fighter planes to Australia when enemy bombers found the venerable old flattop and sent her to the bottom. The last of the ABDA fleet was gone now, and along with it the Dutch East Indies, the conquest of which was completed by March 6. To cap the victory, Chuichi Nagumo's First Carrier Strike Force hit Ceylon in a four day series of brilliantly executed air raids which broke British sea power in the Indian Ocean by sinking the carrier *Hermes*, two cruisers, two destroyers, and a corvette, as well as reducing the Royal Air Force's presence to insignificance. From Burma to Wake Island, Japan now ruled the waves.

Under the terms of the ABC-1 war plan of 1941, Admiral King outlined an immediate Pacific strategy characterized as "defensive-offensive" operations. U.S. naval forces in the Pacific were directed to hold a line extending from Midway Island to Samoa to Fiji to Australia. They could spare no forces to relieve the desperate army of Douglas MacArthur, under siege in the Philippines. Naval units could only hold the defensive perimeter while striking at the enemy when and where they could. As soon as sufficient screening forces could be built up and training was complete, Admiral Nimitz cut orders for the first of a series of long-ranging hit-and-run carrier raids against advance Japanese bases and harassment of enemy shipping. The first of these raiding groups was built around the *Enterprise*

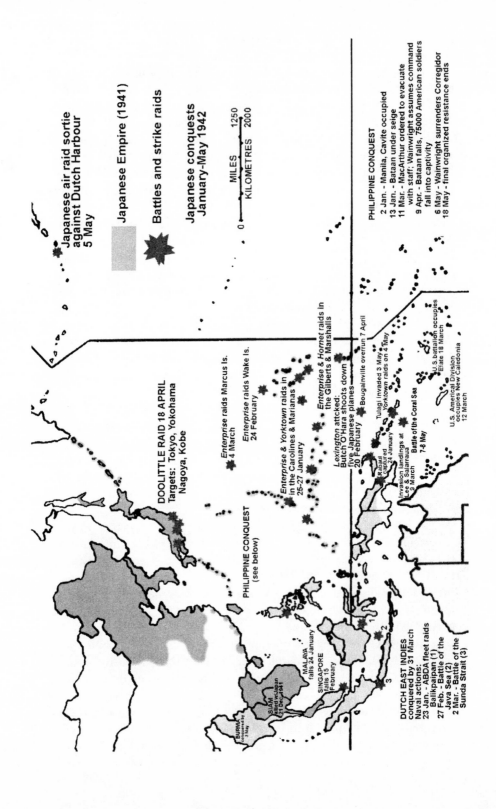

Japanese air raid sortie against Dutch Harbour 5 May

Japanese Empire (1941)

Battles and strike raids

Japanese conquests January–May 1942

MILES 1250

KILOMETRES 2000

DOOLITTLE RAID 18 APRIL
Targets: Tokyo, Yokohama Nagoya, Kobe

Enterprise raids Marcus Is. 4 March

Enterprise raids Wake Is. 24 February

Enterprise & Yorktown raids in in the Carolines & Marianas 25–27 January

Enterprise & Hornet raids in the Gilberts & Marshalls

Enterprise & Yorktown raids in the Carolines & Marianas 25–27 January

Lexington attacked: Butch O'Hara shoots down five Japanese planes 20 February

Bougainville overrun 7 April

PHILIPPINE CONQUEST (see below)

Tulagi invaded 3 May
Yorktown raids on 4 May

Rabaul captured 24 January

Invasion landings at Lee & Salamaua 9 March

Battle of the Coral Sea 7–8 May

U.S. battalion occupies Efate 18 March

U.S. Americal Division occupies New Caledonia 12 March

MALAYA falls 24 January

SINGAPORE falls 15 February

SIAM Allied w/Japan 21 Dec 1941

BURMA Conquered by 3 May

DUTCH EAST INDIES
conquered by 31 March
Naval actions:
23 Jan. – ABDA fleet raids Balikpapan (1)
27 Feb. – Battle of the Java Sea (2)
2 Mar. – Battle of the Sunda Strait (3)

PHILIPPINE CONQUEST
2 Jan. – Manila, Cavite occupied
13 Jan. – Bataan under seige
11 Mar. – MacArthur ordered to evacuate with staff: Wainwright assumes command
9 Apr. – Bataan falls, 75000 American soldiers fall into captivity
6 May – Wainwright surrenders Corregidor
18 May – final organized resistance ends

and commanded by the aggressive William Halsey and on February 1, while the ABDA force was being slowly and steadily whittled down, Halsey's task force struck at the Gilbert and Marshall Islands, bombing Japanese shipping and the new base facilities under construction. At Kwajelin, Halsey's planes sank a transport and two other vessels and damaged eight smaller craft. Carrier strikes then proceeded against Wake and Marcus Islands, and the *Lexington* task force hit the newly seized Japanese air bases at Rabaul on New Britain, the major island in the Bismarck Archipelago just north of Australia. During this attack, enemy defense fighters came up at the raiders and American carrier pilots found themselves in their first real engagement. In the fight that followed, Lieutenant Edward "Butch" O'Hare shot down five Zekes and in so doing became the first Navy ace of World War II. The hit-and-run strikes were little more than pinpricks against the might of Japan, but they served to raise morale both in the Navy and Stateside, provided valuable lessons in conducting carrier strike operations, and more importantly gave American carrier pilots vital combat experience without risking them in a major fleet engagement — a field education which would prove absolutely vital for the ordeals to follow. In the process, the U.S. Navy was learning to adapt itself to a whole new mode of sea warfare, sweeping away old thinking and learning how to achieve the utterly impossible. And in April of that year, they would do precisely that.

The desire for revenge for Pearl Harbor burned deep in the top leadership of the United States, civilian and military. Specifically, they knew the people needed a victory to solidify their conviction that America could win the war. And while achieving a valuable military purpose, Nimitz's quick strike raids were not enough. Something big had to happen, something which would really hurt the Japanese. Something, indeed, which would strike at their very sense of invulnerability and destroy morale. This inevitably led to the only conclusion available — an attack on the Japanese mainland itself.

There were problems with this idea — big ones. The Americans had no bases close enough to launch land-based bombers against Japan, and no carrier could hope to get within strike range and expect to survive that

Opposite: The First Six Months of War — While the U.S. Navy set about rebuilding, Isoroku Yamamoto, as promised, was able to run wild in the Pacific. Burma, Siam, the Dutch East Indies, and the Philippines all fell relentlessly before the Japanese assault, while her navy broke Allied seapower in the Java Sea and in the Indian Ocean. But even as the Empire enjoyed its greatest triumphs, the United States Navy already began striking back — pinpricks at first, but ultimately managing, with very meager forces at its command, to turn back a Japanese invasion and thereby set the stage for the greatest naval battle in history to that time.

deep in Japanese-controlled waters. All forms of conventional attack were ruled out and so it fell to Captain Francis S. Low, one of Admiral King's staff officers, and Captain Donald W. Duncan, a Navy air operations officer also on King's staff, to devise an alternative. The concept they eventually hit upon was unorthodox to say the least: to launch off the deck of an aircraft carrier land-based medium bombers. The two officers managed to sell King on this seemingly lunatic notion and convinced him to go as far as contacting Hap Arnold, the commanding general of the U.S. Army Air Force. But even before the plan had gone through for study, the two Navy captains barged in on Arnold to personally sell the idea to him. Arnold proved most enthusiastic to their proposal and eagerly contacted King to settle upon the division of responsibility. He then called in one of his own staff officers to discuss the particulars— a bona-fide American hero in prewar days— Lieutenant Colonel James Doolittle.

In civilian aviation, Doolittle had been a famous racing, stunt, and test pilot. He was the only man who not only managed to survive flying the infamous Granville Bros. GeeBee R1 racer but also to win the 1932 Thompson Trophy in it. He had set records for speed flights and aerobatics and also had contributed much to the science and engineering of aviation; he invented instrumentation which made possible the flight of a plane without ever looking out of the cockpit and subsequently proved it worked. He was an MIT graduate and a veteran of the Air Corps from 1917, recalled to active duty in 1940. For his time, James Doolittle was one of the world's top aviation experts. So when Hap Arnold asked him what sort of plane could carry a 2,000-pound bombload a distance of 2,000 miles after taking off from a runway space 500 feet long by 74 feet wide, Doolittle's answer was immediate: the North American B-25 Mitchell, which had a wingspan of only 67 feet.

Arnold and King conferred again, and mapped out the details of what became known as the "Special Aviation Project." A two-carrier task force would be required for the mission, one to carry the B-25s which would completely crowd her flight deck and the second to provide fighter cover, since the first ship obviously would be unable to launch her own planes as long as the Army bombers were up top. Volunteers would be chosen for the mission who would train in absolute secrecy and would not be given the details until the combined task force was underway. The planes would launch from the carrier, bomb selected targets in Japan, and then proceed to fly on to unoccupied China or the Soviet Union since landing back on the base ship would be impossible. A date of April 1 was set for the launch of the mission. Colonel Doolittle was chosen to command, and he wasted no time in setting preparations in motion. He initiated the training program while specifying the planes to be used and the modifications and adjustments to be made to their engines for the special conditions the planes would be operating under. The volunteers— all Army pilots— were confused by the presence of a Navy instructor who taught them how to take off with only 500 feet of runway available, but none of them opted out of the mission. They were all willing to follow Doolittle blindly, no matter what sort of flying was required.

On April 1, Doolittle's pilots found themselves at the Alameda Naval Air Station in California, where their sixteen B-25Bs were hoisted aboard the aircraft carrier USS *Hornet*. Once Doolittle's aircrews and planes were safely boarded, the carrier and her escorts weighed anchor and headed out into the Pacific. They would rendezvous with the *Enterprise* and her escorts at sea on April 8, and the ships of the combined Task Force 16, under command of Halsey, would proceed to a point in the ocean 685 miles from Japan. Only when they were underway were the pilots told of their special mission. They would bomb targets in Yokohama, Kobe, Nagoya, Osaka, Yokosuka, and the prize city of Tokyo itself (though the Emperor's palace was declared off limits— a restriction that Doolittle stressed repeatedly in briefing his pilots). For five days, the task force ploughed through the choppy waters of the Pacific with no incident. After an at-sea refueling, the task force's carriers, taking along only a few of their escorts, increased speed to 24 knots to make launch point for April 19. Then, the weather started to deteriorate as the carriers found themselves sailing into rain squalls and increasingly rough seas. Finally, at dawn on the 19th, scout bombers from the *Enterprise* spotted a Japanese patrol craft. Halsey put his ships into an evasive course toward the launch point and encountered high cross-winds and seas lapping over the decks. Time was running out; it would be now or never for the launch — especially as the *Hornet*'s lookouts sighted the picket boat *Nitto Maru* out on patrol. When the American force came into view, the *Nitto Maru*'s skipper sent out a signal which was picked up by the *Hornet*'s radio. Halsey ordered the cruiser *Nashville* to shell the picket boat and had Captain Marc Mitscher turn the *Hornet* into the wind. Doolittle's crews manned their planes, and at 0725 hours the first B-25 roared off the carrier's deck and successfully got airborne — itself a supreme feat of aviation. Once all the Army bombers were assembled in formation, the *Hornet* and *Enterprise* turned tail and headed back to where they left behind their remaining escorts, having necessarily to abort the planned three hour layover until word from the bombers of the attack's success was received, and Doolittle's fliers headed westward.

It was bright and clear over Tokyo that morning. The city was completing preparations to celebrate the Emperor's birthday, which also coincided with the commemoration of a monument to Japanese war dead. The

USS *Hornet* launches James Doolittle's B-25s on the daring Tokyo raid of 18 April 1942. National Archives 80-G-41196.

daily practice air raid was carried out on schedule, though the public did not participate, having become blasé to the continual alarms and excursions. The drill was mostly for the fire and emergency services and defense forces. Indeed, the people had become inured to the routine and the constant assurances that the Homeland was inviolable. They went about their business as usual, as if there was no war.

That pleasant illusion was shattered at 1230 hours when the first of Doolittle's planes arrived overhead. They came in low, skimming at treetop level on their approach to avoid detection by lookouts and defense fighters. The bombers dropped incendiaries— shells loaded with napalm — and quickly pulled away and headed for China. The same took place at the other target cities. Districts full of houses built from bamboo and rice paper burned easily. And despite Doolittle's repeated admonitions regarding the Emperor's palace, some minor damage was inflicted. Most of Doolittle's planes managed to make it to unoccupied territory where crews either bailed out or crash landed. One plane made it all the way to the Soviet Union, where it and its crew were interned for the duration. The sixteenth plane, however, which had suffered propeller damage when a *Hornet* deckhand got too close, came down in Japanese-held territory. The eight fliers were tortured, starved, and after a sham trial three were executed.

Militarily, the strike achieved very little. Psychologically however, it had proven devastating — about as much, if not more so, than Pearl Harbor had been for the Americans. For the first time, the Japanese people were shown, rudely, that the Homeland was not inviolable after all. Immediately after the raid, the propaganda assault upon the population increased tenfold. In the United States, however, the precise opposite effect was being experienced, a perfect yin-yang contrast between the two nations. The American public was inflamed with wild jubilation over the news that they had successfully struck back at Japan itself, and only five months after the Pearl Harbor debacle. It was a feat comparable in history to Stephen Decatur's successful 1804 mission into Tripoli harbor to burn the captured sail-frigate USS *Philadelphia* for the sheer audacity of the action, and its success against impossible odds and in achieving the mission by impossible methods. Addressing the nation by radio, President Roosevelt announced cryptically that the B-25s had taken off from Shangri-La, the mysterious and ageless city which was the setting for the James Hilton fantasy novel *Lost Horizon*.

The shock of the Doolittle raid did nothing to halt the ongoing march of the Japanese war machine across the Pacific. The same week that Task Force 16 set off on its mission, the American bastion at Bataan fell. While some Americans took their chances to desert to the jungle to carry on guerrilla warfare with Filipino natives, the 75,000 soldiers who surrendered in the largest mass-capitulation of American troops in history would suffer the cruelty of the Death March — in which stragglers and the sick and wounded were shot where they fell along the roadside — into prison camps and be forced to endure two and a half years of brutal captivity, starvation, and slave labor; customary Japanese treatment of war prisoners. The final conquest of the Philippines, halted only by the remaining resistance at Corregidor, was only a question of time. And the Dutch East Indies, the prime prize for which the whole war had been fought in the first place, was theirs. Common sense dictated that the time had come for consolidating their gains and tightening their defenses before planning for the next thrust. But common sense had gone right out the window; the Victory Disease had the Japanese in its grips and very few were immune to it. The Victory Disease drove the military forward into an immediate attempt to seize the whole of New Guinea and in particular the harbor of Port Moresby as an advance staging base for the inevitable invasion of Australia. The sec-

America's fighting admirals in the Pacific: Raymond Spruance (top left), Frank "Jack" Fletcher (top right), and William Halsey (bottom) (seen here in a 1944 photograph). National Archives 80-G-14193, 80-G-225341, and 80-G-431108.

Battle of the Coral Sea: the *Shokaku* under dive-bomber attack, takes evasive action. National Archives 80-G-17031.

ondary purpose was to establish a strong enough military presence sufficient to put an end to the hit-and-run strikes carried out by the *Enterprise*, *Lexington* and *Hornet*, which were proving to be a real nuisance.

To secure Port Moresby and the nearby islands of Guadalcanal and Tulagi in the Solomons, the Japanese sent forth a twelve ship invasion force under Vice Admiral Shigeyoshi Inouye, the C-in-C of the Imperial Fourth Fleet, accompanied by a second and larger group specifically targeted for Moresby and consisting of eleven troop transports, a screen of heavy and light cruisers, and the light carrier *Shoho*. Backing both invasion forces were the ships of Rear Admiral Chuichi Hara's Fifth Carrier Division, based around the sisters *Shokaku* and *Zuikaku*. Both had been detached from Chuichi Nagumo's First Carrier Strike Force for this operation and placed under the command of Vice Admiral Takeo Takagi. But waiting for them were the ships of Task Force 17, headed by the carriers *Lexington* and *Yorktown*, under the command of Rear Admiral Frank "Jack" Fletcher, a 22-year veteran and one of the most experienced carrier commanders in the U.S. Navy. Army intelligence had learned of the Japanese invasion thrust and the expected date, and Nimitz had dispatched Fletcher to intercept and destroy the invasion force, augmenting his screening group with two heavy cruisers, a light cruiser, and two destroyers.

Inouye set forth from Rabaul and headed southward into the waters of the Coral Sea while Takagi, after delivering planes there, was making his way around the perimeter of the Solomons to rendezvous with Inouye. He was taking the roundabout way because on May 3, after Tulagi had been taken, American planes bombed the beachhead. This indicated that at least one enemy carrier had to be in their sector. Takagi's intention was to come up from behind, after making an initial feint down the Solomons, to catch the enemy carrier group unawares and destroy it while Inouye's invasion force proceeded on to Moresby. On May 7 (the day after Joseph Wainwright, who took over for Douglas MacArthur when the latter, by direct order of the president, evacuated himself with his family and staff by PT-boat to Brisbane, was finally compelled to surrender the decimated and starving remnant of his army at Corregidor), enemy scout planes spotted what they took to be "a carrier and a cruiser." They were actually the fleet tanker USS *Neosho*, the ship which had miraculously gone untouched while in the middle of Battleship Row, and her accompanying destroyer, the USS *Sims*. On orders from Takagi, Hara launched a force of 78 bombers, torpedo planes, and fighters from both his carriers in an all-out attack on the "task force." The *Sims* went down in minutes under a rain of bombs. The *Neosho* was bombed and torpedoed repeatedly and reduced to a burnt-out wreck lying dead in the water. The surviving crew would have to wait several days until a destroyer arrived to rescue them and scuttle the hulk.

But the Japanese mistake had pulled away planes which might otherwise have gone after the *Lexington* and *Yorktown*, which were at the time vulnerable with all their planes off hunting the enemy. They were in pursuit of a wild goose of their own, a supposed force of two carriers and two heavy cruisers, which was actually a pair of outdated light cruisers. But serendipity played in the Americans' favor, for their course put them right over the light carrier *Shoho*. The scout bombers, dive bombers and torpedo planes of the *Lexington* went in first and all managed to strike the CVL but had not put her out of action. She was turning into the wind to launch planes when the *Yorktown*'s bomber and torpedo squadrons finally arrived and caught the *Shoho* at the moment of maximum vulnerability. They fell upon the flattop, dropping bombs and torpedoes from all sides, and moments later the airwaves were electrified by the announcement of Lieutenant Commander Robert Dixon of the *Lexington*: "Scratch one flattop." The carrier rolled over and sank in minutes with the loss of 500 of her crew.

The sudden destruction of the *Shoho* completely unnerved Shigeyoshi Inouye, and with the threat of repeat aerial attacks weighing on his mind, he chose discretion as the better part of valor, put his invasion force about and headed back to Rabaul, deciding not to proceed until it was certain that no enemy forces remained in the Coral Sea to menace his ships.

The next day, Hara's scouts spotted and definitively identified the *Yorktown* and *Lexington*, whereupon the enemy soon launched another attack force as large as the one sent forth the day before but which had only scored a tincan and a tanker. The *Shokaku* and *Zuikaku* were under cloud cover while the *Fighting Lady* and *Lady Lex* were in clear, sunny weather. Seventy planes fell on the two American flattops while American planes were off hunting the Japanese. They failed to find the *Zuikaku*, which upon sighting enemy planes on the horizon ran deeper into the rain squall for cover, but did find her sister and put three bombs into her.

Though they sank the light-carrier *Shoho* and heavily damaged the *Shokaku,* the American victory came at the heavy price of losing the USS *Lexington.* National Archives 80-G-16651.

Meanwhile, the Japanese strike force had hit the *Yorktown* with one bomb which killed 69 of her crew and inflicted severe damage below decks, while the slower *Lexington*, unable to evade attack as quickly as the newer flattop, was hit by three bombs and two torpedoes which left her listing and afire. The *Lexington*'s damage control crews worked furiously to right the ship and put out the fires. Both she and the *Yorktown* were able to recover their planes while repair and firefighting efforts were underway. In just an hour, the *Lexington*'s engineers succeeded in getting the flooded compartments pumped out and the torpedo damage patched while the fires were brought under control. Prospects for restoring the ship to operational capability seemed good. Volatile fumes had, however, built up to dangerous levels in her holds. An arc-welder, carelessly left on, sparked once. But that was enough. The spark ignited the fumes, and a big blast shook the carrier from stem to stern and wrecked her flight and hangar decks. Ruptured fuel lines went up and the fires soon became uncontrollable.

Many of the *Lexington*'s crew had served with the ship since her commissioning in 1927; in many ways, she was the Queen of the carrier fleet. It was a heartbreaker when Captain Frederick C. Sherman gave the order to abandon ship. The crew did so in such an orderly manner that they were able to finish off the ship's supply of ice cream and rescue Wags, Sherman's pet dog and ship's mascot. The captain was the last man down the lines, and the survivors were picked up by the destroyers *Morris* and *Hammann*. Given the damage to the *Yorktown*, Fletcher decided to withdraw from the area. He ordered the *Lexington* scuttled, and the destroyer *Phelps* went in and put two torpedoes into the carrier's side at sunset. Navy men watched in tears but also with pride as the *Lady Lex* slid beneath the waves, her head up and flying the Stars and Stripes as she sank.

The Americans had no effective strike force left to oppose the invasion. But in the course of the attacks on the American flattops, just about all of the *Zuikaku*'s strike wing had been wiped out, and the *Shokaku* was unable to board her own planes because of the American bomb damage. In and of themselves these difficulties should not have made much difference since the undamaged *Zuikaku* had taken all her sister's aircraft aboard and could still conduct air operations. But thanks to Inouye's retreat the previous day there was now no longer an invasion to cover. Under the circumstances, Takagi and Hara could not justify remaining in the Coral Sea and decided to withdraw back to Rabaul, despite being bombarded by orders from an increasingly furious Yamamoto to turn and attack. It would be two months before the *Shokaku* and her sister would be available for service again, and the absence of both carriers would make a crucial, even fatal, difference just four weeks into the future.

Chester Nimitz was not satisfied that they had traded the *Lexington* for the *Shoho*. Even if the Japanese flattop had been equal to the *Lexington*, the U.S. Navy could not afford to fight a war of attrition and lose a carrier for each one they sank. They had started the war with a two-to-one disadvantage. And he knew what was coming; they similarly could not afford to have the *Yorktown* out of action for three or more months. Nimitz took comfort in the fact that the fight put up by Task Force 17 had proven sufficient to check the Japanese thrust southward. Indeed, it was the first time that the Empire had been compelled to cancel an invasion.

Coral Sea was the first direct clash between the American and Imperial fleets, and the first time ever that warfleets engaged each other with aircraft and at such long ranges that opposing ships never had any visual contact. The face of naval warfare had definitively and decisively changed in two days and the time of the Big Gun was truly over.

It had been six months since Pearl Harbor — and Yamamoto, as he had promised, had run wild in the Pacific. But in that time the United States Navy, in only a few weeks after the devastation of the Pacific Fleet, had begun to strike back. It had maximized the resources available to it and achieved successes far beyond expectations. The navy had hurt Japanese military assets, had inflicted a major blow to Japanese morale, and for an encore had neutralized the Japanese threat against Australia — any one of

Douglas TBD Devastator torpedo bombers, which proved hopelessly obsolescent by June of 1942. National Archives NH77106.

which was supposed to have been impossible. In the process, the U.S. Navy had learned adaptability and in so doing mastered the art of aircraft carrier operations and tactics. As it was, their newfound and increasing proficiency was coming to them just barely in time.

Back on April 19, Isoroku Yamamoto had been at his home in Hiroshima when Commander Yasuji Watanabe, his aide, brought to him the news of the bombing attack on Tokyo. After being assured of the Emperor's personal safety, the only thing Yamamoto was ever truly fanatical about, he reasoned quickly that the strike had to have been launched from aircraft carriers. Anger over the possibility that his fleet could have allowed an enemy force to get so close to the Home Islands gave way to shock when he was told that the planes were B-25s launched from at least one aircraft carrier nearly 700 miles away, which was supposed to be impossible. The Americans had achieved it though, and by utilizing the very assets the Japanese had failed to catch and destroy at Pearl Harbor.

For a long time, Yamamoto had known that Imperial forces could not afford to consolidate their conquests, dig in, and wait for the Americans to attack. He knew that time was on the U.S. side. The war machine the enemy could build up with what he saw on tour in 1923 would destroy Japan. Because of this, he had for the last several months been trying to float a proposal for a thrust which ostensibly was to establish a forward base to anchor their Eastern perimeter but in reality was to fulfill Yamamoto's long held dream of a single, decisive battle against the American navy. Until now, his plan had been resisted because of the distance to the target and the attendant risk. But for Yamamoto's purposes, the American bombing of the capital had been a divine gift. It had proven that Japan was not invulnerable and that the only course of action was to eliminate the threat of the United States Navy. His gambit was the one sure way. The Doolittle raid became Yamamoto's tool in bludgeoning his opposition within the Naval General Staff and winning their assent to his strike plan, code-named Operation MI. He set the plan in motion immediately upon approval. Some half-hearted objections would continue until the defeat at Coral Sea three weeks later, after which all remaining opposition to MI was silenced.

Yamamoto would assemble the mightiest armada ever to sail and use half a year's worth of fuel in the effort to conquer a sandpit of an island in the middle of the Pacific. It was an obscure place which for long had been inhabited only by transient fisher-folk and goony birds before becoming a way station for the Pan American *China Clipper*, the main transpacific air service before the war — a tiny island known as Midway.

CHAPTER 4

Midway

Six minutes. That was all the time it took to change the whole course of the war. And it happened 300 miles northwest of a sandpit island called Midway.

Midway, a tiny atoll consisting of three small islands and a coral reef, lies at the westernmost end of the Hawaiian Islands, 1,150 miles from Oahu, and was so named because it is just about at the mid point in the ocean distances between Asia and the United States west coast. For that reason, in the early and desperate months of the Pacific War it became the forward base for the American Pacific defense perimeter. It had, since August of 1941, been serving as a naval air station with a complement of 800 men. After Pearl Harbor, Midway had been reinforced with additional air units consisting of a Marine Corps fighter squadron, 98 Navy scout and torpedo bombers, and from the Seventh Air Force seventeen B-17 bombers and four B-26s adapted to carry torpedoes. It had become the only frontline fortress between America and Japan, and the latter was now determined to reduce it to rubble, occupy the island, and in so doing to end the war.

Isoroku Yamamoto had pinned all his hopes for Japan's national survival on the chance to draw out what was left of the United States Pacific Fleet and destroy it utterly. Success in this, even if a long-term occupation of Midway proved untenable, would in his calculation render impossible any American effort to strike out into the Pacific and challenge Japanese hegemony again. Quite possibly, the Roosevelt government, embroiled with the struggle in Europe, would be forced to accept peace on Japanese terms. Indeed, if accepting the status quo caused America to turn inward to protect its continental mainland, she would by necessity be forced to withdraw from the war in Europe as well, which would end any further Western threat — particularly from Britain — and the future of the Japanese Empire would be assured. It was a gamble, but with a reasonable chance of success, a situation which appealed to Yamamoto's poker instincts. But he also knew that time was running out. Even as planning and preparation for the Midway Operation was underway, the Americans

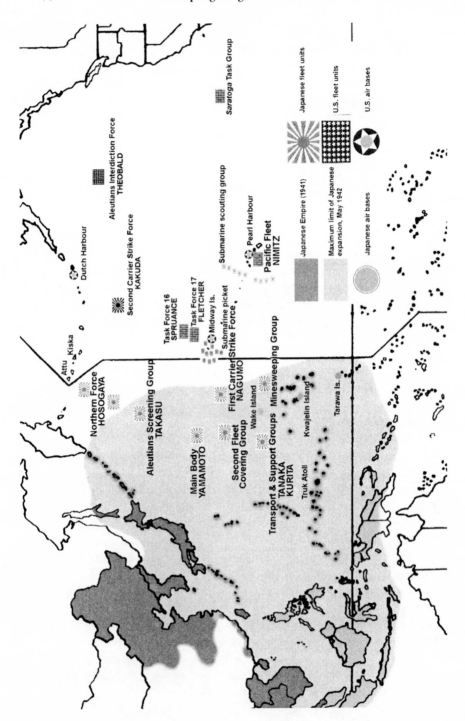

Saratoga Task Group

Aleutians Interdiction Force
THEOBALD

Second Carrier Strike Force
KAKUDA

Dutch Harbour

Submarine scouting group

Pearl Harbour

Pacific Fleet
NIMITZ

Task Force 16
SPRUANCE

Task Force 17
FLETCHER

Midway Is.

Submarine picket

First Carrier
Strike Force
NAGUMO

Minesweeping Group

Attu

Kiska

Northern Force
HOSOGAYA

Aleutians Screening Group
TAKASU

Main Body
YAMAMOTO

Second Fleet
Covering Group

Wake Island

Transport & Support Groups
TANAKA
KURITA

Truk Atoll

Kwajelein Island

Tarawa Is.

Japanese fleet units

U.S. fleet units

U.S. air bases

Japanese Empire (1941)

Maximum limit of Japanese
expansion, May 1942

Japanese air bases

had already won a significant strategic victory at Coral Sea in turning back the invasion aimed at Port Moresby. If this effort failed, and the war progressed past the six months to a year in which Yamamoto knew victory was certain, the weight of American material superiority would inevitably, inexorably crush the Empire. The Midway Operation had to succeed at all costs.

Despite the loss of the *Shoho* at Coral Sea and the laying up of the sisters *Shokaku* and *Zuikaku* for repairs and the replacement of their squadrons, the Combined Fleet had massive resources to draw upon for the Midway Operation. The battle force Admiral Yamamoto would assemble was by all means an impressive and overwhelming one. He would have at his command eight aircraft carriers, eleven battleships, including the newly commissioned superbattleship *Yamato*—the largest and most heavily armed warship in the world—twenty-three cruisers and sixty-five destroyers, along with a large number of long-range submarines, transports, oilers and supply vessels. He also had an array of the finest officers in the navy to draw upon for command of the various elements of his strike force: Matome Ugaki, Tamon Yamaguchi, Boshiro Hosagoya, and most critically, Chuichi Nagumo and his two air operations geniuses Mitsuo Fuchida and Minoru Genda. Helping to formulate the attack plan was another of the architects of the Pearl Harbor raid, the much-renowned "God of Operations," Kameto Kuroshima. With the available force and talent at his command, Yamamoto had every reason to look forward to certain victory against the poor American fleet which had, at best, two operational aircraft carriers, eight cruisers, and an odd number of destroyers and submarines. It was all that was left after Pearl Harbor and the reported loss of the carriers *Lexington* and *Yorktown* at Coral Sea.

The plan developed by Yamamoto's staff was designed to feint the Americans at several points of possible attack and in so doing tempt them to recklessness and the straining of the meager resources left to them. It was also designed to confuse the enemy by using a series of intricate naval maneuvers which would come together at the proper moment when the U.S. fleet was lured out into the Northern Pacific, hundreds of miles from base and the protection of any land-based air forces. Phase One of the plan involved a diversionary strike by a combined force of carriers and

Opposite: The Midway Campaign — With ten task forces simultaneously at sea, Isoroku Yamamoto gambled everything on a bold plan to draw out the remnant of the Pacific Fleet, meet it in open battle in the middle of the ocean, and destroy it. Knowing that Midway Island was the target of the enemy thrust, Chester Nimitz took a bold gamble of his own to block the enemy thrust by striking at its lynchpin, the carrier force of Chuichi Nagumo.

amphibious forces to attack and occupy the Alaskan islands of Attu and
Kiska, presenting a threat to the American mainland from the north. A
second force would hit Dutch Harbor, further up the Aleutians chain, in
support of the Attu-Kiska invasion by suppressing American tactical air
as well as disrupting communication with Alaska. With a clear threat developing there, the U.S. Pacific Fleet would have to charge northward to
attempt to neutralize the invasion. Once drawn out, as would be revealed
by a force of screening submarines dispatched to track the movement of
the enemy, Phase Two, the invasion thrust against Midway Island by three
forces converging from the west-southwest, would be underway. Once
word of the main attack would reach the Americans, they would be obliged
to turn southward and race to Midway's rescue — where they would run
right into the clutches of the First Carrier Strike Force, placed 350 miles
northwest of the island to provide air support for the invasion thrust and
also to strike at the American fleet. Following up on these forces would be
the Main Body, which would have the bulk of the Combined Fleet's battleship and cruiser strength including the *Yamato*, the light carrier *Hosho*
and additional seaplane carriers, and could pivot either towards Midway
or the Aleutians depending upon how the coming battle developed. Converging upon the Americans to close the jaws of the trap would be the
ships and aircraft of the Dutch Harbor strike force. The Pacific Fleet would
be caught in a three-way pincer from which it would not escape, and would
this time be sunk in deep water. With the destruction of the Pacific Fleet,
Midway could be occupied, along with Attu and Kiska, and the remainder of the Hawaiian Islands and even the U.S. west coast would be under
effective threat, forcing the Americans into a permanent defensive position and, ultimately, to terms.

Yamamoto's strategy relied upon a considerable degree of complex-
ity to maximize the confusion of the Americans. As a result, the Combined
Fleet would be spread out into ten separate task forces all over the Pacific
that were expected to converge upon the Midway and Aleutians targets on
schedule, and to head southward or northward depending upon which
way the Americans moved. Yamamoto himself would be riding with the
Main Body in his flagship, the *Yamato*, and the Main Body itself would
trail 350 miles behind Nagumo, to be in that ideal position to either go
eastward to Midway, or north toward Alaska to close the pincer on the
Pacific Fleet. The submarine force, consisting of a dozen boats, had to be
on station by June 1 in a cordon northwest of Oahu and lying between the
main Hawaiian islands and Midway to shadow the American movements
and provide frontline intelligence for the rest of the fleet. His strategy also
turned on the certainty that the Americans would behave in a reckless

manner when confronted with two invasion thrusts. In this, the Japanese anticipated that the Pacific Fleet would be commanded by the U.S. Navy's most daring carrier commander, William Halsey, who had led the raids against Japanese bases and shipping in the Marshall and Gilbert Islands as well as the daring Doolittle raid back in April. He was well known as an aggressive officer who preferred to face his enemy head on. The Japanese planners had every reason to expect that Halsey would be unable to resist the challenge presented and would attempt to rush forward to intercept and destroy the Aleutians invasion force and then, when the Midway threat presented itself, to rush back to rescue the island. That would deliver the Americans right into their hands and certain destruction.

Operation MI also, by definition, depended upon ironclad security so that complete surprise could be achieved. It was therefore quite unfortunate for the Japanese that Yamamoto's opposite number, Chester Nimitz, was reading their every radio message as if all their communiqués had been printed in the afternoon newspaper. The Japanese naval code, JN-25, had been broken after a seven year effort at decryption by HYPO, the U.S. Naval Intelligence's cipher division, and Japanese naval traffic had been available to them since before Coral Sea. As a result, even with the latest variations to JN-25, the Americans were aware of every move the enemy was making. They had naturally picked up on the increased radio traffic which accompanied the coordination of the Combined Fleet's movements across the Pacific and out of Japan. Analysts had identified two codes obviously referring to military objectives — AF and AO — but were thus far unable to determine precisely what they referred to. Admiral Nimitz, himself a good poker player, had reasoned that if Japan meant to win the war, it had to make a strike toward Hawaii to finish up what it had failed to completely achieve with Pearl Harbor and that it had to lure out the Pacific Fleet and destroy it. Nimitz held to this conviction despite insistence from some on his staff and from Washington that the Japanese would attempt to invade the west coast. Complicating the problem of determining the next Japanese objective was the fact that, preceding Pearl Harbor, the enemy had flooded the airwaves with fake messages for deception purposes, and the massively increased radio traffic looked as if the same pattern was occurring again. But Commander Joseph Rochefort and his decrypt experts kept picking up repeated references to AF and AO, and initial Japanese movements were headed toward Midway and the Aleutians, which provided a clue to what the enemy's next target was. Following a hunch, Rochefort suggested to Nimitz that he should order the Midway base to transmit a message in the clear that their distillation plant was out of commission and that they were subsequently running short of fresh water.

Nimitz did so, and Midway sent out the message as instructed. Days later, the HYPO codebreakers picked up what turned out to be a crystal clear message: "AF is short of fresh water." Nimitz had found out all he needed to know, and Yamamoto's grand strategy had been completely undermined.

For a nation which believed so fervently in Fate as the primary guiding force in human destiny, it was a cruel irony when that force seemed, quite suddenly, to have turned completely against the Japanese. Everything which could have gone wrong with the Midway Operation began to go wrong almost immediately. Lacking both the *Shokaku* and *Zuikaku*, Nagumo's First Carrier Strike Force had been cut down to two-thirds strength. Surprise was no longer achievable, though they would not know that as the various task forces set out from their home ports. Furthermore, several of the submarines expected to form the picket line were late in being outfitted and, thanks to further delay by bad weather, would set forth late and therefore had no hope of being on station by the scheduled date of June 1. They would not know, going in, when the Americans left port or where they would be. Of particular bad luck for Nagumo was the fact that both Fuchida and Genda were down with the flu and confined to sickbay as his force set sail. And in what would prove to be a truly cruel twist of fate, the one element of the Japanese plan on which its entire success was predicated suddenly was no longer in the equation. Halsey was beached.

The pressure of continuous combat since Pearl Harbor and an acid temperament had triggered an outbreak of shingles so severe that Halsey had to be hospitalized. He would not be able to return to duty for weeks afterward, and certainly could not command his task force for the coming battle. Given this, Nimitz visited his favorite admiral in the hospital and asked his recommendation for a replacement. Without hesitation, Halsey gave one: Raymond A. Spruance. Nimitz balked at first; Spruance was a "cruiser skipper" with no real experience with aircraft carriers and cautious by nature. But Halsey stuck with his recommendation. He knew Spruance well, having had him as his second in command. Despite his apparent record, Spruance was familiar with carrier tactics and was an able strategist who had planned several of Halsey's raids in the Gilberts. He trusted him, and that was sufficient for Nimitz to override his own objections and those of his staff and to hand over the *Enterprise* and *Hornet* to the "cruiser skipper." This one change would upset all the Japanese equations on which their grand strategy was based; Spruance would not charge impulsively after the Japanese headed toward the Aleutians or charge back in haste and carelessness to Midway and into the jaws of a trap. He was cautious, comparatively unimaginative, and certainly less daring than

Halsey. But this was enough to change the whole picture. In overall command of the combined force would be Nimitz's veteran carrier commander, Frank "Jack" Fletcher, who had recently triumphed at Coral Sea and had just succeeded in bringing back the wounded *Yorktown* from across the Pacific.

Fletcher's feat had also added a new element the Japanese hadn't anticipated, a third aircraft carrier. Japanese intelligence had reported the *Yorktown* either sunk or so badly damaged that she would be out of action for several months. It might indeed have taken that long to properly recondition the battered flattop, but the U.S. Navy had neither the time nor the luxury of reinforcements to draw upon. Nimitz had three whole shifts of shipfitters, welders, damage control engineers, and technicians, many drawn off the work on other vessels, waiting to swarm aboard the damaged carrier as soon as she docked. In less than three days, working around the clock, they achieved the impossible. The *Yorktown*'s battle damage from Coral Sea was substantively repaired and she was operational once again, available to sail on May 30 to link up with Spruance's Task Force 16, which was already heading out into the Pacific.

Nimitz had everything in place. He knew where Yamamoto was heading and the details of his plans. He had three aircraft carriers and Midway's land-based planes, which gave the U.S. forces the equivalent strength of four complete carrier air wings. In addition, his ships and Midway had an additional advantage — the new radar technology which had come of age in 1939 and had already helped to win the day for the Royal Air Force in the Battle of Britain. He had two capable combat officers in command out on the Pacific, one of whom the Japanese hadn't figured on (though no one on the American side could have known the difference that would make). But there was still the outside chance that the Japanese main target was the Aleutians. Or that the whole thing was a ruse and therefore a trap. Nimitz was gambling literally everything on one round; either the United States would triumph in the coming battle, or Nimitz would lose the fleet and possibly the war. There was no third possibility.

By the morning of June 3, Task Forces 16 and 17 were gathered at a place known as Point Luck, an arbitrary spot located 350 miles northeast of Midway Island, while a token naval force under Admiral Robert Theobald was headed to the Aleutians to cover the possibility that the main Japanese thrust might be aimed there after all. Meanwhile, long-range Catalina flying boats were covering sweeps in a 180-degree arc out to 700 miles from the island when one of the scouts, piloted by Ensign Jewell H. Reid, spotted a large force of ships to the west. He had found the transports of Rear Admiral Raizo Tanaka which were attached to the Midway

Invasion Force, and kept to the clouds while tracking them on their course eastward. Tanaka's lookouts spotted the Catalina and sent up antiaircraft fire, but it was far too late. They had been seen and now any hope for surprise was irretrievably lost.

Upon the report from the Catalina, Midway air operations swung into high gear at once, and nine B-17 bombers were launched just after noon to intercept the Japanese formation. They found the enemy task force 570 miles to the west and went in for the attack. The Japanese ships took evasive action while filling the sky with flak. The bombers, at altitudes of 10,000 and 12,000 feet, dropped a total of thirty-six 600-pound bombs—which completely missed the targets. Not a single hit on surface ships or planes was scored by either side. While this somewhat inconclusive round was being played out, the initial shelling at Dutch Harbor in the Aleutians had commenced.

Simultaneously, Nagumo's First Carrier Strike Force was ploughing through heavy seas and heavier fog and cloud cover. The terrible weather prevented all possibility of launching scout planes, and with no intelligence coming from submarines which had not been on station when Spruance and Fletcher sailed, he was literally going into battle with no idea where the enemy was. Nor was any intelligence from Yamamoto available, even though the radio aerials aboard the *Yamato* had picked up on increased communications in and around Hawaii. The Commander-in-Chief was strictly observing radio silence. He assumed that, as Nagumo was hundreds of miles closer to the enemy, he must surely have picked up on the radio traffic. This was not so, however, due to the *Akagi*'s poorer radio apparatus. Nagumo was therefore forced to hope that any American carrier forces were still in the Solomon Islands, where intelligence had last placed them.

Fletcher, for his part, studied the reports of Ensign Reid's contact with Tanaka's transports and of the B-17 attack. Because no carriers had been spotted, he reasoned that the main strike force had not been involved and had to be somewhere else. He knew of a weather front to the northwest, and drew on an instinct that if the carriers would be anywhere, it would be in the thick of that squall, approaching under cover, which was what he would do. As a result, he drew the task forces further in to 200 miles north of Midway to be in a better position to intercept the enemy the next day.

Dawn rose at 0430 on the morning of June 4. Nagumo's carriers reached a relative clearing in the weather, turned into the wind, and at 0445 hours launched 108 planes for the initial bombardment of the Midway shore installations. The Vals and Kates under the command of Lieutenant Joichi Tomononga formed up into two V-shaped echelons while Zeke fighters formed up into a combat air patrol. As the first strike was getting into the air, Midway-based Catalinas were already fifteen minutes airborne and headed out westward in search of the enemy force. They were followed up shortly by B-17s from the 5th and 11th Bomb Groups of the Seventh Air Force to proceed to the attack as soon as the scouts sighted the enemy.

When Nagumo launched his first strike, he had been confident that there was no American task force anywhere near his area and that they were unaware of their plan or his approach. But before long, his natural caution was reasserting itself. He had ordered a second wave of 108 planes prepared with torpedoes and armor-piercing bombs to deal with ships, and further directed the launching of scout planes to commence air search operations to the south and east, as well as all sectors north of Midway Island. The search plan was devised by a barely recovered Minoru Genda, who coaxed himself out of sickbay to return to duty when his admiral needed him the most. But things began to go wrong again and at the worst possible time for the Japanese. Seven scouts were scheduled to take off, but only two managed to lift off on time. One plane developed engine trouble and was forced to return before accomplishing a significant portion of its assigned search mission, and others of the scout force were forced back to their base ships by bad weather. But the worst breakdown of operations occurred with the half-hour delay in launching the scout plane from the cruiser *Tone* because of malfunctions in the ship's catapult system. Its search pattern was to have encompassed the area of ocean 200 miles to the north and a few degrees slightly east of Midway Island: right where Fletcher and Spruance were lying in wait.

Fletcher and the Midway command were having considerably better luck launching their own air search operations. Ten Dauntless dive bombers from the *Yorktown* were in the air as were five Catalinas from the island. The Dauntlesses failed to sight anything in the weather front to the northwest, but Flight 58, under the command of Lieutenants Howard Ady and William Chase, spotted through clear patches in the cloud cover the telltale wakes of Nagumo's aircraft carriers and escorts. Hurriedly, they radioed back a report of the contact, but said only "Enemy carriers sighted." Not how many or their exact location. Nor did they have time to clarify the details; they had been sighted by the ships and were coming under antiaircraft fire, and Zeke fighters were boring in for attack. Fortunately, they lost them in a cloud bank. In the meantime, they had spotted Tomononga's formation while circling back for another look, flying right below them and already halfway to Midway, and radioed an immediate message: "Many enemy planes heading Midway, bearing 320 degrees, distance 150." The Catalina then sent a follow up message which gave the details Fletcher desperately needed. Two carriers and battleship were on the same bearing and distance, heading on a southeast course at a speed of 25 knots. With that information, Fletcher radioed Spruance and ordered him to launch bombers and torpedo planes immediately, with information that he would follow as soon as his search planes were recovered.

As soon as the message warning of the approach of Tomononga's attack force had been received, air search radar on Midway spotted the planes, and the ground staff scrambled planes and prepared for air assault. The bombers heading for Tanaka's transports were redirected to the position of Nagumo's carriers to hit them instead, and the four torpedo-equipped B-26s were launched to join them in the strike, along with six Grumman TBF Avenger torpedo bombers, the first combat mission for these aircraft in the war. Additionally, a squadron of Dauntless dive bombers and a squadron of semiobsolescent Vindicator bombers were launched to strike at the carriers. To meet the oncoming attack by Tomononga, Midway lofted a force of 25 fighters. Unfortunately, most of these were the decidedly inferior Brewster F2A Buffalo fighter, a plane whose design was based on air combat as conceived in the '30s and therefore totally unsuited for the war which had actually developed. The remainder were reliable F4F Wildcats. The lead Wildcat pilot, Major Floyd Parks, spotted the Zekes which were heading down for strafing runs on the base and the rest of Tomononga's planes, which weren't expecting an attack. The Wildcats and Buffaloes dove in to strike. The result was a virtual massacre; thirteen Buffaloes and two Wildcats were shot down in exchange for only five or six Japanese planes. Ten Marine fighters returned to the airfield, and of those, only two were operational for any subsequent action. For the Buffalo fighter, however, this was its first and last action in American service.

Tomononga's squadrons arrived over Midway at 0630 hours and proceeded methodically to pound the base. In twenty minutes through heavy antiaircraft fire the Japanese dropped around five hundred bombs on Midway, Sand, and Eastern Islands, demolishing barracks, a generator house, the post exchange, and the command post. They demolished the seaplane hangar and set the fuel stores afire. But through the strike, little damage was done to the airfield itself. The runways were still clear and operational, and almost none of Midway's planes were on the ground. And despite the heavy bombardment only thirteen Americans lost their lives in the course of the attack, though one was the base commander, Major William Benson. Tomononga led his planes away from the burning islands aware that

A Wildcat fighter launches from the USS *Yorktown* at the Battle of Midway.
National Archives 80-G-312016.

his strike had accomplished very little. Antiaircraft defenses were still in
place and the airfield was still available for action. A second strike at least
would be necessary to reduce the base and he so radioed to the *Akagi* at
0700 hours.

The Tomononga report, innocuous and direct as it was, began, imperceptibly at first, to set off a chain-reaction of confusion which would hin-
der the smooth execution of air operations for the First Carrier Strike
Force. Nagumo was already becoming nervous over the possibility that
enemy carriers might be in the vicinity and now the message from his
attack wing indicated that Midway could still launch airstrikes against his
own force. The Americans were surely aware by now that he was in their
sector. Where would the threat materialize from? He was torn between
authorizing a second strike against the island installations or preparing for
carrier-based assault. Making matters worse was the conflicting advice he

was getting from his staff officers, particularly in the form of an increasingly heated argument between Rear Admiral Ryonsuke Kusaka and Minoru Genda over which potential threat was the greater. As the bridge of the *Akagi* filled with the rancor between the officers, the alert klaxons began to blare, the first and only warning of attack since none of the Japanese ships had radar sets. Four B-26s and six Avengers appeared over the horizon and bore down on Nagumo's flagship. Antiaircraft fire and a trio of Zeke fighters, as well as gunfire from the cruiser and destroyer escorts, cut the first attack to bits in minutes and not a single torpedo was launched within effective range. Nagumo and his officers were able to watch in safety as the *Akagi* easily evaded the fish. But the dispute between Kusaka and Genda continued until Genda, when pressed by Nagumo, conceded that Tomononga's planes could be armed for anti-ship strikes. With that, Nagumo made his decision: the second wave planes on the *Akagi* and the *Kaga* were to be rearmed with contact bombs for the second strike against Midway.

Planes were hastily taken below to the hangar decks and worked over by the armorers. Because speed was vital, the torpedoes and armor-piercing bombs could not be properly stowed and so were simply left piled up on the decks, to be taken below to the magazines later. While the rearming was taking place, air raid sirens sounded again. The new attack came in the form of 14 B-17s which flew over at 10,000 feet and dropped their loads at the *Hiryu* and *Soryu*. But both ships remained untouched; great geysers of water were thrown up but not a single bomb scored a hit. The second American attack had failed, and the fact that these had been land-based bombers confirmed the decision to ready the second Midway strike as soon as possible. But then, as rearming was about to be completed, the *Akagi* received a radio report from Scout Four, the plane from the cruiser *Tone* which was a half-hour delayed in launching because of the faulty catapult. The plane had finally reached its assigned search sector and had spotted American ships: ten of them, though there was no identification as to their type. Now the confusion began to build, as well as the tension on the *Akagi* bridge, as Nagumo sent out orders to cease arming the planes with contact bombs and to switch back to the anti-ship ordnance instead. Effort reduplicated as the crews sweated over the switchover, and again bombs and torpedoes were left stacked on the decks, or were sent back down to the magazines without being properly disarmed.

In the middle of this mad ant-dance on the carriers, the air raid siren sounded for the third time. Marine SBD Dauntless and Vindicator bombers appeared. The Dauntlesses went in first, but because their pilots had not been trained in dive-bombing attacks, they instead came in on a glide-bombing approach and were intercepted at 800 feet by Zekes. Half the Dauntlesses were shot down and none scored a single hit or even came close. Next in were the slower Vindicator bombers which were out of range of the carriers and so bore in on the escorting cruisers. Yet another ineffectual American attack had been effortlessly beaten off, but the reports from Scout Four gave conflicting information which did nothing for Nagumo's state of mind. The first dispatch stated that the American surface force consisted of only five cruisers and five destroyers. The next one, however, was the first indication of the American aircraft carriers Nagumo feared: "Enemy force accompanied by what appears to be an aircraft carrier bringing up the rear." The third report, received ten minutes later, gave no more details, but by now it was impossible to discount the possibility of at least one carrier. But Nagumo was in a quandary. If a carrier was with that force, where were its planes? In the midst of his confusion, Tamon Yamaguchi aboard the *Hiryu* radioed Nagumo advising an immediate attack on the American task force. And complicating matters was the fact that Tomononga's planes would be running out of fuel; launching the strike against enemy surface ships now would mean leaving the first strike wave to ditch in the sea.

It took several painful minutes for Nagumo to finally make a decision; he would recover the returning Midway strike force, which would be refueled and rearmed for action against the American surface forces as soon as possible. The readied planes on the *Akagi* and *Kaga* were cleared from the decks to recover the Tomononga force. With that, Nagumo set his force heading northward to close to optimum range of the American force. He radioed his intentions to Yamamoto and to Nobutake Kondo, commanding the Invasion Force, and proceeded to attack position. Aboard the *Hiryu* and *Soryu*, planes were being rearmed from bombs to torpedoes. And as the First Carrier Strike Force steamed northward, Nagumo's prized ships were crowded on flight and hangar decks with fueling and fueled planes, avgas lines, and loose, live ordnance.

On the American side, things were going much more smoothly than for the Japanese. The *Enterprise* and *Hornet* had launched a full attack force of bombers and torpedo planes at around 0700 hours; at roughly the same time Tomononga's planes were swarming over Midway. Spruance had originally intended to wait until he had closed to within a hundred miles of the last reported enemy position, but on the advice of Captain Miles Browning, who reasoned that the enemy would wish to launch a second strike against Midway as soon as possible and therefore could possibly be caught at the worst moment of vulnerability — preparing to launch planes on the decks — had decided to speed up his timetable. The *Hornet* put up a total of 60 aircraft; 15 Douglas Devastator torpedo bombers verging on obsolescence which composed Torpedo Squadron VT8 under the command of John C. Waldron, a man who flew by instinct and, being part Sioux Indian, could supposedly "feel" his way to the enemy, along with 35 Dauntless dive bombers and 10 Wildcats. The *Enterprise* also launched 60 planes, and these were followed up with the *Yorktown*'s own squadrons a half-hour later. One hundred fifty-five planes were on their way to the expected interception point. But en route to the Japanese force, a slight mishap occurred. Max Leslie, commander of the *Yorktown*'s VB8 squadron, had signaled his pilots to arm bombs as soon as they reached cruising altitude at 10,000 feet. The planes were recently equipped with a new electrical arming switch. When Leslie pushed the button, he felt his plane lurch upward. His 1,000-pound bomb had released prematurely. Three other SBDs lost their bombs as well. The electrical switch was obviously malfunctioning, and Leslie quickly radioed the rest of his squadron to use manual arming. Leslie was now leading only thirteen properly armed planes but there was nothing for it but to press on. Meanwhile, while four of Leslie's planes were losing their ordnance, Stanhope Ring, air group commander of the *Hornet* who was leading the *Hornet* and *Enterprise* bombers, had lost Nagumo. While his ships were under cloud cover, they had changed course to the north. Ring continued to follow the line of his base course, then realized that the enemy must have altered their heading. He turned his planes toward Midway atoll, but again found no evidence of enemy ships, only the smoke columns from the burning islands. He had guessed wrong, and now was losing some of his force as planes began running low on fuel. Some planes managed to make it back to the *Hornet*. Others were forced to land on Midway or, the ones running out of avgas, to ditch in the seas around the island.

Though Ring has gotten lost, Commander Waldron hadn't. The part–Sioux had guessed correctly that Nagumo's carriers would change course if they meant to intercept Task Forces 16 and 17 and swung his Devastators northwest, as did the Devastators of the *Enterprise*'s Torpedo 6 squadron. Keeping watch over them were ten Wildcats from the *Enterprise* led by Lieutenant James Grey. As the Devastators made their approach to the Japanese task force, Waldron ordered his planes to drop to wave-level to make their run and once in range sighted on the nearest carrier, the *Akagi*.

Fifty Zeke fighters were flying cover overhead, and they dived on Waldron as soon as they sighted him. Because of a lack of coordination between groups, there was no signal for Grey's fighters to come to Waldron's aid, and Torpedo 8 went in without protection. The Devastators were slow and lumbering planes, equipped with only one .50 caliber machine gun for defense and barely able to make 200 mph in full flight; they were moving targets. The Zekes swooped down on the hapless planes from all sides and literally shot them to pieces. The last plane in was piloted by the squadron's navigator, Ensign George H. Gay, who watched helplessly as his squadron mates were killed plane by plane, which all burst into flames and tumbled into the sea in echelon without launching a single torpedo. Before takeoff from the *Hornet*, Waldron had attached a letter to each man in the squadron to the attack plans issued to them in which he stated that every man was expected to do his utmost to press the attack, even if they found themselves the last plane left. Gay's was now that last plane, and he bore on in toward the *Akagi*. He kept flying on, trying to keep the flattop in his sights even as it was maneuvering out of the crosshairs, despite the thudding of machine gun shells into his fuselage and as shells and shrapnel dug into his arm and thigh. His gunner was killed almost immediately and flames began rising. Every Zeke in the formation and the *Akagi*'s anti-aircraft fire were focused on him, but still he pressed on. With his left hand useless, he held the stick between his knees as he pulled the manual release on his torpedo. His plane bobbed up, suddenly free of the torpedo's weight, and he kicked his rudder while taking the plane into a steep climb. Doing so, he barely skimmed over the *Akagi*'s bow, but his plane was so badly shot up that it stalled. Gay managed to flatten her out and ditched in the water. Quickly, he was scrambling out of the sinking Devastator and inflating his lifejacket, but not his raft for fear that he would be sighted and either captured or shot up by the Japanese. Instead, he swam over to where a seat cushion from his plane was floating and hid himself under it.

Nagumo barely had time to even smile at the triumphant report of the fighter squadron commander when the klaxon sounded yet again. The Devastators of Torpedo 6 were now coming forth, split into two groups which ran at the *Akagi* from port and starboard. Again, a lack of coordination between squadrons resulted in Grey's fighters still circling overhead as the Devastators went in without cover, and again there was another massacre. Four of Torpedo 6's planes managed to launch their fish and escape the murderous defensive fire and fighter attack, but without result. Minutes after that, yet another torpedo attack, this time from Lieutenant Commander Lance Massey's VT3 squadron from the *Yorktown*, who at least had some fighter cover from six Wildcats of VF3 squadron. And as with the previous two squadrons, Massey's was also shot to pieces. Only five of the twelve Devastators lasted long enough to launch torpedoes, and three of those were splashed by Zekes minutes afterward. Two escaped to return to the *Yorktown*.

The gods seemed to be smiling on Nagumo. In a half hour, they had faced attack by 41 torpedo planes, of which 35 had been shot down in quick succession and not a single hit on any of his ships was scored. He could not help admiring the almost samurai-like bravery of the crews who had pressed on with their doomed attacks, but he was glad that his sky seemed at last to be clear. And in the whole time of the attacks, his squadrons were at last fully armed and ready for launch. The Admiral gave the signal at 1020 hours and his four carriers turned into the wind. Four minutes later, the first Zeke roared off the *Akagi*'s deck when a lookout shouted a warning. On the bridge, Nagumo and his officers looked upward in stunned horror as the high-distant specks of Dauntless bombers seem to hang in the air for a moment, then began to peel off one by one.

Max Leslie's Dauntlesses aimed themselves in a 73 degree dive right for the *Kaga*, which was getting its first plane in position for takeoff. Leslie intended to strafe the ship and distract the antiaircraft gunners as did the other three SBDs without bombs. They were met with only sporadic machine gun fire, and the sky was free of enemy planes. Thanks to the sacrifice of the Devastators, the fighter cover had been pulled down to wave-level and had been scattered all over the area. Some planes were on long return arcs and making their way back to the fleet formation, but it was far too late. The carriers were totally naked to attack and at the worst possible moment with the decks crowded with fully fueled, fully armed planes. Leslie's wingman, Lieutenant Paul Holmberg, sighted on the invitingly big red circle painted on the carrier's flight deck — a perfect bullseye — and released his bomb. The thousand-pounder struck just forward of the ship's island and detonated among the parked planes awaiting takeoff along with a tanker cart full of avgas. Flames and explosions spread across the flight deck in seconds, with a rising fireball roasting the bridge, instantly killing the captain and most of the ship's senior officers, which ended any possibility of a coordinated effort at damage control or evacuation of the crew. Three more bombs added to the carnage, setting off fuel, explosives, and machine gun shells. Planes were flung into the sea. Airmen still strapped in were killed inside their craft. Deckhands were blown off the ship or ended up diving overboard; screaming human torches. The fires soon spilled into the hangar deck, among the avgas lines and the loose ordnance, and a new series of explosions rent the ship from stem to stern, transforming the *Kaga* into an inferno.

Nagumo and his officers, watching from the flagship, didn't even have time to register the horror of the *Kaga*'s devastation unfolding before them when the planes from the *Enterprise* arrived overhead.

Lieutenant Commander Clarence McClusky, having gotten lost along

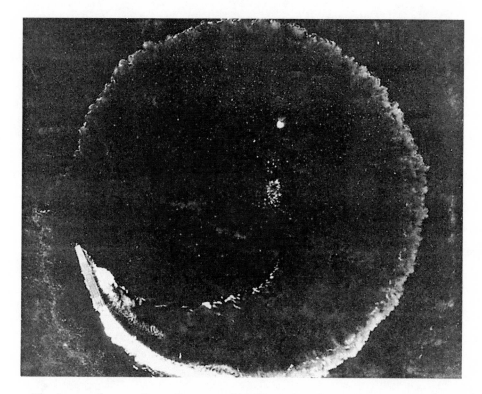

The *Soryu* takes evasive action to avoid Midway-based B-17 bombers, 4 June 1942. National Archives USAF ID4585.

with Stanhope Ring, had figured that Nagumo must have changed course the same as Commander Waldron had. He then got lucky and sighted a Japanese destroyer which was moving at full speed toward the northeast. The *Arashi* had been under harassment by the submarine USS *Nautilus* and had proceeded to drive it away from the position of Nagumo's formation. McClusky took a gamble that its captain was now heading back to the main Japanese task force and put his planes on the tincan's wake. The gamble paid off, and his pilots spotted three carriers, one of which was already in flames. McClusky split his formation in two; one group headed for the *Akagi* and McClusky's for the *Soryu*. Again, with no fighter opposition the Dauntlesses of Bombing 6 dove in on their targets. Two bombs struck the *Akagi*; one detonating right in the middle of the planes gathered on her deck, the other dropping right through an open lift to the hangar deck and then exploding — again in the middle of loose ordnance and avgas lines. As on the *Kaga* whole aircrews were killed immediately along with deckhands, plane handlers, and armorers. Those who survived the initial blasts either ended up set afire themselves or, wounded, roasted alive when they couldn't escape the spreading fires. Over on the *Soryu* the holocaust was repeated as three bombs scored direct hits on her flight deck, amongst parked planes. And, as the loose ordnance and fuel lines in her hangar were touched off, yet another chain-reaction of explosions rended the carrier. The engines died and the *Soryu* wallowed to a stop; a floating, devastated wreck.

The *Akagi* was still operational but only by a rather selective definition of the word. The blasts on the flight deck had demolished her bridge, killing half the men there. Nagumo was slumped on the deck, unhurt but in a state of complete shock. He didn't even hear what Admiral Kusaka was shouting at him. It took several minutes before he finally registered that Kusaka was urging that he leave the stricken carrier and transfer his flag to the light cruiser *Nagara*, which had pulled alongside to aid in the firefighting effort. He still had to command what was left of the fleet, but Nagumo made no motion to leave his ship. Whether he thought that perhaps she could be saved or was thinking of going down with her is unknown, but it took heavy persuasion by Kusaka and the *Akagi*'s captain, Taijiro Aoki, to finally convince him to transfer to the *Nagara*. Fires blocked the ladderways leading from the bridge, and so the old Admiral had to slide down a rope to the outboard portion of the flight deck, then make his way to a waiting rope ladder on the anchor deck to climb into a launch.

Meanwhile, the *Hiryu* was left as the only fully operational flattop on the scene. The evasive maneuvers that Nagumo's ships had to undertake to escape the earlier torpedo and bomber attacks had placed the last carrier 30 miles farther to the north and so spared it the devastation visited upon the other three carriers. Tamon Yamaguchi wasted no time launching his bombers into the air. Led by Lieutenant Michio Kobayashi, a veteran of Pearl Harbor, the eighteen Vals and six Zekes—all that was left of the First Carrier Strike Force's airpower other than various orphan planes from the now flaming carriers—took sighting on Bombing 3, headed back to the *Yorktown*, and formed up to follow behind and so be led by the Americans back to their base ships. On the way, some of Kobayashi's more enthusiastic fighter pilots peeled away to attack the stragglers of Leslie's squadron and were shot down. And en route his formation was jumped by Grey's Wildcats. By the time the Wildcats were forced to break off, Kobayashi had only half his bombers left to him.

Around noon, the *Yorktown*'s radars picked up Kobayashi's formation on their screens, and the carrier and her escorts prepared to meet the attack. Refueling and rearming operations were suspended, with engineers

The USS *Yorktown* suffers the attack which forces the crew to abandon ship. National Archives 80-G-17062.

taking the extra precaution of draining the avgas lines and filling them with fire-retardant carbon dioxide. Watertight doors were closed and Leslie's returning flight was waived off. Kobayashi's decimated force bore in for the attack. Two planes were shot down almost immediately but six pressed on through a murderous curtain of antiaircraft fire. Kobayashi's bombers succeeded in planting three bombs on the *Yorktown*, one of which penetrated the side of her hull and detonated inside, setting off fires in a storage compartment full of oil-soaked rags. A second bomb dropped right into the ship's stack, and the shock of the blast knocked her boilers out, killing engine power. Damage control crews worked quickly and efficiently to put out the fires, but for the time being the *Yorktown* was dead in the water and Fletcher was obliged to transfer to the cruiser *Astoria*.

While the *Yorktown* attack was in progress, a single scout plane from the *Soryu* landed on the *Hiryu* and brought to Yamaguchi the location of the American fleet and the presence of three aircraft carriers in its formation. The plane had found the flattops during the time its base ship was being turned into a funeral pyre but had been unable to signal back to the fleet due to a malfunctioning transmitter. The pilot even named the ships for the admiral: *Enterprise*, *Hornet*, and *Yorktown*— the third of which was supposed to be at the bottom of the Coral Sea. When five surviving bombers from Kobayashi's group returned minus their leader and some strays from the *Akagi* and the *Kaga* arrived, Yamaguchi ordered their immediate refueling and rearming. All he had left to finish off the *Yorktown* and destroy her sisters was a poor force of ten bombers— a mix of Kates and Vals— and six Zekes. Joichi Tomononga assumed command of the bomber force and took off in a plane with a wing tank which had been punctured in the morning's raid on Midway, knowing full well that he would not have enough fuel to make it back. The planes were all in the air by 1245 hours.

At the same time Tomononga's planes were launching, the *Yorktown*'s damage control crews had finally gotten the fires put out and were repairing the damage to her hull and flight deck. Her engineers worked furiously on the boilers and got four of them relit. By 1345 hours, the carrier was moving under her own power at a respectable 18 knots and was able to recover Max Leslie's Dauntlesses, which had been forced to wait out the attack and the efforts to repair the flight deck and were now running out of fuel. Some were forced to ditch near the *Astoria*, and the crews were quickly rescued. But just an hour later, Tomononga's bombers arrived and dove in on the *Yorktown* from all sides. Fighters and heavy antiaircraft fire whittled down the attack group, but the survivors managed to put two torpedoes into the carrier's port side. Tomononga, one of the pilots who managed to hit the carrier, was blasted out of the air seconds after releasing his fish. Only eight planes managed to leave the area to return to the *Hiryu*. Aboard the stricken *Yorktown*, the situation was bad; her powerplants were dead and free-flooding from the two torpedo hits was causing the carrier to list dangerously — with no way to pump or counterflood. It seemed as if the *Yorktown* was in imminent danger of capsizing and her captain, Elliot Buckmaster, felt he had no choice but to order the crew to abandon ship.

The surviving pilots returned to the *Hiryu* and reported to Yamaguchi that they had left a second *Yorktown*-class carrier afire and dead in the water. They had not known that they had merely hit the same ship Kobayashi had attacked earlier. They and now Yamaguchi were under the impression that the Americans were reduced to one carrier. The odds were now even again — they thought — and Yamaguchi figured that he could possibly get off a third attack and destroy the last American aircraft carrier. There was still the chance to accomplish the main objective of the mis-

sion. With the last carrier gone, the far superior gun power of the battleships and cruisers of Yamamoto's Main Body would easily dispatch the
remaining cruisers and destroyers left to the Americans, and they could
go on to invade and occupy Midway. The war, Yamaguchi believed, was
on the verge of being won that day. But because his pilots had been in continuous combat since early morning, they were exhausted and in no condition to go out immediately a third time. So he had food quickly prepared
and granted a period of rest while a single search plane was sent out to
determine the position of the surviving enemy carrier for a twilight attack.

On the American side, Fletcher had transferred tactical command to
Spruance, being unable to properly coordinate carrier operations from
the *Astoria*. And as the *Yorktown* was suffering her second attack, one of
her scout planes found the *Hiryu* and radioed her exact position back to
the fleet. Bombing 6's Dauntlesses on the *Enterprise* were prepared for
launch and rearmed with 500- and 1000-pound bombs. Also joining in

A dramatic but inaccurate diorama depiction of the *Hiryu* under torpedo attack
from the submarine USS *Nautilus*, based on uncomfirmed reports at the time.
National Archives 80-G-71087.

were some SBDs from the stricken *Yorktown*. Aboard the *Hornet*, sixteen Dauntlesses were rearmed and refueled and now also ready for launch. The first of the forty planes began lifting off from their flight decks at 1530 hours.

At 1700 hours, the last of the *Hiryu*'s planes were fueled and armed. The pilots and aircrews were finishing off the rice cakes served to them and were about ready to launch for the planned twilight attack when the lookouts spotted the planes from the *Enterprise* overhead. It was now Yamaguchi's turn to experience the same horror his boss had gone through six hours ago on the *Akagi*. The *Hiryu*'s captain, Tomeo Kaku, ordered hard right rudder to evade the dive bombers and his gunners put up heavy antiaircraft fire, but it was far too late to save the doomed ship. Four bombs landed on her flight deck and, just as on the other three ships of Nagumo's once impressive force, the detonations amongst fully fueled and armed planes touched off a roaring inferno which would soon engulf the ship. By the time Bombing 8's SBDs arrived on the scene, an attack on the *Hiryu* was pointless and so they instead went after the cruisers *Tone*, *Haruna*, and *Chikuma*, but failed to hit any of the ships, as did a second force of B-17s launched from Midway which arrived in the middle of the attack on the last Japanese carrier.

Night fell, and the skies in the area where the remainder of Nagumo's force lay were lit by the four burning flattops. The *Soryu* was the first to go, finally sliding beneath the waves shortly after 1900 hours after having burned all afternoon. Her captain, Ryunsuke Yanagimoto, remained on the bridge singing "Kimigayo." She was followed by the *Kaga*, which went down burning and exploding twelve minutes later. The *Akagi* was left with a crew still attempting to quench the fires on board, but when the *Hiryu* began to list to 17 degrees, Captain Kaku commenced evacuating his wounded and ordered the crew to prepare to abandon ship. Yamamoto, however, still had plenty of fight left in him and was determined to salvage a victory in the face of the looming disaster. He detached the *Hosho* from the Main Body and ordered the light carriers *Ryujo* and *Junyo*, attached to the Aleutians force, to race toward Midway to reinforce what was left of Nagumo's force, which was ordered to close with the American fleet along with the escorting battleships and cruisers of the Midway Invasion Force. He also ordered the Main Body to proceed at top speed to join them. He would get within range and destroy the American fleet in a night action, when they would be unable to launch planes. But the effort was utterly unrealistic. The carriers from the Aleutians force were too far away and would not be in effective strike range for two days. Neither would Yamamoto's Main Body. And further, the cautious Raymond Spruance,

obeying his instincts and sensing the possibility of an attempted night surface or submarine attack by the enemy, had ordered the task forces to withdraw eastward. He also had no desire to get out too far from Midway and
decided to draw in closer to be in position to either protect the atoll or
pivot out again for follow-up on the enemy if the opportunity presented
itself the next day. So the Japanese were caught in a race eastward they could
not win. Yamamoto stubbornly remained confident he could close in on
his pressed enemy. But Nagumo, still aboard the *Nagara*, had taken somehow to magnifying the size of the American fleet until he had attributed
to the enemy a large force of five carriers, six heavy cruisers, and fifteen
destroyers. Yamamoto, oppressed by stomach pains which seemed to get
worse with each passing minute, relieved Nagumo of what was left of his
command and placed Nobutake Kondo in charge of all surface forces in
the vicinity of Midway. Kondo prepared eagerly for battle, but the American move eastward would make it impossible to close upon them before
dawn. And once the sun was up, the Americans would be able to launch
planes and the Japanese would be caught with no air cover.

Some alternative plans were floated in the conferences aboard the
Yamato through the night, including a suicidal plan to have all surface
ships close to shelling range of Midway — which would also place them
within air attack range of Midway's bombers and whatever carrier planes
were left. Before long, these realities became impossible to ignore, and any

The *Hiryu* burning and adrift at Midway in the late evening of the 4th. National
Archives NH23064.

notion to shell Midway without air support was recognized as sheer lunacy. Matome Ugaki, Yamamoto's chief staff officer, was the first man to voice the possibility of their defeat in this battle.

A stunned silence overtook the room, and one of the junior officers, wrestling with the unspeakable, nervously asked, "But how can we apologize to His Majesty for this defeat?"

"Leave that to me," Yamamoto finally said, as unavoidable realities sunk in. "I am the only one who must apologize to His Majesty." At 0250 hours on the morning of June 5, he finally transmitted permission to Captain Aoki to scuttle the *Akagi*. She would be the first Japanese warship in the history of the Imperial Navy to meet such an ignoble fate. Five minutes later, the Commander-in-Chief of the Combined Fleet issued a blunt order whose first line read: THE MIDWAY OPERATION IS CANCELLED. Two hours after the *Akagi* went down, Tamon Yamaguchi finally arranged for the scuttling of the *Hiryu* and, assuming full responsibility for the loss of her and the *Soryu*, elected to go down with his flagship. Captain Kaku chose to stay with his admiral, and destroyers torpedoed her after the remaining survivors and the Emperor's portrait were taken off. By noon, the four flattops of the First Carrier Strike Force were gone.

June 5 was a day of mostly inconclusive action in the wide-ranging Battle of Midway. At around 0300 hours in the early morning, as the *Akagi* was vanishing beneath the surface of the Pacific, the submarine USS *Tambor* found four heavy cruisers and two destroyers all under the command of Rear Admiral Takeo Kurita, which had been dispatched to attempt a night bombardment of Midway but were now retreating upon Yamamoto's orders. At the moment the *Tambor* spotted the Japanese, they had sighted the sub and Kurita ordered evasive action. The cruisers *Kumano*, *Suzuya* and *Mikuma* all turned hard to port, but the last ship in the line, the *Mogami*, somehow failed to receive the maneuvering order and ended up ramming the *Mikuma*, losing her bow in the collision. Both ships were able eventually to get underway again but at reduced speed, and the *Mikuma* trailed a long oil slick in her wake.

During the day a lone Navy PBY Catalina, searching the area where the First Carrier Strike Force had been lost for signs of enemy units, spotted a life raft with a single man aboard and landed nearby. Drawing up, they saw that he was American. The Catalina crew helped Ensign George Gay, the sole survivor of Torpedo 8, on board. He had remained hidden under his seat cushion through the whole of the previous day and literally had a ringside seat for the destruction of Nagumo's carrier force. He had escaped the notice of the Japanese by blending in with the surrounding debris and waited until the middle of the night to inflate his raft.

Through the night, the destroyer USS *Hughes* stood by the derelict *Yorktown* to observe her sinking and to prevent anyone from boarding her. But as dawn rose, it became clear that somehow the *Yorktown* was not going to sink. Her list had stabilized at 25 degrees. The minesweeper USS *Vireo* was ordered to take the abandoned carrier in tow, and a boarding party from the *Hughes* found four men left behind along with a number of secret papers and decoding devices. As the morning wore on, Captain Buckmaster gathered a volunteer salvage crew of 170 officers and men and went over to the destroyer USS *Hamman*, which set out for his wounded ship accompanied by the destroyers *Balch* and *Benham*.

While the *Yorktown* was being towed to a rendezvous with the *Hamman* and her escorts, American air strikes dogged the damaged *Mikuma* and *Mogami*. The first was a force of six Dauntlesses and six Vindicators of Marine Air Group 22 from Midway, followed up by a formation of B-17s in a high-altitude attack. The Dauntlesses and B-17s scored only near-misses. The Vindicators came in for a glide attack on the *Mikuma*, but the flight leader, Captain Richard Fleming, took a hit from antiaircraft fire. He released his bomb but was unable to pull away and crashed into the cruiser's number 3 turret aft of the bridge. The flames from Fleming's plane were sucked into the air intakes and ended up detonating fumes built up in the starboard engine room, killing its crew and inflicting greater damage than either his bomb or the earlier collision with the *Mogami*.

Sunrise on June 6 saw the *Hamman*, *Balch* and *Benham* finally drawing up alongside the doughty *Yorktown*. Buckmaster and his salvage crew boarded and began assessing the condition of the ship. Before long, the cooks had chow preparing and the dead were being identified and tagged. Antiaircraft positions were manned, and electrical lines were strung from the *Hamman* to provide power. The remaining fires were put out at last and the pumps were working again, clearing first the engine rooms. By mid-afternoon, the carrier's list had been reduced by two degrees and there was some prospect of restoring internal power. The ship which refused to die at Coral Sea looked as if she was going to return again to Pearl Harbor to be fully refitted to fight another day. But unfortunately, the *Yorktown* had used up the last reserves of her luck. A Japanese submarine, the I-168, had slipped through the cordon surrounding the carrier. Originally dispatched to shell Eastern Island, she was withdrawing when a seaplane spotted the *Yorktown* under tow. On hearing of this, Yamamoto ordered the I-168 in to sink the carrier. The moment he had the ship in his crosshairs, Yahachi Tanabe, the boat's skipper, fired a spread of four torpedoes. One missed, one struck the *Hamman* amidships, which almost immediately broke in two and sank, and the remaining two hit the carrier on her starboard side. Without the destroyer, the *Yorktown* lost power to her pumps and once more began to list. Again, Buckmaster had to leave his ship.

But it would be tit-for-tat this day. At the same time the salvage effort on the *Yorktown* was beginning, planes from the *Enterprise* and *Hornet* caught up with the crippled *Mikuma*. A combined force of fifty-seven dive bombers, three torpedo bombers and two dozen Wildcats in three successive waves battered the *Mikuma* and *Mogami* further. The former ship suffered worse for the strikes, having already been heavily damaged, although the *Mogami* suffered heavier casualties. Finally, the Dauntlesses finished the *Mikuma* in the afternoon. Five direct bomb hits set off fires and internal explosions which eventually sent the cruiser to the bottom. The *Mogami* managed to escape destruction and eventually made its way to Truk, the major Japanese naval base in the Caroline Islands, but was so heavily damaged that she would be out of action for a whole year. Additionally, two destroyers assigned to accompany the two wounded cruisers, the *Arashi* and *Asashio*, suffered heavy casualties from strafing attacks by *Enterprise* Wildcats, which because of the complete lack of air cover were able to sweep over the ships at will.

The *Yorktown* lingered through the remainder of the afternoon and all the following night. Amazingly, she still refused to sink, and some fleeting hope was held out that somehow they would be able to save her. But when dawn broke on the morning of the 7th, the Americans could see she was seriously down in the water and clearly doomed. Officers and men on the accompanying destroyers removed their hats, watching in silent mourning as the carrier underwent her final death throes. Some were in tears. Flags were lowered to half-mast as the sounds of loose machinery rattling free inside the dying vessel could be heard as she shifted. Eventually the *Yorktown* began to heel to port, and then she rolled over and sank beneath the waves. It was a sad postscript to what had been an astounding triumph for a U.S. Pacific Fleet that had been on the edge of annihilation. With the Japanese clearly in retreat and mindful of the need to preserve American naval forces, Spruance and Fletcher put about and returned to Pearl Harbor.

Midway was the first major naval defeat suffered by the Japanese since 1592 and as a result, the expansion of the Empire had ground to a halt. Four attack aircraft carriers, one-third the carrier strength of the Imperial Fleet, had been lost along with 3,500 men. Far worse was the complete loss of four carrier air wings, over 300 aircraft and 100 irreplaceable veteran pilots. The Japanese claimed two American aircraft carriers destroyed but only one had been sunk (though Radio Tokyo would report the destruction of the *Enterprise* as well as the *Yorktown* in the false announce-ment of a great Japanese victory at Midway, the first of eight times the *Enterprise* would be claimed sunk by Japanese propaganda). They would never be able to exploit the toehold gained in the Aleutians and a long, wasting campaign would continue for another year for a territory which, without Midway in their grasp, was militarily useless to Japan. The sur-vivors from Nagumo's carriers were transferred, under dead of night, from hospital ships to security holding areas at the Yokosuka Naval Hospital and were forbidden all contact with the outside world. Until they recov-ered sufficiently to return to duty, they were held as virtual prisoners so that no word of what really happened at Midway would leak out. Yamamoto would eventually recover from his stomach cramps and regain his powers, but he would live under the shadow of his prophecy of Japan's eventual downfall from that moment forward. For his part, Chuichi Nagumo, the victor at Pearl Harbor and Ceylon, now found himself under a cloud of disgrace, having ingloriously lost his command. Nagumo would return to battle another day, but he would never again occupy the lofty heights he once enjoyed before the destruction of his precious carriers.

The Midway Operation had resulted in a loss more serious even than that of four aircraft carriers, their planes, pilots, crews and several top officers. On May 3, a month earlier, a force of Kate torpedo bombers accompanied by Zeke fighters had been launched from the *Ryujo* to strafe Dutch Harbor and destroy any moored flying boats there as part of the pre-invasion softening-up. One of the Zekes, piloted by Tadayoshi Koga, took a small hit which punctured a fuel tank. Koga, rapidly losing fuel, picked out what looked like a good piece of ground on Akutan Island but which was actually a bog. His landing gear caught in the spongy turf, the plane flipped over, and Koga died from a broken neck. Five weeks later, a U.S. Navy patrol found the plane and a landing party discovered that it was virtually intact. The wreck was salvaged and sent to San Diego, where engineers learned every detail of its construction. The navy had gotten its hands on wrecked Zekes from Pearl Harbor, but this was a prize. Virtu-ally intact, it proved easy to restore to flying condition. In tests the plane yielded up every last detail of its flight characteristics, capabilities, and vulnerabilities, and the data gleaned went into the design for the fighter plane to succeed the Wildcat in carrier service, the Grumman F6F Hell-cat. It would outclass the Zeke in nearly every aspect and would increas-ingly tip the balance in the Pacific.

Midway was a disaster for Japan, at war for eleven years, more or less with successive victories. It had taken nearly four decades to build a mod-ern blue-water navy but only six minutes to destroy her hopes for empire.

CHAPTER 5

Offensive

It had now become a question of which side would stop bleeding first.

In the six months of war since Pearl Harbor, America and Japan had crippled each other. The Japanese for the moment enjoyed a theoretical two-to-one superiority in aircraft carrier strength, having four operational flattops to the Americans' two. But the limited supply of available oil, reduced considerably by the expenditure in the failed Midway effort, rendered that advantage moot by severely curtailing the range of Japanese naval operations. In point of fact, the total destruction of Nagumo's strike force at Midway had neutralized the Imperial Fleet for at least a month; for all their overwhelming superiority in battleships and cruisers, they were valueless without sufficient airpower to back them. So quickly had the new realities of naval warfare imposed themselves even upon Big Gun admirals in both navies. And on the day the *Yorktown* went down, the *Saratoga* arrived back at Pearl Harbor after a full refit. Three days later the *Wasp*, transferred from the Atlantic, passed through the Panama Canal and would be joining the *Enterprise* and *Hornet* in just a little over a week, so the Americans regained a rough equivalency with the enemy for the first time since before December of 1941. On balance, the odds were now even again.

But neither side was up for another major engagement in the weeks immediately following Midway. Japan was now forced to consolidate her position and as a result could not even support the invasion of Attu and Kiska. The Navy General Staff were now obliged to cancel plans for an invasion of the Samoan Islands, and the Alaska invasion was reduced to a permanent diversion in the hope that the United States would expend men and matériel to drive them off North American soil while they followed up on the initial drive of conquest southward, toward Australia.

The Americans weren't about to expend any more matériel than could be afforded. The priorities imposed by the Europe First strategy saw to that, particularly in the wake of the Operation Torch landings on the Moroccan coast in July and continuing pressure upon Washington and

London by Josef Stalin to open a Second Front against Nazi Germany to relieve the pressure on the Soviet Union. But Ernest King in Washington now began increasingly to press for a primary offensive in the Pacific, a view which was picking up powerful advocates in Congress. Many of them wanted the main thrust of that effort to go right where the Japanese hoped, to expel the invaders from Attu and Kiska. But King and the rest of the strategic planners knew that a renewed Japanese drive against Australia could materialize soon. For that reason any possible threat in that direction had to be neutralized.

It was the where and how of neutralizing that threat which was still up for debate. General Douglas MacArthur in Australia was pressing for overall control of the Pacific war effort and demanded a Marine division and two carrier task forces to invade Rabaul immediately, arguing that he could drive the Japanese out in two weeks. The Navy wasn't about to allow an Army general to control what was primarily an amphibious war, which was their province. The long-distance infighting between the service chiefs ultimately came to involve the Navy and Army staffs in the Pentagon and roiled until George C. Marshall put his foot down and imposed a compromise. Command in the Pacific would be shared equally between Nimitz and MacArthur. Next, Marshall outlined a three-phase campaign: the Navy and Army would move in parallel to one another to oust the Japanese from the Santa Cruz and Solomon Islands combined with a simultaneous drive on New Guinea. Once Guadalcanal and New Guinea were secured, the effort to reconquer Rabaul would proceed to conclude the rollback of the enemy from the Southwest Pacific. To avoid any conflict between the Navy and Army, the Joint Chiefs shifted the responsibility for Guadalcanal and the Solomons to CINCPAC, specifically to Admiral Robert Ghormley, Nimitz's South Pacific Area commander.

As the strategies unfolded in the planning sessions, Joseph Rochefort's HYPO team at Pearl decrypted new JN-25 intercepts which indicated that the enemy were rushing to complete an airstrip on Guadalcanal Island. If it became operational, the Japanese would be able to wield effective air control over all the air and sea approaches to Eastern Australia. Guadalcanal now assumed first priority and Operation Watchtower was altered to reflect the new threat developing rapidly on their flank. The plan to establish advance bases in the Santa Cruz islands was shelved for the time being. Guadalcanal and Tulagi, a tiny islet right offshore of Florida Island, were scheduled for simultaneous invasions with a target date of August 1.

It took six weeks for Admiral Ghormley and Marine Corps Major General Alexander Vandegrift to assemble their forces. The difficulties involved had in fact obliged the planners to push back the timetable by a week while ships and troops were pulled together from places as disparate as Auckland, New Zealand and San Francisco. Further hampering the effort was the very poor intelligence Ghormley and Vandegrift had at their disposal. All their information on the two islands they were to invade was derived entirely from articles and pictorials in *National Geographic* magazine, old Imperial German charts of the area, and interviews with missionaries, tramp captains, and Melanesian fishermen who had plied the waters in and around the Solomons for decades. It was an inauspicious beginning and was indicative of the hasty, slapdash nature of the Watchtower preparations. But the delays imposed by the foul-ups in the logistics allowed Ghormley to refine his strategy and gather needed photoreconnaisance of the enemy airstrip and the beaches at Lunga Point, the planned landing zone. The troops of the First Marine Division would come in on nineteen transports backed by three cruisers and six destroyers for gunnery support under Rear Admiral Richmond Kelly Turner. His immediate support would be provided by three cruisers and five destroyers of the Royal Australian Navy under the command of Sir Victor Crutchley and reinforced by the heavy cruiser USS *Chicago*. The main striking power for the invasion would be provided by the carriers *Enterprise*, *Saratoga*, and *Wasp*, reinforced by five cruisers, four destroyers, and the fast battleship *North Carolina*, all under the command of the veteran Frank "Jack" Fletcher.

While the shoestring Operation Watchtower preparations had been underway, the Japanese on Guadalcanal had been working desperately to hack out a runway through the dense jungles on the island. The crews and the 2,300 Imperial Marines who made up the occupation force mostly lived on Tulagi. Another 1,400 men of the Imperial Navy Airfield Construction Unit had been shipped out to complete the work on the base. The workers and troops ferried themselves over each day rather than hacking out a permanent residence as yet.

Guadalcanal is an island roughly 100 miles long by 50 wide, and in addition to dense jungles also features a mountain range, with peaks up to 8,000 feet above sea level, which traps moisture into very dense tropical rain clouds, bathing the island in monsoon-like weather most of the year. The optimum landing zone was on the northernmost end where the beaches just east of Lunga Point are to be found. Around midnight on August 6, the 62-ship armada slipped around the perimeter of Cape Esperance and into the strait dominated by Savo, the volcanic island lying between the two main islands of Guadalcanal and Florida. It was at 0430 hours that the task force split in two formations and took station, transports in front with the bombardment groups formed up in line of battle behind them.

The first warning the Japanese had of the presence of this armada was when lookouts on shore began to make out very large silhouettes against the rising dawn. Seconds later, at 0613 hours, the heavy guns of the fleet opened fire. The commander on Tulagi had just enough time to radio the Imperial Fleet base at Rabaul, saying that he would defend to the last man against the overwhelming enemy force which had suddenly appeared on his doorstep, before several shells from the warships demolished his radio shack with him still inside. The first wave of attack planes from Fletcher's carriers swept over the islands minutes later, destroying the two seaplanes assigned to Guadalcanal as they revved their engines and scrambled desperately to take off. The fighters then peeled off to strafe ground targets. Sixteen thousand Marines swarmed ashore on the two islands at 0815, finding only light resistance on Tulagi and virtually none on the beaches east of Lunga as construction workers panicked and fled into the jungle. It was when Marines began moving farther inland that they encountered their first taste of the fanaticism of Japanese warriors driven by the codes of Bushido. Of the 2,000 defenders on the island, only 23 were taken alive. None of them surrendered, and 100 Marines lost their lives in putting down the last of the enemy resistance. The island was secured in three days.

It had been a quick triumph in this first American offensive of the war, at least on the ground. Thankfully, Japanese intelligence had been caught so totally flatfooted that the enemy never bothered to ensure that Guadalcanal would have been invested with the forces necessary to have blown the slipshod and badly coordinated invasion off the beachhead. In large measure, the American invasion had been saved by the fact that the Imperial General Staff had opted to make their next main thrust against New Guinea, where 16,000 crack troops of the Seventeenth Imperial Army were mired down against Allied forces on the Owen Stanley mountain range which divided Papua in two. So complete was the surprise that the Japanese at Rabaul could not even organize an immediate counterattack when it would have been most effective, while invasion supplies were piling up on the beaches faster than the Marines could clear them off. Guinichi Mikawa, the Imperial Fleet commander at Rabaul, had already committed his bombers to airstrikes at New Guinea, and his ships were scattered on convoy escort duties. Despite a flurry of orders from Isoroku Yamamoto to recapture Guadalcanal with all haste, the 500 Marines and seven cruisers Mikawa had at his disposal were inadequate to the task when he discovered the size of the American force before him, and he withdrew his squadron back to Rabaul. The first day, he could only offer up token airstrikes with what planes he had available. The next morning, however,

Mikawa was able to call in heavier raids which pressed through a heavy fighter screen to sink a transport and damage a destroyer so severely she later had to be sunk. Admiral Turner sped up the offloading of invasion supplies in response, while the already landed Construction Battalions—civilian employees of the Navy Department who were contracted to build advance bases in invasion zones and who would come to be known by the famous appellation of Seabee—immediately set to work with the equipment left behind by the Japanese workers to finish the airbase for the Marines. When it was finished, the strip, code named Cactus Base, would be formally christened as Henderson Field, in honor of Major Lofton Henderson, one of the first Marine airmen to die in the defense of Midway.

The Solomons are arranged in two groups of islands which run almost perfectly parallel to one another. At the lower leg of the archipelago lies the sprawl of the New Georgia group: New Georgia, Munda, Rendova, Kula Gulf, Vella Gulf, and Vella LaVella. The upper leg is bounded by the large islands of the Santa Isabel chain: Choiseul, Santa Isabel, and Malatia. Bougainville, immediately east of New Britain, and Guadalcanal define the ends of the archipelago, and running right between them is a natural highway which made for a perfect amphibious invasion route, a 600 mile channel which would come to be known as "the Slot." It was for this route that Japanese and Allied forces would contend for the next four months of heavy and costly fighting.

First blood, however, would be drawn by the Japanese.

Vice Admiral Mikawa reassembled his cruiser force, five heavies including his flagship *Chokai*, two light cruisers and a destroyer, and set out from Rabaul on the morning of the 8th, following a course right down the Slot. Mikawa's plan was to come up on the enemy forces in the dead of what would be a moonless night in the early morning hours of the 9th to ambush the beachhead and enemy naval forces in the area. The gamble was worthwhile since his gunners were specially trained in night fighting and they had intimate knowledge of the littorals around Savo. Nevertheless, Mikawa was taking a massive risk, especially in broad daylight. Were his force to be spotted by enemy scout planes and a carrier strike launched, he would stand no chance of leaving the Slot alive.

But Mikawa was incredibly, almost stupidly, lucky. An Australian seaplane had in fact spotted his ships, but the radio report sent out was garbled in transmission and incomplete. Radar operators on the picket destroyers, exhausted from 36 hours of combat, were not put on alert. There was not even any sort of clear indication of how and where the enemy was moving since for the time being, the Americans had lost their intelligence edge; the Japanese had modified the JN-25 code and it was going to take two weeks for the HYPO cryptologists back at Pearl to break it. Mikawa was also inadvertently aided by the decision of Admiral Fletcher to withdraw his carriers. Citing the losses to his squadrons in beating off the previous day's air raids and the need to refuel, he radioed Robert Ghormley for permission to take his ships out of the Guadalcanal area and, as the afternoon progressed, had them get underway without waiting for confirmation of his request. This in turn caused Turner to make preparations to withdraw his transports and cruisers as soon as possible. This would leave Vandegrift's Marines stranded on the beaches, but without air cover Turner felt he had no choice. He was not going to let his ships get caught by enemy bombers and destroyed. Fletcher was already long gone by 2000 hours, nobody was watching the Slot either by airborne or electronic eyes, and by the time midnight rolled around the inky black skies were lit only by lightning flashes over the mountains. Nobody spotted the single seaplane scout which was using the mountains as cover while surveying the Savo area for Mikawa, who was coming right down the Slot unobserved.

Assembled around Savo was a nearly equal force of eight American and Australian cruisers, the USS *Quincy*, USS *Chicago*, HMAS *Canberra*, USS *Astoria*, USS *Vincennes*, USS *San Juan*, and the HMAS *Hobart*, screened by the American destroyers *Blue*, *Patterson*, *Ellet*, *Bagley*, and *Ralph Talbot*. Victor Crutchley's flagship, HMAS *Australia*, was still anchored 30 miles away to cover Kelly Turner's transports. Mikawa's force was entering the strait at around 0140 hours and lookouts were probing the darkness for silhouettes. The destroyer *Blue* had in fact turned about almost as the lead ship in Mikawa's van was coming on top of him and had failed to spot the enemy on their fantail. It was a lookout on the *Patterson* who spotted the Japanese and signaled to the rest of the squadron: WARNING WARNING STRANGE SHIPS ENTERING HARBOR. Green flares dropped by a seaplane fluttered down upon the Allied formation and it was not long before Japanese searchlights had the *Chicago* and *Canberra* in their beams.

A savage mêlée began with an opening torpedo salvo from the *Chokai*, which was immediately followed up by a barrage from the cruiser's 8-inch guns. The *Chicago* and *Canberra* never even had a chance to aim their own turrets before torpedoes and shells slammed into both ships. The first salvo damaged the *Canberra*'s bridge and knocked out her boilers, killing all engine power and rendering her guns useless. Several more shells hulled the helpless ship through and she began flooding belowdecks. A torpedo strike on the *Chicago* blew off a big chunk of her bow, compromising her maneuverability and making it difficult to bring guns to bear, though she was able to score one hit on the *Tenryu* as she sailed past, while the *Patterson* and *Bagley* engaged the enemy formation with 5-inch guns and torpedoes and scored a hit on the *Kinugasa* before they followed the *Chicago* retreating to the west. Mikawa then headed his ships on a course rounding the perimeter of Savo and split his force into two formations with the intent of enveloping the Northern group in a classic pincers movement.

The bridge watch on the *Vincennes* awakened Captain Frederick Riefkohl but for some reason did not inform him of the *Patterson*'s dispatch. Riefkohl spotted the distant flares and concluded that the Southern group were engaging some sort of enemy force but otherwise was working completely in the dark. Over on the *Quincy*, Captain Samuel Moore rushed to the bridge as soon as general quarters was sounded. But before either captain could act, their ships were illuminated by enemy searchlights and within seconds found themselves under heavy fire, *Quincy* taking hits on her fantail and bridge and *Vincennes* riddled and set afire before any of her guns began firing. The *Astoria*, which trailed in the formation, was the last to go into action. The rapidly deteriorating situation seemed to have caught the *Astoria*'s officers completely unawares, and the resulting disorganization on the bridge prevented an even remotely effective response. The three ships soon found themselves bracketed on both sides and on the receiving end of a murderous barrage at point-blank range. The *Vincennes*' guns managed to inflict steering damage on the *Kinugasa* before she received more shells and torpedoes, forcing Captain Riefkohl to give the abandon ship order at 0230 hours. The *Astoria* managed to put the forward 8-inch turret on the *Chokai* out of action before she too began to go down. The *Quincy*, for her part, charged forward despite taking hit after hit after hit. Captain Moore was determined to give his enemy hell before he went down and his gunners poured fire onto the *Chokai*, destroying her chartroom and killing several officers within. But at 0210 hours, a shell hit destroyed the *Quincy*'s bridge. A lone surviving signalman at the helm tried to carry out the captain's last order to beach the ship and had turned her toward Savo, but there was no hope; she was already flooding. A further torpedo hit finished any chance to run aground and the cruiser capsized.

But on the edge of his triumph, Guinichi Mikawa was suddenly overcome by extreme caution. It was coming onto 0230 hours and though he had a prime opportunity to destroy the invasion transports which were still desperately offloading supplies and protected by only a single cruiser and destroyer, the Admiral became worried that pressing the attack would mean his ships would be caught in the strait as dawn was rising, after which the American carriers which had to be prowling around Guadalcanal would be able to launch planes. It would be suicide to remain in the area in the face of that threat, even though Mikawa had no way of knowing that Fletcher's carriers were in fact gone. As a result, the Japanese commander threw away his opportunity to reclaim Guadalcanal in one stroke and ordered his ships to exit what came to be known as Ironbottom Sound, for the number of wrecks that would rest there, and head back to Rabaul. On the way back up the Slot, one of his cruisers, the *Kako*, was torpedoed and sunk by the submarine USS *S-44*, but otherwise the Japanese triumph was about as complete as it could be under the circumstances.

Savo was the single worst defeat suffered by the United States Navy in a surface battle in its entire history. It was as much attributable to the complacency and confusion which had reigned among Allied officers as to Mikawa's aggressive determination and the lack of air support from Fletcher. Four cruisers were sunk and one heavily damaged, with an additional two destroyers damaged and only minor damage on two ships inflicted in return. The casualties numbered at 1,077 dead and 700 wounded, including *Quincy*'s Captain Samuel Moore, who died on his bridge, and *Canberra*'s Captain Frank Getting, who died of his wounds the next day. The one positive to be drawn from the bleak situation was that Mikawa withdrew in the face of the phantom threat of Fletcher's carriers, which saved the Marines from annihilation. Kelly Turner continued to offload supplies even during renewed air attacks until he determined he could no longer risk remaining in the area. He pulled out with a thousand Marine reserve troops, most of the division's heavy artillery and equipment, and most of its rations still aboard the ships. For the time being, Vandegrift's Marines and the Seabees were left on their own.

Guadalcanal by itself was of marginal importance. Either side could have made the decision to bypass it altogether and attempt to establish bases on one of the other islands in the archipelago. But now, both the American and Japanese leadership became obsessed with Guadalcanal. The Americans were not about to abandon the first island they had captured in the war, especially after the blood that had already been spilled to retain their hold. Guadalcanal was now a symbol as much as a strategic objective and the icon of their determination not to abandon the offensive against the enemy now that it had begun in earnest. To the Japanese, Guadalcanal's loss would be utterly unacceptable, a failure of the first magnitude and a further surrendering of the initiative after the disaster of Midway. Bushido demanded that the island be reconquered at all costs. All costs. As a result, neither side was going to let go of this small, overgrown, malarial island now.

The real bloodletting was just about to begin.

For five days, the whole war seemed to be hanging in limbo. The Seabees continued their work on the airstrip and support buildings, pushing to get the base operational as soon as possible and knowing that it might become necessary to destroy the whole thing to deny it to the enemy. Vandegrift's men dug in and braced themselves for the inevitable attack which they were sure had to come any day now, and with no support from the Navy and not even any means of escape available, they knew they were preparing to make a last-ditch stand. Each day, they watched for enemy planes, expecting a massive bombing attack at any moment. But luck had shifted back to the American side; the raids on the landing and the airstrikes on New Guinea had severely depleted Rabaul's total air strength. Vice Admiral Mikawa, returning to Rabaul in triumph on the 9th, found himself under severe reprimand by Admiral Yamamoto for failing to destroy the American beachhead and demanded that action to dislodge the enemy be taken immediately. But until Mikawa could get his air force rebuilt and bring up reinforcements, there was little he could do about the Guadalcanal situation. The General Staff, however, started moving immediately to remove the American presence. Nobutake Kondo and his Second Fleet, backed by the Third Carrier Division consisting of the recently refitted sister ships *Shokaku* and *Zuikaku* under Chuichi Nagumo, rehabilitated from disgrace, along with the 10,000 ton light carrier *Ryujo* and the heavy cruiser *Tone* under Chuichi Hara, were sent to reinforce Mikawa. But Japanese intelligence, still underestimating both the numbers and determination of the American force on Guadalcanal, saw fit to detach only 6,000 troops from the Seventeenth Army engaged at New Guinea to retake the island.

The Marines faced their first enemy bombing raid on the 14th. Still lacking planes or any sort of antiaircraft defenses, they could only hunker down and take it. This had to be the opening phase of the enemy's campaign and they assumed that an equal or superior force would soon be on its way. As yet, they had no idea that the Japanese were proceeding in as slapdash a manner as they had with their own invasion, and that enemy resources were as strained as their own. The first glimmer of light for the Americans came the next day when four ships arrived. They were navy transports, loaded with aviation gas, bombs, and ammunition. The Seabees rushed to complete the airfield, since this was a sure sign that planes would soon be delivered, and in five days, their task was complete. Henderson Field was now operational just in time for the delivery of nineteen Wildcat fighters and twelve Dauntless dive bombers attached to Marine Air Group 23. This seed unit of the "Cactus Air Force" had flown to Guadalcanal off the USS *Long Island*. The appearance of this ship was the first deployment in the Pacific of a new type of vessel, the CVE — the escort or "jeep" carrier. Converted from a cattleboat, she was literally a "baby flattop," a miniature aircraft carrier with a small island and a 500-foot flight deck. The *Long Island* herself arrived the next day bearing additional planes from the Fifth Air Force's 67th Fighter Squadron. Slowly, the Cactus Air Force began to grow in strength.

The opening gambit of the Japanese campaign of reconquest was played on the night of the 18th, when a convoy of six destroyers under Captain Torajiro Sato came into Ironbottom Sound at midnight and slipped silently past the Lunga beachhead to Taivu Point, 22 miles to the east. The six ships were the advance unit of the invasion convoy commanded by Rear Admiral Raizo Tanaka. Sato's mission was to land Colonel Kiyano Ichiki and the first 900 of his 2,000-man strong Advance Detachment of Marines as secretly as possible and, while proceeding on the way back out of the Sound, to shell Henderson Field and the Marine positions on Tulagi. The nightly shore bombardment, along with the bombing raids of the Japanese Eleventh Air Fleet coming every day precisely at 1300 hours—"Tojo Time"—would become characteristic of the brilliant strategy devised by Tanaka to keep the enemy off balance while men and supplies were slipped in quietly in night amphibious runs up and down the Slot. Tanaka organized his runs with the regularity of a railroad timetable, and so efficient was the conduct of the operation that it came to be known famously as the Tokyo Express. It was such a good strategy that the Americans copied it and similarly ferried in men, supplies, ammunition, and fuel by destroyer. In the first of these runs the destroyer *Blue*, a survivor of the Savo massacre, clashed with a Japanese destroyer inside Ironbottom Sound. With a torpedo hit, the *Blue* joined the wrecks on the floor of the sound.

Ichiki was supposed to wait for the remainder of his 1,100 Marines to arrive to engage in a coordinated pincer on Henderson, but the good colonel decided that he could drive what he believed was a small American force completely off Guadalcanal all by himself and proceeded to march westward. But General Vandegrift was alerted to the presence of an enemy force on his island by Jacob Vouza, a native scout for Australian Captain Martin Clemens' coastwatcher unit which had been secreted on the island since the Japanese occupation. Vouza succeeded in making it to the American positions to raise the alarm despite having been tortured, bayoneted, and left for dead.

Confident of their coming victory, Ichiki and his men were anything but cautious and an advanced patrol, marching out in the open, walked right into an ambush set up by a Marine patrol in Alligator Creek and were wiped out to a man. Vandegrift now had confirmation, with the fresh uniforms on the corpses, that newly landed troops were headed his way and he had a defense line set up at the creek. Two days later Ichiki had moved up his whole unit and, slightly after midnight on the 21st, without even bothering to scout out the enemy ahead of him, charged across the sandbar at the mouth of the creek. Vandegrift's Marines were set up behind well-entrenched positions with barbed wire and strategically placed machine gun nests. Ichiki's troops were relentlessly mowed down, wave by wave, as they came forth. Unable to believe that he could be defeated, Ichiki withdrew no further than 200 yards and dug in. The Americans spread out to cover his flanks and by the afternoon hours had the Japanese pinned down in a killing zone, with the lagoon at their backs—a dead end. The Marines hit them with machine gun and mortar fire and then charged Ichiki's position with tanks.

One wounded trooper was the sole survivor of Kiyano Ichiki's Advance Detachment. The rest were gunned down trying to escape across the mouth of the lagoon or died trying to stop tanks with only machine guns and pistols. Ichiki and his officers committed seppuku—ritual suicide in which the belly was deliberately cut open with a tanto dagger. The site of the battle was renamed Hell Point.

Meanwhile, out at sea, Raizo Tanaka's larger convoy of slow transports was proceeding down the Slot with the rest of Colonel Ichiki's troops, unaware that their commander and all but one of his advance force were now lying dead on a sandbar. Following the convoy were the three carriers and other units of the Combined Fleet sent to back up the Guadalcanal reconquest. Chuichi Nagumo and Chuichi Hara, in addition to their primary mission to back Tanaka, were also out hunting for Jack Fletcher's Task Force 61, which had now returned to the Solomons area and was also hunting for the Japanese in addition to acting as a screen for the resupply convoys going into Guadalcanal. But despite the possibility that a serious enemy invasion effort against Guadalcanal might be underway, Fletcher weakened his forces by detaching the *Wasp* and her escorts for refueling. As a result, he had only the *Enterprise* and *Saratoga* on hand when the *Ryujo*, positioned roughly 200 miles north of Guadalcanal, launched an airstrike on Henderson Field in the late morning hours of the 24th to coincide with the daily Tojo Time raid from Rabaul.

Fletcher had launched an air search mission consisting of thirty Dauntless dive bombers and eight Avenger torpedo bombers from the *Saratoga* to seek out the *Ryujo*. Navy PBY Catalinas had been shadowing Tanaka's convoy all through the 23rd and the 24th, so Fletcher knew that a large Japanese operation was in progress, but ordered the *Enterprise* to launch only 23 Avengers on a scouting run. As a precaution, 54 Wildcats were put up as a combat air patrol to screen his carriers. It was at this point that things got confused. When a Catalina spotted the *Shokaku* and *Zuikaku* just a few miles further north of the *Ryujo*'s position, Fletcher was thrown into a quandary. He didn't have sufficient air strength to launch a full strike against the two larger ships and it was too late to recall his planes. Further, a Jake floatplane had spotted Fletcher's two carriers at about the same time the Catalinas had spotted Nagumo and doubtless had radioed his position to the Japanese force.

The leader of the *Saratoga*'s bomber force had intercepted the radio dispatch on the position of Nagumo's two carriers and had taken it on his own head to seek them out and attack. But after finding nothing in the sector he took his group to, he cut his search short and doubled back to strike at the positively identified and positioned *Ryujo*. They came upon Hara's flagship at 1600 hours while she was refueling her bombers returned from the Henderson raid. Her own fighters were engaged in attempting to beat off an attack by Cactus Air Force B-17s when the *Saratoga*'s dive bombers arrived. As a result, the *Ryujo* had virtually no cover and the Dauntlesses screamed down upon the hapless flattop. She was maneuverable enough to evade most of the strike, but not sufficiently; four bombs still landed on her flight deck, and Avengers came in from both sides and put two torpedoes into her stern quarters. Steering control was destroyed and the ship was burning abovedecks as she circled helplessly. Her surviving planes, no longer able to land on their own base ship and not having enough fuel to reach Nagumo's fleet carriers, tried to fly on to Bougainville, where a Japanese garrison was located. Most crashed into the sea. The *Ryujo* would finally capsize and sink four hours later, and the Japanese lost yet another air wing.

At the same time the *Ryujo* was being destroyed, 27 Val dive bombers and 10 Zeke fighters launched from Nagumo's two carriers flew through heavy cloud cover to evade the CAP screen over Fletcher's task force and they gathered in a pack when they spotted a large flight deck below. The Zeke pilots went in first, and due to poor management of the Wildcat squadrons and the greater experience of the Japanese veterans, the Wildcats were scattered and diverted, leaving the *Enterprise* wide open to attack. The Vals headed down, coming in one every seven seconds upon Fletcher's flagship, and flew their way through very heavy antiaircraft fire put up by both the carrier and the new fast battleship *North Carolina*. Two bombs slammed into the aft end of the flight deck, jamming the stern deck elevator, while a third one exploded just aft of the island. Three Vals put their bombs on the stern of the *North Carolina*, but the battleship's heavier armor protection and the efficiency of her firefighting crews minimized

A bomb blast on the deck of the *Enterprise* during the Battle of the Eastern Solomons, in which the photographer was killed taking this shot. National Archives 80-G-17489.

the damage. Thick columns of heavy black smoke rose from the stricken carrier, causing the Japanese strike wing commander to report that the *Enterprise* was mortally wounded.

Such was far from the truth. The damage control parties on the carrier were succeeding in getting the fires under control and quickly welded steel plates to patch up the holes in her flight deck. Fifteen minutes later, the fires were out, the deck was intact, the stern elevator was freed and recovery of aircraft began. But then, unexpectedly, the carrier suddenly lost all steering control, her rudders jammed to starboard. Far worse, the destroyer *Balch* was right in her path, and the carrier was about to ram the tincan at 24 knots. Fortunately, the skipper of the *Balch* ordered full power and was able to speed out of the *Enterprise*'s way just in the nick of time.

For the next harrowing 38 minutes, Fletcher anxiously watched the radar screens as they tracked a second strike wave of planes headed for his helpless flagship. So long as the carrier was circling, they couldn't recover the remainder of their own aircraft or keep her turned into the wind long enough to launch fighters. Nagumo's planes would have a perfect sitting duck to blow apart. But, for a third time since the beginning of the war, the strange luck which seemed to protect the *Enterprise* intervened. The leader of the second attack group miscalculated their position and changed course too soon, going off 50 miles to the west. Finally, an engineer managed to battle his way through choking fumes which had built up in the steering control compartment and switched over to the auxiliary motors. The rudders unjammed and the *Enterprise* was brought back under full control. Fletcher was able to board the last of his planes just as they were running out of gas. In the last action of the day, two Dauntlesses from the *Saratoga* came across the seaplane tender *Chitose* and dove upon her. Both 1000-pound bombs dropped from the planes missed the ship, but just barely. The concussions from the close-aboard blasts bracketing the ship opened up seams in her hull plates and she nearly foundered before a cruiser from the Main Force came to take her in tow during the night.

Fletcher took the opportunity to pull the damaged *Enterprise* out of the area and rushed back southward to meet up with his tankers to refuel again. As a result, they were well clear when a group of heavy cruisers swept the area in a search pattern. The next day, the *Enterprise* and *Saratoga* picked up the *Wasp*'s group heading back toward them. Meanwhile, Tanaka's transports continued ploughing toward Guadalcanal, now 150 miles away, when the Cactus Air Force struck again in the early morning hours. Bombs fell close aboard Tanaka's flagship, the light cruiser *Jintsu*, before a third bomb struck the forecastle, wiping out the radio room and its crew. Tanaka himself was knocked unconscious for a time, during which the largest of his transports, the *Kinryu Maru*, was bombed and began sinking. The destroyer *Mutsuki* drew alongside to take off survivors when three more planes, B-17s, appeared and dropped enough bombs to pot the tincan and sink her in short order.

Aboard his flagship, the superbattleship *Yamato*, Isoroku Yamamoto listened glumly as the reports of the debacle in the Eastern Solomons came in. They had lost the *Ryujo* along with 60 more planes and aircrew. A heavy transport had been sunk along with a destroyer and it was now obvious that the slow, ponderous transports would not be able to run swiftly enough in a sea for which they had not established either full sea or air control. The Americans had succeeded in getting their airbase operational and obviously were being reinforced and resupplied by sea. A whole battalion of Imperial Marines had been wiped out in a stupidly suicidal attempt to take the island from enemy forces which had to be much larger than intelligence assumed them to be — and certainly more determined than they had expected. Reluctantly, but bowing to the realities of the situation, Yamamoto formally terminated Operation KA and ordered the Combined Fleet to turn about and return to Truk.

By August 31, the Tokyo Express had succeeded in landing the rest of the late Colonel Ichiki's 1,100 troops and another 1,000 infantry under Seventeenth Army Major General Kiyotake Kawaguchi. Two days had been lost when a destroyer had been sunk on the 28th in a Cactus Air Force attack which had damaged two other destroyers and forced a retreat. Morale had been lifted by news that the submarine *I-26* had found a large American aircraft carrier and sent her to the bottom of the Solomon Sea days after another enemy flattop had been left burning and dead in the water. Furthermore, the success of his four-destroyer convoy in landing Kawaguchi had convinced Tanaka's superiors that the fast night runs by destroyers were the way to build forces on Guadalcanal to annihilate the Marines hanging on there. Meanwhile, the "sunken" aircraft carriers *Enterprise* and *Saratoga*, the latter suffering only minor hull damage and a broken down turboelectric drive engine from a single torpedo strike, headed back to the drydocks at Pearl Harbor for refit. But for the time being, both would be out of service, leaving only the *Hornet* and the *Wasp* to hold a very precarious line.

By September 8, the Japanese invasion effort on New Guinea had bogged down. Though the forces of the Seventeenth Imperial Army had finally succeeded in breaching the Allied defense line covering the Gap, the main pass in the Owen Stanley mountain range through which lay the open route to Port Moresby, the stiff resistance of Allied ground troops, constant air attacks, the cutoff of their supply lines, and the tropical diseases contracted in the thick, pestilential jungles had taken their toll on the Japanese invasion force. Once again, the Imperial General Staff had underestimated both the numbers and determination of their opposition, and in the final three days of fighting, a push to take Milne Bay was shattered as Japanese battalions fanatically staged one suicidal frontal assault after another against ten-to-one odds. When the order terminating Operation RE, a two-pronged thrust at Port Moresby, came through and all surviving forces were ordered to fall back to Buna, they were forced to undertake a hellish retreat through the jungle which few survived. With the downfall of the Moresby operation, troops originally allocated for that effort would instead be shifted increasingly to the Guadalcanal campaign.

Tanaka's Tokyo Express operation continued to run right on schedule, landing more men nightly. General Kawaguchi's forces steadily grew to 6,000 men. Though not nearly enough to guarantee superiority over

Vandegrift's Marines, they were already too many to ensure a continuous unbreachable defensive cordon around the base and Henderson Field. Now, Kawaguchi's forces were moving through the jungles toward Henderson, to hit the Marine positions in a night attack, timed to coincide with the nightly destroyer bombardment. If Kawaguchi and the navy could knock out Henderson Field, even if they couldn't overrun the base completely, the American position on Guadalcanal would be rendered untenable.

Martin Clemens' scouts kept Vandegrift apprised of the enemy movements, and the 840 men of the First Raider Battalion under Colonel Merritt Edson were transferred from Tulagi to block the one clear pass through the thick jungles of the island, a ridge just east of the Lunga River. Edson, a 45-year veteran of the service who had fought in World War I, knew just where to place his defenses and dug entrenchments protected by barbed wire and mines. The Japanese would be forced to come in through the narrow 1000-yard passage and right into the teeth of Edson's earthworks, which would also be on the high ground. By the time Edson's battalion had completed their preparations, the troops under Kawaguchi were still slogging their way through steamy jungle, which was putting them behind schedule and breaking up his formations. It wasn't until the night of September 13 that 2,500 men assembled before the ridge and charged in wave after wave after wave right into heavy machine gun and artillery fire. Only one battalion managed to actually make it to the east end of the Marine position on Bloody Ridge and were repulsed with heavy casualties. Kawaguchi was forced to retreat back through the jungle, with no rations— since he counted on capturing American food stocks—and men dying of their wounds and disease every step of the way.

Every night, the destroyers which ferried in Japanese troops and supplies shelled Henderson Field on their way out through Ironbottom Sound. Every morning, the Seabees were out with the bulldozers and heavy machinery filling in craters and re-laying steel netting to restore the airfield to operability. Kawaguchi's retreat was harassed by Marine fighters strafing his disorganized columns. Now, a major resupply convoy was headed toward Guadalcanal to bolster Vandegrift. Six transports were carrying the 7th Marine Regiment, 3,000 strong, with 147 vehicles, 1,000 tons of rations, and an additional 4,000 gallons of avgas. The convoy was being shepherded by the aircraft carriers *Wasp* and *Hornet*, the battleship *North Carolina*, and a screen of escort destroyers. They were proceeding on the final leg of their course to Guadalcanal on the afternoon of the 15th and the *Wasp* had just landed her combat air patrol for refueling when a periscope broached the surface. The skipper of the I-15 could hardly credit his eyes as a large carrier moved through the crosshairs, but he wasted no

The USS *Wasp* burning out of control and sinking after a submarine attack, 15 September 1942. National Archives 80-G-16331.

time maneuvering his boat into position. He took range and bearing, and fired two Long Lance torpedoes at 1445 hours. Both fish slammed into the *Wasp*'s starboard side, and the shock from the blasts ruptured avgas lines and knocked out the fire mains, so that when flames touched off a conflagration fueled by the spilling avgas, the efforts of the damage control crews to control the fires were already severely compromised. Five minutes later, a second submarine, the I-19, had fired a spread of torpedoes at the *Hornet* and the *North Carolina*. The carrier's lookouts had spotted the tracks headed toward their ship and Captain Charles Mason was able to take evasive action, but one torpedo hit the *North Carolina*, opening a 30-foot hole in her port side while another hit a destroyer which later foundered trying to steam away from the area.

Aboard the *Wasp* the situation was deteriorating rapidly. The inability of the engineers to effectively control the fires soon led to a inferno which, within a half hour, was consuming the ship. The flames spread to an ammunition magazine and detonated the ordnance within, gutting the

Wasp's innards and destroying part of her bridge. There was no choice now but to abandon ship. The crew went down the slidelines shortly after 1500 hours, and 24 fighters managed to launch off the deck before flames overtook it. The carrier was finally put out of her misery by a destroyer-launched torpedo at 2100 that night. Back at Pearl, the loss of the *Wasp* was counted as a disaster. They had not even traded her for the destruction of an enemy flattop and Nimitz was seeing exactly the sort of attrition of his ships he had desperately sought to avoid since the war began. The advantage in carriers was shifting dangerously in Japan's favor once more.

Kelly Turner steamed on, undeterred by the loss of the *Wasp* and retreat of the *North Carolina*, and succeeded four days later in landing the reinforcements and resupply for Vandegrift's beleaguered force. The *Hornet* task force would remain in the area to provide additional air support for the Cactus Air Force. In the meantime, Catalina flying scouts reported to fleet command that two light aircraft carriers had joined the *Shokaku* and *Zuikaku* in the Solomons sector, the converted cruisers *Junyo* and *Hiyo*.

By the time October rolled around, the Tokyo Express had landed a total of 21,000 troops on Guadalcanal to face Vandegrift's 19,000. The disaster suffered by General Kawaguchi had decided the issue of the importance of Guadalcanal's reconquest; the island was now the number one military priority. Kawaguchi was relieved of command by his immediate superior, the commanding general of the Seventeenth Army, Harukichi Hyakutake. He arrived on the 9th to personally take charge after yet another defeat on the ground in which the Army had lost forward positions that had been chosen as assembly points for the final push on Henderson Field and so threw Japanese preparations again into disarray. That same day, Kelly Turner left the allied base at New Caledonia with another convoy carrying an additional 2,800 U.S. Army troops to reinforce the Marines, bringing total American strength to nearly 22,000. Accompanying the convoy were three task forces in support. Part of their mission was also to disrupt the Tokyo Express and any sea support Hyakutake hoped to count on. Spearheading these forces were a group of four cruisers, the USS *Helena*, USS *Salt Lake City*, USS *San Francisco*, and USS *Boise*, under the command of Rear Admiral Norman Scott. On October 11, Scott had received word that an enemy force of two cruisers and six destroyers were coming down the Slot. The "cruisers" were in fact seaplane carriers ferrying artillery, including four large howitzers, crucial to Hyakutake's coming assault, along with more ammunition and additional reinforcements. Scott determined to ambush this convoy before the entrance to Ironbottom Sound and destroy it. He was unaware, though, of a larger force following behind the convoy — three heavy cruisers and two destroyers assigned to shell Henderson Field and under the command of Rear Admiral Aritomo Goto.

At 2325 hours, Scott's column was patrolling the southwest channel entrance to Ironbottom Sound when the radars on the *Helena* and *Salt Lake City* picked up surface contacts steaming toward them at 30 knots. The two columns were headed for a rendezvous in the waters immediately off Cape Esperance, which defined the southern bank of the entrance to the sound. The Japanese ships could have come up on Scott's cruisers while they were retracing their course to form a perfect broadside line to the ships formed in a column, a maneuver known in classic naval strategy as "crossing the 'T'," but none of Goto's ships had radar and were heading in blind and unawares, operating on the assumption that no American ships would be on hand to challenge the convoy. On the American side, some confusion reigned when Scott ordered the *San Francisco*, his flagship, to turn to port to cover the next leg of their patrol pattern. The next four ships in the formation followed Scott's lead, but a breakdown in communications resulted in the trailing destroyers in the van not getting any word of the course change, and in order to catch up they turned where they were. This split Scott's formation into two columns, and when the gunnery radars picked up the lead elements of Goto's formation coming into range, Scott at first assumed these to be his own destroyers. The contacts now closed to three miles and the captains on the other ships waited anxiously for Scott to give the order to open fire. With Goto's ships now closing almost on collision course, the captain on the *Helena* decided not to wait any longer and opened fire.

As it turned out, despite inadvertently splitting into two columns, Scott's ships had in classic fashion, albeit accidentally, crossed Goto's "T" and now with the *Helena* opening up shells slammed into the lead vessel, which was in fact Goto's flagship, the *Aoba*. Admiral Goto himself was mortally wounded when his bridge was demolished with the first salvo. But at the moment of destroying the Japanese column, Scott, still confused by the situation before him and convinced that they were firing on their own destroyers, ordered a cease-fire to confirm the identity of his targets. The Japanese captains, now having to act without orders, split formation and turned about. As they were turning, however, the captains on the other cruisers recommenced fire, pounding the *Aoba* and *Furutaka* even further and inflicting massive damage on both vessels. An accompanying destroyer was pounded into scrap and went down quickly, while the *Furutaka*, attempting to limp out of the sound with all haste along with the *Aoba*, fell further behind as she flooded, the rest of the formation turning to cover them on the retreat.

Coming onto midnight, Scott ordered his ships to regroup and pursue the now positively identified and retreating enemy formation. But the *Kinugasa*, undamaged and not having engaged in the first exchanges of gunfire, now charged forward and fired a spread of torpedoes which narrowly missed both the *Helena* and the *Boise*. *Kinugasa* then spotted a searchlight which had unexpectedly turned on, marked range and bearing, and opened up with a salvo of 8-inch shells which straddled the *Boise* before one hit her directly in the forward turret, setting off raging fires that spread toward her forward ammunition magazines. But fortunately, the blasts from further shell hits on her thin-skinned hull allowed seawater to flood her forward sections, including the magazines. The fires were doused and *Boise* was saved. Scott's formation then turned southwest, and the *Salt Lake City* maneuvered to cover the damaged *Boise* while the badly mauled Japanese force retreated. The shattered enemy formation made it only a few miles back up the Slot when Goto finally died and the *Furutaka* began to go down. Two more destroyers would be caught and sunk by planes from Henderson Field the next day. For the cost of only two destroyers (one damaged and one which had to be beached after being unfortunately caught in the crossfire) and one cruiser damaged, the American force had sunk a heavy cruiser and three destroyers. But the triumph was far from complete; the enemy convoy was able to slip in, offload General Hyakutake's artillery and reinforcements, and slipped right back out of Ironbottom Sound while Scott's cruisers were engaged with Goto's.

That same morning, Kelly Turner came back into Ironbottom Sound with his convoy carrying the U.S. Army's 164th Infantry Regiment, Americal Division, and offloaded them. The jubilation over the overnight successes, however, would be counterbalanced by the midnight bombardment of the airfield by the field guns delivered the previous night by the Tokyo Express and also by the battleships *Haruna* and *Kongo*, firing 14-inch shells at the base. During the shelling, Tanaka, who had also brought in six destroyers to screen the two battlewagons, now pulled off his single greatest feat of the whole campaign by slipping onto the island an additional 4,500 troops in one landing. However, for all the destructiveness of the bombardment by both army and navy guns, the Seabees had the runways quickly repaired once again and the next day, Cactus Air Force planes caught and sank three of the transports retreating back up the Slot. Nothing, it seemed, could dislodge the stubborn American resistance, which hung on despite constant shellings, air attacks, assaults on the line, and the torrential rains, constant flooding, humidity, pestilential insects, and the diseases which struck indiscriminately at American and Japanese alike.

Chester Nimitz grimly assessed that his fleet was not controlling the sea in the Solomons area and that the battle situation was becoming critical. Robert Ghormley's hands-off leadership and cautious approach to combating the Japanese was proving ineffective — especially where the Tokyo Express was concerned. Nimitz was particularly displeased with the amount of leeway Ghormley allowed Jack Fletcher to withdraw his carriers entirely at his discretion, which had left Kelly Turner's cruisers open to destruction at Savo. On the third week of October, Nimitz relieved Ghormley of command and replaced him with the aggressive and outspoken William F. Halsey, who had just recovered from the shingles that had beached him before Midway. The effect upon morale on Guadalcanal was almost immediate. The embattled Marines were elated, knowing that at last they had a fighter backing them to the hilt, just as a similar morale boost spread through the personnel of the South Pacific forces.

In the first few days of his new command, Halsey himself was concerned that he didn't have the assets to do the job, with the *Wasp* having been sunk and the *North Carolina*, *Saratoga* and *Enterprise* all out of action. But on October 23, the *Enterprise* returned to Noumea, New Caledonia, with her task force and the new fast battleship *South Dakota* in tow. "Now," said the pugnacious admiral, "we have a fighting chance!" One of Halsey's first moves was to replace Jack Fletcher in command of his carriers with George Murray, the former captain of the *Enterprise* under Halsey, and Thomas C. Kinkaid, who would be riding aboard the *Enterprise* with Task Force 16. Neither Halsey nor his men could know that the next three weeks were going to be the crisis point in the whole campaign for Guadalcanal.

CHAPTER 6

Crisis

Since October 14, the Japanese had stepped up both their air attacks and nightly bombardments on Henderson Field, reducing the flow of supplies and avgas to a mere trickle and softening up the Marine base for their next big push. Harukichi Hyakutake now felt he was ready to make his assault to overrun Henderson. He had nearly 23,000 troops at his disposal, but as with his two predecessors, he had seriously underestimated the enemy lying in his path. Hyakutake had no inkling that the Marines now had more than double the 10,000 man garrison he assumed they had. And Guadalcanal was now teaching Hyakutake the harsh lessons of the ground and weather which Kiyotake Kawaguchi had meted out to him before and after Bloody Ridge. Once again, infantry troopers were exhausted from hacking their way through dense jungle and the ranks were thinned by disease while approaching well dug-in defenders behind solid earthworks on high ground. Hyakutake's columns were so slowed down by the jungle that his operation was falling behind schedule. Eventually, 8,000 men in two formations and backed by light tanks and artillery were making their way to positions west and south of the Henderson perimeter. In addition to their own artillery, they would also be counting on offshore support from the big guns of the blockade fleet to participate in a coordinated shelling to wipe out the Marine entrenchments and destroy the airfield once and for all.

Unfortunately for Hyakutake, that was where everything began to unravel. Isoroku Yamamoto had been forced to recall the fleet from the area for refueling and transmitted that a 24-hour delay in the ground assault would be necessary to allow time for his cruisers to return. But somehow, that information was not communicated to General Tadashi Sumiyoshi, who commanded three mechanized battalions, and he charged forward across the sandbar at the mouth of the Matanikau River on the night of the 23rd as originally planned. The Marines, anticipating the assault thanks to Martin Clemens' scouts, decimated Sumiyoshi's tanks with 37mm antitank guns and simply wiped out each wave of charging soldiers as they came up to the lines. The 5,000 men under Lieutenant General Masai Maruyama were not only being slowed more and more by the jungle, they were placing their artillery to cover positions the Americans had abandoned weeks ago. They set fires to the rice fields to try to clear the way forward — and were promptly spotted by Clemens' scouts, who radioed the information in to Vandegrift. The nearest position to the enemy's approach was the 1st Battalion commanded by Lieutenant Colonel Lewis Puller, who had clear fields of fire cut through the grass thickets. The barbed-wire laid on their perimeter was hung with shell fragments, which made perfect makeshift noisemakers, a trick he had used in the Banana Wars in Nicaragua back in 1912. They provided Puller's men and the accompanying Army platoons both warning and location when enemy soldiers hit the wire while crawling through a torrential downpour at around 2130 that evening. The Americans opened up with machine guns, semiautomatic rifles, and mortar fire. The Japanese tried charging forward through a field which was now a mud swamp pocked-marked with mortar holes. In a repeat of the carnage at Bloody Ridge, the Americans held their line at the cost of only 100 dead while killing over 2,000 of Maruyama's warriors. Hyakutake's assault had been broken. Returning with the survivors through another hellish jungle retreat, he reasoned that he still had 15,000 effective troops at his disposal and, by calling in his 38th Division held in reserve all this time, he would be able to return to the offensive with 37,000 men — this time enough to overwhelm any American force before him. He radioed Rabaul with his orders to begin the transport of his reserves by destroyer convoy to be followed up with the large transports.

The next big naval clash between the American and Imperial fleets came about when the two opposing forces literally blundered upon one another. William Halsey had Task Forces 16 and 17 headed for Guadalcanal to finally drive the Japanese out of the Solomons altogether. Navy PBY Catalinas, specially adapted for night action, had on the night of October 25 found Chuichi Nagumo's strike force — the *Shokaku* and *Zuikaku* along with the light carriers *Zuiho* (replacing the *Hiyo*, which had been forced to return to Truk because of machinery problems) and *Junyo*, accompanying elements of Nobutake Kondo's Second Fleet, headed to reinforce the Guadalcanal invasion campaign — and pressed the attack with torpedoes, which caused the ever-cautious Nagumo to head his carriers into a retreat northward. Kondo followed Nagumo in the retreat in order to get his ships out of range of Espiritu Santo, where Marine fighter and bomber squadrons were now located. His course headed him right for *Enterprise* and *Hornet* and their escorts less than 200 miles away, east of the Santa Cruz Islands.

Halsey had picked up the radio reports from the Catalinas of their attack on Nagumo's task force and immediately signaled *Hornet* and *Enterprise* to attack at once. Thomas Kinkaid, who had not had any information on the PBY contact with the enemy, was at a loss as to where to attack, but went ahead and launched a precautionary force of sixteen SBD Dauntlesses to scout ahead as soon as dawn rose the next morning. As it turned out, Kinkaid's simple prudence paid off; the Dauntlesses ended up overflying the lead elements of Kondo's formation and at 0650 hours sighted Nagumo's three carriers. Evading the Zekes coming up after them by going into a cloudbank, Lieutenant James Leed of the *Enterprise* formed up the rest of his planes and pointed them into a dive on the *Zuiho*. The light carrier scrambled its planes before two 500-pound bombs landed on the aft end of the flight deck, setting the smaller flattop's stern ablaze. The *Zuiho* quickly put about and retired northward.

Just barely ten minutes later, Chuichi Nagumo was receiving a radio report from the *Shokaku*'s own scouts identifying the American task force ahead, which included at least one aircraft carrier. Nagumo wasted no time launching a full strike of 60 aircraft. On the way out, the Japanese formation sighted 29 planes headed in the opposite direction — bombers from the *Hornet*. Following behind them were 19 planes from the *Enterprise*. The Zekes in the *Shokaku* strike group's formation peeled off to attack the *Enterprise* planes and soon went after the others. This left the *Shokaku*'s bombers without fighter cover, and while the aerial mélée was underway, a second flight of 23 strike craft also from the *Enterprise* slipped past.

The radars on the *South Dakota* and the *Enterprise* picked up the Japanese formation on their screens shortly before 0900 hours. The battleship and the cruisers and destroyers immediately formed into a ring around the carrier so as to provide overlapping fields of fire for antiaircraft. The *Hornet*'s own cruiser-destroyer screen executed the same formation as the two task forces braced for the attack. Both carriers had their CAP screens up as well, but because the air controllers were inexperienced, they had the fighters drawn in close to the carriers and had denied them full freedom of movement, so the enemy planes were able to close to target. But once again, luck intervened for the *Enterprise*; a sudden rain squall blew up not far away, and the carrier and her escorts went right into it for cover.

This left the *Hornet* to bear the brunt of the attack. First blood was drawn when the lead Val in the enemy formation, hit and set ablaze, went into a suicide dive and crashed through the flight deck, its two bombs detonating in the hangar. Two Kates then launched torpedoes which struck the *Hornet* on her stern quarter, knocking out all engine power, while Vals landed three more bombs that burrowed deep into the ship's innards before

An out-of-control Japanese plane about to crash into the USS *Hornet*, under heavy attack at the Battle of the Santa Cruz Islands, 26 October 1942. The loss of the *Hornet* would leave only the *Enterprise*, a motley assortment of cruisers and destroyers, and the squadrons at Henderson Field to hold a very precarious line in the campaign for Guadalcanal. National Archives 80-G-33947.

exploding. In only ten minutes, the carrier was wrecked and laying dead in the water. Destroyers drew alongside to aid in the firefighting as well as to attempt to put the stricken flattop under tow.

But while the *Hornet* was being mauled, her planes had at that moment caught up with the *Shokaku*. Boring their way in through heavy fighter defenses, the Dauntlesses put six 1,000-pound bombs onto the flight deck, ripping it apart and rendering the carrier useless for further air operations. Avenger torpedo bombers had also arrived for the strike, but unfortunately the actions of the two groups were uncoordinated and the Avengers were easily beaten off by the *Shokaku*'s own guns, otherwise Nagumo's flagship might have been destroyed right there and then. The *Hornet*'s first strike wing and that of the *Enterprise*, which had been jumped by the Zekes on the outbound leg of accompanying the flagship's bombers, were left uncoordinated and all the second strike racked up was a single hit on one cruiser. Nagumo was once more forced to leave his flagship for a cruiser but was still fully in command of the battle and knew, thanks to undisciplined American pilots talking in the clear, that he was facing only two aircraft carriers. In the equation, he had sufficient airpower at his command to destroy both, and one was already burning and stopped dead. His second strike wave, 64 planes strong from the *Zuikaku* and *Junyo*, was on its way. The battle and possibly the whole war would turn on the success of their attack.

Thomas Kinkaid knew he was in a very precarious position. His fighters were down on the decks of the *Enterprise*, refueling, and the rain squall he had run his flagship into for cover was dissipating quickly. Slightly after 1000 hours, he received a radio flash from the *South Dakota*; enemy planes sighted on radar were bearing in from the northwest, only 50 miles and closing. His air operations officers sped up the refueling of fighters and scrambled them off the deck as quickly as possible. This time, however, the planes were deployed in a wide arc covering the area around the carrier to better intercept the enemy strike force with a layered defense.

The Kates and Vals arrived 15 minutes later and ran into a wall of Wildcats. Ten planes were shot down by the first defensive wave before the rest of the formation broke through and made their runs on the *Enterprise*. Another five were blasted out of the sky by the carrier's new Bofors 40mm quad antiaircraft guns, which would repeatedly prove effective in battle as the war progressed. Two bombs struck the *Big-E* on the forecastle and the other on the flight deck, jamming the forward elevator. The rest exploded close aboard, but the concussions opened several weakened hull plates on the starboard side, as well as knocking an auxiliary drive turbine off its mountings. Despite this, the *Enterprise* was still fleet enough to evade the torpedoes put down by the Kates. The surviving planes broke off and returned to their base ships. But Kinkaid would have only a forty minute respite. The *SoDak*'s radars picked up a third attack wave, 29 planes launched from the light carrier *Junyo*. All planes from the two carriers now gathered into a pack to protect the *Enterprise* as the attackers came forth. The Wildcats and Bofors guns cut the strike wave by a third and so harassed the survivors that they scored one hit on the cruiser *San Juan* and another on the *SoDak*'s forward turret, inflicting only superficial damage. No additional bombs fell on the *Enterprise*, a ship which was proving unkillable. The attackers broke off again, and Kinkaid was able to recover his planes, some of which from the *Hornet* were running out of gas. They came in first and were quickly fueled and launched off to make landfall at Espiritu Santo, since with a stuck deck lift the *Enterprise* couldn't board her sister's aircraft as well as her own.

While the battle had been raging, the cruiser *Northampton* had been laying close aboard the *Hornet* to aid in the firefighting effort and finally got the blaze under control just as the *Enterprise* beat off her attackers. The wounded flattop was taken in tow by the cruiser and Kinkaid and Murray, with both their carriers damaged, gave the order to withdraw from the area with all haste. But while the task force was proceeding slowly, at 1400 a fourth wave of strike planes assembled from the air groups of the surviving Japanese carriers dove in on the helpless carrier and her escort. A torpedo struck the *Hornet* sternward, and her engine spaces began free flooding. With no power, damage control was impossible and the ship took on a dangerous list. Captain Mason and his crew abandoned ship quickly. While they were being picked up from the sea by the accompanying destroyers, 10 bombers from the *Junyo* pounced and, believing they had an active warship in their sights instead of a dead hulk, dropped their bombs on the *Hornet*. The flattop was soon burning from stem to stern once again, and Admiral Murray ordered her scuttled. But now, radars had picked up surface contacts; two battleships, two cruisers and their escort destroyers were coming up on their position, pursuing the retreating task forces. The screening destroyers scrambled to sink the *Hornet* before the Japanese could capture her, firing nine torpedoes and four hundred 5-inch rounds into the burning wreck. But like her lost sister *Yorktown*, the *Hornet* stubbornly remained afloat. They were finally forced to retreat when the lead destroyers of Vice Admiral Hiroaki Abe, in advance of Nobutake Kondo's main formation, were closing the range and opened fire on them, and so had no choice but to leave an American man-o'war to fall into enemy hands. But the fires aboard the wreck were now raging so furiously that Abe couldn't send over a boarding party, and in all likelihood the carrier would sink before they could tow her all the way back to Truk. Abe decided the *Hornet* was unsalvageable and contented himself with delivering the coup d'grace on the ship, unknown to him, that had launched the bombing raid against Tokyo six months earlier.

Santa Cruz had been a vicious battle of attrition in which both fleets seriously mauled one another. The Japanese could claim a tactical victory by virtue of having sunk another of Nimitz's precious carriers and shooting down 74 planes. But while Nimitz was running out of carriers, Yamamoto was running out of planes and pilots. One hundred had been lost in the fight for Guadalcanal so far. The *Shokaku* had been so badly damaged that she would be in the repair dock for the better part of a year. But he was able to content himself with the fact that the *Zuikaku* and the *Junyo* were intact, the damage to the *Zuiho* was not as extensive as that on the *Shokaku*, and the *Hiyo* was scheduled to be back in service soon while the Americans were down to their last aircraft carrier — the wounded *Enterprise.*

The U.S. Navy was down but certainly far from out; a PT-boat base had been established on Tulagi and together with Cactus Air Force bombers they now began to seriously put a dent in the Tokyo Express operation. On November 7, a convoy of 11 ships got badly shot-up by both planes and PT-boats and was forced to withdraw back up the Slot, while the Pacific Fleet continued its own resupply parcel-delivery service to sustain Alexander Vandegrift's motley army, which now began to strike forth against the battered and exhausted remnants of Harukichi Hyakutake's advance forces in two big sweeps across the Matanikau River and east toward Koli Point. The two offensive prongs scattered the enemy into the jungles. But on the verge of success, Vandegrift pulled his men back into defensive positions. He had received intelligence of a massive enemy operation scheduled for the night of November 13. It would prove the opening round in the decisive fight for the possession of Guadalcanal as the battered fleets of both sides once again groped toward one another.

Raizo Tanaka was going to be bringing 11 large transports down the Slot, bearing an additional 7,000 troops with enough ammunition and other supplies to service a force of 30,000 men. Accompanying this largest run of the Tokyo Express was Nobutake Kondo's Second Fleet battlewagons under the command of Hiroaki Abe: the battleships *Hiei* and *Kirishima*, the heavy cruiser *Nagara* and 14 destroyers. Following up for further reinforcement were Gunichi Mikawa's cruisers and destroyers. The mission of this armada was to successfully execute the landings while also reducing Henderson, and this time with sufficient offshore gunnery to finally level the base once and for all. Coming up from the south, however, was an American convoy bearing 5,500 troops and supplies, accompanied by the hastily patched-up *Enterprise*, which was bringing with her the two most powerful and heavily armed ships in the sector, the fast battleships *Washington* and *South Dakota* under Rear Admiral Willis Lee.

While the Japanese may have had nominal numerical superiority, quality was definitely on the American side. The *Hiei* and *Kirishima* were old World War I–era ships which had been rebuilt extensively between the wars but were still ponderous, insufficiently armored and under-gunned, while the *Washington* and *South Dakota* were two of the newest battleships in the U.S. Navy, both as fast as an aircraft carrier and highly maneuverable, heavily armored, and both sporting a main battery of nine 16-inch guns and secondary batteries of twenty 5-inch guns each. The *Enterprise* carried her complete complement of aircraft; 80 plus. The Cactus Air Force plus the Marine squadrons on Espiritu Santo gave the Americans the equivalent of another carrier air wing, while two of the Japanese flattops were light carriers which between them just about accounted for the strike force of a single large carrier. Plus, the Americans enjoyed the invaluable advantage of radar, while not even the flagships of the Japanese force mounted a single set between them. The South Pacific task forces were far from disadvantaged, though the Japanese believed otherwise and were steaming into battle once more underestimating the enemy before them.

It was around 0130 hours on the morning of the 13th when Abe's battleships entered Ironbottom Sound. The gunnery crews were loading the turrets with high explosive ordnance in preparation for the planned shelling of Henderson Field and signalmen were waiting to communicate the orders to the group to change formation and then commence firing. But waiting for him in the darkness were Admirals Norman Scott and Daniel Callaghan with their cruiser-destroyer forces which had escorted in two troop convoys and then, detaching only minimal escorts, had stayed to intercept the Tokyo Express. Scott, the senior officer by virtue of battle experience rather than date of commission, rode in the light cruiser *Atlanta*, while Callaghan flew his flag aboard the *San Francisco*. The rest of the force consisted of the *Portland*, *Helena* and *Juneau*, and the destroyers *Cushing*, *Laffley*, *Sterett*, *Barton*, *Aaron Ward*, *Fletcher*, *Monssen* and *O'Bannon*. The ships were formed in a van column and were patrolling up and down the Sound. The radar set on the *Helena* was the first to pick up Abe's formation as it sailed towards their position at 18 knots. Abe's ships were arrayed in a "V" formation with the *Nagara* and nine destroyers spearheading the way for *Hiei* and *Kirishima*. But neither Scott nor Callaghan fully appreciated the advantage radar gave them (being a relatively new invention, conservative officers were unwilling to rely fully on it as yet) and wasted precious time waiting for the enemy force to emerge from a rain squall for visual aiming. They ended up giving the two battleships a full fifteen minutes to switch from high explosive to armor piercing shells, which the crews did when the lookouts sighted the Scott-Callaghan force maneuvering to cross their "T." Thus, the Americans squandered a prime tactical advantage. It was at 0151 when a searchlight beam from the *Hiei* fell upon the *Atlanta*, and with that, Scott gave the order to illuminate the enemy formation and then to commence firing. As the battle developed, both sides came straight forward and crossed into each other's formations.

American and Japanese ships opened up on one another at almost point-blank range. The skies lit with flashes for the next twenty-four savage minutes. Orderly maneuvering degenerated into ship-to-ship mélées as the Americans found themselves bracketed on both sides. Fifteen-inch shells from the *Hiei* crashed into the *Atlanta*'s bridge, killing Admiral Scott, the captain, and all but one of the bridge crew. More salvos poured into the stricken cruiser while destroyers fired a full spread of torpedoes, two of which struck the late admiral's flagship. The *Cushing* and the other seven destroyers rushed headlong toward the Japanese formation, firing torpedoes and 5-inch guns. Both *Cushing* and the *Laffley* were pounded into scrap metal trying to protect the *Atlanta*. Their puny shells did nothing toward putting the *Hiei* out of action, but did start fires in her upper works which forced the battleship to break off action.

There was a momentary lull as both sides stopped to take new bearings on their targets. The *Kirishima* was the first to reload; she got her spots on Daniel Callaghan's flagship and promptly opened up a full broadside. Most of the ordnance slammed into the *San Francisco*'s superstructure. The bridge was destroyed in the bombardment and Callaghan joined his superior in death, along with most of his senior staff. The *Portland* was struck by a Long Lance astern, and was sent circling out of control because large hull plates bent backward by the blast acted like a huge rudder. But her own 8-inch batteries continued to fire away on the *Hiei*, along with the other ships, inflicting massive damage and crippling her steering machinery. The *Juneau* also took a torpedo astern and was put out of action. A third destroyer, the *Barton*, got cut in two by a Long Lance, while the *Monssen* was destroyed when she put on a searchlight and made herself a perfect target.

And then, at 0215, the guns suddenly fell quiet. Abe was abandoning his mission and the rest of the force put about, following the flagship out of Ironbottom Sound. With dawn rising in only four hours, the admiral chose to withdraw in the face of inevitable American airstrikes. Two Japanese destroyers had sunk, along with the *Cushing, Laffley, Monssen,* and *Barton*. The *Atlanta* would follow them to the bottom of the Sound after nightfall, adding to the growing population of wrecks gathering there. One thousand Navy men and both commanding admirals had died in the successful blunting of Abe's assault on Henderson Field, which had not a single gun trained on it the whole course of the battle. It was a tactical loss yet a clear strategic victory for the Pacific Fleet.

The *Helena*, least damaged of the ships in the Sound, led the crippled *Juneau* and *San Francisco* out of the channel with three destroyers in escort and then headed southward to shepherd the battered cruisers to Espiritu Santo. Once into clear sea, however, the periscope of Imperial submarine *I-26* sighted on the *Juneau*. One torpedo tracked all the way to the wounded cruiser and, at 1100 hours, struck and touched off a massive explosion which sank her immediately. The rest of the formation went to maximum steam to escape the area, leaving 700 survivors to fend for themselves in shark-infested waters. Among the dead were all five sons of Mr. and Mrs. Thomas Sullivan of Waterloo, Iowa; brothers who had enlisted the same day, went through basic training together, and sought assignment to the same ship to remain together. Following this tragedy, the Navy forbade the assignment of brothers or relatives to the same vessel, a ruling which subsequently went into force in all the services and stands to this day.

Through the daylight hours of the 13th, the crippled *Hiei*, escorted by the *Kirishima*, a light cruiser and five destroyers, slowly made their way up the channel leading out toward the Slot. The battleship, still smoldering and trailing oil, suffered from further machinery breakdowns and was forced to steer by varying the revolutions of her screws, which rendered her about as maneuverable as a garbage scow. The first air attacks came at dawn, as Cactus Air Force Dauntlesses and Avengers followed her smoke trail and bore in for the attack. Despite heavy antiaircraft fire from the destroyer screen, two Avengers successfully launched their torpedoes into her. Successively through the morning, more dive bombers and torpedo planes would come forth to harass Abe. Because of his decision to send the *Kirishima* away to save her, the *Hiei*'s protection was greatly diminished. Next came another fifteen planes: nine Avengers and their fighter escort which had been sent on ahead to Guadalcanal by the *Enterprise*. They spotted the cripple as they were making their roundabout approach to Henderson and pounced, putting another three torpedoes into Abe's flagship.

For the rest of the day, Henderson and the *Enterprise* simply rotated attack runs back and forth on the *Hiei*, progressively whittling her down. At one point a squadron of B-17s from Espiritu Santo joined in and added their bombs to the ones which had already battered the wounded battlewagon into a wreck. Finally, at 1600 hours, Abe ordered the crew to abandon ship. Scuttling charges were set off after the Emperor's portrait was successfully transferred to the destroyer *Yukaze*, and the *Hiei* sank at about roughly the same time as the *Atlanta*. She was the first battleship scuttled by the Imperial Japanese Navy, and for that disgrace on top of his utter failure to carry out the mission he had been assigned — which forced Tanaka's convoy to turn back to Rabaul — Hiroaki Abe was dismissed from command. Isoroku Yamamoto saw to it he would never get another.

Hoping to regain the initiative, Yamamoto had his fleet press on with the overall campaign despite Abe's failure. Right on schedule, three heavy cruisers and one light cruiser under Gunichi Mikawa went into Ironbottom Sound the night following the cruiser action and, despite fierce attacks by the Tulagi-based PT-boat flotilla, lobbed a thousand shells onto Henderson

Field. However, the ordnance the Japanese brought to bear wasn't heavy enough to cause any destruction beyond the odd plane or two being pasted. Seabees were out in force re-laying steel matting and clearing debris. By sunrise on the 14th, the airstrip, as usual, was ready for full combat operations once again. Both Henderson Field and the *Enterprise* sent out search missions which spread over the whole area for the enemy convoy that was expected to be proceeding down the Slot that day.

It was 0949 when Lieutenant Doan Carmoday from the *Enterprise* overflew a large formation located 150 miles northwest of Guadalcanal and moving at 14 knots. Eleven transports bearing 14,000 troops were accompanied by a cruiser with a screen of 12 destroyers and a squadron of Zeke fighters from the *Hiyo*. Raizo Tanaka was headed to what he believed was a safe landing zone thanks to the reported destruction of Henderson. That assumption was going to cost him dearly in the hours to follow. Carmoday promptly radioed his sighting back to the *Enterprise* before diving his Dauntless, followed by another SBD piloted by Lieutenant W.E. Johnson, onto the lead ship in the formation. Their bombs missed the targets, and seven Zekes wasted no time splashing the SBDs. But it was only the beginning of what was to follow.

Admiral Murray on the *Enterprise* relayed Lieutenant Carmoday's sighting to Guadalcanal and had his squadrons prepped for launch. Within minutes, Dauntless and Avenger bombers were lofting off the flight deck, while at the same time Henderson was launching Marine bomber and torpedo squadrons. Both the carrier and the base already had strike missions out which, at 1000 hours, had found Mikawa's ships and sank the *Kinugasa*, set the *Isuzu* afire, and damaged both the *Maya* and Mikawa's flagship *Chokai*. Originally intending to rendezvous with Tanaka's convoy, Mikawa was forced to retreat with all haste and Tanaka was now alone.

For the rest of the afternoon, carrier and land-based bombers and torpedo planes, accompanied by Wildcat fighters, struck at the convoy. Because Nobutake Kondo was reluctant, in the face of the losses already suffered so far in both planes and veteran air leaders, to commit the squadrons of the *Zuikaku* and *Hiyo*, Tanaka had only token air cover to stand against the successive waves of U.S. Navy, Army Air Force, and Marine attack planes that came at him. After a rain of bombs from a B-17 squadron from high altitude, there came the eighteen Dauntlesses of Marine bomber squadron VSMB 142 along with seven Avengers of the *Enterprise's* VT 6 torpedo squadron. The 1000-pound bombs and torpedoes struck three transports and the cruiser as Wildcats strafed all the ships in Tanaka's force. Unarmored, the transports were easy victims and were soon sinking in flames. Because each ship had been overloaded with troops, the carnage was massive. Men by the thousands were spilling into the sea as the thin-shelled transports cracked up on the surface. And to ensure that none of the troops would be picked up to contribute to the reinforcement of the enemy on Guadalcanal, the Wildcat pilots carried out their grim orders to machine-gun survivors in the water. The directive had been for total destruction, and despite the sickening inhumanity of the action, the pilots carried it out to the letter.

By 1645 hours, Tanaka had lost seven of his transports as well as nine destroyers and every vessel in his convoy had sustained damaged by the continual air attacks. With his remaining four transports all burning as they closed upon the Tassafaronga landing zone near midnight, he ordered them to beach, whereupon they quickly evacuated their troops and crews. Only 3,000 of the men who had rode with the convoy made it to Guadalcanal, and they were without most of their ammunition, supplies, and rations. The ships which had managed to make it all the way would find themselves under renewed air attack the next morning and also under shelling by the destroyer *Meade* and land-based artillery. It would be total destruction.

As laid out in the strategic planning, Nobutake Kondo's battleship force was spearheading the way for Tanaka's convoy, and was also charged with carrying out the mission both Hiroaki Abe and Gunichi Mikawa had failed so miserably to achieve — the reduction of the Marine airbase. Kondo's command consisted of the battleship *Kirishima*, the heavy cruisers *Atago* and *Takao*, the light cruisers *Nagara* and the *Sendai*, and the destroyers *Anayami* and *Uranami*. Once again, as had happened two nights ago, a force of American ships was already in Ironbottom Sound waiting for them. But this time, it was Willis Lee's Task Force 64, formed around the *Washington* and *South Dakota* with the destroyers *Walke*, *Gwin*, *Benham*, and *Preston* in support. And unlike the late admirals Scott and Callaghan, Lee had a full understanding and appreciation of radar and the tactical advantages it afforded him.

Kondo's force had been under surveillance by both Catalinas and patrol submarines which had been shadowing the enemy movements since 1600 hours and Admiral Lee had been kept updated since first contact. With the battle group 150 miles from Ironbottom Sound and moving at 17 knots, Lee anticipated that the enemy would be within range by 2300. Through the evening the *Washington*'s and *South Dakota*'s screens tracked Kondo's warships as they closed the distance. The closest was only nine miles off of Savo Island, the *Sendai* bird-dogging the trail ahead. The enemy move in splitting their formation to sweep into the inlet on either side of Savo was observed, and at 2110 Lee had his ships form into a column sweeping in a reciprocal east-west course across the entrance to the Sound to cross the "T" on Kondo. Then Lee waited patiently for him to come forth.

Just as Lee had figured, the *Sendai* reached the area of Ironbottom Sound at almost exactly 2300 hours and her movements were tracked clearly on the *Washington*'s radar plot. The two Task Force 64 battleships simply bided their time until the cruiser was in optimum range. While on board the *Sendai*, lookouts kept their eyes peeled as they sighted two silhouettes ahead; sleek, black shapes which they reported to the bridge as cruisers. Seventeen minutes passed while the lookouts struggled to positively identify the ships before them. Suddenly, flashes illuminated them for just a moment or two—followed by a rain of 16-inch shells which straddled the cruiser. The destroyers of both sides rushed forth at one another, the Japanese tincans coming from behind Savo while the four American escorts charged ahead. They exchanged shellfire and torpedo salvos, which sank only one Japanese destroyer but left two American destroyers sinking and a third with her bow blown off.

The *Washington* and *South Dakota* now moved to close the passage between Savo and Cape Esperance. As they joined the battle, the *SoDak* suddenly suffered a shortout of her entire electrical circuitry, which blanked the radars and radio and cut the power to her turrets. While the *SoDak*'s engineers raced to restore power and communications, the *Washington* continued to pound the *Sendai* mercilessly while still ploughing ahead. They reached the other side of Savo and found themselves face to face with the *Kirishima*, the *Atago* and *Takao*, and two destroyers. The *SoDak* was the lead vessel closing the distance and, with electrical power restored just in time, she opened fire on the enemy formation. Searchlight beams found her, and the *Kirishima* responded with her own 14-inch batteries which struck the *SoDak*'s superstructure and cut her radio masts down, depriving her of contact with the *Washington*. But while the Japanese were concentrating on the wounded *South Dakota*, the *Washington* was coming upon them undetected, and with radar-directed aiming by Lee's expert operators, they caught *Kirishima* perfectly in salvo fire from a range of five miles. The 16-inch shell hits demolished the vintage battlewagon's pagoda-like superstructure and crippled her, forcing her to drop out of the line. More shell hits cut her steering, and the battleship circled out of control while the *Washington* continued to blast away on her as if she were nothing more than a gunnery target. Fires were raging all over her upper works while shells penetrated to her vitals, knocking out boilers, which deprived her of all engine power even as the captain was trying to bring the vessel back under control by varying her screws. She would finally be abandoned and sunk by torpedoes from the four destroyers which stood station over the burning hulk at 0300 hours on the 15th — one more wreck to litter the floor of Ironbottom Sound.

Under the rapidly deteriorating battle situation, Nobutake Kondo proved to have little more stomach for the fight than Hiroaki Abe had and withdrew northward with his surviving ships while he still had the chance. The *Washington* and *South Dakota*, suffering only minor damage, pursued for seven miles until the destroyers in Kondo's screen fired torpedoes to ward them off. With no escorts of their own, Lee called it a battle and headed his dreadnoughts back to Savo.

Isoroku Yamamoto had played his last card and lost. The Combined Fleet's resources, already severely strained when the Guadalcanal operation had been initiated, were now so thin that drastic economies had to be imposed. The Imperial Navy could no longer support the army landing in any substantive way, and as a result pulled out of the campaign, excepting for the nightly destroyer resupply runs of the Tokyo Express, which would never be able to adequately supply or reinforce Hirokichi Hyakutake's remaining troops, now being progressively reduced by disease, air attack, and the constant pressure put on by 50,000 new U.S. Army troops beginning in December. On the night of November 30, eight Japanese destroyers attacked an American force of five cruisers and six destroyers, in which the *Northampton* was sunk. But there would never be another attempt at a large reinforcement convoy; the Imperial General Staff was not about to send more men to what they now referred to as the Island of Death. At every step of the way, the Japanese had underestimated both the numbers and sheer tenacity of their American enemies and it had cost them dearly. The United States had lost more ships in the naval battles in and around Guadalcanal. But as Admiral Yamamoto had always known and dreaded, they could be replaced more easily than Japan's losses. As the year rolled around to 1943, Japan's power in the South Pacific, along with the myth of her invincibility, had been irretrievably broken and the Tokyo Express shifted into a withdrawal operation, evacuating General Hyakutake's surviving forces as quietly as they could. By February 8, the last of them would be gone, and the only flag left flying on Guadalcanal was the Stars and Stripes.

For the last six weeks of 1942, the *Enterprise* continued to cover the Guadalcanal area as the sole American aircraft carrier in the Pacific Theatre. But she would patrol the waters around the island unopposed. Had even one of the aircraft carriers Chuichi Nagumo lost at Midway survived, the *Enterprise* might very well have been destroyed at Santa Cruz along with the *Hornet*, which would have tipped the balance in Japan's favor.

Both sides had bled each other almost white in the six month struggle over Guadalcanal. But now, the American industrial machine was kicking into full gear. The *Saratoga* would return to service early in 1943. But she would not be returning alone.

At the very end of the old year, December 31, the United States Navy commissioned into service the brand new warship USS *Essex*, a vessel carrying a proud name dating all the way back to before the War of 1812. She was the first of a whole new class of fast attack aircraft carrier: 38,000 tons, heavily armed with four dual 5-inch gun turrets and an array of 40mm and 20mm antiaircraft guns, capable of 33 knots and carrying an air wing of nearly 100 planes. The design for the *Essex*-class had been laid down in 1938 and represented the ultimate development of American aircraft carrier evolution to that point. In every way the new flattop was a modern vessel. As she headed out on her shakedown cruise, her first sister ship was already building on the slipway. When she entered service, the second *Essex* carrier would be named for — and embody the ghost of — the proud ship lost at Midway which, like the battle itself, would haunt the Japanese for the rest of the war.

Yorktown.

CHAPTER 7

Cartwheel

On April 3, 1943, Isoroku Yamamoto boarded a twin-engined Mitsubishi G4M2 Betty bomber to fly out to the Empire's Southwest Pacific bastion at Rabaul, New Britain, to coordinate with the Army area commander, General Hitoshi Immamura, on a combined Army-Navy air operation designed to destroy all American air forces in the Southwest Pacific. This would relieve the pressure against their remaining positions on New Guinea as well as blunt the renewed American offensive in the Solomons Sea area. Designated Operation I-GO, the campaign involved the launching of air strikes down the Solomons and the Papuan peninsula, where Douglas MacArthur's combined Allied forces had prevailed in months of bloody, bitter fighting to clear out the last of the Japanese forces originally sent to take Port Moresby. The backbone of the campaign was provided by the Eleventh Air Fleet based at Rabaul, and to back them up, every plane from the naval base at Truk as well as from the aircraft carriers *Zuikaku*, *Junyo*, *Hiyo* and *Zuiho* had been stripped from their commands and sent to Rabaul. Bad weather kept 200 planes grounded for four days, finally launching in the early dawn hours of April 7. Pilots returning from the strike eagerly reported having sunk dozens of warships and transports as well as destroying American planes by the squadron. In reality, the first strike wave had succeeded in sinking only a tanker, a destroyer, and a corvette; while the Eleventh Air Fleet squadrons suffered disproportionate casualties in prosecuting the attack.

A week and a half later, on April 18, Admiral Yamamoto took off with his staff in two Betty bombers, the second one carrying his Chief-of-Staff Matome Ugaki, and accompanied by an escort of six Zeke fighters to make a tour of the airfields on the surrounding islands. He wanted to see to it that operations were being carried out to his design, to bolster the morale of the pilots. His first stop would be at Bougainville to inspect the garrison at Ballale, then to proceed on to the Shortland Islands and Buin. The ever-punctual admiral took off at exactly 0600 hours for what was expected to be an hour and forty-five minute flight.

The admiral's punctuality, ingrained in him by a lifetime of duty and habit, would prove to be his doom. Back at Pearl Harbor, the HYPO team three days earlier had decrypted the C-in-C's complete itinerary, which showed that Yamamoto's formation would come within range of fighters based at Henderson Field. Chester Nimitz immediately decided to take advantage of this prime opportunity to assassinate the Number One Japanese commander in the Pacific, depriving the enemy of its top strategist as well as delivering a hammer-blow to its morale. After securing permission from Franklin Roosevelt himself, Nimitz ordered William Halsey to carry out the mission designated Operation Vengeance.

Halsey coordinated with the Marine and Army Air Force commanders at Henderson. Following on the operational plan they thus developed, a force of seventeen P-38 Lightnings of the Fifth Air Force's 339th Fighter Squadron led by Major John Mitchell took off in the predawn hours of the 18th to be in position to intercept the Yamamoto formation. The Lightnings were twin-engined, twin-tailed fighters designed for long-range intercept and fitted with belly-tanks to extend their range to a maximum of 2,260 miles. The admiral arrived at their position over Bougainville precisely on schedule. The Lightnings dropped their tanks and eight peeled off to deal with the fighter screen while the remaining nine put themselves on the two Bettys which were taking evasive action in a desperate bid to escape. Since Mitchell's pilots hadn't expected more than one Betty bomber and consequently didn't know which plane was carrying their target, they simply opened fire on both. One plane went down in the jungle at the edge of Bougainville while the other, losing a wing, spiraled into the sea.

Matome Ugaki managed to escape his plane before it sank, waded ashore, and made his way to the nearby village of Aku, where an Imperial Army unit was stationed. They hacked their way through the jungle the next day and finally found the Commander-in-Chief's bomber. Inside the wreck, Isoroku Yamamoto, who had celebrated his 58th birthday twelve days earlier, was found dead in his seat, blood streaming from his temple and his left hand clasped around his sheathed katana.

There was no one in the entire Imperial Naval officer corps who could replace Yamamoto. The only man who had any significant measure of his strategic brilliance combined with fighting spirit was Tamon Yamaguchi. But he was dead now; having decided in all honor to go down with the *Hiryu* at Midway. The very conservative and unimaginative Mineichi Koga was appointed as the new C-in-C of the Combined Fleet and its operations soon reflected the limits of Koga's abilities. Yamamoto's ashes were brought home aboard the superbattleship *Musashi* and a national day of mourning was declared by the Emperor himself. A pall hung over the

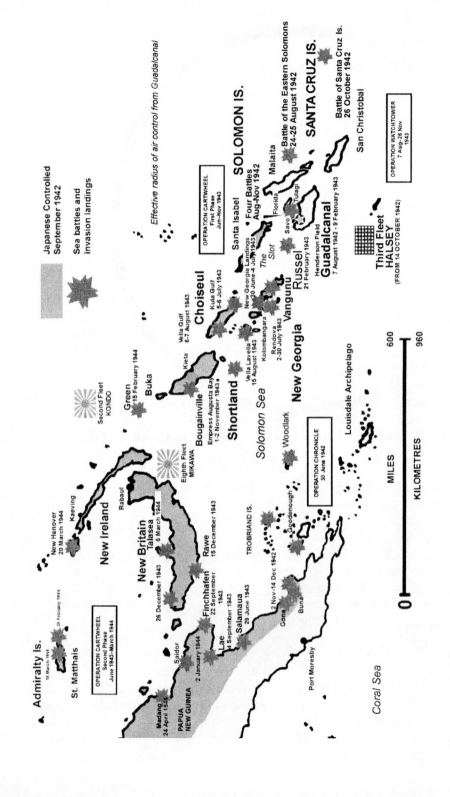

Japanese Controlled
September 1942

Sea battles and
invasion landings

Effective radius of air control from Guadalcanal

OPERATION CARTWHEEL
First Phase
Jun–Nov 1943

OPERATION WATCHTOWER
7 Aug–26 Nov
1943

Battle of the Eastern Solomons
24–25 August 1942

Battle of Santa Cruz Is.
26 October 1942

SANTA CRUZ IS.

SOLOMON IS.

San Christobal

Santa Isabel

Malaita

Four Battles
Aug–Nov 1942

Florida

Savo

Tulagi

Third Fleet
HALSEY
(FROM 14 OCTOBER 1942)

Guadalcanal
7 August 1942 - 9 February 1943

Henderson Field

Russel
21 February 1943

Vangunu

New Georgia

Kolombangara

Rendova
2–30 July 1943

New Georgia Landings
30 June–4 Jul 1943

The Slot

Vella Lavella
15 August 1943

Kula Gulf
5–6 July 1943

Vella Gulf
6–7 August 1943

Choiseul

Kieta

Buka

Green
15 February 1944

Second Fleet
KONDO

Empress Augusta Bay
1–2 November 1943

Bougainville

Shortland

Solomon Sea

Woodlark

OPERATION CHRONICLE
30 June 1942

Eighth Fleet
MIKAWA

Louisdale Archipelago

Rabaul

Kaeving

New Ireland

New Hanover
20 March 1944

New Britain

Talasea
6 March 1944

26 December 1943

Finchhafen
22 September
1943

Rawe
15 December 1943

TROBRIAND IS.

Goodenough

2 Nov–14 Dec 1942

Buna

Gona

Salamaua
29 June 1943

Lae
4 September 1943

2 January 1944

Saidor

Medang
24 April 1944

PAPUA
NEW GUINEA

Port Moresby

Coral Sea

OPERATION CARTWHEEL
Second Phase
June 1943–March 1944

Admiralty Is.
16 March 1944

29 February 1944

St. Matthais

0   600

MILES

960

KILOMETRES

officers and men of the Imperial Japanese Navy and though no one would speak the thought, though many still clung to belief in ultimate victory, the death of Isoroku Yamamoto was the beginning of the end.

After the punishment both sides suffered in the Guadalcanal campaign, neither navy was up for another engagement any time soon. The recent Battle of the Bismarck Sea, an American victory in which air strikes had wiped out eight transports and four destroyers carrying reinforcements for the Japanese invasion force on New Guinea, had been an Army Air Force operation. William Halsey had only the *Saratoga* and the *Enterprise* with him. The latter was badly in need of a long-delayed refit and under the circumstances he did not want to risk his flattops against land-based air. He would not take his South Pacific Force into combat until he had sufficient reinforcements to meet the enemy force one-on-one, or preferably, with better odds in his favor. The Japanese for their part had flattops with few planes, thanks to the losses suffered from I-GO. The *Shokaku* was still laid-up having her flight deck rebuilt and the *Hosho*, the world's first keel-built aircraft carrier, was finally withdrawn from service as too antiquated. A program of ship conversions in addition to new carrier construction was undertaken to replace the flattops lost in last year's fighting. The seaplane tenders *Chitose* and *Chiyoda* were undergoing conversion to light carriers, while two World War I–era battlewagons, the *Ise* and *Hyuga*, were having their aft turrets replaced with short flight decks. Additionally, two *Yamato*-class battleships already building on the slips were reordered as carrier conversions. Construction on the brand-new aircraft carrier *Taiho* was underway, along with the first five of fifteen planned vessels based on a modified *Hiryu*-class design and five "improved-*Taihos*." It was an ambitious program, the aim of which was to bring the Imperial Fleet up to twice the carrier strength they had at the outset of the war. The target dates for the delivery of all these vessels lay between November of 1943 and April of 1945.

The mounting losses were already sapping Japan's industrial strength. The flow of oil and raw materials was reduced to a trickle and was barely sufficient to sustain just the effort to replace units lost in the fighting. The very thing the late Admiral Yamamoto had feared since before the beginning of the war was now coming to pass: the American industrial machine

Opposite: Watchtower and Cartwheel — After Midway, the Pacific war turned to a bitter contest over the Solomons and New Guinea. Once Guadalcanal was finally won, William Halsey began one prong of Operation Cartwheel, leapfrogging up the Solomons chain while MacArthur's allied forces began their amphibious thrusts up New Guinea's northern coast. The island-hopping concept isolated the Japanese strongholds of Rabaul, Kaeving, and Bougainville.

USS *Essex*, the lead ship in a new class of heavy attack carrier. Commissioned at the very end of 1942, the *Essex* and her sisters would form the nucleus of a new and far deadlier carrier fleet than anything that had ever been seen. National Archives 80-G-68097.

was swinging into full gear. It had already been seven times the size and scope of Japan's at the beginning of hostilities and was sustained by a wealth of resources and raw materials which the Americans had within their own territory. Now, that industrial machine was itself expanding, while the Japanese industries were barely keeping their own pace. Japan was losing the all-important battle for production.

American shipyards by stark contrast were turning out ships of all types almost once every six weeks, particularly the ubiquitous Liberty Ships which Henry Kaiser's yards were producing on an assembly-line basis, almost like automobiles. On February 17, the first of the *Essex*'s sisters to join the fleet was the new USS *Lexington*, while the *Yorktown* was commissioned only three days before Admiral Yamamoto's death over Bougainville, and four more were building and expected to all be in service by December of 1943, while a further 16 were on order. In addition to these heavies, nine *Cleveland*-class cruiser hulls were reordered as light carrier (CVL) conversions, entering service as the *Independence*-class: *Independence, Princeton,*

Belleau Wood, Cowpens, Monterey, Langley, Cabot, Bataan, and *San Jacinto.* These ships, like all light carriers, were limited in their plane-carrying capacity, because of their smaller size and narrower hulls, to a maximum of 40 aircraft. Nevertheless, they represented a significant tactical asset in and of themselves, able to provide fleet air cover in addition to augmenting tactical air operations against enemy fleet units and ground targets. What had been initiated as an emergency measure in the dark days of 1942 would add the equivalent of three complete carrier air wings to the Pacific Fleet's overall strength. In addition to these combat carriers, more of the tiny escort or "jeep" carriers—550-foot merchant ship conversions based on the *Long Island* pattern — were also being turned out. Many of these little vessels were units of the *Bogue, Sagamon,* and *Casablanca* classes. Thirteen already existed and these, along with several built for the British Royal Navy, served in both the Atlantic and Pacific. Before war's end, 120 of these stout little vessels would be built and commissioned. The escort carriers, too small to support the sort of air operations required of fleet engagements, were mostly used in the Atlantic for convoy escort and antisubmarine warfare, and in the Pacific to ferry replacement aircraft to both island bases and to the larger fleet aircraft carriers. Eventually though, they would be used for invasion support missions and become combat vessels in their own right. The CVLs and CVEs were a testament to American adaptability under the worst conditions, to provide the fleet with operational flightdecks as quickly as possible.

In addition to the carriers, American shipyards were launching the new *South Dakota*–class fast battleships *Massachusetts* and *Alabama* and also the largest, most heavily armed warships ever built by the United States up to that time, the four dreadnoughts of the *Iowa*-class; *Iowa, New Jersey, Missouri,* and *Wisconsin.* Each had nine 16-inch guns in three massive turrets and displaced 58,000 tons. Only the *Yamato*s were larger. They would soon be joined in service by those battleships damaged at Pearl Harbor but now being rebuilt and modernized. The first twenty of the *Fletcher*-class fast destroyers were also being completed, along with heavy and light cruisers, long-range fleet submarines, landing craft, cargo vessels, assault transports, oilers, and PT-boats by the squadron. Even without those vessels allocated for the war against Hitler, this massive industrial machine had, in just one year, built up from scratch a fleet which outnumbered that of the Imperial Japanese Navy at its apex.

American industry also had no problem turning out enough aircraft to supply this new carrier fleet. The venerable F4F Wildcat was steadily being replaced as the Navy's main carrier-based fighter by the new F6F Hellcat, although the older but still reliable Wildcat would continue in ser-

The escort carrier USS *Wake Island*. The CVEs represented an innovative solution to the problem of getting operational flightdecks to sea in large numbers. Serving as both tactical air platforms in the Pacific and antisubmarine ships in the Atlantic, 120 of these stout vessels would be built by war's end. U.S. Navy, catalogue number unavailable.

vice the rest of the war. The Grumman TBF Avenger torpedo bomber had already replaced the antiquated Devastator after Midway and had proven its value in the Guadalcanal campaign. In addition to these two superb combat aircraft, there was also the unique Chance-Vought F4U Corsair, a large but fast fighter with a gull-wing design and capable of mounting a maximum bomb-load of 1,300 pounds. At first rejected by the Navy as a carrier fighter, she entered service with the Marine Corps but would soon be accepted by the Navy when carrier-based Marine fighter units increasingly were composed of Corsairs. The Corsair was deceptively fast for its size, capable of 478 mph. She was also an agile craft. Her two wing-intake scoops and large propeller blades caused a characteristic whistling noise which led the Japanese to dub the Corsair "Whistling Death." The venerable Douglas SBD Dauntless would soon be augmented by a larger, longer ranged dive bomber, the *Curtiss* SB2C Helldiver.

It was not only in raw numbers but also technological superiority that the Americans exceeded the best efforts of the Japanese. One of the greatest handicaps suffered by the Imperial Japanese Navy was the near-total lack of radar of any sort, and what radar sets they had were quite primitive — indeed, for the time, they were the worst in existence. Not only did the Pacific Fleet have radar even from the beginning of the war, each and every ship in the Navy was now being fitted with the newest radar being developed to provide full ship-tracking and plane-tracking capability in addition to dead-reckoning tracing for navigation. Plane-tracking radar was also increasingly being integrated into antiaircraft coordination as well, with radar operators and gunners operating in tandem. To counter the threat posed by Japanese land-based night fighters and bombers, a new type of plane-mounted radar was developed to equip carrier planes with night-fighting capability. In addition, carriers and other capital ships were being outfitted with a new type of four-channel VHF radio which would permit multiple ship communication and at short range to prevent enemy radio receivers from intercepting their transmissions. Finally, the Americans adapted a British innovation; the usage of an Identification Friend-or-Foe (IFF) transponder to enable American planes to automatically identify themselves to the ships of the fleet, making the identification of hostiles in the skies far easier (excepting those pilots who forgot to flip on their IFF devices). This new technology all allowed the Pacific Fleet's carrier task forces to more easily coordinate surface, submarine, and air operations over long distances and to act in concert with one another.

By the first anniversary of Isoroku Yamamoto's death, Chester Nimitz would have at his command a brand new navy — a large, modern, deadly armada powerful enough to overwhelm and annihilate the Japanese Imperial Navy. It would be the most destructive war machine ever to sail the oceans, and Nimitz would be eager to unleash it on his enemies 4,000 miles away. But in May of 1943, Nimitz's new navy was still building. He and his commanders had to deal with the menace of the Imperial Navy with the resources at hand. They were still living the hand-to-mouth existence they had become accustomed to, and they could not as yet take on the enemy directly. The Japanese force anchored inside Truk lagoon, now designated the Mobile Fleet, acted as a deterrent against further American advance in accordance with Operational Plan Z, devised by the late Admiral Yamamoto as a stopgap measure in the hopes of buying time. With their carrier squadrons decimated, however, that fleet dared not venture into the Pacific. Japan's brief rule of the waves had come to an end. The first direct results of that brutal reality were the loss of their distant Alaskan footholds, the islands of Attu and Kiska.

The failure to capture and occupy Midway the previous year had rendered the whole Aleutians operation pointless except as a diversion for American resources. The Americans had devoted no more of their combat strength to fighting off the Japanese invasion effort than they absolutely had to, but it had been enough to stall the operation. While the Guadalcanal campaign was in progress, there was no question of reinforcements being devoted to the expansion of their toehold on Attu and Kiska. A resupply convoy under Boshiro Hosagoya, accompanied by the entire strength of his Fifth Fleet—four cruisers and four destroyers—had set forth from the Kurile Islands on March 26. But unfortunately for Hosagoya, Rear Admiral Charles McMorris was prowling the area with the heavy cruiser *Salt Lake City*, the light cruiser *Richmond* and a pair of destroyers. He had arrived on February 18 to shell Attu Island and had sunk a previous convoy of two transports. Hosagoya came upon him with two-to-one odds in his favor in addition to a measure of surprise, since Naval Intelligence had failed to provide any warning of the enemy sortie. But McMorris, known to his compatriots as "Socrates," applied the whole of his tactical brilliance in fighting a four hour gunnery duel off the Komandorski Islands in which he managed to drive off the enemy convoy, thanks in large measure to Hosagoya's own cautious nature. Two destroyers were similarly unsuccessful in their attempt to run McMorris' very effective blockade and now Attu and Kiska were cut off from the rest of the world.

The Japanese presence on Attu and Kiska was little more than an annoyance but, a decision having been made to eliminate it, a large invasion force was dispatched toward the Northern Pacific. The fleet under the overall command of Rear Admiral Thomas Kinkaid, who had replaced Robert Theobald in January, consisted of transports carrying 11,000 troops of the U.S. Army's 7th Infantry Division taken from Douglas MacArthur's command (thus delaying his operations) and were accompanied by the escort carrier *Nassau* for tactical air support and also by the battleship *Idaho*. Also sailing with this fleet were the rebuilt *Pennsylvania* and *Nevada*, the first of the Pearl Harbor battleships to return to duty. Guiding the fleet were the submarines *Narwhal* and *Nautilus*, necessary in the treacherous arctic conditions the invasion force was sailing into.

Kinkaid decided to bypass Kiska and concentrate on the larger island of Attu, farther down the Aleutian chain. This would totally isolate the Kiska garrison, which could be left to freeze and starve. His fleet, cloaked by the mists, closed to bombardment range on May 11, and the battleships opened up with a radar-guided shelling of Holtz Bay, where the enemy's main base and airfield were located. Navy and Army Air Force planes flew when the skies were clear enough and added to the pounding. The 11,000 troops went ashore with only light opposition, but the garrison commander, Colonel Yasugo Yamakazi, retreated with his forces toward Chichagcof Harbor, a cul-de-sac which also afforded his men the advantage of semi-frozen mud that would bog down enemy armor and vehicles, forcing them to come forth on foot. Yamakazi was outnumbered five-to-one, but his men were firmly dug in and ready to fight it right to the last ditch.

Back at Truk, Minechi Koga had hastily scrambled the Mobile Fleet for a rescue mission, but he was subsequently overridden by the Imperial General Staff. The Empire could not afford to send its deterrent away from their main defense perimeter to rescue a doomed garrison from a distant outpost of no military value. The fleet was recalled and Yamakazi and his men were abandoned to their fate.

Two weeks later, with food, supplies, and ammunition running out, Yamakazi's surviving troops threw themselves at the American lines surrounding Engineer Hill on which they had chosen to make their last stand. They came by the hundreds, in human-wave attacks, with pistols, knives and swords against machine gun nests. In a final banzai charge in the dawn hours of May 30, the last 500 men rushed forward to the slaughter. The remaining survivors pulled the pins of their grenades, and put them to their heads in a grisly act of mass suicide. The Americans lost 1,000 and took only 28 prisoners. The Stars and Stripes was run up on Attu that afternoon. Kiska was isolated and subject to almost daily bombing attacks by the Eleventh Air Force. Two months later, under cover of heavy fog, two cruisers and six destroyers slipped in toward the coast and evacuated the last 5,000 Japanese off of the North American continent. American and Canadian troops who finally swarmed ashore on August 15 found Kiska Island occupied only by three half-starved dogs.

The first advance into the Central Pacific, Operation Cartwheel, began on July 2. Its strategy, designed by Halsey and MacArthur in a round of intensive planning sessions with their staffs from April 15th to the 18th, was to move up the Solomons and New Britain archipelagos step-by-step in thirteen landings which would push the Japanese perimeter all the way back to New Guinea, which would be hit last, between July and December. At each stage, MacArthur's forces would seize islands ahead of the fleet to use as forward bases while the Marines riding with Halsey would secure and occupy the islands which were the main invasion targets. Each wing would operate in tandem, taking the strongholds with each subsequent leap. Ultimately, the object was to be in position to seize New Britain and Bougainville in order to launch a two-pronged offensive on Rabaul for the early months of 1944.

Halsey's Third Fleet, as the South Pacific Force was now designated following a reorganization of the U.S. Pacific Fleet's command and force division structures, closed on New Georgia with the carriers *Saratoga* and *HMS Victorious*— temporarily seconded to his fleet when the *Enterprise* was sent back for overhaul— six battleships, and seven divisions backed by 1,600 Navy, Marine, and Army Air Force planes. The troops swarmed ashore on nearby Rendova Island, across the channel from Munda Point

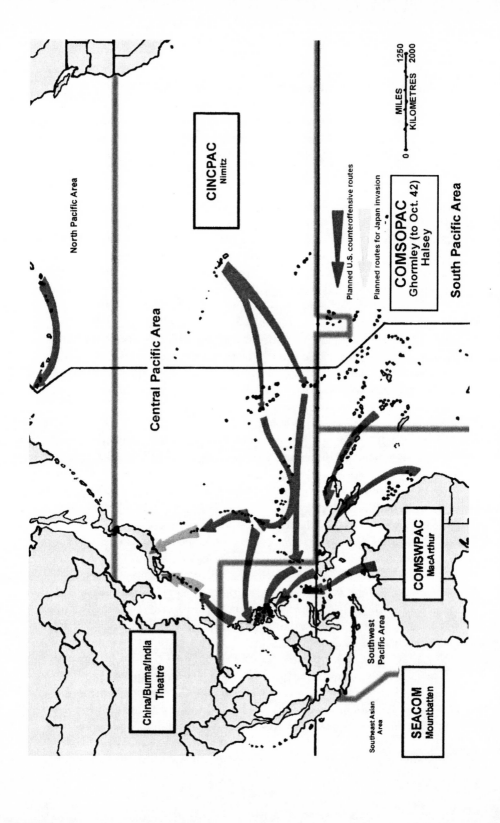

North Pacific Area

CINCPAC
Nimitz

Central Pacific Area

Planned U.S. counteroffensive routes

Planned routes for Japan invasion

COMSOPAC
Ghormley (to Oct. 42)
Halsey

South Pacific Area

COMSWPAC
MacArthur

China/Burma/India
Theatre

Southwest
Pacific Area

Southeast Asian
Area

SEACOM
Mountbatten

MILES 1250
KILOMETRES 2000
0

on New Georgia itself. Intelligence that the enemy was rushing to complete an airstrip had compelled Halsey to land the men of the 4th Marine Raider Battalion ten days early. Colonel Michael Currin and his men succeeded in getting ashore at Segi Station and took the small fishing port at Viru, vital for establishing a PT-boat base to support the invasion. It took Currin's Marines twelve hours to hack their way through dense jungle, harassed by Japanese snipers every step, just to gain seven miles. They had fallen twenty-four hours behind schedule of the main landing, but in spite of their ordeal, they were able to fight off Japanese units for four solid hours to aid the main assault. Rendova was secured by the 30th and was prepped as the staging base for the landing on New Georgia itself.

The Japanese garrison pulled back to Munda and heavily fortified their position to protect the airstrip. Mirroring the tactics employed by Alexander Vandegrift the previous year on Guadalcanal, the canny and resourceful Japanese garrison commander, Major General Nabor Sasaki, centered his perimeter on the airbase and set up a chain of machine gun nests which provided overlapping fields of fire and augmented the strength of his main position with an outer ring of pillbox strongpoints. All positions were fortified with log and earthen barriers and heavily camouflaged. General Hitoshi Immamura, the Imperial Army commander on Rabaul, vetoed Sasaki's plan to try to retake Rendova in favor of concentrating all defense forces on their base. Coordinating with Admiral Koga, Immamura set up a new Tokyo Express operation to attempt to reinforce the Munda garrison. A convoy carrying 4,000 reinforcements set out from Rabaul on July 3. However, they ran right into the task force of Rear Admiral W. L. Ainsworth — three cruisers, including the *Helena* and the Royal New Zealand Navy's *HMNZS Leander*, and four destroyers. In the ensuing battle, the *Helena* and the destroyers *Gwin* and *Strong* were sunk and the *Leander* heavily damaged, but the superior gunnery radar of the American force scored the destruction of the Japanese light cruiser *Jintsu* and one troop-carrying destroyer, with another forced to run aground. The remainder of the convoy was compelled to return to Rabaul.

Outnumbered three-to-one, Sasaki's garrison put up a determined resistance. It took the Army and Marine troops five weeks to finally over-

Opposite: The Plan for Reconquering the Pacific — The Allies divide the Pacific Theatre into four combat sectors, then formulate a strategy centering upon a two-pronged thrust through the Central and Southwest Pacific. Chester Nimitz led the Navy through the Mandates in combination with Douglas MacArthur's thrust up from Australia to strike at the heart of the Empire. The conceptual leap of island-hopping, bypassing heavily fortified stronghold islands, would greatly speed up the Allied campaign.

run Munda on August 5. But Sasaki succeeded in pulling out his survivors and crossed over to Kolombangara Island, where he took charge of the garrison and had them dig in an equally tough chain of defenses to await the American invaders. Sasaki would have a total force of 10,000. They were being reinforced by the Express runs from Rabaul despite harassment by PT-boat squadrons. But a subsequent Express convoy sailing five days later was caught and suffered the loss of three destroyers at the guns of a unit of U.S. destroyers, operating independently of a screening cruiser and winning the U.S. Navy's first night destroyer action.

But Admiral Halsey, and Nimitz back at Pearl, were appalled at how long it had taken just to advance ten miles on New Georgia, and equally tough defenses were awaiting his forces at their next target, Kolombangara. Computing on that rate of advance, the war in the Pacific would end up lasting another eight years. This was utterly unacceptable and Nimitz urged Halsey to reconsider their strategy to devise a faster way to advance through the Central Pacific.

Halsey found his inspiration in the recent victory in the Aleutians campaign. Thomas Kinkaid's brilliant move in bypassing the more heavily fortified Kiska Island to take Attu had proven so successful that Halsey decided to apply this strategy to his own campaign. By island hopping, instead of taking every fortified bastion, they would seize lightly defended islands which nevertheless could serve as forward bases and staging points for the eventual invasion of New Britain. By establishing total sea and air control over the area, the presence of fortified Japanese garrisons would actually be quite insignificant. They would be isolated and completely neutralized, cut off from all resupply or possibility of escape.

Nimitz readily concurred and approved of Halsey's modified strategy. Kolombangara would be bypassed and instead the Third Fleet hit Vella LaVella further up the archipelago. The small Japanese garrison was quickly overwhelmed and the island proved large enough to accommodate seven Marine Corsair squadrons. Combined with their positions on Guadalcanal and Espiritu Santo, the Americans now had virtually complete ownership of the skies over the Slot. For little cost, Halsey's island-hopping had already gained the Americans a vital military asset. But the stratagem, which at the time was merely a matter of military expediency, would prove to have far-reaching consequences as it began, imperceptibly at first, to speed up the whole tempo of the Pacific War. It would prove to be beyond the ability of the Japanese to adapt. From that point forward, the Empire's main enemy was not the American navy, but Time.

CHAPTER 8

Spearhead

Through the summer of 1943, the strength of the Pacific Fleet was greatly augmented by the gradual arrival of the new aircraft carriers *Essex*, *Yorktown*, *Lexington*, *Independence*, *Princeton*, and *Belleau Wood* along with two battleships, two cruisers, and twenty destroyers. The fleet's numbers had been restored and its airstrike capability was now massively greater than it had been before December of 1941. With the arrival of so many new aircraft carriers and other vessels, the Central Pacific Force was subsequently made into the Fifth Fleet and placed under the overall command of Midway veteran Raymond Spruance. The growing presence of the new flattops also forced Nimitz to address the problem of fully integrating air operations with the overall naval campaign and in the most efficient and effective manner. Nimitz's air operations chief, Rear Admiral Jack Towers, conferred with the captains of the new flattops and the flag officers who rode with them. In the course of their deliberations the air officers developed the concept of the fast carrier task force. In theory, such a unit would be composed of three heavy and, if available, two light carriers upon which the fleet's striking power would be based. The air wings would conduct direct tactical air support for amphibious landings, provide air defense for task forces with no carriers of their own, and actively seek, attack, and destroy enemy land, sea, and air forces wherever they were found. Battleships, cruisers and destroyers would exist to provide an integrated screen and operate in tandem with the flattops. The air officers all concurred that such a formation would most efficiently concentrate offensive power in the most devastating manner instead of dispersing carriers to various surface-based task forces, where they would be little better than auxiliaries. It was also recommended that the officers to command such task forces should be thoroughly trained in carrier tactics and coordinated fleet air operations.

Towers' recommendations were all based on the logical conclusions derived from the Pacific Fleet's operational experiences in the war to date. They were obvious enough to anyone who looked at how the fleet had

Armorers prepare bombs in the hangar deck of the USS *Yorktown*. National
Archives 80-G-419959.

survived and prevailed at Coral Sea, Midway, and Guadalcanal, as well as
looking at what went wrong in those campaigns. But Big Gun thinking
still tended to linger in the minds of Nimitz's senior officers, and while
there were admirals who were "air minded," the new mode of warfare
which Towers' theories laid out dictated that top command slots be filled
by specialists in fast carrier tactics.

   It was decided to put the theories to the test with a hit-and-run raid
on Marcus Island. Rear Admiral Charles Pownall would set forth with a
battleforce designated Task Force 15, which would be based on his new
flagship *Yorktown*, the *Essex*, the *Independence*, the fast battleship *Indiana*,
two light cruisers and ten destroyers. The carriers would sail in the center of the formation, circled by the battleship and cruisers with the destroyers forming an outer defensive ring to provide maximum antiaircraft
protection with omnidirectional, overlapping fields of fire. Following in
the formation would be an oiler and a submarine, the USS *Snook*, to not
only screen the task force's way ahead but also to stand by to rescue downed

An F6F Hellcat, the more advanced fighter plane in the Pacific from mid–1943, revs for takeoff from the USS *Yorktown*. National Archives 80-G-204747-A.

aviators. This subsequently would become the pattern for all fast carrier task force operations through the remainder of the war.

The U.S. Navy last visited Marcus Island in the bleak late winter of 1942, when William Halsey was conducting his hit-and-run raids to harass the Japanese. Now, the Navy was returning to conduct an experiment. Intelligence on Marcus was based entirely on the Halsey raid of a year and a half ago, but the *Yorktown*'s air group commander, Captain James Flatley, and the *Essex*'s air operations officer, Captain Wallace Beakley, developed an airstrike plan based on the assumption that the enemy would still be following the same air search pattern they had operated from since the war began. When the task force arrived in position on August 31, Beakley's faith in the Japanese and their lack of tactical creativity would be vindicated. The *Yorktown*'s radars picked up a single snooper plane which had conducted its sweep and, reaching its range limit, had turned and headed back to base. Pownall's radar operators kept a track on the aircraft while he had his ships increase speed to 30 knots, to provide a boost for takeoff in a sea which was dead calm with little wind in the air. The first planes began rolling off the decks at 0422 hours.

The American strike force caught the Japanese totally unprepared. Planes ranged over the base at will, destroyed seven Betty bombers parked on the ground, and pounded the airstrip and the surrounding hangars and outbuildings. What antiaircraft fire was offered up in return was badly coordinated but was heavy enough to claim three planes from the group. The task force closed to 110 miles and launched a second strike. But Pownall became increasingly cautious as the mission went on, and decided to withdraw his task force in haste rather than staying long enough to totally destroy the base. Operating bombers from the *Independence* was deemed unwieldy in Pownall's view and he subsequently recommended that light carriers be devoted exclusively to boarding fighter squadrons for task force air cover and scouting. On review, however, it was decided to keep mixed air groups aboard the light carriers for tactical flexibility.

After Marcus, the next target on the schedule was Baker Island, located in an ideal spot east of the Gilberts. The Navy and Marines had earlier established occupation forces on nearby Phoenix and Ellice, two atolls to the west and southwest of the Gilberts. Baker would complete a triangle on which Marine airbases and staging areas were to be established in preparation for the eventual invasion of the Gilberts. Willis Lee led Task Force 11, built around Rear Admiral Arthur Radford's two CVLs, the *Princeton* and *Belleau Wood*, on September 1 to land a Marine battalion to occupy the tiny islet. This operation was carried off with virtually no opposition.

Marcus and Baker were easy and relatively insignificant affairs in the scope of the Pacific War, but they had proven that the theory of the fast carrier task force was indeed a viable one, and had provided invaluable combat training for new pilots. But it also exposed a need for capable, aggressive officers commanding both the task forces and the ships themselves. *Independence*'s captain had to be replaced when he proved unable to withstand the stress of the Marcus operation. Charles Pownall's own conduct on the mission left something to be desired as well, but it was decided to allow him to continue in command of his task force, since one operation was not sufficient to judge an officer and Pownall's observations had a great deal of validity to them, and some degree of allowance was granted since these initial missions were regarded as vital battle training. Not only theory, but men as well, were being tested by fire.

While Nimitz's officers were practicing and refining fast carrier tactics, Douglas MacArthur's forces were proceeding against Japanese strongholds on New Guinea. The previous month, Fifth Air Force planes hammered enemy bases on the island and swept over the waters around Huon Peninsula and the Bismarck Sea. They destroyed over 150 transport barges which the enemy utilized to shuttle troops between their garrisons at Lae, Salamaua, and Finschhafen. On their best day of the campaign, August 17, Fifth Air Force planes wiped out 200 aircraft on the ground at the Japanese airbase at Wewak, just about the whole of their air strength on New Guinea at the time. Starting on September 4, MacArthur led the 41st U.S. and 9th Australian divisions to a landing 20 miles east of Lae and moved quickly to arrive outside the port the next day. Forming his siege ring, MacArthur effectively cut off Lae, and it was too late for the enemy to try to move in reinforcements. Lae fell by September 25, three days after Salamaua was taken. On that same day, the 22nd, the 22nd Infantry Battalion of the Australian 9th Division landed on the tip of the Huon Peninsula despite heavy resistance by 5,000 Japanese troops.

The next fast carrier task force experiment was slated for a pre-invasion strike against the Japanese base on Tarawa atoll; it was the main target for the pending Gilberts operation scheduled for November, so aerial reconnaissance was a primary objective of the mission in addition to bombing the airfield and garrison. Task Force 15 was reformed to further test operations using primarily light carriers providing the balance of striking power. Charles Pownall transferred his flag to the new *Lexington*, which would be on her first combat mission and backing up the squadrons of *Princeton* and *Belleau Wood*. The screening force was composed of three light cruisers and ten destroyers, and following the formation would be one fleet oiler and the submarine Steelhead to be on station for rescue operations. The task force's attack would be prefaced by a raid conducted by 25 Seventh Air Force bombers on the night of September 17 while Pownall's force was making its final approach to launch point.

The Tarawa mission, however, turned into a botch-up. During the night of the 17th, Pownall spent several hours outlining procedures to be undertaken in the event of his death in action, a needless effort since Navy policy already dealt with such possibilities. The bombers and carrier planes destroyed several planes and boats as well as hitting targets on nearby Makin and Apamama, but one of the photo-reconnaisance planes was shot down, depriving the Americans of vital vertical images of the planned invasion beachhead, and Pownall again developed a case of nerves and rejected recommendations to launch a second scouting mission for fear of his ships being caught and destroyed in the open. Clever camouflaging had concealed many valuable targets from the American strike planes. And what was worse, the airstrikes tipped off the Japanese to the possibility of an invasion attempt against the Gilberts. The same morning that Pownall's squadrons were sweeping over Tarawa, the Japanese sortied the *Shokaku*, *Zuikaku*, and *Zuiho*, two battleships, and ten cruisers plus destroyers in escort from their main base at Truk.

By the time the Mobile Fleet arrived in the area of Eniwetok on September 20, Pownall's force was already long gone from Tarawa and no approaching invasion force was evident, so they put about and returned to Truk. But subsequent to the Tarawa raid, the Japanese in reactionary fashion decided to devote the bulk of their defenses to protect Rabaul, which they perceived as the main target of the American thrust with Halsey making his way up the Solomons and MacArthur's amphibious landings on New Guinea.

The timetable for Operation Galvanic, the invasion of Tarawa, was steadily winding down toward D-Day. Fast carrier tactics had been practiced and were being refined, but Nimitz and his officers had decided that one more experiment was needed, not only to provide a definitive test of the entire strategic concept but also to provide more training for pilots and task force officers in advance of the coming invasion. This time, the target would be Wake Island, the bastion which had fallen within days of the Pearl Harbor strike and among the first of the occupied islands hit by William Halsey back in early 1942. This time, the U.S. Navy would be returning with no less than six aircraft carriers, the largest assemblage of flattops in a single formation since the beginning of the war. But for this operation, Rear Admiral Alfred Montgomery, who would command Task Force 14, added a twist to this latest experiment; he would divide his force into two "cruising groups" of unequal size. The first, under Montgomery himself, would consist of the *Essex*, *Yorktown*, *Independence* and *Belleau Wood*, escorted by four light cruisers for bombardment support. The second group, under Van Hubert Ragsdale, would assemble around the *Lexington* and the newly commissioned *Cowpens* with three heavy cruisers. Also riding with the force would be a screen of twenty-four destroyers, two oilers, and the submarine *Skate* to do lifeguard patrol. The task force launched its planes in the predawn darkness of October 5. Over Wake, the squadrons ran into serious opposition: thirty Zeke fighters which had hastily scrambled to meet the attackers. However, the Zekes were massively outnumbered, and the subsequent combat was the first trial by fire of the new Grumman Hellcat fighter. The Zekes, totally outclassed as well as outnumbered, were nearly all annihilated and the squadrons proceeded to paste the garrison base with three times the number of bombs dropped on Marcus, Baker, and Tarawa combined. An attempted retaliatory strike of twelve fighters and twelve bombers launched from the Marshalls was intercepted and driven off by Ragsdale's own combat air patrol. The next day, the cruisers shelled the island and two more airstrikes completed the exercise. Only twelve American planes were shot down, and six of the pilots were successfully rescued by the *Skate*. Leaving Wake in flames, Task Force 14 put about and returned to Pearl, its mission a complete success. The fast carrier concept had now been proven beyond doubt. Formations would work with any size force as Montgomery and Ragsdale demonstrated by varying between two-, three-, and six-carrier cruising groups. Radar picket coverage ensured both full warning of enemy retaliation as well as coordination of carrier operations, and the circular formation combined with the Combat Air Patrol effectively shielded a task force from retaliation, affording it full freedom of movement and tactical flexibility.

The Japanese overreacted once again, sortied the Mobile Fleet back to Eniwetok and, as before, found nothing in the area and were forced to return to Truk by October 26. Not knowing that Wake was nothing more than an exercise, the Imperial General Staff carried out the plan to mass all available defenses to cover Rabaul, and pursuant to this stripped away every plane from the Eniwetok and Tarawa bastions as well as the Mobile Fleet's carriers. The outer defense line was now nothing but an empty shell. If the American fleet hit before they could restore their air strength in the area, the Gilberts and Marshalls would be lost.

While the Fifth Fleet's carriers were conducting their experiment across the Central Pacific, Halsey's Third Fleet continued moving up the Solomons. The day after the Mobile Fleet returned to Truk, Halsey arrived off the coast of Bougainville Island, the cap of the Solomons archipelago. But neither Halsey nor MacArthur were eager for a battle on a 150 mile long island occupied by a force of 35,000 crack troops, including the 6th Imperial Division, which had participated in the infamous Rape of Nanking. Additionally, the island was riven by active volcanoes and jungle-clad mountain ranges, terrain which favored the defenders. But there was no question of bypassing Bougainville. Its position was too vital for total control of the Slot, and the six Japanese airbases on the island had to be neutralized. Trying to avoid a bloody beachhead, Halsey and his planners studied the maps and finally decided to land the first troops on the southern end of Bougainville, where the land stretches into a narrow peninsula around Empress Augusta Bay and there establish an airbase. The landing site itself was far from ideal, but from a host of bad choices it was all they had, a swamp located at Cape Torokina, the only place which offered level ground.

To feint the enemy defenders and secure ground for advance airstrips, airstrikes and offshore bombardment would be directed not at Torokina

but on the main strongholds of Buin and Bonin, while another diversionary raid was made against Shortland Island. A battalion of the 2nd
Marine Division would be landed at Choiseul for a week long raiding expedition. While this was in progress, the 8th New Zealand Division would
land on the largest of the nearby Treasury Islands to set up the airstrips.
The landing at Choiseul took place first in the early dawn hours of the 27th.
Four days later, A.S. "Tip" Merrill's Task Force 39, built around the carriers *Saratoga* and *Princeton*, four light cruisers and eight destroyers,
shelled Buka, Bonin, and Shortland while also conducting airstrikes on the
strips located on Bougainville's northern side, a mission augmented by a
Henderson Field–based bomber raid on Buin. The ruse worked; thousands of troops were rushed to Choiseul and the New Zealanders were left
to build their airstrips completely unmolested. Meanwhile, on the 28th the
spearhead assault on Empress Augusta Bay was carried out by the 3rd
Marine Division, who caught the beachhead defenders—positioned within
eighteen potentially deadly pillboxes—totally by surprise. The landing
might have been wiped out, but the Japanese reinforcement convoy of two
heavy cruisers, two light cruisers, six destroyers and 1,000 troops had been
successfully beaten off by Merrill's cruisers and destroyers in a devastating display of radar-directed gunnery. It had claimed the heavy cruiser
Sendai and drove two destroyers into a collision which sank one before
the convoy turned and retreated in complete confusion.

Back at Truk, Minechi Koga decided to send in a large surface force
to escort the reinforcement convoy and detached six heavy cruisers from
the Mobile Fleet to Rabaul. Air search reconnaissance spotted the ships in
Simpson Harbor three days later. Now, Halsey was faced with a very
difficult decision. If that force assembled together and was further augmented, the landing at Empress Augusta would be destroyed. Every heavy
cruiser had been recalled for assignment to Ray Spruance's Fifth Fleet and
Merrill's own cruisers had withdrawn to Purvis Bay for replenishment. He
did not have heavy enough surface forces to protect the landing zone and
so he had no choice but to take a big gamble. Halsey detached the *Saratoga*
and *Independence* under Rear Admiral Frederick Sherman, formerly the
captain of the old *Lexington* at Coral Sea, and with whatever destroyer
screen could be put together dispatched them to hit Rabaul and destroy
the enemy cruiser force before it could set forth. To back the two flattops,
Halsey also radioed Nimitz for additional support, as well as requesting
bombing runs by George Kenney's Fifth Air Force.

Sherman's two carriers made their approach under the cover of heavy
weather and on the morning of November 5 launched a 96 plane strike
force. They went in under heavy antiaircraft fire over Simpson Harbor but

faced badly organized resistance from the 100 enemy aircraft assembled at Rabaul. Twenty-five were shot down in the first raid and the American planes damaged six cruisers and four destroyers while losing only ten planes in all. Throughout the day, every B-17 under Kenney arrived to hit the harbor, wreaking additional destruction. The raids were so heavy that it caused the increasingly timid Koga to recall his ships back to Truk.

Within three days, the carriers Nimitz had detached from the Fifth Fleet in response to Halsey's call for reinforcements, the *Essex*, her newly commissioned sister *Bunker Hill* and the new CVL *Monterey* along with four light cruisers, arrived at Bougainville. With a total of five carriers under his command, Halsey decided that it was time to pound the base at Rabaul into sand and end the threat of its air force once and for all. The combined force set forth and on November 11 launched the single largest air strike ever attempted by the U.S. Navy. Through the course of the day, five waves of strike planes hit Rabaul, coming in on Simpson Harbor from both north and south. Along with land-based F4U Corsairs, they wiped out most of the Japanese air forces located there, all the while that a 120 strong force of land-based bombers launched against the carriers were beaten back by Alfred Montgomery's combat air patrol and the task force's own antiaircraft guns. Additionally, the raiders sank a light cruiser and two destroyers remaining in the harbor after the recall of Koga's damaged ships. By dusk of that day, Rabaul's air force had been decimated. Neither Hitoshi Immamura nor Minechi Koga could protect the Marshalls, the Gilberts, or Bougainville, much less Rabaul, and now Koga's fleet dared not venture forth from Truk. His aircraft carriers, stripped of planes, were as useless as prison hulks.

The reality of the situation dictated that the Solomons archipelago was now irretrievably lost. But Harukichi Hyakutake on Bougainville refused to recognize this. Still stinging from his defeat at Guadalcanal, Hyakutake was determined to hang on at all costs and planned to launch a devastating counterattack on the enemy invaders. But he misjudged completely the American position and decided that the beachhead at Torokina was just another diversion designed to feint him into weakening his defenses around the airfields. As a result, he gave the Seabees three weeks to build an airfield in the swamp and the Marines to dig out a one mile deep defensive perimeter extending in a semicircle five miles around the landing zone, as well as to seize the high ground on the ridge around Empress Augusta Bay. Additionally, starting on November 8, the troops of the U.S. Army's 37th Infantry Division began pouring ashore, and by the time Hyakutake's men started hacking through the jungles to meet the invasion, 34,000 troops would be waiting to greet them in heavily reinforced

Marine F4U Corsair fighter launches rockets against an invastion beachhead. National Archives 127-GR-97-126420.

dugouts. The Tokyo Express operation set up to reinforce Hyakutake was intercepted on November 25 by five destroyers under Captain Arleigh Burke. Three enemy destroyers were sunk and the remainder of the reinforcement convoy was forced to retreat. From that point on, Bougainville was cut off. Constant air raids by the U.S. Navy and the Fifth Air Force neutralized the airfields at Buka, Buna, and Bonin. By December 9, the Seabees had completed the airstrip and by the time the first of Hyakutake's troops reached the perimeter around Helzapoppin Ridge, they discovered two full infantry divisions and a fully operational airbase ready to blast him off the island if he attacked. Hyakutake was faced with another Guadalcanal, only this time he was completely trapped with no hope of reinforcement or rescue, while more Americans would be landing on the island. His men retreated into the jungle to carry on a guerrilla war which would last well into the coming year.

While William Halsey was busy neutralizing Bougainville, the Fifth Fleet set out from Efate Island in the New Hebridies on November 11 on course for the Gilbert Islands. Operation Galvanic was finally underway. The carriers which Nimitz had dispatched to Halsey's aid would proceed independently to rendezvous back with the fleet, after detouring to launch airstrikes against the Japanese bases on Naru Island situated 350 miles southwest of the primary invasion objective: the bastion island of Tarawa. The main spearhead of the fleet was a formation which was the first of the properly constituted fast carrier task forces, Task Force 50. Divided into four task groups, the operational form of the experimental cruising groups Alfred Montgomery tested in the Wake raid, Charles Pownall's Task Force 50 was built around six heavy carriers—the veterans *Enterprise* and *Saratoga*, the *Essex, Yorktown, Lexington,* and *Bunker Hill*—and the light carriers *Independence, Princeton, Monterey, Belleau Wood,* and *Cowpens*. The total strength of the invasion fleet headed for Tarawa consisted of these 11 carriers, 8 additional escort carriers for direct tactical air support of the landings, 7 battleships, 6 cruisers, 44 destroyers, and over 1,000 planes to support the 5th and 6th Amphibious Groups with a total of 150,000 troops. With this formidable armada, the United States was making its first move to breach the now thin-shelled outer defensive ring and, once the Gilberts were secured, to threaten the bulwarks of the Empire's Pacific defense perimeter.

The initial airstrikes were launched as early as the 13th, hitting Tarawa and nearby Makin along with diversionary attacks on Wake and Marcus. This was enough to cause Minechi Koga to misread American intentions and dispatch the Second and Third Air Fleets under Takeo Kurita and Jisaburo Ozawa to the Marshalls, thus further reducing the decimated airpower available to defend the Gilberts. Wide ranging attacks carried out by the bombers of the Seventh Air Force added to Koga's confusion until he simply recalled his remaining planes back to Rabaul. Seven days later, the Fifth Fleet closed in on Makin and Tarawa. The U.S. Army's 27th Infantry Division swarmed ashore on Makin on November 20 led by General Ralph

C. Smith. Makin atoll was lightly defended by only a few hundred troops on the ground. They were overwhelmed in three and a half days, allowing Ralph Smith to announce the success of his phase of the operation with the laconic report, "Makin taken."

Tarawa would be a different and far bloodier story. The main objective at Tarawa was the airstrip on the two mile long sand reef of Beito. Waiting for the invaders was a network of coconut-log barriers, coral sand machine gun nests, and a chain of concrete bunkers behind which stood the 4,836 Imperial Marines under Admiral Keiji Shibasaki. To fire up his troops, Shibasaki declared that "a million Americans could not take the island in a thousand years." Neither the carrier strikes, the Seventh Air Force's raids, nor the three day pre-invasion bombardment had reduced these positions. Worse, the landing force was not going in with full reconnaissance information thanks to Admiral Pownall's failure to launch a second aerial scouting mission when he was last at the atoll in September. Kelly Turner, the amphibious forces commander, and Marine General Holland M. "Howling Mad" Smith, would be forced to rely on charts over a century old to guide the invasion forces on the beachhead and gauge the tides.

The 2nd Marine Division hit the beaches starting at 0330 hours on the 20th, simultaneously with Ralph Smith's landing on Makin. The first wave of the assault came in on vehicles first tested in the Operation Torch landings at Morocco the previous year, Amphitracs. Armed with a single machine gun, they were designed to "swim" to the shore and roll up onto the beach on their own tracks, each carrying 20 soldiers inside an armored compartment. They were ideally suited for landing on coral reefs where standard landing craft would have their bottoms ripped out before hitting the sand.

The failure of the shelling to soften up the enemy positions became apparent from a hundred yards out from the shore as machine gun fire came at the amphitracs almost, as one Marine described it, as thick as sheet-rain. In the nine hours of vicious fighting which followed, the first invasion wave had suffered 20 percent casualties. Fewer than 1,500 Marines were ashore and were pinned down by heavy fire and the beaches were rapidly clogging with landing craft and corpses. Only very slowly had a pair of Sherman tanks followed by an amphitrac managed to push 100 feet inland. The continuing naval bombardment was the only thing preventing Shibasaki from rallying his defenders into a concerted attack on the landing zone, and Colonel David Shoup signaled back to the fleet that his situation was desperate. But neither Kelly Turner nor Holland Smith had properly gleaned the nature of the situation on the Beito beachhead, being some 85 miles out of contact, and it took several hours before they authorized the release of the reserves.

The confusion which reigned aboard Kelly Turner's flagship *Pennsylvania* reflected some serious defects in the planning of the operation. Trying to coordinate two invasions of objectives 85 miles apart with only one command ship was already resulting in delays reinforcing one of the beachheads. An even more glaring weakness had been exposed in the disposition of Task Force 50. Instead of heeding the lessons learned in the fast carrier raids on which the entire concept had been proven, Admiral Spruance had lapsed into Big Gun thinking and relegated the carriers to a defensive support role, especially upon the insistence of Kelly Turner, who had no faith in the fast carrier theory. Spruance over-relied on offshore bombardment to do the job instead of unleashing the full power of his air forces, and worse, their actions were slaved to officers aboard the battleships instead of the flattops. As a result, airstrikes were poorly coordinated and were far less effective than they might otherwise have been. The assignment of the carriers to defensive sectors also prevented proper coordination of strategic air operations. Sixteen Betty bombers from Kwajelin and Maloelap, which Pownall had been denied permission to strike, came in for a counterattack at dusk. Nine of the planes were shot down by fighters and antiaircraft, but not before one managed to put a torpedo into the *Independence*, damaging her badly enough for a six-month stay in the drydock. Back at Pearl Harbor, Jack Towers used the *Independence* incident to press Chester Nimitz on the necessity of ordering Spruance to shift his carriers to full offensive operations at the first opportunity. With a valuable warship having already been knocked out of action, Nimitz concurred.

The second day, Spruance committed all his available airpower to close invasion support. With more reserves pouring in, the Marines on Tarawa began to make progress against Shibasaki's troops. They poured gasoline into each pillbox and ignited it with grenades while using flamethrowers to drive machine-gunners from their nests. It would take another day's fighting to finally capture the airstrip. Tarawa fell simultaneously with Makin. One thousand Marines were killed and another 2,301 were wounded. Ninety-seven percent of Keiji Shibasaki's troops were killed outright. The admiral himself along with his officers were buried alive in one of his own bunkers. Marines then, as with the other pillboxes, poured gasoline down the ventilation shafts and popped in a grenade. It was, to date, one of the most horrifying spectacles of mass slaughter in the Pacific campaign. The heavy death toll suffered by the Americans was increased on the morning of the 25th when a submarine, the I-175, crept through the screen covering Task Group 50.2 and torpedoed the escort carrier *Liscombe*

Bay. The carrier had no armor protection on the hull and the torpedo detonated inside, setting off her ammunition magazines in a rapid chain-reaction which engulfed the little vessel. Her burning hulk sank twenty minutes later, taking 644 dead to the bottom, including Rear Admiral Henry Mullinix and ship's captain I.D. Wiltsic. She was the first CVE lost in the war.

For two days, the fleet had intermittent contact with planes snooping out the edges of their formations just after sundown. They generally hung just outside of radar range but strayed within its effective radius enough times to tip off the Americans that they were up to something. The Japanese actions were eerily similar to their night air sorties against ships at Guadalcanal and there was now every reason to believe they would again attempt night bombing attacks, presuming that the darkness would cover their planes until it was too late. However, this time, the Americans had something up their sleeves to deal with the new threat.

Aboard the *Enterprise* was a specially modified Grumman Avenger torpedo bomber, which mounted a radome on one wing. The Avenger

Grumman TBF Avengers bombing Japanese targets. National Archives 80-G-490232.

could function as a spotter plane at night, to provide radar direction for an accompanying pair of Hellcat fighters. Available to lead the U.S. Navy's first night fighter screen was the *Enterprise*'s new air group commander, Edward "Butch" O'Hare, the ace who had singlehandedly saved the old *Lexington* from destruction at the first Rabaul raid early the previous year.

The plan developed by O'Hare and the air staff officers was a simple one: the Avenger would launch first followed by O'Hare and his wingman, Ensign Warren Skon. The spotter plane would concentrate exclusively on searching out enemy aircraft while maintaining a constant link with the flattop's radar operators, who would be able to keep track of all planes in the sky simultaneously. The two fighters would maintain a constant radio link with the radar Avenger and when it spotted something, it would fire a starshell flare in the direction of an enemy attacker to illuminate it as a target for O'Hare and Skon. On November 25, the three planes lifted off from the *Enterprise* as dusk was falling. For a couple of hours, their search revealed nothing as the last light faded and the three planes found themselves in inky blackness. Suddenly, O'Hare and Skon spotted a flare from three miles away. It burst into full illumination and slowly floated toward the ocean below. It clearly lit up a formation of Betty bombers which were headed toward the fleet. The Bettys fired wildly in all directions. One had attempted to veer off when it spotted the navigation lights on the American planes. It was quickly downed as the fighters swooped in, knocking down at least two while the ball-turret on the Avenger opened up on a third Betty attempting to jump them. The Japanese raiders were beaten back, but somehow, Butch O'Hare got caught in the crossfire. His plane spiraled into the ocean, and the Navy's first air hero of the war was gone.

The next target of the Fifth Fleet was slated to be the Marshall Islands group. Three bastions were located in this sector — Kwajelin, Eniwetok, and Majuro. These, along with the islands of Taroa and Wotje, were the keys to controlling the entire archipelago and would provide large anchorages and staging bases from which U.S. forces could pivot either deeper into the Pacific or to finally hit Rabaul and Truk. The ultimate objective, of course, would be to place U.S. forces in position to impose an ever-tightening blockade of Japan which would shrink its domain relentlessly, contain its fleet, and strangle all of its lifelines until she was brought to her knees. At the strategic planning conferences held at Cairo on December 3, 1943, it was decided that the forces under Nimitz and MacArthur would continue making their separate ways in the general direction of Formosa and the Philippines. However, the ultimate course of Pacific operations would be left open-ended to allow for a number of strategic options to select from to successfully prosecute the war. The Marshalls and Marianas soon took on significantly greater importance because of the advent of the newest long-range bomber, the Boeing B-29 Superfortress. While some would be based in China, it was recognized that having untouchable island bases for the new bomber would be the ideal option, and while Kwajelin and Eniwetok might be too distant from Japan, they would put the Fifth Fleet in strike range of Tinian, Saipan, and Guam, from which the Home Islands would fall under the sweep of the Superfortress. And so the direction of the campaign was already being altered by the onset of new strategic options as they manifested themselves.

The coming campaign would also be shaped by the appalling blood-bath which had taken place on Tarawa. Both Holland Smith and Chester Nimitz, inspecting the beachhead afterward, likened the scene to the battlefields of World War I. In reviewing the operations logs from Spruance, Pownall, Turner, and Smith and other carrier flag officers, Nimitz determined that the failure to gather adequate intelligence combined with the inadequate exploitation of the fleet's airpower while attempting to conduct simultaneous invasions of two widely separated targets had resulted in the needless loss of over 1,800 officers and men, including the deaths from the *Liscombe Bay* and the *Independence*. Following on Admiral Towers' recommendations as well as those from several of his flag officers, Nimitz would ensure that carriers and their air groups would no longer be relegated to a purely defensive role in future operations. In addition, Nimitz had replicas of Shibasaki's bunkers constructed on an outlying Hawaiian island for bombardment tests to determine how much punishment they could withstand and the best way to reduce them. Finally, it was agreed among all of Nimitz's commanders to concentrate all forces on one objective at a time instead of dispersing the invasion force's strength, to avoid another bloodbath such as Tarawa.

On the same day of the Cairo Conference, Pownall's carriers conducted a raid at Kwajelin for necessary softening-up as well as to keep the Japanese command off balance. The far more important purpose was reconnaissance. The photos revealed the presence of airstrips on Wotje and Maloelap to the east and Mili and Jalut to the west. Additionally, Eniwetok had its own large airbase from which the strike that crippled the *Independence* had been launched. In the planning sessions for Operation Flintlock, Spruance, Turner, and Holland Smith lobbied for the seizure of every island surrounding Kwajelin lest American forces find themselves surrounded. But Rear Admiral Forrest Sherman, John Towers' Chief of Staff, argued the aviators' point of view—from Kwajelin and Tarawa, when its airfields became fully operational, and the fast carrier task forces, the surrounding islands could be bombed continuously and neutralized, in addition to ranging outward to neutralize any threat from Truk, Eniwe-tok, or any of the enemy bases in the Marianas. Sherman's view was in accordance both with lessons learned from the fast carrier experiments and the bitter experience of Tarawa, as well as the overall island-hopping strategy of bypassing heavily defended concentrations of enemy troops. As a result, Nimitz overrode the objections of Spruance, Turner, and Smith, and told his officers that they were going to Kwajelin — though he would later accede to Spruance's request to seize nearby Majuro atoll in addition to Kwajelin because of its potential as a fleet anchorage.

While planning and logistical preparations for Operation Flintlock were underway, back in the Southwest Pacific area, William Halsey was moving steadily against Rabaul. Halsey's fleet had, through the month of December, attacked and seized the islands east and north of New Britain, where Seabees began airfield construction as soon as the beachheads were secured. On Christmas Day and again on January 4, 1944, Halsey sent Frederick Sherman with the carriers *Bunker Hill* and *Monterey* to hit Kavieng, New Ireland. The raids netted little in the way of kills, but the suppression of the Kavieng base aided in the overall pressure being placed on Rabaul. Simultaneously, on December 26, the 1st Marine Division landed at Cape Gloucester. Fifth Air Force P-38s beat off wave after wave of attack planes launched from the Rabaul base, which further decimated the remaining Japanese air strength in the Southwest Pacific. Discovering that the area marked on the maps as Damp Flats was actually a pestilen-tial swamp, it took the Marines three days of slogging through thick marsh as well as jungle to secure Cape Gloucester and its airfield. It would be another three weeks of vicious hand-to-hand combat before 10,000 enemy troops were cleared from the Cape altogether. But once the Americans had Cape Gloucester in their hands, they had nailed the last door shut on the Japanese. One hundred thirty five thousand enemy soldiers were now trapped in the interior of the island, and Rabaul was bottled up tight, so there was no hope of resupply or escape, and what was left of the Japanese air forces on New Britain had been eliminated. In short, Rabaul was out of the war; for all intents and purposes it was another huge prison. While on New Guinea, Douglas MacArthur's divisions continued to squeeze the remaining Japanese troops into an ever shrinking perimeter.

D-Day for Kwajelin was scheduled for January 31, 1944. Once again, it would be a combined operation involving the Seventh Air Force pro-viding the initial softening-up bombing in tandem with tactical airstrikes launched from the Fifth Fleet. The Seventh Air Force would now be able to operate from their new bases on Tarawa and Makin, launching squadrons of B-24 Liberator and B-25 Mitchell bombers. The airstrikes commenced on the 29th with carrier-launched attacks at Majuro, Roi, Tarora, Wotje, and Kwajelin. While the attacking formations met heavy antiaircraft fire, there was virtually no fighter opposition due to the steady annihilation of the Japanese air fleets and the squadrons of the First Carrier Division. There were no more planes to defend the islands. But on the 29th a tragic mishap occurred when a flight of Mitchells from the 820th Bomber Squadron were misidentified as enemy Nell bombers and were subsequently attacked by the ships and planes of the fleet. Before the mistake was recognized, one Mitchell was shot down and two others badly shot up with the loss of one life. Two of Spruance's task groups were exclusively committed to Kwajelin, along with a heavy bombardment from his battleships and cruisers.

The first troops of the U.S. 7th Infantry Division swarmed ashore on Kwajelin on the 31st, while the 4th Marine Division hit the two islets of Roi-Namur on the northern side of the island and a battalion of the U.S. 27th Division landed on Majuro. All total, Raymond Spruance was debarking 55,000 troops to take the three islands. In the meantime, he had another of his task forces proceeding to intercept position off Truk in case Minechi Koga decided to scramble the Mobile Fleet to attempt to meet the invasion. This new unit was recently created but would soon become famous in the history of the Pacific war as well as its commander, Task Force 58 under Rear (soon Vice) Admiral Marc Mitscher.

Majuro was secured by 0950 hours that day. One by one, the islands of the atoll were overwhelmed by the sheer weight of numbers in the American invasion force, which took three days to finally subdue the Japanese garrison of 8,000. The first phase of Operation Flintlock had gone so smoothly and in such a short time that Raymond Spruance implemented a speed-up of phase two. The transport convoy which had been dispatched in the direction of Eniwetok was now ordered to land its two Marine battalions, while the mission of Task Force 58, with a total strength of 12 aircraft carriers, 8 fast battleships, 6 cruisers, and 36 destroyers, was altered

Opposite, top: The Fast Carrier Task Force 58 at sea. The influx of new aircraft carriers into the fleet required a whole new strategic approach in the Pacific centered upon carrier-based airpower as the primary striking instrument, led by aggressive and innovative air-minded admirals. The result was a flexible and deadly armada capable of simultaneously supporting amphibious invasions, bombing enemy installations at very long ranges, and effecting the destruction of enemy battlefleets in direct combat. National Archives 80-G-301351. *Bottom*: Vice Admial Marc A. Mitscher, the model fast carrier commander, led Task Force 58 from its formation in January 1944 through to the invasion into the very heart of the Japanese Empire. National Archives 80-G-236831.

Top: "Murderers' Row," a formation of Task Force 58 carriers at Ulithi Atoll in December 1944. The establishment of these distant anchorages enabled the Pacific Fleet to operate far from its main bases at Pearl Harbor and New Caledonia. National Archives 80-G-294131. *Bottom*: Enlisted seamen return to the USS *Casablanca* after a few days of R-and-R at Rara in the Admiralty Islands — another vital function of the anchorages. National Archives 80CASA-618.

Launching of the USS *Boxer*, the 21st *Essex*-class carrier, in December 1944. By this point in the war, Japan had definitely lost the battle for production with America. National Archives NH56560.

to an offensive one — to reduce the Japanese naval base at Truk, the "Gibraltar of the Pacific," to ruins.

By the middle of February 1944, the United States had command of a massive armada in the Pacific which had in just six months completely wrested control of the seas from Japan. Furthermore, the island-hopping

The USS *Randolph* with a repair tender moored alongside at Ulithi, March 1945. The ability of the U.S. Navy to refuel, rearm, resupply, and even repair at sea was crucial to achieving victory in the Pacific. National Archives 80-G-344541.

strategy developed by William Halsey had not only seized the entire South Pacific in that same time but also had taken nearly 200,000 enemy soldiers and the bastion of Rabaul right off the board. The steady destruction of Japan's naval air forces in the South Pacific had left their island bastions completely defenseless before the sweeping advance of the American navy and now there was no more outer defense ring. Far-sighted Japanese officers began to see that it was no longer a question of holding the perimeter secure but how long it would be before the Home Islands themselves were threatened. Minechi Koga and the Imperial General Staff shifted their focus upon holding "to the death" the Inner Defense Perimeter; an arbitrary line which ran from the Kurile Islands and curved toward the Chinese coast. Anchoring that line were the three islands of Saipan, Tinian, and Guam. The focus of both sides in the war was now being turned inevitably, inexorably, toward the Marianas.

CHAPTER 9

Marianas

As the sun rose over the Imperial Naval base at Truk Island on the morning of February 17, 1944, Japanese pilots found themselves hastily scrambling every aircraft they could man into the air. The defenders of the great "Gibraltar Of The Pacific" had barely any warning of a large attack wave of 72 Grumman F6F Hellcat fighters which even as they were climbing from the island's airstrips were already beginning their run on the base. The Japanese managed to get four of the Hellcats before 50 of them were shot down in mere minutes. The remaining 68 Hellcats thereupon pounced Truk's airfields, docks, hangars, and any ship found in the harbor. Before withdrawing, the fighters also strafed the parked formations of Zeke fighters left on the ground, some attempting to get off the ground before they were blown up by tracer shells puncturing gas tanks. Next came the second wave of Avenger torpedo bombers carrying incendiary charges in addition to their normal ordnance. The incendiaries were dropped on the already stricken base and soon ignited a conflagration which swept over every ground facility, while the planes broke off to deal with the ships in harbor. Following the Avengers was a third-wave strike with Dauntless dive-bombers. And as the shell-shocked defenders were to discover, these three attack waves were only the beginning.

As the sun, partially obscured by great columns of black smoke rising miles into the skies, set over the former Imperial Naval base at Truk Island on the evening of February 18, 200,000 tons of shipping lay on the bottom of the harbor. The base itself was burning and in ruins, and 275 attack planes were destroyed — planes which were now not available for the defense of Eniwetok, which was being simultaneously invaded by Kelly Turner's amphibious forces 360 miles away. The combat vessels of the Mobile Fleet had fled to the Palaus only days earlier with Minechi Koga, but much of its support auxiliaries were now reduced to scrap and the "Gibraltar Of The Pacific" was no more. The total destruction of the base actually negated any reason to invade the Caroline Islands and so they were added to the atolls and lonely outposts which had been bypassed by

USS *Enterprise* recovers Hellcat fighters after a bombing sweep against Turk Island, February 1944. National Archives 80-G-39314.

the American juggernaut as it proceeded farther westward toward the next target of opportunity, the Marianas Island group.

In three days, the Japanese war effort had suffered a double disaster. The declared Inner Defense Perimeter had already been breached, and Vice Admiral Koga quickly returned to Tokyo to confer with the Imperial General Staff. In emergency session, Koga and the planners quickly developed Operational Order 73. The Palaus, almost proximate to the Philippines bastion, were now a front-line position, and of necessity the new principal naval base in the Pacific. The new Inner Defense Line was anchored on the Kurile Islands, Palau, and the Mariana Islands, principally on Saipan. This put the front lines directly opposite the paths of MacArthur and Halsey in their separate thrusts. The combat plan called for targeting the American aircraft carriers for destruction; stopping them would deprive the Americans of their invasion support and put the Imperial Fleet back on par in big gun firepower backed by superior air in the effort to hold the line "to the death."

A Hellcat lands aboard the *Lexington* to refuel and rearm during the Great Marianas Turkey Shoot, in which 344 Japanese planes were shot down in a single day's fighting. National Archives 80-G-236955.

Unfortunately, the primary anchor for the new Inner Defense Line itself fell under attack on March 30, when American forces arrived in the area and launched another massive strike mission against the Palaus and Yap Island. Koga managed to scramble most of the Mobile Fleet out of the anchorage, but 36 ships which couldn't get underway were caught and destroyed as American planes simply roared over the island virtually without opposition. The next day, Koga himself was flying to Davao Island just off the Philippines to establish a new headquarters when his plane was lost in a storm. Minechi Koga was declared missing and soon presumed dead. In early May, Vice Admiral Soemu Toyoda was commissioned the new Commander-in-Chief of the Imperial Combined Fleet. And upon his shoulders fell the entire weight of what was becoming an impossible task: stopping the United States Navy.

Just days before Christmas 1943, Chester Nimitz undertook a major command reshuffle of the Pacific Fleet. Charles Pownall was removed from field command due to his overly cautious and, in at least a couple of critical cases, inept handling of his carriers, particularly in the hasty decisions to withdraw from Marcus and Kwajelin and the decided failure to collect full aerial reconnaissance at Tarawa, which led to the subsequent bloodbath. The war, which was rapidly evolving, would permit no margin for error. The Navy would have to hit the enemy harder, faster, and at longer ranges. Decisive action was now an absolute requirement and though Raymond Spruance could not understand the perceived faults with Pownall's command style, Nimitz's more air-minded staff officers and more importantly William Halsey were in full agreement that carrier task forces needed commanders who would employ them aggressively and decisively. The officer Nimitz selected to assume the primary fast carrier command proved to be an ideal choice. The efficient and thorough devastation of Truk had been executed by a U.S. Navy combat unit which was to become virtually as destructive as a force of nature in its own right — Task Force 58. This formidable war machine, as of January 5, 1944, was proceeding into battle under the command of a soft-spoken yet skilled and aggressive officer who possessed a thorough grasp of fast carrier tactics: Vice Admiral Marc A. Mitscher.

"Pete" Mitscher, 56, had bound his whole career to naval aviation. He had graduated from Annapolis in 1910, had started as a pilot in the heady days of pre–World War I aviation and participated in many of the air operations experiments conducted from the old USS *Langley*. When World War II broke out, he was riding the bridge of the *Hornet* as her first captain and as a consequence would pilot her under William Halsey on the famous Doolittle mission against Tokyo. Two months later, he was at Midway and held the terrible responsibility of launching Torpedo 8 on its brave but doomed mission which indirectly led to the swift destruction of three enemy flattops and changed the course of the war. Mitscher was a natural leader who, childless, tended to adopt his fliers and crews as his "sons." These men would follow him to the death; he knew how to lead them into battle and get them back out again. He trusted his officers and task group commanders and in return the strong-minded admirals under Mitscher fell right into line and obeyed his orders to the letter. Mitscher, for his part, would never interfere with the way his officers performed their tasks as long as they got the job done, telling them what he wanted done and leaving the hows to their discretion.

Mitscher flew his flag aboard the new *Lexington* and enjoyed almost absolute command of Task Force 58 when engaged in carrier battles or raiding sweeps against Japanese shipping and bases, having only to defer tactical command in the event of a major surface engagement to Rear

Admiral Willis Lee, whose battleships and cruisers would form a combined force which would carry the designation of Task Force 54. And as the war progressed, the tag-team combination of Mitscher and Lee would prove to be one of the most effective in the history of naval warfare.

The main striking power of Task Force 58 was in its fifteen flattops. In addition to the *Lexington*, Mitscher had at his command the *Yorktown*, *Essex*, *Wasp*, *Bunker Hill*, *Hornet*, and the veteran *Enterprise*, the light carriers *Bataan*, *Belleau Wood*, *Princeton*, *Monterey*, *Cowpens*, *Cabot*, *San Jacinto* and the new *Langley*, and an air force of over 900 planes; Hellcats, Dauntlesses, Avengers, and the new Curtiss SB2-C Helldiver. Willis Lee's big guns were mounted aboard seven new fast battleships: his flagship *Indiana*, the *Washington*, *North Carolina*, *South Dakota*, *Alabama* and the brand-new *Iowa* and *New Jersey*. The remainder of the task force's support rested upon a phalanx of 8 heavy cruisers, 13 light cruisers and 69 destroyers. With 112 ships in array, not counting auxiliaries, Task Force 58 exceeded in numbers the entire prewar strength of the Pacific Fleet and was a thoroughly modern war machine, carrying the latest in military technology and weaponry and capable of crushing just about any target in its path. It already had left Truk, Yap, and Palau all burning in its wake and was employed to devastating effect helping Douglas MacArthur leapfrog his way up Hollandia and the Admiralties. It was an armada the likes of which had never before been seen on any ocean in the history of the world.

At about the same time that this formidable armada was beginning to make its power felt in direct combat, another force was coming into its own and proceeded to inflict equally devastating damage on the entire enemy war effort. When hostilities broke out in 1941, and the United States had pitifully few resources to prosecute the campaign against Japan, she turned to one of the few weapons she had left to her in the wake of the Pearl Harbor debacle — submarines. In the Atlantic, the German U-boats were having a devastating impact upon Britain's ocean lifeline, sinking several hundred thousand tons of shipping almost each month. The submarine had established itself as a viable war weapon in the last World War, in which the U-boats of the Imperial German Navy had nearly succeeded in strangling Britain entirely and had threatened to accomplish that goal in this war. Chester Nimitz declared a policy of unrestricted submarine warfare in the opening weeks of the Pacific war. But the few boats available to the United States were comparatively primitive craft, of limited range and armament. Some older boats of the S-class were prone to leaking oil while submerged; this was a significant disadvantage not only in terms of operational range but also in compromising the boat's position.

American submarine commanders lacked aggressiveness and did not know how to coordinate attacks on enemy shipping, and their torpedoes tended to malfunction more than 75 percent of the time. As a result, American submarines managed in the first six months of war to score only 35,000 tons of enemy shipping, while a typical U-boat ace in the *Kriegsmarine* scored that much in a single patrol. This dismal situation, however, was soon to change considerably for the better with the appointment of a new Commander of U.S. Submarine Forces, Pacific, Vice Admiral Charles Lockwood.

Lockwood began the war as an attaché to the Royal Navy, and as a result was able to study firsthand the effects of the German U-boat tactics on Allied shipping. Recalled from London, he was assigned to command a submarine flotilla based in Brisbane and attempted to apply U-boat tactics in the Dutch East Indies, but the deficiencies inherent in American subs and their torpedoes soon became apparent to his keen judgment. His continual caustic reports on the performance of American torpedoes ultimately led to a series of experiments carried out by the Bureau of Ordnance in Hawaii, in which the causes of poor torpedo performance were uncovered: the magnetic fuse, which more often than not failed to detonate within proximity of a hull's magnetic field, and a poorly designed depth-control mechanism which caused fish to run below the targets. These evaluations led to the production of the Mark 28 torpedo. The Mark 28 had only half the speed of the Japanese Long Lance, but it also left almost no telltale wake on the surface and was fused with a simple but effective contact pistol. The first examples of this device began arriving at the front lines in September 1943 although it still had some teething problems, but once submariners got used to the mechanics of the new torpedoes, kill-rates began to climb.

Next, Lockwood replaced a full third of American submarine skippers, seeking aggressive officers who would take independent initiative and risk the survival of their boats to carry out a mission. He initiated an aggressive training program aimed at teaching sub captains to make direct frontal attacks on targets as well as shooting from the stern. The result was that captains gained experience in a broadly expanded set of tactical possibilities; they could exercise greater control over the target, since with "up the kilt" or "down the throat" shots, the target's speed could virtually be ignored in computing the firing solution, and if a ship made a turn, the sub captain had a broader target to shoot. Lockwood would also partially adopt the *Kriegsmarine* tactic of the U-boat Wolf Pack. But instead of adhering to the strict German model of shepherding whole formations of attack boats by radio, controlling the strike from a shore command base,

Lockwood organized submarines into squadrons, assigned them to attack sectors along enemy convoy routes, and allowed his captains full freedom of action in their areas of responsibility. The German methodology had not only restricted the potential operational range of U-boats but also, by slaving their actions entirely to radio direction, had provided Britain's Bletchley Park codebreaking team with the means to decrypt their Enigma transmits, and as a result, not only led to the tracking and destruction of Wolf Packs but also compromised nearly every secret German military communication. American submarines would operate independently and maintain strict radio silence, relying on their natural stealth as their chief weapon while enjoying the benefits of independent initiative and enterprise.

Finally, the U.S. Navy, starting in 1942, had undertaken the construction of modern fleet boats to replace the inadequate and in some cases woefully obsolete submarines America had started the war with. The direct result of this building program was the *Balao*-class fleet submarine. These fine boats measured 312 feet in length and displaced 1,500 tons on the surface. Generally, they were armed with ten 21-inch tubes (six bow and four stern) and carried a combat load of twenty-four Mark 28 torpedoes, and a variety of armaments from .50-caliber machine guns to 40mm antiaircraft to 5-inch bow guns, depending upon the particular boat. They also mounted the latest in sound gear and modern firing computers, far superior to anything carried by any Japanese vessel on or below the surface. Before the end of the war, 174 *Balao* and the improved *Gato*-class boats, both built to the same general design, would be commissioned into fleet service.

The coming together of Lockwood's reforms, the new torpedoes, and the steadily growing number of modern submarines had yielded startling results. In 1943, American submarines had managed an average kill-rate of slightly under 125,000 tons of enemy shipping per month, but Japanese ship production managed to keep up with the loss rates to their merchant fleet to the extent that, at the end of the year, they were slightly ahead in tankers. In January of 1944 alone, U.S. submarines sank nearly 300,000 tons of Japanese shipping. Furthermore, the advancing conquest of the Pacific islands provided new forward bases for the submarines to operate from, greatly extending their reach right into the heart of the Empire. Enemy antisubmarine and convoy organization measures were inadequate, and the Japanese seemed unable to analyze the problem of defending against submarine warfare on even the most basic level, just as they had never figured out how to exploit the full strategic possibilities of the submarine in the first place. American submarines not only doubled the tonnage they sank but also scored warships, impacting directly on the combat effectiveness of the Imperial Navy. So great was the impact of submarine warfare that when 1945 began, the Japanese war effort and economy were both dying.

While the American war effort was showing increasing strength, organization, and effectiveness, the Japanese war effort was beginning to fall apart at the seams. Near-hysteria was breaking out in the highest levels of the Japanese leadership, and a split between the Army and Navy chiefs flared into open conflict which deadlocked the Empire's military command. The Navy still clung to Yamamoto's dream of forcing the U.S. Navy into a single, decisive, showdown battle in which it could be caught and destroyed before it penetrated into the innermost reaches of the Empire's Pacific domain. The startling expansion of the U.S. Navy in just a year rendered that dream increasingly untenable. The Army bitterly castigated the Navy for its failure to accomplish what they had promised back in 1941 and lobbied for a strategy of concentrating all their manpower and air strength on major island bastions such as Formosa and the Philippines, where the Americans would have to invade and upon which the battle would shift to land, where the Army had always been unconquerable — or so they said. Prime Minister Hideki Tojo's solution to the deadlock was to sack both Chuichi Nagumo, the Navy Chief-of-Staff, and Hajimi Sugiyama, the Army Chief. Tojo then appointed a puppet officer, Shigetari Shimada, to run the Navy, and directly assumed the post at the head of the Army himself, in effect creating an executive dictatorship.

In the end, both Army and Navy stratagems would be adopted in much the forms proposed. For the present, Tojo and his officers analyzed the American campaign, noting its two-pronged nature and the thrust of what appeared to be the main enemy naval force through the Central Pacific and the direction it was headed — toward the Marianas bastions of Saipan, Tinian, and Guam. Stopping the American thrust over sea would cut one of the prongs off the overall enemy offensive and deprive General Douglas MacArthur the support he would need to prosecute an invasion of the Philippines or Formosa. This task was handed to Soemu Toyoda upon his appointment as C-in-C of the Combined Fleet.

Before his death, Minechi Koga had formulated the essential Navy strategy of luring the American navy to close range of their island air bases where a united assault of land and carrier-based air would crush it as part of Operational Order 73. Toyoda, upon inheriting Koga's fleet, made only a few changes in detail to Order 73 and incorporated it into his Operation A-Go, which adjusted the plan for the expected point of interception of the enemy fleet.

Despite the losses suffered by the Imperial Navy, Toyoda still had a formidable battle force at his command, and the building program was about to add a pair of brand-new flattops to the fleet's roster. The bulk of surface strength was going to be combined into a new force designated the First Mobile Fleet. Its main striking power would devolve upon an array of nine aircraft carriers; the conversions *Chitose* and *Chiyoda*, the light carriers *Junyo*, *Hiyo*, *Zuiho*, and *Ryuho*, the veteran sisters *Shokaku* and *Zuikaku*, and the newly commissioned heavy carrier *Taiho*, a 64,000 ton vessel carrying an air wing of over 90 aircraft, roughly equivalent to the American *Essex*-class carriers. Together, the nine flattops would be able to field an air force of 450 aircraft. In addition, they would have the 500 planes of Vice Admiral Kakuji Kakuda's First Air Fleet, based at the airfields on Saipan, Tinian, Rota, Guam, Iwo Jima and Chichi Jima, to bring their full air strength up to par with that of the American carrier air forces. They also enjoyed the advantage of aircraft with half-again the range of the American Hellcats and Avengers, enabling them to strike the enemy when they would still be 300 miles from their formations. Providing the defensive screen for the carriers would be a force of 5 battleships, including the *Yamato* and *Musashi*, 13 cruisers, and 28 destroyers. In toto, this force of 73 ships was the largest Japanese surface fleet assembled for one battle since Midway.

To command this armada, Toyoda appointed Vice Admiral Jisaburo Ozawa. Nicknamed "the Gargoyle" years ago by his academy mates, Ozawa was a tough, capable officer and a good commander to the men under him. He would be riding into battle aboard the *Taiho*. But there was one great negative weighing against the Japanese: inexperience. So many of the veteran pilots which had supported Japan's drive across the Pacific were dead now, killed in two years of hard fighting with the Americans. The training the new pilots received was inadequate by anyone's standards, but the lack of veteran officers to educate the new recruits plus the necessity to husband precious resources such as aviation fuel had greatly restricted this most vital aspect of military preparedness. Furthermore, the inexperience reached right to the top; Jisaburo Ozawa had never commanded carriers in battle before. Toyoda and other veteran officers were forced to stomach this and comforted themselves with the material advantages they had at their command, particularly the range advantage of their planes. A further sign of encouragement was the knowledge that Ozawa's opposite number for the coming battle was going to be Raymond Spruance, profiled by Japanese intelligence as a cautious, conservative officer lacking tactical brilliance.

Soemu Toyoda dreamed of the coming battle as a Japanese Midway, the chance to reverse the course of the war and turn it once again in the

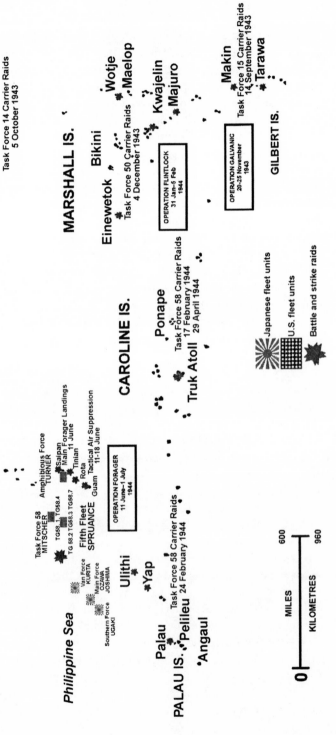

BATTLE OF THE PHILIPPINE SEA
19-20 June 1944

MARIANA IS.

Philippine Sea

Task Force 58
MITSCHER
TG 58.2 TG58.3 TG58.7
TG 58.1 TG58.4
Fifth Fleet
SPRUANCE

Van Force
KURITA
Main Force
OZAWA

Southern Force
UGAKI

Amphibious Force
TURNER
Saipan
Main Forager Landings
11 June
Tinian
Rota
Guam Tactical Air Suppression
11-18 June

OPERATION FORAGER
11 June–1 July
1944

Ulithi
Yap

Palau
PALAU IS. Pelileu
Angaul

Task Force 58 Carrier Raids
24 February 1944

CAROLINE IS.

Ponape

Truk Atoll
Task Force 58 Carrier Raids
17 February 1944
29 April 1944

MARSHALL IS.

Einewetok
Bikini
Task Force 50 Carrier Raids
4 December 1943

OPERATION FLINTLOCK
31 Jan–5 Feb
1944

Wotje
Maelop
Kwajelin
Majuro

Wake
Task Force 14 Carrier Raids
5 October 1943

Makin
Task Force 15 Carrier Raids
14 September 1943
Tarawa

GILBERT IS.

OPERATION GALVANIC
20-25 November
1943

Japanese fleet units
U.S. fleet units
Battle and strike raids

MILES 600
0
KILOMETRES 960

Empire's favor. It was, therefore, a most cruel twist of irony that much the same thing which had happened to the Japanese at Midway had just happened to them again. Koga's Chief-of-Staff, Rear Admiral Shigeru Fukudome, had survived the April storm which had claimed the life of his boss on the way to Davao but was himself forced to ditch and ended up washing ashore at Cebu, where he and his briefcase containing the full details of Order 73 wound up in the hands of Filipino guerrillas. By now, those plans, translated and annotated, were in the hands of Chester Nimitz back at Pearl Harbor and as a consequence the Americans more or less knew what sort of reception to expect as they headed toward the Marianas. Toyoda, of course, had no way of knowing of this and proceeded to implement Operation A-Go, confident of victory.

June 6, 1944 (the same date but because of the International Date Line a full 24 hours before the D-Day landings at Normandy half a world away), was the day that Task Force 58 weighed anchor and departed Majuro, proceeding on course for the Mariana Islands as the spearhead for Operation Forager. Following in their wake would be an invasion force of Kelly Turner's 423 vessels carrying 127,571 troops with tanks, amphitracs, vehicles, guns, Seabees and all their equipment. Once out at sea, the task force redeployed into five task groups, each ringed by a screen of cruisers and destroyers: TG 58.1 based around the *Belleau Wood, Bataan, Hornet,* and *Yorktown;* TG 58.2 with the *Cabot, Wasp, Monterey,* and *Bunker Hill;* TG 58.3 at the center of the formation and formed up around the *Princeton, Enterprise, Lexington,* and *San Jacinto;* TG 58.4 bringing up the rear with the *Cowpens, Langley,* and *Essex.* Willis Lee's battleships formed the nucleus of TG 58.7. On orders from Spruance, riding with the force in his flagship, the cruiser *Indianapolis,* TG 58.7 would take up a forward position at the van of the task force, deploying its ships into a defensive array to face any enemy strike force with an antiaircraft barrier. The ordnance for the 5-inch guns of the fleet consisted of shells fitted with a VT proximity fuse, designed to detonate the charge at a set altitude. The charge itself consisted of shrapnel — ideal for knocking down massed formations of aircraft.

Five days after setting off, the Forager invasion force and Task Force 58 were closing range on their first island objective, Saipan. A fighter sweep launched by Mitscher put 200 Hellcats, Avengers, and Helldivers over Saipan, Tinian, and Rota, destroying 150 planes on the ground which

Opposite: The Central Pacific Thrust — While MacArthur and Halsey island-hopped their way up the Solomons, Nimitz unleased his new fast carrier task forces in the Central Pacific, culminating in the June 1944 clash between Raymond Spruance's Fifth Fleet and its spearhead, Marc Mitscher's Task Force 58, and Jisaburo Ozawa's First Mobile Fleet in the Battle of the Philippine Sea.

effectively ensured a landing free of enemy air resistance. Kelly Turner's battleships, some of them rebuilds of the vessels damaged at Pearl Harbor, opened up with a massive bombardment, and the next day 600 amphitracs carried a first-wave assault of 8,000 Marines onto the beaches. They were kept pinned down in their landing zones by a fierce bombardment conducted by General Yoshitsugu Saito's artillery, but because he had mistaken where the expected landing was to take place, most of his division were on the western end of the island and could not be brought into the battle. Eventually, 20,000 Marines got ashore and began to press inland, their main objective being the Aslito airstrip. An attempted banzai charge in the early morning hours of the 14th was cut to shreds by offshore destroyer bombardment, costing Saito 75 percent of his troops. He withdrew his survivors to entrenchments on the slopes of Mt. Tapotchau and determined to wait for the Imperial Navy to score a decisive victory at sea and then relieve him.

Ozawa finally set off from the fleet base at TawiTawi in the Sulu Archipelago on June 13, when Japanese scout planes from Guam spotted Marc Mitscher's formation two days earlier and the Marianas had finally been identified positively as the next American objective. Once at sea, his fleet redeployed into two formations. In accordance with the plan Ozawa laid out, the Van Force under Takeo Kurita was organized into three task groups, each with a carrier: the *Chitose*, *Zuiho*, and *Chiyoda*. The Main Body, under Ozawa's direct command, was organized into two task groups; one centred on the carriers *Junyo*, *Hiyo*, and Ryuho, the other formed around the heavies *Taiho*, *Zuikaku*, and *Shokaku*. As Ozawa neared the vicinity of the Marianas, he would have the two halves of his fleet separate farther apart, ultimately spacing out to a distance of 100 miles from one another. The idea behind the deployment was to allow Spruance to sight Kurita, who would withdraw westward and encourage pursuit. Once the two groups were again within range of one another, they would be able to launch a united air assault which would catch Spruance with a wall of aircraft on his front, while land-based air would follow up on the Americans and so catch their fleet between them in a crushing air pincer. Planes launched from carriers would land on bases at Guam and Rota, refuel and rearm there, and return for a second strike, subjecting the surviving American units to shuttle-bombing. All in all, it was a simple but potentially effective strategy. As the First Mobile Fleet proceeded farther eastward, Ozawa signaled his ships and delivered to the officers and men of his battle force the message which Heihachiro Togo gave to his officers on the eve of Tsushima, the same message Isoroku Yamamoto addressed to the First Carrier Strike Force on the eve of Pearl Harbor: "The rise and fall of the Empire depends upon this battle. Everyone will do his duty to the utmost." Banzais sounded aloud on the decks of all Ozawa's warships as the crews fired themselves up for the battle ahead.

Spruance had already considered the possibility of the Japanese shuttle-bombing his fleet and determined that the first task at hand was to eliminate the enemy's land-based air power while he had the chance. Pursuant to that, he had Task Force 58 divide in two, sending seven carriers north to hit airfields on Iwo Jima and Chichi Jima on the 11th and 12th simultaneously with the strikes on Saipan, Tinian, Rota, and Guam. Zekes roared up from the stricken airfields to do battle with the Hellcats, but inexperienced pilots had no chance against veterans flying superior aircraft, and the comparatively few defense fighters which had risen to challenge Mitscher's pilots were shot down in short order. Most of the rest were destroyed on the ground.

The raids had immediately deprived Jisaburo Ozawa of the bulwark he had counted on in the A-Go battle. To make matters worse, Vice Admiral Kakuda reported none of this to the First Mobile Fleet, and as a consequence Ozawa would end up sailing into battle unaware of the fact that his air strength had already been cut in half. He was also running right toward a line of six picket submarines, ordered by Nimitz to "report first and shoot later."

Four days later, on the 16th, Spruance received reports that the pickets had observed the passage of two large ship formations through the San Bernardino and Surigao straits, and the USS *Cavalla* began shadowing Ozawa on June 17 when his force was within 800 miles of Guam. As the First Mobile Fleet entered the Philippine Sea, Ozawa gave the order for Kurita to take his Van Force out ahead of the Main Body. Scout planes launched from Ozawa's carriers spotted the lead elements of Task Force 58, but it was nearing dusk and Ozawa did not know the condition of the Guam airfields where his pilots would have to land were he to launch an attack so late in the day, so he refrained from any action and ordered the scouts to return.

Radio intelligence and the appearance of blips on the radar screens of Mitscher's carriers finally gave Task Force 58 its first direct sighting of the enemy. Mitscher began moving his carriers westward and had his aviators prepare an air search plan. Through the course of the day on the 18th, the two fleets warily felt one another out, unsure as to where the other lay exactly. But late that evening, Ozawa broke radio silence to confer with Toyoda, who was coordinating the battle back at the Combined Fleet's headquarters in Hiroshima, and in so doing gave away his position at 335 miles WSW of Mitscher's position. Mitscher immediately radioed

Spruance requesting permission to get Task Force 58 into position to hit Ozawa by 0500 hours the next morning.

It was here that Spruance made one of the most crucial decisions of the war. He saw his mission as primarily to protect the Saipan beachhead, which he assumed to be the enemy's main target and, just as at Midway, he was not going to allow himself to be drawn too far away from his area of responsibility. He suspected a trap, dismissing Ozawa's transmission as a mere diversion and acted accordingly. As a result, he denied Mitscher permission to move any farther than a 300 mile radius from Saipan and ordered him to swing eastward again.

Spruance's order sent waves of bitter disappointment and even resentment through the ranks of Mitscher's pilots and captains. In their view, Spruance was allowing the enemy the option of striking at dawn after having steamed unmolested to Saipan, and in so limiting the carriers to a defensive role instead of taking the initiative, they were running the distinct risk of being caught in a hemmed-in position in which many of their pilots and perhaps one or more of their valuable flattops would be destroyed. As a result, Spruance would come in for a great deal of criticism after the fact, but the admiral was determined to husband as much of his air strength as possible to meet the aerial assault he suspected was coming the next day. Unknowingly, Spruance had also, in acting conservatively, saved many of his pilots from withering antiaircraft resistance from Kurita's Van Force, which would have made an American attack a bloodbath even with their present advantage in numbers.

As the dawn hours of the 19th approached, Spruance ordered Willis Lee's battleships to execute the planned maneuver to place themselves in a line 15 miles ahead of the carrier task group, taking the point in anticipation of an enemy attack. Shortly after sunrise, Mitscher launched an attack against Guam to ensure that Orote Field remained neutralized. As it was, the Americans caught the last 35 planes which managed to remain intact through the previous raids and shot them down as they came up to meet them, then proceeded to drop more bombs on the base.

Ozawa turned his carriers into the wind as soon as dawn broke, and the first wave of aircraft launched from the decks as early as 0600 hours; a force of 69 scoutplanes, bombers, and fighters from Kurita's van carriers fanning outward in a general sweep. Rain squalls threatened and the imperfect conditions presented another problem for the Japanese; experienced pilots would have easily compensated for the bad weather, but these were rookies who in many cases were flying their first missions. Next was a wave of 48 Zekes, 54 Yokosuka D4Y2 Judy bombers, and 27 Nakijima B6N2 Jill torpedo bombers—replacements for the Air Fleet's venerable Val and Kate bombers—which launched from the *Shokaku, Zuikaku,* and *Taiho.* All total, Ozawa had sent 198 aircraft to form up his first strike on the American fleet, and he ordered his carriers to ready another 130 planes for the second strike to follow immediately upon the first.

But even as Ozawa was launching the remainder of his killer force against the Fifth Fleet at 0900 hours, he had no idea that his shiny, brand-new flagship, considered unsinkable by her builders and officers, was lined up in the crosshairs of the submarine USS *Albacore,* which had pursued Ozawa's carriers since crossing the picket line. The *Albacore*'s skipper, Commander J.W. Blanchard, had *Taiho* dead in his sights and bided his time until he had the firing solution computed. Once the numbers came up, he fired off two torpedoes.

Warrant Officer Sakio Komatsu was lifting off the *Taiho*'s deck at 0910 when he spotted a torpedo wake closing in on his base ship. Without hesitation, Komatsu dove his plane directly in the torpedo's path, crashing into and exploding it. Doubtless, the young pilot believed he had saved the flagship at the moment of his death, but unfortunately the second fish ran true and struck the *Taiho* on her starboard bow. The hit jammed the forward elevator and blasted a hole which opened her forward compartments to the sea. The shock also ruptured avgas lines belowdecks. Damage control crews got to work immediately, sealing off flooded compartments and beginning repairs to free the stuck deck lift. The ship apparently was still quite operational and could make 26 knots, which satisfied Ozawa. But nobody aboard the flagship, however, even suspected that deadly, inflammable fumes from leaking avgas were beginning to build up in sealed-off compartments down below.

The first wave of Ozawa's planes appeared on Mitscher's radar screens at 0730 hours, 150 miles away and closing rapidly. The admiral himself took the microphone of the Talk Between Ships (TBS) radio system and issued an old circus call indicating trouble: "Hey Rube."

Immediately, antiaircraft defenses on all ships were put on combat alert. Radar operators trained their searches in the direction of the given coordinates for the coming attack wave and planes were readied for launch. The Wildcats which had accompanied the Guam strike mission turned about and headed back out to sea, leaving the Helldivers and Avengers to continue pasting the airstrip. When the enemy force was within 45 miles of Task Force 58 bearing 333 degrees, at about 1007 hours, Hellcats from the *Lexington, Cowpens, Bunker Hill, Essex,* and *Princeton* launched into the skies and formed up into a combat air patrol screen ahead of Willis Lee's battleships. The chaos of earlier American air operations had been eliminated in a year of preparation, drills, and combat experiments. Chatter was kept to only a succinct exchange of orders and vector instructions between pilots, and crisp direction from radar plot officers coordinating the fighter defenses. As a result, several waves of green Japanese pilots were about to run right into a well-organized air defense backed up by a massive and lethal antiaircraft cordon. It was going to be a slaughter — and all on the Japanese side. The 220 Hellcats formed up into a two-tiered formation and orbited in position to await the oncoming wave, the first 69 planes launched from Kurita's carriers.

The enemy tactics reflected the woeful inexperience of the pilots. The planes gathered into a rendezvous point at 20,000 feet and waited until they were completely regrouped instead of flying in a united formation and boring in for the attack, which allowed the Hellcats all the time in the world to get up to altitude. Then, instead of proceeding in formation, planes wheeled off individually or in small numbers to challenge the American CAP waves. The result was that 25 planes were knocked down immediately, either charging straight ahead or falling prey to the most basic dogfighting tricks in the book. They would make runs on ships but veer off before getting into range. Worse, the enemy flight leaders would send instructions in clear Japanese, which Lieutenant Charles Sims was able to understand and interpret. He relayed the Japanese instructions to the fighter directors on their own base ships, who in turn sent the Hellcats to ideal intercept vectors. Another 17 planes were splashed within minutes of the first. The remaining 11 which managed to make it through both CAP formations ran into a curtain of murderous antiaircraft fire, managing to put a single bomb on the *South Dakota* but inflicting only minor damage. The entire first-wave engagement lasted 34 minutes and only 28 enemy planes survived to return to their carriers. One pilot from the *Lexington* commented upon the mass slaughter that "It was like an old-time turkey shoot down home." The phrase soon spread like wildfire throughout the fleet and the fighter ranks and thus, in future, the battle would be known famously as the Great Marianas Turkey Shoot.

More turkeys were on their way. Just ten minutes after the retreat of what was left of the first-wave attack, Ozawa's second wave appeared on radar, 128 planes in all. The Americans patiently awaited their quarry to come right on ahead. The lead planes of the second wave reached them at about 1139 hours and were immediately attacked by David McCampbell, the commander of the *Essex*'s VF9 fighter squadron. His first kill was a Judy dive bomber which he blew out of the sky the moment he had it in his sights. McCampbell, who would end the war as the Navy's leading ace with 34 total victories, scored five kills and one probable for the sortie. But the most courageous performance was put in by *Lexington* pilot Alex

Vraicu. Vraicu wove in and out of the loose Japanese formations and chased planes right into the midst of his own side's antiaircraft fire. He followed one Judy bomber into a steep dive to shoot it down before it could plant a pair of bombs on the deck of a destroyer, barely managing to pull out before plunging into the water himself. Finally forced to return to the *Lexington* low on fuel and ammunition, he was nearly shot down by his base ship's own antiaircraft until he frantically radioed that he was on their side. Upon landing, he saw Admiral Mitscher on the flying bridge and, with an exhausted smile, held up six fingers to indicate his kills. The second Japanese attack wave lost a total of 97 planes.

A third wave of 47 planes was reduced when half of them got lost and were forced to turn back to their base ships. The remainder managed to make some attack runs of TG 58.4 but inflicted no damage whatsoever and seven more planes were lost in the bargain. The final fourth-wave strike, which arrived at around 1420 hours, consisted of 82 aircraft. Forty-nine of them got lost along the way and attempted to land on Guam, where waiting Hellcats shot down 30. The remaining thirty-three concentrated their attacks on TG 58.2, with nine planes making runs on the *Wasp*. Captain Clifton Sprague had to put his ship into a hard evasive zig-zag to avoid bombs and torpedoes but managed to get away with only superficial damage from bomb and plane fragments and phosphorous from an exploding incendiary raining onto the foredeck. With that, Ozawa's last shot had been spent. The remaining and badly mauled survivors of the fourth wave limped back to the First Mobile Fleet. In all, fewer than 100 planes from the whole attack managed to return to their base ships. Raymond Spruance's losses for the day so far amounted to 22 planes and 60 men. It was already one of the most lopsided victories in history, and the day was not yet done. Ozawa's ordeals were only beginning.

The *Taiho*'s damage control crews were still shoring up the vessel from the morning's torpedo attack. As it was, they remained unaware of gasoline fumes which were already at dangerous levels inside the great flagship. One engineer opened ventilating ducts to lessen the danger of buildup of volatile fumes in the bunker tanks which could be touched off by a single spark. It was a particular danger because Japanese warships at this time were directly burning unrefined light crude — a wartime economy measure to keep the fleet fueled on schedule and sufficiently to maintain large-scale sea operations. But the engineer's action only allowed the further spread of the avgas fumes into compartments throughout the lower levels of the ship. *Taiho* was now a time-bomb waiting for one tiny accidental spark to ignite her fuse.

At about this time, while Mitscher's airmen were chopping up Ozawa's air wings, silent killers beneath the waves stalked Ozawa's fleet. The submarine *Cavalla* had finally closed to attack range with the Main Body, and her skipper, Commander Herman Kossler, took his sighting on one of the enemy's heavies. The ship Kossler had in his crosshairs was none other than the *Shokaku*. She and her sister *Zuikaku* were the remaining two survivors of Chuichi Nagumo's First Carrier Strike Force, and now she was a sitting duck. Shortly after noon, as soon as he had his bearings fixed, Kossler fired a full spread. Observers on the *Taiho* saw four great water geysers erupt on the *Shokaku*'s port side before she dropped out of the line. Fires soon spread throughout the Pearl Harbor raider and defied every effort of the damage control crews to quell them. Within two hours, the *Shokaku* was engulfed in flames. Huge columns of smoke marked her wake, and a new chain-reaction of explosions erupted within her hangar spaces and lower decks. Finally, at about 1500, one of the six ships which had started the war with the United States rolled over and sank beneath the waves with 1,250 of her crew.

And then, the pending disaster awaiting the *Taiho* finally happened. No one knows exactly what touched off the fumes which by now filled every lower space and compartment, but 22 minutes after the *Shokaku* went down, a massive series of explosions wracked Jisaburo Ozawa's "unsinkable" flagship. The armored flight deck was heaved upward, allowing a great sheet of flame to shoot high into the air, while the sides of her hull were blown out. The great carrier had been thoroughly gutted and there was no saving her. The Borneo crude which had fueled her engines now fueled the fires which were consuming the wrecked ship, producing such great heat that destroyers could not draw close to take off survivors. It was with great persuasion that a suicidal Ozawa was convinced to save himself, and the Admiral, along with his staff and the Emperor's portrait, were successfully evacuated to the destroyer *Wakatsuki*. A second blast finished her, and the mighty *Taiho* was no more. Sixteen hundred fifty of her crew joined those of the *Shokaku* in their watery grave at the bottom of the Philippine Sea.

Reestablishing his command aboard the heavy cruiser *Haguro*, Ozawa was faced with some desperate decisions as dusk fell and the remaining survivors of his decimated air groups returned to the fleet. Two of his carriers, including the newest commissioned capital ship in the Imperial Navy, were gone. So were 346 planes. Throughout the day, he had received radio reports that the land-based air force he had counted on as support for his carrier wings had indeed struck and inflicted massive damage on the enemy, but it was evident now that those reports had either been misleading or exaggerated at best. Ozawa intended to refuel his ships and strike back with every plane he had left at his command, but Soemu Toyoda instead ordered Ozawa to draw off westward beyond the range of the American fleet. Bitterly, he complied but planned to strike back again on the 21st and transferred his flag to the *Zuikaku* at 1300 hours on the afternoon of the 20th to better coordinate his counterattack.

It was not until 2000 hours on the night of the 19th that Spruance finally unleashed Marc Mitscher, ordering Task Force 58, minus one carrier group to continue air operations against Guam and Rota, to move westward at maximum headway to hunt down Ozawa. Mitscher and his staff were already charting air search patterns and planning a daylight strike. But as dawn arose on the 20th, Mitscher's carriers were still chasing Ozawa westward. The first search missions were launched at 0600 hours and proceeded throughout the morning without finding the enemy.

That afternoon, roughly a half hour after Ozawa had completed his transfer to the *Zuikaku*, Lieutenant R.S. Nelson took off in his Avenger and headed out on the first leg of his assigned search sweep. After two hours of flying, Nelson was at the end of his fuel range and was about to return to the *Enterprise* when he spotted distant wakes on the ocean surface. He was right over Ozawa's fleet — and it was taking on fuel from tankers and thus proceeding slowly enough for the task force to close to strike range. Excitedly, Nelson radioed the *Lexington*, but atmospherics garbled his transmission, requiring him to repeat his reports longer than specified to give clear information to the flagship. But the longer he remained on the air, the more his signals were picked up by the light cruiser *Atago*. Its captain immediately signaled the *Zuikaku*, and Ozawa knew his position had been compromized. All refueling operations were terminated and he had his ships increase speed to 24 knots.

After 15 minutes of continual transmissions, Nelson's reports finally made sense enough to determine the position and disposition of the enemy. Ozawa's fleet was located to the northwest at a distance of 275 miles, which was just about maximum range for Mitscher's attack planes. It was already 1605, late in the afternoon, and night would be falling in three hours. If Mitscher launched an attack now, his planes would be flying right to the very edge of their fuel endurance and would be returning at dusk at the earliest. And the enemy were already increasing speed to escape. Asking advice, Mitscher's operations officer, Commander W.J. Widhelm, replied bluntly that it was going to be tight; the strike missions would have only a limited time over the target area and there was the distinct possibility that it would already be night before the squadrons made it back. As a result, a lot of pilots were probably going to be lost. Mitscher weighed all this in his mind, and made a hard decision: the opportunity to destroy the main strike force of the Japanese Navy could not be passed by, no matter the cost. He ordered his carriers to increase speed to maximum and sounded battle stations. By 1641 hours, the carriers turned into the wind, and the first of 216 planes began roaring off the decks.

It was two hours of hard flying before the first strike wave caught up with the trailing elements of the First Mobile Fleet, six oilers which had been left behind in Ozawa's desperate retreat and were scrambling west at best speed. Helldivers pounced upon the ships and inflicted such heavy damage upon the *Genyo Maru* and *Seiyo Maru* that they had to be abandoned and scuttled later that evening. All were burning as the squadrons passed overhead on the way to their primary objective.

Minutes later, the bulk of the First Mobile Fleet finally came into view. Eight Avengers from the carriers *Belleau Wood* and *Yorktown*, led by Lieutenant George Brown, set themselves upon the *Hiyo*. After circling briefly, the planes peeled off one by one and dropped down to make their torpedo runs. The four Avengers from the *Yorktown* split off to hit the *Zuikaku* while Brown's mates continued on their way. Brown found himself flying through very heavy antiaircraft and with part of his left wing blasted away. The rest of the crew bailed out while he continued his run and managed to launch his torpedo while Lieutenants Benjamin Tate and Warren Omark also put down their fish. At least two struck the *Hiyo*, setting off a chain-reaction of fires and explosions within the light carrier. Tate and Omark managed to evade enemy Zekes, and Brown's crew were later rescued, but Brown himself was lost.

A ragged force of 75 Zekes was hastily scrambled to protect Ozawa's flattops, but they were simply overwhelmed by the American strike force. Avengers, Dauntlesses and Helldivers all pounced upon the *Zuikaku*, *Junyo*, *Ryuho*, and *Chiyoda*, inflicting heavy damage on each. They also hit the battleship *Haruna* and the heavy cruiser *Maya*. Hellcats and Avengers shot down 65 Zekes, virtually destroying what was left of Ozawa's air force. It was all over in twenty minutes; as the sun was setting, the *Hiyo* was gone. Four of Ozawa's surviving flattops were no longer serviceable and his remaining air strength was a paltry 35 planes. With dusk falling, Mitscher's airmen turned and headed back. The burning tankers they had hit on the way in made for a perfect navigational marker as they set course for home. But shortly thereafter, the pilots had nothing but their instruments to go by. Nights in the Pacific entailed such total darkness that there was no view of the ocean or the horizon. All the pilots saw ahead was blackness.

From the first launch, Marc Mitscher remained on the *Lexington*'s bridge, following the progress of the strike over the radio and watching the daylight fade quickly. The moment that his pilots reported that their mission was complete and that they were heading back, he ordered his task groups to spread out to a station-keeping distance of 15 miles apart to provide maximum coverage for rescue and recovery operations. He could hear the chatter from the pilots, desperately searching for their base ships, some taking votes on whether or not to ditch in a group. Finally, radar indicated that the returning squadrons were coming overhead, and lookouts could hear the steady drone of their engines. The planes would be running out of fuel just about now. All these things, and an innate humanity, formed in Marc Mitscher's mind and at 2045 hours, the admiral turned to his chief staff officer, Captain Arleigh Burke: "Turn on the lights."

With Mitscher's soft command, all ships in the task force turned on their searchlights, trunk lights, every running light they had. Every 5-inch gun fired starshells which illuminated the entire area. Search beams either pointed directly up as beacons or were trained right onto flight decks. It was a massive risk Mitscher was taking: lighting up his ships like Christmas trees while they were slowed for recovery made them perfect targets for any Japanese submarine lurking in the area. Mitscher ignored the danger; his pilots simply were not expendable. Planes which were fast running out of gas settled on the first ships they could reach, while others could not wait even that long and ditched nearby. There was one incident where two planes landed simultaneously on the *Lexington* and somehow managed to avoid smashing into one another. Other planes crashlanded on the decks and were quickly cleared off for the next plane coming. By 2230 hours, the last of the pilots had either been landed or plucked from the water, and the task force resumed pursuit of Ozawa, but Willis Lee's battleships were obliged to slow in order to pick up additional survivors— 50 in all—from the sea. Night-fighting rigged Avengers launched on air search missions and managed to reestablish contact with Ozawa, but he was already steaming at 20 knots for Okinawa and was too far away with Task Force 58 having to slow to rescue more downed airmen. The chase was fruitless and ultimately Mitscher broke off the pursuit.

In writing up his report of the battle, Mitscher expressed his own bitter disappointment, albeit in neutral wording, that the Fifth Fleet had let a badly crippled enemy escape instead of effecting their total destruction. But he was speaking for his captains, air staffs, and pilots, nearly all of whom blamed Raymond Spruance for not allowing them to strike first when they had the chance. William Halsey was much more vocal in his criticisms, blaming Spruance directly for his failure to wipe out the Imperial Japanese Navy when they had the golden opportunity to do so. Even Spruance began second-guessing himself and criticized his own decision-making and lack of aggressiveness against the enemy. These opinions, however, were not shared either by Ernest King in or Chester Nimitz back at Pearl Harbor — and their opinions were the only ones which counted.

It was the great clash of the carrier fleets, the greatest naval engagement since Jutland. By any judgment, Raymond Spruance and Marc Mitscher had achieved an overwhelming triumph. In two days, not only had they preserved the striking power of their fleet, they had supported the Saipan invasion with devastating airpower, had destroyed 900 enemy planes, sunk three carriers and put four others plus a battleship and a cruiser out of action — and all at a cost of only 130 planes and 76 airmen while not losing a single ship. What power was left to the Imperial Japanese Navy had been irretrievably broken and for all intents her fleet air arm was no more. Without planes, the surviving Japanese aircraft carriers and those now building on the slipways were useless for anything other than ferry ships or decoys, and without air power, their remaining ships would be targets to be struck and destroyed at will. Beyond that, in just two days' fighting, the Americans had collapsed Japan's Inner Defense Line, and with their fleet nearly destroyed the Pacific Ocean was now wide open. There was nothing to stop Douglas MacArthur or Marc Mitscher and their relentless advance toward the Imperial Homeland itself.

Saipan fell two weeks later. Yoshitsugo Saito's remaining 4,000 men, many armed with knives or sharpened bamboo spears, would hurl themselves against the American positions surrounding their last redoubts on the slopes of Tapotchau and Hill 500 in massed banzai charges, storming right into heavy machine gun, artillery, and flamethrower fire. Corpses would pile up on the barbed wire and sandbag barriers, and toward the end, even clerk-typists and cooks would add their bodies to the mountains of the dead which would be cleared away with bulldozers to fill mass graves. On the night before the final suicidal human-wave attacks, Saito sent a last message to Tokyo, blaming his defeat on the failure of the Navy to reinforce him by air as he was promised, and offering an apology to the Emperor for his inability to do better by the Nation.

In another bunker on Tapotchau was Vice Admiral Chuichi Nagumo. Although he held the commission as Commander, Pacific Fleet, it was an empty title and his "fleet" consisted of a pathetic collection of coastal gunboats. It was a crushing humiliation for the man who had so reluctantly gone to war in the first place and despite that had become the hero of Pearl Harbor and Ceylon. His successes had led him to his ruin. There was no possibility of escape for Nagumo, certainly none for victory, and no way for him to redeem his honor. And now, the end had come. He was trapped on an island, in a hole in the ground with fanatics preparing to throw their lives away for a war which was clearly lost. For all that, Nagumo was still his Emperor's soldier, an Imperial officer, and surrender was as unthinkable for him as it was for Saito or his men.

After Saito finished his radio message, he shared a bottle of sake with his officers and gave his men a final order for the dawn attack, exhorting them to take seven enemy lives for each of theirs. At about the same time the general committed seppuku, Nagumo put a gun to his head.

The day that Saipan was invaded, a force of B-29 Superfortress bombers of the U.S. Fourteenth Air Force launched from China and bombed the Japanese steel production facility at Yawata on the southern Home Island of Kyushu. It would be only the first of many bombing raids; the war had come right to the enemy's front doorstep. Once the Marianas were completely conquered, fleets of B-29s would begin launching from Saipan, Tinian, Rota, and Guam on a daily basis as soon as the Seabees finished their work building the new bases. The day Saipan fell, the Japanese Fifteenth Army was forced to retreat from Burma before the advance of Lieutenant General William Slim and his British Fourteenth Army. The string of military disasters greased the way for the downfall of Hideki Tojo. The cabinet and the Emperor's own advisers had combined against him to force his resignation. Emperor Hirohito subsequently approved the appointment of General Kaniaki Kosio as the new Prime Minister. Kosio chose as his deputy the former prewar Prime Minister, Admiral Mitsumasa Yonai — who had opposed the war along with many in the Navy prior to 1941 — and appointed officers to a new, formally constituted Supreme War Council charged not with a mission to win the war so much as to find a means for the Empire to effect a political solution. Time was no longer on Japan's side, and Soemu Toyoda bluntly advised the government that the Combined Fleet would not survive the year.

On July 26, Franklin Roosevelt met with Douglas MacArthur and Chester Nimitz at Pearl Harbor to settle the details for the next phase of the campaign. Nimitz and many of Roosevelt's own advisers had pushed for Formosa to be the next target, since it was closer to the Home Islands. This would afford the opportunity to support military action against Japanese armies in China while simultaneously exercising full sea and air control to neutralize the Philippines, as well as serving as the staging point for an eventual invasion of Japan itself. MacArthur, driven by his emotional commitment to the Philippines, argued in persuasive terms that it was a matter of military practicality that the archipelago could not simply be bypassed, given the concentration of both troops and airpower the enemy would still have and that there was, beyond matters of strategic necessity, a moral obligation on the part of the United States not to renege on its commitment to return and liberate seventeen million Filipinos suffering under the yoke of Japanese oppression. Filipino resistance fighters and American guerrillas had sustained themselves against the enemy for two years on the promise of an American return in force. They could not be abandoned now. Finally, to win his argument, MacArthur pointed out that Luzon, Leyte, and Mindanao offered a much larger staging base and fleet anchorage than Formosa could.

In the end, MacArthur's views won out. He had successfully sold Roosevelt on his plan and returned to Brisbane jubilant that his cherished dream to lead the liberation of the Philippines, as he had vowed to do on the day of his humiliating retreat, was going to be a reality. Ernest King, who privately believed that Douglas MacArthur was a megalomaniac and in no way trusted him, reluctantly concurred that the conquest of the Philippines would require fewer troops than any invasion of Formosa and its mountainous coastline. The Joint Chiefs of Staff approved the invasion of the Philippines on September 8 and named December 20 as D-Day. That same day, William Halsey was informed by Nimitz that he would be assuming command of the Fifth Fleet and as a consequence it was to be redesignated the Third Fleet. The move was in accordance with Nimitz's policy of rotating the command of the Pacific forces periodically, and Halsey responded eagerly with a series of airstrikes against Luzon, Leyte, Yap and the Palaus as soon as he had the fleet reorganized.

Four days later, Halsey radioed Pearl Harbor that his airstrikes had suppressed virtually all Japanese air power in the Philippines sector and had swept the seas of shipping. He reported that the Philippines were wide open to attack and urged that the Third Fleet's upcoming Pelileu operation be transformed into a full-scale invasion of Leyte itself. CINCPAC was not amenable to calling off the Pelileu invasion. The plans were too advanced and the anchorages there and at Ulithi too vital for future operations. Nimitz did concur with Halsey that the timetable against Japan should be speeded up, giving the enemy far less time to prepare. He received the Joint Chiefs' approval to begin assigning invasion troops and advanced D-Day against Leyte to October 20.

But as a result of CINCPAC's determination to press on with the Pelileu invasion, a waste of manpower ensued in the bloody campaign to take a militarily useless island, exterminating the Japanese in vicious cave-to-cave fighting at a cost of two months, over 2,000 American dead, and many times that number of wounded.

Time was running out for Japan. As the Empire's defenses were beginning to collapse, the ever expanding American war machine now began to swing itself in the direction of the Philippines.

CHAPTER 10

Sho

Japan was doomed.

No one with even the least measure of military sense could fail to appreciate this reality. The Marianas had fallen. On Saipan, Tinian, and Guam, the Americans were constructing bases for their long-range B-29 Superfortress bombers and it was certain that the Home Islands, already suffering bombing raids from Chinese bases, would soon fall under massive aerial attack.

These realities were not lost on Soemu Toyoda, particularly now that the Americans were closing in on the Philippine Islands. Now the southern anchor of the Empire's defensive perimeter, if that bastion fell, the Americans would have a major staging base for an eventual invasion of the Japanese mainland itself. The only way this could be avoided would be for the invasion to be stopped dead in its tracks and for the American fleet to be destroyed in detail. Consequent to that, he prepared what was one of the most complex battle plans in the history of naval warfare, and on it were pinned Japan's remaining hopes for national survival. In that spirit, the plan was christened by the Japanese word for victory: Sho.

There were actually three Sho plans, each designed to cover the places where the next American strike was expected: the Philippines, Formosa, or the Ryukyu Archipelago, only 300 miles from the Home Islands. When the Philippines clearly became identified as the target of the next American thrust, the Japanese activated Sho-1 for operation.

Sho-1 involved dividing the Combined Fleet into three main task forces. The Northern Force, under Jisaburo Ozawa, was to play the role of decoy; its mission was to lure away the aircraft carriers and fast battleships of the main American force guarding the beachheads by presenting itself as a threat requiring immediate action. With the American fleet off chasing Ozawa, a second Southern Force, approaching from two different directions, would form the lower jaw of a pincers movement on that beachhead; the first group of battleships and cruisers under Soiji Nishimura would move through the Surigao Strait while Kiyohide Shima would lead a second unit of cruisers and destroyers and rendezvous with Nishimura in the Mindanao Sea and combine their units into a single formation. The Center Force, under Takeo Kurita, would simultaneously be proceeding through the Sibuyan Sea and the San Bernardino Strait, skirting the perimeter of Samar until both would converge upon the expected landing site, Leyte Gulf, where they would wipe out the beachhead. United, the two forces would then proceed northward to intercept the Americans, heading back with all dispatch to rescue the invasion forces, only to be caught between the Northern and Southern Forces and thus annihilated. Air support was to be primarily drawn from land-based squadrons and those few planes still available to the Combined Fleet. Their tasks were to harass the landing forces, attack and weaken enemy naval units chasing Ozawa, aid in the destruction of the invasion forces when the Southern and Center Forces achieved linkup, and then to combine into a united wing to destroy the American naval forces afterward. Timing for the plan was critical; Shima and Nishimura were to converge after setting forth from Japan and Brunei, respectively, on October 17 while Kurita was starting from Singapore. Ozawa had five days to be on station to advertise his presence by the time Nishimura, Kurita, and Shima were in Philippine waters approaching from the west. For their part, they had to make the convergence point at the moment the landing was proceeding and the American invasion troops would be at their most vulnerable. The plan also depended upon one crucial element: that the Americans would behave as predicted; in particular the driven, aggressive Third Fleet commander William Halsey, whom Japanese strategists knew to be a man who charged eagerly to the attack. But only two years earlier, the plan at Midway also turned on Halsey and his aggressive propensities to deliver the Americans into the jaws of their trap. Because he failed to be the one in command, disaster befell the First Carrier Strike Force, which was the beginning of all Japanese reverses in the war. Sho was a gamble with long odds against it, but it was Japan's last chance to avoid the disaster which was beginning to loom over the horizon.

Fortunately for the Japanese, Halsey was in command and would fulfill the expectations of the strategists by behaving as predicted. Unfortunately, it was every other element of the plan which was off. For a start, the American naval forces were divided into two fleets under two independent commanders; Halsey of the Third, and Thomas Kinkaid of the Seventh. Additionally, because the Americans had sped up their invasion timetable by two months, by the time any Japanese unit would be in Leyte Gulf the troops would already be ashore. Even more critically, Sho absolutely depended upon airpower comparable to the Americans in both

numbers and training to work. But most of what was left of the Imperial
Navy's veteran air arm had been destroyed in the Turkey Shoot five months
ago, and Halsey's carrier raids of October 10 against Formosa and Okinawa decimated the land-based air forces and airfields. What pilots were
left were green recruits hastily trained and nowhere near the quality of
those precious veterans who were now all dead. There simply would not
be enough in numbers to sufficiently reduce American air or seapower,
and rookie pilots would be no match for veterans. Because of all this, Sho-
1 was doomed even as it was being set into motion.

While Ozawa, Nishimura, Shima, and Kurita were all underway to
make their stations, Douglas MacArthur, on October 20th, was already
landing on the beaches at Leyte with the troops of Walter Krueger's Sixth
Army and waded ashore with Filipino president Sergio Osmeña. There
was no air resistance. Commando units and Filipino resistance fighters had
already been creating havoc with the occupation forces, and escort carrier
task groups of the Seventh Fleet under Rear Admiral Thomas Sprague had

Douglas MacArthur wades ashore at Leyte along with his staff officers and
Philippines President Sergio Osmeña, 20 October 1944. National Archives 111-
SC-402101.

spent three days launching sorties which pounded Japanese airfields while a force of battleships under Jesse Oldendorf and Willis Lee provided gunfire support and shelled the beach for two straight days. Now the troops were ashore, and the long-promised liberation of the Philippines, the dream of MacArthur, had begun.

Three days later, the Imperial Navy was arriving in Philippine waters. Ozawa had with him mostly empty carriers, the *Zuikaku*, the light carriers *Chiyoda*, *Zuiho*, and *Chitose*, and the hybrid carrier-battleships *Ise* and *Hyuga*, hastily converted earlier that year. Between them, the six aircraft carriers had a grand total of 116 planes, only slightly more than the full complement of a single American fleet carrier. Protecting him was a light screen of cruisers and destroyers, with such insufficient numbers and firepower that it would never provide enough cover against a large air assault or a heavy surface attack. Ozawa knew that he was on a suicide

The decimated First Mobile Fleet proceeds to the Philippines, 22 October 1944. The great Sho-1 plan in which they are to participate has already launched too late to halt the American invasion at Leyte. National Archives (captured Japanese Archival photo) NH63435.

mission, but if he succeeded in drawing off the main forces of the Americans, the effort would be worth even the destruction of his whole force if it came down to the worst-case.

Meanwhile, Kurita's Center Force, with its five battleships (including the superbattleships *Yamato* and *Musashi*) and twelve cruisers, was rounding the southern portion of Mindoro when he was spotted by the submarines *Dace* and *Darter*. After radioing the position of the enemy force to Admirals Kinkaid and Halsey, the two subs moved in for the attack. Kurita was still 220 miles from the San Bernardino Strait when four torpedoes slammed into his flagship, the heavy cruiser *Atago*. Two more fish put her sister *Takao* out of action. Even as Kurita was making a hasty transfer to the *Yamato* and the *Atago* was going down, the *Dace* fired four torpedoes into the cruiser *Maya*, which blew up on the spot. It was a bad omen for the rest of the operation.

Responding to the presence of Kurita in the approaches to the Sibuyan Sea on the morning of the 24th, Halsey ordered three of Marc Mitscher's carrier groups in toward the eastern Philippines, where they would be in optimum strike range while enjoying the screen of the islands. A fourth, Task Group 38.1, under Frederick Sherman, was replenishing fuel and ammunition when Japanese land-based bombers found his force and bore

The superbattleship *Yamato* proceeds into battle against the U.S. fleet for the first time in the war. National Archives (captured Japanese archival photo) NH73082.

in for the attack. Joining in the strike were 76 of Ozawa's planes to provide support and to contribute to the effort to get Ozawa's forces noticed by the Americans.

Spotting the attack force on radar, Sherman's carriers put up a CAP screen at once. All of Ozawa's planes failed to achieve anything and most were shot down. The survivors, untrained in making carrier landings, proceeded to Luzon to land and thus reduced markedly the tiny air force Ozawa had available to him. The planes of the Second Air Fleet were decimated, but one of them managed to get through the screen and put a bomb on the deck of the light carrier *Princeton*, setting off severe fires and explosions which the crew, determined to save their ship at all costs, fought with considerable energy. But unfortunately the fires spread to the torpedo magazine, detonating ordnance and blowing off the carrier's stern. The blast rained shrapnel on the cruiser *Birmingham* which had come alongside to aid the firefighting effort, and it suffered heavy damage and casualties as a result. The *Princeton* was doomed, and Sherman gave the order to evacuate the survivors and destroy the ship.

The disastrous effort to pound TG38.1 left Kurita with no air cover whatsoever and the other three task groups were free to hit him at will. Making a very rough passage through the Sibuyan Sea, Kurita's ships came under repeated attack by five waves of torpedo planes, dive bombers and fighters from Mitscher's carriers in the course of the day's action. All of Kurita's battleships were damaged and he lost another heavy cruiser when the *Myoko* was put out of action and forced to retire. The *Musashi*, however, had been crippled and began to trail behind the rest of the formation as it reversed course to evade the air strikes. In the fifth and final strike of the day, Mitscher's planes found the wounded supership alone, down at the bow and moving slowly, trailing a long oil slick in her wake. The whole formation fell upon her like jackals and put 19 torpedoes and 17 bombs into her, after which one of the two largest and most powerful battleships ever built rolled over and sank with the loss of 1,000 of her crew. In the course of her operational life, the *Musashi* never had a chance to fire her great guns in battle.

By the time dusk fell on the 24th, Kurita had already been bloodied and slightly unnerved. He had lost 30 percent of his force and now, due to his evasive maneuvers to duck the airstrikes, would be more than an hour off schedule for the rendezvous with Nishimura and Shima off Leyte. Sho-1 was beginning to fall apart. However, even while disaster was already befalling the Japanese, one critical part of the plan was about to succeed in its purpose. As Sherman's force was fighting off furious air attacks and the *Princeton* was suffering her death throes, scout bombers from that ship had finally spotted Ozawa's Northern Force 190 miles NNE of TG38.1's

The CVL *Princeton* explodes following a Japanese air attack at Leyte Gulf. National Archives 80-G-281663.

position in the mid-afternoon. It had been a frustrating day for Ozawa up to that point. Making smoke, zig-zagging, breaking radio silence and sending messages in the clear, and even sending his planes in on the attack against Sherman had accomplished nothing. Japanese communications remained as poor as ever and so Ozawa had no idea of the mauling Kurita was taking. So from his perspective, the Gods were smiling upon him when the *Princeton*'s scouts appeared in his sky at last.

What was about to happen next came as a direct result of the divided command structure of the naval forces in the Philippines, the turn of one man's driven ego, and a certain amount of confusion regarding the fleet roles between Halsey and Kinkaid—conditions which were just perfect for a critical miscommunication between the two fleet commanders.

Halsey's natural aggressiveness was now further exacerbated by the fact that, after two years of the press following him around across the Pacific and writing endless stories of "Bull" Halsey the Fighting Admiral, he had begun, perhaps unconsciously, to believe in his own legend. There was also the fact that, following the Marianas campaign, he had been one of the most vocal critics of Raymond Spruance's decision to not follow up on Jisaburo Ozawa's First Mobile Fleet to annihilate it after it had lost its air wings. Now, in Halsey's view, that force had returned to menace the Leyte invasion. It was the most dangerous threat conceivable, since carrier strike forces carried the longest and heaviest punch and without air support the Japanese thrust made no sense whatsoever. Halsey could not know that Ozawa had virtually no planes, but no commander in his right mind ever assumes weakness on the part of his enemy. Furthermore, according to the way he interpreted his orders, he had a duty, upon discovering the presence of any significant enemy force in his area, to shift his priority to the destruction of that force.

Kinkaid, for his part, saw that his and Halsey's duty was to cover Leyte. They had already been in combat with enemy fleet units in the Sibuyan sector, and though Kinkaid had no problem in general with the imperative to seek out and destroy enemy naval units which could pose a threat to MacArthur, he assumed that both fleets would pivot that effort on the defense of the Leyte position. The miscommunication entered into the picture on the afternoon of October 24, when Halsey and Kinkaid conferred via radio on a plan to form up Willis Lee's Task Force 34, adding fourteen destroyers drawn from two other carrier groups, and assigning it to "engage decisively at long ranges" any enemy units reported approaching Leyte. Kinkaid was satisfied and understood this would be put into effect. But when Mitscher's relayed report of Ozawa's presence reached Halsey, the whole picture of the campaign changed for him in an instant. Here was his chance to finish up what Spruance had failed to do and eliminate what he judged to be the remaining and more dangerous threat to the Leyte position. Turning to his chief of staff, Rear Admiral Robert Carney, Halsey put his finger on the marked position of Ozawa's force on the plot board and said, "That's where we're going, Mick. Start them north." And, by "them," Halsey meant the entire Third Fleet.

This had not been adequately communicated to Kinkaid, who only heard that Halsey was taking three carrier groups north to attack Ozawa in the morning. Kinkaid assumed that Halsey had executed his intention to form up Task Force 34 and that it would be covering the San Bernardino Strait and furnishing backup for the task groups providing aerial support. Halsey managed to satisfy himself that the badly mauled Kurita — who according to the last reports on him had reversed course and was retiring from battle — no longer posed a threat and that he could therefore take as large a force as he felt necessary to ensure the total destruction of Ozawa. So, with four battle groups ordered to start forth to rendezvous with the main body of the fleet, Halsey set off at 1800 hours that evening in pursuit of what was only an empty shell of a task force, and in so doing left not so much as a single destroyer to cover the San Bernardino Strait. Kurita, who had not been observed returning to his base course toward the Strait, would find it obligingly wide open the next morning.

While these movements were taking place east of the Philippines, Nishimura and Shima were making their way through the Mindanao Sea but not quite as planned. Shima was trailing 40 miles behind Nishimura and could not achieve linkup, particularly because Nishimura, on receiving reports of the attacks on Kurita and the losses suffered by the Center Force, had increased speed to link up and reinforce Kurita but had not communicated that intention to Shima. Between them, Nishimura and Shima had only two battleships and three heavy cruisers, not quite enough to make up for the ships already lost by Kurita, particularly the *Musashi*. The divided Southern Force had been spotted by a search plane the morning of the 24th as the lead units were approaching the strait between Negros and Mindanao. They suffered a superficial airstrike at 0920 hours but were left unmolested the rest of the day while Task Force 38 was engaged with Kurita. Their movements, however, were kept under constant shadow.

Kinkaid knew where they were heading, and detached Jesse Oldendorf's shore bombardment task group to cover the expected exit point — the Surigao Strait. Oldendorf, who had been at Savo Island, was determined that this time the enemy would be wiped out once and for all. No second chances. He set three picket lines of 39 PT-boats to cover the approach path between Leyte and Dingat and formed his battleships and cruiser-destroyer screen in a perpendicular line to blockade the exit. By a delicious irony, Oldendorf's force read like an honor roll of ships damaged at Pearl Harbor, reconstructed and now offering an opportunity for vengeance and a last measure of glory before the age of the battleship ended forever: *Maryland*, *West Virginia*, *Tennessee*, *California*, and *Pennsylvania*, with the *Mississippi*, another prewar battlewagon, bringing up the rear.

Nishimura entered the pass at midnight and came under attack by the PT-boats. As his ships dodged the torpedoes, they shelled the boats, inflicting heavy casualties. That tiny triumph was very short lived, however, and they found themselves under heavier attack by two destroyer squadrons which bore in for torpedo attack and succeeded in sinking the battleship *Fuso* and damaging the *Yamashiro* while escaping damage themselves. When the two forces at last came into range of one another, Oldendorf engaged what all sea commanders dreamed of and after this night would never happen again in naval warfare, a classic battleship duel. The Japanese force was formed up in a column, while Oldendorf's heavies were arrayed in a full broadside line and able to employ maximum firepower. They had successfully crossed Nishimura's "T" and true to form Oldendorf's battleships opened fire on each of Nishimura's ships as they came up the line, one by one. His cruisers and destroyers added support fire, and the main body of the Southern Force was wiped out. And with the admiral dead aboard his blazing flagship, the surviving cruiser *Mogami* and the destroyer *Shigure*, heavily damaged, turned tail and headed back the way they came, retiring at best speed. When Shima's paltry cruiser-destroyer group arrived at the far end of the Strait, a PT-boat torpedoed the cruiser *Abukuma*. Shima tried to press on when the retreating survivors of Nishimura were heading out, providing cover with misaimed torpedo attacks. Shima's own flagship, the *Naichi*, rammed the already battered *Mogami* and with that, what was left of the Southern Force put about and retreated. The burning *Yamashiro*, the crippled *Abukuma* and the bowless Asagano were all torpedoed and sent to the bottom of the Strait in the morning. It would be the last ever clash of big guns at sea.

The morning of the 25th was a deceptively quiet beginning for what would prove to be the most desperate and confused day of action in the entire battle for Leyte Gulf. Kurita's Center Force sailed unopposed through the San Bernardino Strait at 0540 hours, right at dawn. As the officers and men saluted the rising sun, the ships turned southward and ploughed on toward their objective, only three hours at maximum headway. As the Center Force proceeded on its way south, it seemed that the Sho-1 plan was going to work after all. So far, Kurita enjoyed a clear sea and not a plane was to be seen in the skies above. It looked as if the Americans had acted as they had hoped, and had gone off leaving the beaches completely unguarded. His force, reduced in strength, still had plenty of firepower including that of the mighty *Yamato*, pride of the Imperial Navy, and there was the chance of salvaging some measure of victory by destroying the invasion forces and halting the American advance.

However, the way ahead to the Leyte beaches was not quite as wide open as Kurita thought. Off Samar lay a force of 16 baby-flattops, the CVEs of Rear Admiral Thomas Sprague's Task Group 77.4, divided into three task units, "Taffy 1," "Taffy 2," and "Taffy 3," with four to six escort carriers and a light destroyer screen each. These ships had been providing tactical air support for the landings while effecting suppression of enemy airfields. They were completely unaware of what was coming toward them, a battleforce with so much heavy firepower that their little ships stood no chance whatsoever in a stand-up fight. However, Kurita had no idea that any ships lay in his path at all. The presence of the task group was as much of a shock to him as Kurita's was to the Americans.

Admiral Kinkaid ordered the beginning of aerial search operations at dawn that day, but not a single scout managed to launch off any of the CVEs until 0700 hours. As a result, the appearance of Kurita's battleships came as a very ugly surprise. Indeed, one search plane spotted the ships and the pilot assumed that they had to be Third Fleet units until antiaircraft fire came up at him. Taffy 3's commander, Rear Admiral Clifton Sprague, ordered an identification of the ships. At that moment, his own lookouts spotted them on the horizon and recognized their pagoda masts just as gunfire opened up.

Taffy 3 was at the front of the developing battle line, and Kurita was stunned to find himself falling upon carriers—and he had no air cover to protect his ships. Instead of a tiny force of tiny ships, Kurita perceived what had to be the lead elements of Marc Mitscher's fast carrier task force before him. With the savaging he endured yesterday still very fresh in his mind, the single, deadly equation of carriers vs. battleships flashed before him in an instant; if those flattops managed to turn into the wind and get planes off, he was doomed. His only chance was to finish them now or suffer utter annihilation, and he set the entire Center Force upon Taffy 3. But in his haste to strike first, Kurita gave the confusing order of "General Chase" just as his ships were changing formation, whereupon attack coordination soon became impossible.

For his part, Clifton Sprague, faced with giants bearing down to squash him like a bug, with insufficient force and no help immediately available, fell back upon the only resource he had left to draw upon —common sense — and had his ships take evasive action to the east, laying down smokescreens as cover. The course selected put his jeep carriers right into the wind and Sprague launched every plane which had not been sent off earlier for tactical air operations on Leyte and with any ordnance which could be loaded: bombs, depth-charges, torpedoes, fragmentation bombs, and armor-piercing and incendiary machine gun shells. He ordered in the small escort destroyers to attack with torpedoes while running his carriers

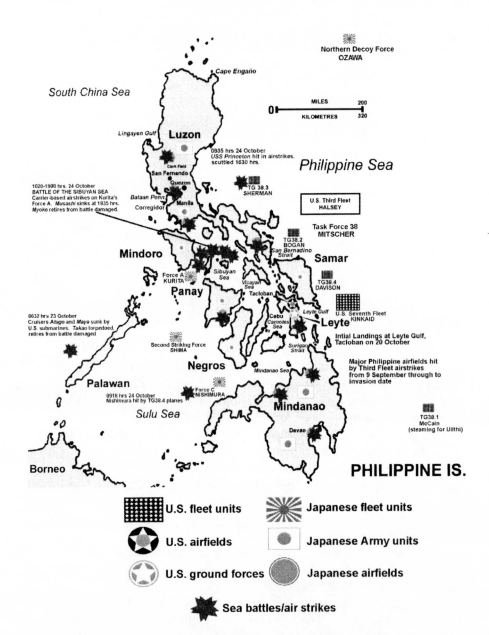

Above and opposite: Leyte Gulf, October 1944 — The liberation of the Philippines begins with the invasion of Leyte. The Japanese pull together the remnants of the Imperial Fleet for one last desperate shot at victory in the doomed Sho-1 strategic plan. Sho-1 does draw away William Halsey's Third Fleet, which sets off in pursuit of a carrier force which is only a decoy. Map graphics by Patrick Degan.

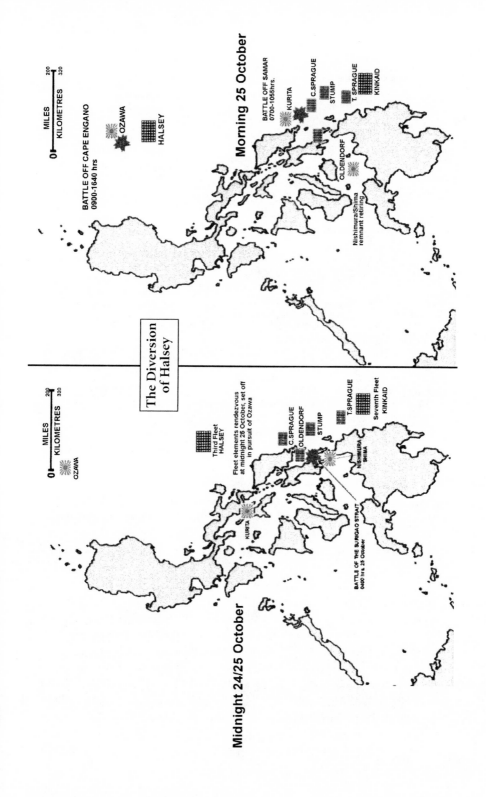

The Diversion of Halsey

Morning 25 October

MILES | 0 | 200
KILOMETRES | 0 | 320

BATTLE OFF CAPE ENGANO
0900–1640 hrs

OZAWA

HALSEY

BATTLE OFF SAMAR
0700–1055hrs.

KURITA

C.SPRAGUE

STUMP

T. SPRAGUE

KINKAID

OLDENDORF

Nishimura/Shima
remnant retiring

Midnight 24/25 October

MILES | 0 | 200
KILOMETRES | 0 | 320

OZAWA

Third Fleet
HALSEY

Fleet elements rendezvous
at midnight 25 October, set off
in pursuit of Ozawa

C.SPRAGUE

OLDENDORF

STUMP

T.SPRAGUE

Seventh Fleet
KINKAID

KURITA

NISHIMURA
SHIMA

BATTLE OF THE SURIGAO STRAIT
0400 hrs, 25 October

The CVE *Gambier Bay* is bracketed by Japanese shellfire at Samar. National Archives (captured Japanese archival photo) 80-G-287505.

into a nearby rain squall. His three larger destroyers, meanwhile, to provide cover for the carriers, charged full toward Kurita, employing torpedoes and gunfire and closing to point-blank range even while running at evasive action. Against the odds, these ships succeeded in temporarily scattering Kurita's force, compelling *Yamato* to reverse course and head northward for ten minutes while torpedoes from the *Johnston*, *Hoel*, and *Samuel B. Roberts* put the heavy cruiser *Kumano* out of action and inflicted damage on the *Chokai* and *Chikuma*. While his gallant ships fought the impossible battle, Sprague put out desperate calls in plain english — and in the clear — for help from any nearby naval unit. Taffy 2, under Felix Stump, was able to launch planes to assist Sprague and provide tactical advice. Thomas Sprague, however, was still 130 miles away, too far to lend a hand. And until Stump's planes arrived on the scene, Taffy 3 was all alone.

Things then turned ugly. Out of torpedoes and in close range, the three destroyers came under murderous fire from Kurita's main body. The *Hoel* was pounded by more than forty shells and her upper works wrecked before she rolled over and sank. The *Samuel B. Roberts*, a 40 foot hole in her hull, also went down. Kurita reformed his ships to bear down upon the flattops, but the *Johnston* interposed herself to allow the carriers a chance to escape, whereupon the Japanese circled the hapless destroyer and kept firing into her until she sank. The three tiny escort destroyers, badly mauled, retired to the Taffy 3 formation.

With the destroyer screen gone, the Japanese charged the little jeep carriers and opened up on them with every heavy gun that could be brought to bear. Sprague's flagship, the *Fanshaw Bay*, took four 8-inch hits from Kurita's heavy cruisers. The *Kalinin Bay* took thirteen hits. However, because the shells were all armor-piercing and the escort carriers were totally unarmored, they passed through the thin-skinned little ships without exploding. Instead, they were hulled through, particularly the unfortunate *Gambier Bay*, which took so many hits, quite a number of them from the massive 18.1-inch shells of the *Yamato*, that the damage control crews were unable to cope. Even as the *Gambier Bay* was capsizing, the *Chikuma* was still firing into her from close range.

However, while Sprague's carriers lay naked before Kurita's battleships and cruisers, Kurita himself was wide open to air attack, paltry as it was yet managing to have effect. Sprague's planes dropped what ordnance they had. They made strafing runs on the Japanese ships. Even those planes which had no ammunition made dummy runs to harry and distract the antiaircraft defenses. The "first-wave attack" was soon joined by the returning planes from the latest Leyte strike and added to the aerial harassment. As the fighting progressed, Taffy 2 planes arrived on the scene and began to inflict real damage. The cruiser *Suzuya* was hit and slowed, and fell out of the battle along with the *Kumano*. As planes ran out of ammunition and were forced to withdraw from lack of fuel, they made their way to Stump's carriers or to the recently captured Tacloban airstrip on Leyte to refuel, rearm, and rush back to Taffy 3's rescue. A haphazard second strike, this time more heavily armed than the first, arrived to finish the crippled *Suzuya* and sank the *Chikuma* and *Chokai* as well.

The combined air and surface attacks mounted by Taffy 3 and Taffy 2 were, comparatively speaking, like gnats swarming around elephants. But while Clifton Sprague was figuring that perhaps he would be dead sometime in the next fifteen minutes, Takeo Kurita was becoming increasingly unstrung and continued to magnify both the size and numbers of the forces before him. He was now solidly convinced that he had Mitscher's large carriers by the tail. He also believed that the planes hitting him in increasing waves—like they did the day before—were originating from additional carriers just over the horizon, and that reinforcements from Halsey must be converging upon him. He knew that Nishimura had been destroyed and that evidently, the Americans had either ignored or destroyed Ozawa's decoys with just a detached force which would soon be returning. The Center Force now faced possibly being caught in a pincer and

The crew of the *Zuikaku*, last of the Pearl Harbor raiders, prepares to abandon ship at Cape Engaño, 25 October 1944. National Archives (captured Japanese archival photo) NH73070.

crushed. Further, by now, the American invasion forces would already have been landed, and it made no military sense to risk destruction to destroy empty boats. All these factors, only a tiny portion of them real, added up and Kurita's nerve broke. As a result, at 0911, just minutes after the *Gambier Bay* disappeared beneath the waves and just as Taffy 3 was on the edge of annihilation, the battered yet still formidable Center Force turned about and retired to the southeast, ostensibly to attempt to regroup. After further attacks from Taffy 2 and Taffy 3 planes which struck the battleship *Nagato* and heavy cruiser *Tone*, Kurita eventually withdrew back the way he came. Back to the San Bernardino Strait, and thence, to Singapore.

And where was "Bull" Halsey and the Third Fleet during the desperate fighting off Samar? He and Marc Mitscher had spent the night chasing Ozawa farther and farther northeast of the Philippines, led on by the Japanese just as Sho-1's planners had envisioned. Night scout fighters from the light carrier *Independence* finally spotted Ozawa's six carriers, three light cruisers, and eight destroyers at 0200 hours. Upon making contact, Mitscher, in tactical command, ordered Willis Lee to execute the formation of Task Force 34, a unit meant to have been back at the San Bernardino Strait, and expand its numbers with all the battleships of Task Force 38 including Halsey's own flagship, the *New Jersey*. Task Force 34 took the point ahead of the fleet in anticipation of night action. Mechanical difficulties had compelled the scouts to turn back and they had temporarily lost track of the Northern Force. But the last contact had indicated that Third Fleet was closing to optimum range, and just after dawn, Mitscher's carriers turned into the wind and launched the first of the 787 planes available to form the first attack wave and the CAP umbrella over the fleet.

Ozawa's decoy force was found just after 0800. A dozen of his remaining 29 planes went up, managed to shoot down one Avenger torpedo bomber — and were quickly splashed. Heavy antiaircraft fire proved little protection, given how few ships were available to cover each other. A destroyer got it first; hit by a bomb amidships, it disappeared in a large explosion. Dive bombers then swarmed on the *Chitose* and landed three bombs on her, one blowing a hole below the waterline, after which she capsized and sank. The cruiser *Tama* and Ozawa's flagship, the venerable and lucky *Zuikaku*, took torpedo hits but remained afloat.

Having planned to go down with his flagship, Ozawa was obliged to transfer from the stricken *Zuikaku* when command from there became impossible. Steering motor damage had left the carrier unmanageable. Her radio aerials had been shot away, so Ozawa could not communicate with Kurita to the south and report his success — a breakdown that would turn the tide at Samar. Meanwhile, the second strike was proceeding apace at 1000 hours. A second destroyer was bombed and sunk, and the carrier *Chiyoda* was left dead in the water, listing and afire.

Halsey was almost rubbing his hands together with glee; what seemed to be left of the Imperial Japanese Navy was about to be wiped from the surface of the Earth and he would be the chief engineer of its destruction. It was the battle he had sought since missing Midway. He even anticipated surface action to mop up what cripples were left and ordered his ships to increase speed to 30 knots to be on hand for the kill.

Mitscher's third attack left the *Zuiho* crippled and afire with torpedo strikes which also further damaged the *Zuikaku*. Indeed, for her, it was the end of the line. The *Zuikaku*, whose name translated from the Japanese as "Fortunate Crane," had been almost as lucky a ship in this war as the *Enterprise*. She had lost her entire air wing at Coral Sea yet escaped destruction. She had cheated destruction at the Solomons and the Marianas, escaping the very battle in which her sister, the *Shokaku*, had met her end. She was the last of the Pearl Harbor attack force still afloat and in service. But now, the *Zuikaku*'s luck had finally run out. The veteran flattop slowly began to heel to starboard until she rolled over completely and disappeared forever beneath the Philippine Sea. The pilots from the *Lexington* observed this delicious spectacle while driving off ships which had drawn close to the *Chiyoda* in an attempt to rescue her.

But Halsey himself, at the moment of triumph, was not there to share in the kill. The day had soured for him; he was overwhelmed by the confusion he and Kinkaid had left in each other's wakes since the previous night and which had left Taffy 3 open to near destruction at Samar.

Not since the breakdown of communication between Robert E. Lee and Jeb Stuart at Gettysburg had two commanders been thrown into such confusion going into battle. Dispatches long-delayed through the night finally reached the bridge of the *New Jersey* at 0648 while the first strike was on its way to Ozawa — a message which reported that Seventh Fleet units were engaging enemy units in the Surigao Strait and to which was attached a question: IS TF34 GUARDING SAN BERNARDINO STRAIT? Halsey radioed back that it was with him, engaging enemy carriers. A later dispatch from Kinkaid reported that the enemy force at San Bernardino had been beaten back. After 20 minutes came another message: one of Seventh Fleet's escort carrier groups was under fire off Leyte. Minutes after that, a message in the clear from Kinkaid described in detail what was actually Kurita's Center Force and requested immediate assistance from Willis Lee, and carrier support. More messages became increasingly frantic. Halsey relented and ordered a carrier group under John McCain to turn back from its intercept-rendezvous course with Third Fleet, return to Leyte Gulf, and attack any enemy units in the area.

All during the morning of the 25th, Admiral Nimitz back at Pearl was listening with alarm to the frantic radio traffic from Samar and to the Halsey-Kinkaid exchanges. At first, he resisted the urge to issue direct orders, not wishing to interfere with his admirals at sea. But after a while the situation appeared intolerable and he ordered the transmission of a message intended to be a gentle inquiry and a "prod" to take action in response to the plight of Clifton Sprague. The message was spelled out with random character strings and doggerel meant to throw off Japanese decryption. Nimitz's communiqué began with TURKEY TROTS TO WATER GG. But somehow, this first part of the code string was left off the dispatch, and what went out, with carbon-copies to Admiral King in Washington and Admiral Kinkaid, read like this: FROM CINCPAC ACTION COM THIRD FLEET INFO CTF77X WHERE IS RPT WHERE IS TASK FORCE THIRTY FOUR RR THE WORLD WONDERS....

This made all the difference between the message being understood for what it was and its being taken by Halsey, already under heavy pressure, to be a public rebuke and humiliation. In front of his staff officers and the *New Jersey* bridge crew he threw a fit of rage, then retreated to his cabin to sulk. When Halsey calmed down, he returned to the bridge and reluctantly gave the order for Task Force 34 to return at full speed to Leyte to destroy Kurita's attack force. He detached Mitscher to finish off Ozawa, with a group of cruisers and destroyers under Laurence DuBose to furnish surface and antisubmarine cover. En route, he picked up Gerald Bogan's carrier task group and they steamed all day to the relief of the Seventh. After 14 hours, though, they would arrive to find Kurita long gone.

Task Force 34 set off at 1115 hours while the third strike against Ozawa was underway. Mitscher would launch three more strikes through the remainder of the afternoon. The *Zuiho*, damaged in the third attack, managed to get underway and was retreating at high speed when she was caught and destroyed in the fourth strike. It was more revenge for the U.S. Navy, since *Zuiho* had participated in the destruction of the old *Hornet* at Santa Cruz. The last two strikes of the afternoon converged upon the hybrids *Ise* and *Hyuga* but achieved only near misses on the two ships, which would escape the day. With that, and with dusk falling, Mitscher dispatched DuBose's task group to clean up on the survivors. They found and sank the abandoned *Chiyoda* and later, in a night action involving torpedo and gunfire exchange, sank one of three destroyers scouring the area for Japanese survivors. Later on that evening, the limping cruiser *Tama* was found by a sub and also sent to the bottom of the seas off Cape Engaño. (Translated from the Spanish, the word *engaño* means "deception.")

It had been foolish of William Halsey to take the whole of the Third Fleet — excepting a single carrier group — off to destroy Ozawa when Mitscher's task force and additional surface support would have done the job adequately. Halsey's presence in the general Leyte Gulf sector would have spared the agony Taffy 3 suffered that morning, and Takeo Kurita would instead have run into his own annihilation. As it was, though, Kurita's own panic turned what would have been a Japanese triumph, perhaps not a long lasting one, into a rout driven by nothing more than the sheer determination of men faced with certain destruction and therefore having nothing further to lose. Jisaburo Ozawa succeeded beyond all reason in his mission to lure the American fleet away from the beaches at Leyte, but his triumph was as hollow as the threat his decoy force had represented. He lost the few planes left to the Imperial Air Fleet and half his force to no object because the plan he played such a vital part of, on paper, had been doomed from the jump. The remaining strength of the Imperial Navy had in essence been thrown away on a one-shot, impossible gamble. The Japanese couldn't hope to succeed without large air forces manned by veteran pilots. At Leyte Gulf, they had faced two complete, modern warfleets with a vitiated force which was nowhere near the strength or quality of the navy which existed at the beginning of 1942.

The Japanese, for their last, desperate naval gamble, had relied upon a plan so complicated, depending upon a precise timing it could not achieve and upon a date for action which proved too late, a plan which had so little margin for error to begin with, that the whole operation was destined to collapse. And, by the circular nature of war, because the Americans had advanced their timetable in accordance with William Halsey's recommendation to speed up the campaign back on September 12, Toyoda and Ozawa never had the chance to assemble and train the forces they would have needed to make their gambit work. So while Halsey may have foolishly fallen for Ozawa's bait, it had been his strategic insight in the first place that had rendered Sho-1 a failure before it had begun.

Now, the last four operational aircraft carriers Japan had left were gone. The few flattops which remained no longer had planes and aircrews to garrison them. Or they were still building on the slipways, when steel was available. Or they were in drydock undergoing repair, when materials were available. The warships remaining to the rapidly shrinking Imperial Fleet would be needlessly sacrificed as the end came ever nearer. All that would render even the one real triumph left to Ozawa — managing to bring back ten of his ships intact — hollow.

Few could appreciate that they had borne witness to the death throes of a once proud navy. Perhaps, though, the Americans could not have appreciated it because, even in the hour of this latest and most sweeping victory, a new and savage element had entered into the Pacific War.

As the Taffy 3 ordeal was beginning, 130 miles to the south Taffy 1 came under attack at around 0800 by planes from a Japanese airfield still operational on the Philippine island of Luzon. The four bomb-laden planes, instead of making standard attacks, came straight into a dive on the four escort carriers. Two were shot down, but two crashed into the *Santee* and *Suwanee*, blasting large holes in both flight decks and wreaking considerable hangar damage. The *Santee* would also suffer damage from a single torpedo, but both ships were well-built converted oil tankers and were operational again within hours. Around 1100 hours, after Kurita had retired from battle, the already battered Taffy 3 came under a similar attack. One plane struck the *Kitkun Bay* glancingly, but its bomb exploded, causing considerable damage. The hapless *Kalinin Bay*, already wounded by thirteen shell hits, received two planes on the flight deck which inflicted further massive damage. But the *St. Lô* would suffer worst: a plane punched through the flight deck and detonated in the hangar amongst unstowed bombs and torpedoes, setting the little ship blazing stem to stern as she began to disappear beneath the waves. This new form of attack drew its name from Japanese legend, a name that would become well known to Americans and infamous in history: *kamikaze*.

CHAPTER 11

Kamikaze

November 26, 1944, was the third anniversary of the day the First Carrier Strike Force weighed anchor and slipped out of the fog-shrouded waters of the Tankan Bay to begin the first leg of its journey to start a war. In the three years since that fateful day, Japan's empire had shrunk to almost nothing and the fleet which had built that empire was now a shattered ruin.

Just days ago, the Imperial Navy, increasingly a navy in name only, commissioned the brand new aircraft carrier *Shinano* into service. Converted on the slipway from the hull of what was to have been the third *Yamato*-class battleship, the Shinano, at 69,000 tons, was the largest aircraft carrier ever built and the most modern in the Imperial Navy. She was Japan's answer to the *Essex*-class, a fast ship with large hangar spaces which could accommodate an attack wing of over 90 aircraft, heavy antiaircraft defenses, and an armored flight deck to withstand heavy pounding. She also incorporated a hurricane-bow, a feature common to British flattops for better handling in rough seas. The Shinano represented the apex of Japanese aircraft carrier development and would be a proud addition to what was now a desperate, shrinking fleet.

On the 27th, the Shinano was undergoing a very abbreviated shakedown on the way to her final fitting out in the Inland Sea when she sailed right into the crosshairs of a periscope belonging to the submarine USS *Archerfish*, herself a newly commissioned fleet boat out on her first combat mission. Commander J.F. Enright could have licked his chops at the prize before him. He bided his time, took range and bearing, and fired a full spread at the carrier's starboard side. Four torpedoes struck the unprotected ship. She had no watertight doors; they had yet to be installed. The compartments began free-flooding, damage control crews panicked, and with no effective countermeasures in operation, the brand new Shinano, without seeing so much as a single day of front line service, rolled over and sank, taking 500 of her crew with her. Also going down with the ship, stowed on the hangar deck, were 50 newly built Okha suicide bombs, the

219

Third Fleet battleships enter Lingayen Gulf in the Philippines. Envisioned as the ultimate weapon as far back as World War I, the battleship by this time had been relegated to the role of offshore artillery. National Archives 80-G-59525.

deadly cherry blossoms developed for service in the new Special Attack Corps: the Kamikaze Corps.

Only a desperate nation steeped in the belief in Divine Assistance, whose culture was awash with the history and legend of noble sacrifice and honorable suicide in the service of the Emperor, all in combination, could have conceived of anything like the Kamikaze. The inspiration was taken from the distant past. In 1281, Japan faced national annihilation from the forces of Kublai Khan and the expanding Mongol Empire. The Khan's fleet was sailing into Japanese waters carrying an invasion force to conquer the Home Islands when an unexpected typhoon blew up at the moment the enemy were approaching the shores, when Japan needed Divine Assistance the most. The storm wiped out the fleet and the Mongols never again attempted to invade Japan. The typhoon was christened in legend as the Divine Wind: kamikaze.

Kamikaze — the new and deadly element in the equation of war. The *Essex* takes a hit from a suicide plane. National Archives 80-G-273032.

The Special Attack Corps, as it was officially designated, was the brainchild of Yamamoto's former staff officer, Vice Admiral Takijiro Onishi, who helped to plan the Pearl Harbor attack. Formed as part of the Sho-1 defense plan to resist the American invasion of the Philippines, the practical concept was that the antiaircraft defenses on the American ships were too formidable for conventional attack to succeed, as were the Combat Air Patrols which had scored such devastating successes against Jisaburo Ozawa's squadrons months ago. But a manned bomb, so to speak, disregarding fighter attack and antiaircraft and boring into the target, would have a better chance of success. The calculus was certainly tempting: one man with his bomb-laden aircraft could trade his life for the destruction of an entire warship and its crew, or even for an entire aircraft carrier and its air wing, either directly if it happened upon the ship when its planes were boarded, or indirectly by denying the enemy squadrons their landing platform at sea. The appeal of the plan was also hypnotic, striking every deep chord of emotional and spiritual belief in the indomitability

of the Japanese spirit. To die gloriously in the destruction of the enemy
would set one among the Gods themselves, a well-earned divinity achieved
with the sacrifice of a mortal life which was itself a mere shadow of existence. The prospect of such a perfect merger of myth and reality, of poetry
and war, proved irresistible. The first volunteers for the Special Attack
Corps were overwhelmed with emotion at their selection, while those
rejected cried bitterly at failing to qualify.

The kamikaze appeared too little and too late to halt the Leyte invasion. But the results achieved were far greater than the conventional air
attacks carried out by the Japanese land-based squadrons and those
Ozawa's planes had scored, sinking the CVE *St. Lô* and putting another,
the *Santee*, totally out of action. While the Americans battled to retake the
whole of the Philippines, there remained the chance of repulsing the invasion by striking at its sea-based support. On that basis, Onishi received
150 aircraft (out of 300 requested) to use for his Special Attack squadrons.
The aircraft were scraped up from whatever was available from untouched
airfields and training centers, regardless of condition since all they had to
do was fly long enough to reach and dive into the target. The same went
for the later recruits, exceedingly young and inexperienced pilots given
only a minimal amount of flight training, as much as was needed to learn
to take off in a plane, fly straight, and put the craft into a dive. Two weeks,
if that. The targets would be the transports bringing in reinforcements
and supplies as well as their fleet protectors. Specially targeted would be
the carriers, whose air support was vital to sustaining the American invasion effort. With their elimination the invasion would die on the vine.

The next appearance of the kamikaze occurred as American task forces
were launching strikes against Luzon to disrupt the new Tokyo Express
reinforcement and resupply operation set up to sustain the enemy defenders. The carrier *Ticonderoga*'s squadrons had finished sinking the heavy
cruiser *Kumano* while savaging two coastal convoys when she and the rest
of Task Force 38's carriers fell under attack by thirteen suicide planes.
They came in two waves and were escorted in by nine fighters. The planes
scored hits and inflicted severe damage on the *Essex* and her sisters *Intrepid* (a hapless ship which seemed to attract torpedoes, bombs, and
kamikaze planes in such profusion that she earned rather quickly a bad
reputation and was known in the fleet as the *Evil I*; also *Dry I* and the
Decrepid for the amount of time she spent in drydock) and *Hancock*, and
the light carrier *Cabot*. American operations continued unimpeded, however, a fact which would continue to be lost upon the Japanese as the
kamikaze campaign wore on.

The American invasion next moved on to Mindoro, vital stepping stone to Luzon, the main Philippine island. Kamikaze planes were transferred to Luzon on December 15 as MacArthur's forces were swarming ashore — thirteen suicide Zekes in addition to the last forty Japanese planes still operational in the whole of the Philippines. Too late to affect the outcome on Mindoro, they were held in reserve for the eventual American effort against Luzon. As the ships of the Third and Seventh Fleets entered Lingayen Gulf on January 6 to commence minesweeping operations in advance for moving in Oldendorf's battleships for the pre-invasion shelling, the planes appeared. Three days earlier, a single kamikaze had crashed into the jeep carrier *Ommaney Bay*, which sank the next morning with over a hundred dead. Now, the suicide planes struck the CVEs *Manila Bay*, and *Savo*, the battleships *New Mexico* and *California*, the heavy cruisers *Louisville* and *Columbia*, a destroyer escort, an LCL landing craft and the Australian cruiser HMAS *Australia*. Most of the kamikaze planes were shot down, but it took heavy firing of nearly every gun in the fleet to knock down the planes before they could strike their targets. The skies were literally filled with the black puffs of antiaircraft fire. In what would become characteristic of defense against the kamikazes, the gunners would have to keep firing until the suicide plane was utterly destroyed, merely shooting it down was no longer sufficient in the face of this new form of attack. When the actual landings were underway, kamikazes reappeared and crashed themselves into the baby-flattops *Kadashan Bay* and *Kitkun Bay*, the battleship *Mississippi*, and again the *Columbia* and three more hits on HMAS *Australia*. In addition to the air attacks, the Japanese introduced the Kaiten manned suicide torpedoes with 500-pound explosives in the nose which sank two LCL landing craft and damaged a further four LST craft and an invasion transport. By the time this first kamikaze campaign had ended on the 13th, thirty-nine ships had been damaged and four sunk with a cost of 738 dead and 1,400 wounded. And Halsey's task force, returning from the South China Sea on a commerce-raiding sortie in which forty-four merchant ships were sunk, was attacked by Formosa-launched kamikazes which struck and damaged the carriers *Ticonderoga* and *Langley* and a destroyer. And all this was only a foretaste of what was to come.

As MacArthur's forces crossed the Sulu Sea to land on Luzon in December, the Japanese hastily scrambled the new aircraft carrier *Unryu* into action. The ship had been commissioned six months ago, and though a fine new vessel, she seemed condemned to spend her entire career in the Inland Sea because of the danger from American submarines as well as from a lack of planes, fuel, and crews to man her and the remaining vessels of Japan's disintegrating navy. The imminent invasion of Luzon provided the new carrier with her first opportunity to proceed into battle —

but as a ferry ship. Her hangar deck was loaded with planes, torpedoes, suicide boats and another 30 Okhas such as were carried aboard the ill-fated *Shinano*. The Okhas were piloted bombs, designed for air-drop and, using a powerful rocket engine, could attain a maximum speed of 550 miles per hour, over 100 mph faster than the best carrier plane the Americans had, and crash into a ship at almost 600 mph at maximum dive.

The *Unryu* departed Kure on the 18th with the destroyers *Hinoki*, *Shigure*, and *Momi* as escorts to deliver the kamikaze aircraft to the Japanese defenders at Manila. This time, the force avoided the passage through the Bungo Strait, which was crawling with enemy subs. Instead, Konishi Kaname, the *Unryu*'s captain, took his flattop west through the Shimonoseki Strait, where the USS *Wyoming* had fought the Japanese 81 years ago, and into the China Sea. Unfortunately, the course selected took the small task group right toward the submarine USS *Redfish*, which had been hunting enemy shipping off the China coast. Obligingly, the carrier's zig-zag put her perfectly in the sub's sights, and Commander L.D. MacGregor fired a spread of six torpedoes at his target. The carrier went into a sharp evasive turn to starboard at full speed, managing to avoid all but one of the fish which struck under the island. The hit inflicted severe machinery and control damage which cut electrical power and reduced her speed, as well as setting off fires in the crew spaces and on the hangar deck, where the kamikaze ordnance was stored. MacGregor fired his stern tubes at one of the destroyers but missed. The three destroyers then started a depth-charge run on the *Redfish*, but MacGregor was determined to stick around to get the carrier and had his torpedo crews scramble to reload the tubes while making an evasive circle to get back into position to attack. MacGregor was lucky that day; he had one fish ready in the tube and was lined up on his target just as *Unryu* began to get underway again. He fired while he had his chance. The torpedo ran true and struck the flattop's starboard side — this time abreast of her forward deck lift and nearby ammunition magazines and avgas storage tanks. The results were disastrous. As fires and explosions quickly spread through the bow area, the conflagration reached the hangar deck and set off the Okhas one after another. The flying bombs, meant to be used against enemy ships, blew out the carrier's side instead, and she soon rolled over and sank with the loss of 1,238 officers and men.

The next target for the American thrust across the Pacific was Iwo Jima. Laying right between the Marianas and Japan, it was critical for both sides. It controlled the sea approaches to the Ryukyus and the Home Islands themselves and its capture would bring all the Japanese mainland under the sweep of the B-29s. The newly redesignated Fifth Fleet, with Raymond

Spruance rotated back in command, hit the island starting on February 16, 1945, with a massive offshore bombardment while planes from Task Force 58, six hundred miles away, engaged in sorties against Tokyo itself, destroying planes held in reserve for Iwo's defense. Thirty thousand Marines landed three days later and began the opening round in what would prove to be a vicious, bloody struggle against a fanatical corps of defenders hiding in pillboxes and caves and who would have to be rooted out at the cost of very heavy casualties. The kamikazes reappeared in this campaign. Several ships were crashed into on February 21, inflicting severe damage on the carrier *Saratoga* and sinking another baby-flattop, the *Bismarck Sea*. While fighting would continue to mid–March, the Marines and the Army secured enough of the island to have effective control of it. Land-based Betty bombers hit Task Force 58 on March 19, striking conventionally as well as in suicide attacks and damaging the *Yorktown, Wasp, Enterprise,* and *Franklin.* The latter suffered one of the worst ordeals of any

The kamikazes fail to stop the American advance; U.S. Marines raise the flag on Mt. Suribachi on Iwo Jima, 23 February 1945. National Archives 80-G-413988.

ship of the U.S. Navy in the whole war. Two 500-pound bombs hit the carrier with her decks full of fully armed and fueled planes, the first wave of which were readying for takeoff on the next sortie. Severe fires and internal explosions spread in the same sort of chain-reaction which had destroyed Chuichi Nagumo's carriers at Midway almost three years earlier and took seven hours to quench. The firefighting effort was aided by the heavy cruiser *Santa Fe* which put itself at extreme risk doing so. It was doubtful for a time that she could be saved, and before it was over, half the ship's crew were casualties, 830 dead and 300 wounded. The *Franklin* had to be towed out of the battle area by the heavy cruiser *Pittsburgh* but her engineers were eventually able to restore internal power, and she would make her way back Stateside on her own.

On March 21, the radars of the Fifth Fleet picked up another force of Bettys with a fighter screen heading their way. One hundred fifty Hellcat fighters from the *Hornet*, *Bennington*, *Wasp* and *Belleau Wood* quickly scrambled to meet this force. The first group were disposed of in short order with the loss of only two Hellcats. The main force was set upon shortly thereafter as they came up. The American pilots were surprised to find the Bettys maneuvering slower than usual and showing what appeared to be sets of additional, tiny wings underneath. The enemy bombers were all shot down, but the American pilots did not know that they had busted up the first attempted attack of Okha manned flying bombs. It was the latest loss suffered by a program which as a whole was an operational failure, plagued by misfortune almost at every turn. And of the 800 manufactured, only 50 made it into the field and only three of those ever crashed into a target.

But for all the devastation inflicted in the ultimately futile campaign to defend Iwo, all of it was only a prelude to what awaited the Americans at their next objective: Okinawa. The main island of the Ryukyu Archipelago, it lay only 350 miles south of Kyushu, the southernmost of the Home Islands of Japan. If Okinawa fell, the Americans would have the last stepping stone they needed toward a future invasion. The loss of this island would spell certain disaster for the Empire. It had to be defended at all costs. *All* costs.

The Fifth Fleet closed to bombardment range of Okinawa on April 1 to begin the pre-invasion softening up while Task Force 58 staged air raids against Kyushu which destroyed whole squadrons on the ground and their landing strips; it was a devastating blow which actually paralyzed any Japanese counterattack for several critical days while the troops poured ashore. The kamikazes reappeared on April 6 — 355 in the first assault. The squadrons managed just by weight of numbers to break their way through

USS *Belleau Wood* afire after a kamikaze attack, October 1944. The *Franklin*, in the background, is also afire from a suicide plane strike. National Archives 80-G-342020.

the CAP screen put up by the fleet only to run into the guns of the picket destroyers. Combined, the carrier planes and antiaircraft defenses knocked down 333 of the planes. Twenty-two survived to sink the destroyers *Bush*, *Calhoun*, and *Emmons* with heavy loss of life. They would come in wave after wave after wave for two months.

During the height of the kamikaze siege, not only aircraft carriers were targeted for destruction but also in particular the destroyers which were set out in radar-picket formations circling the fleet and providing advance early warning. Crews on the tincans, in reactive black-humor, took to fashioning large arrows out of bedsheets pointing away from their ships and with "This Way To The Carriers" emblazoned on them. The most savage mauling of the destroyers was suffered by the *Aaron Ward*. Starting at 1822 hours on May 3, a Val dive bomber made the first run at the destroyer. Ploughing its way through thick antiaircraft fire focused on the lone plane, the Val managed to inflict minor damage on the ship when it blew apart and crashed into the sea and pieces of it rained onto one of the gun mounts. The engine smashed into another. The propeller sliced into the aft deckhouse, jamming the entrance door. Cleanup crews found the boot of the pilot with his foot still in it nearby. Minutes later, a second Val appeared and was splashed 1,200 yards from the destroyer. Then, almost at the same instant, a Zeke came in from the port side, slipping in under the radar. It released a 500-pound bomb which detonated below the waterline and jammed the rudders, locking the ship into a circular path, while the plane itself slammed into the superstructure.

The fact that the destroyer was crippled seemed to bring the kamikazes right to her like vultures closing in on a dying animal. In the ensuing attacks, the nearby pickets *Little*, *Luce* and *Morrison* were hit and sunk. More kamikazes appeared to add to the *Aaron Ward*'s ordeal. Her batteries knocked down ten planes before the next one got through to make another hit. Planes from the task force and from Marine airfields already operational on Okinawa appeared to rescue the wounded destroyer. They shot down kamikaze planes left and right, and some Corsair fighters were knocked down by friendly fire. The destroyer was under such murderous attack that the gunners took to simply shooting at anything that was in the skies above, friend or foe.

The attacks continued with no letup. A fifth plane, a twin-engined Betty, was shot down just short of the destroyer's side when two more Vals appeared. One was shot down, but the other was in its dive. Gunfire from the ship and a Corsair on its tail managed to knock the plane from what would have been a fatal crash into the bridge, but the wings clipped the radio masts and sheared off the top of the number one funnel before veering off into the sea. The hit on the funnel also opened the steam valves to the whistle and siren, which blasted forth in what seemed to be the ship's screaming out in its own agony. Then, another Val aimed itself at right at the bridge. One of the forward guns kept up firing and managed to knock the Val off just enough so that it fell short and crashed onto the foredeck instead. Its bomb detached and exploded in the water, but the blast ripped another hole in the already damaged hull. The fireroom flooded, which killed the engines, and the destroyer wallowed to a stop. Another plane came up, a Zeke, which crashed into and wiped out one of the gunnery stations and its crew. Barely a minute after that, there came in another plane low on the deck to starboard. This one slammed into the aft funnel, its bomb blowing the stack, the searchlight tower, and two gun stations into the air and raining shrapnel on the ship, inflicting more casualties. Finally, night fell, and that proved the salvation of the ship. In the morning, rescue ships could see the results of the multiple suicide attacks. The upper works were wrecked, the decks resembled a junkyard coated with blood and shrapnel, and the ship had sunk almost down to its main deck, which remained mere inches above the surface of the water. But somehow, the *Aaron Ward* remained afloat. Her total casualties amazingly numbered only 45 dead and 49 wounded.

On May 11, two bombers threaded their way through the murderous antiaircraft fire put up by the fleet and headed right for Marc Mitscher's flagship, the *Bunker Hill*. One skidded across the flight deck and over the side, but its bomb penetrated to the hangar deck, setting off explosions and fires when avgas lines were ruptured. The second plane slammed into the ship's stern gallery deck, the plane's 500-pound bomb causing more massive damage while the motor flipped up and destroyed the flag office, killing several of Mitscher's staff. After three hours, fires still raged belowdecks. Men roasted alive in the corridors and passages and firefighters were overcome by the smoke and heat. The water poured onto the hangar deck seemed only to float the flaming mixture of avgas and oil and for several minutes it seemed that the captain might be forced to give the abandon ship order. But he came up with a last desperate idea and ordered a 70 degree turn which caused the carrier to heel sharply to starboard. The maneuver spilled the burning fluids overboard, and soon afterward the remaining fires were brought under control, but by the time it was over, the *Bunker Hill*'s casualties numbered at 396 dead. The ship was so heavily damaged that command from there was impossible and Mitscher was forced to transfer his flag to the *Enterprise*, which three days later came under attack from another suicide bomber. The plane skimmed the flight deck until it came down and crashed forward of the island. Its bombs blew out the nearby deck elevator and demolished the forward hangar spaces, and Mitscher was obliged to shift carriers again, this time to the *Randolph*. That hit put the *Enterprise* out of action for what turned out to be the rest of the war; with her other battle scars and hastily repaired damage from the March 19 attack, it was decided to send her back for a full refit and she wouldn't leave the drydock again until October of 1945. By contrast, aircraft carriers of Vice Admiral Sir Bernard Rawlings' British Carrier Task Force, which was now attached to the Fifth Fleet as Task Force 51, suffered

The USS *Bunker Hill* burns 11 May 1945 after suffering two kamikaze hits. The ship was saved, but at the cost of 396 of her crew. Her sister ship, the *Franklin*, suffered over 800 dead as a result of a bombing attack during the kamikaze assault on March 1945. Both ships were put out action for the rest of the war. National Archives 80-G-274266.

comparatively light damage from kamikaze attacks by virtue of fully armored flight decks. There were considerably less vulnerable than the wooden decks of American carriers, though the armour protection cost the ships in plane-carrying capacity and had taken twice as long in building as any American flattop. Nevertheless, the lessons of the British carriers were put into a new carrier class which was building in the United States but would not launch its first unit until after the end of the war.

By the end of the Okinawa operation, 34 ships would be sunk and 368 took damage to varying degrees with the loss of 4,900 men. The kamikaze campaign ultimately petered out from the inevitable depletion of planes available but also, in the end, from a growing disenchantment of the later recruits, many of whom were sent in to die either drunk or even drugged. In the later weeks of the campaign, the kamikaze spirit dried up as increasingly pilots felt like sheep being led to the slaughter — especially after the High Command began simply drafting fliers for suicide duty outright — and an increasing number returned to base claiming they could not find their targets. And when Okinawa fell anyway, and the Americans continued to come on with ever increasing numbers of ships and men and planes, pilots could get no good answer when they began to question their commanders as to what they were accomplishing. And indeed, after Okinawa, the U.S. Navy roamed Japan's seas and American planes ranged over Japan's skies at will. The B-29s, after trying high-altitude precision bombing to bring the Japanese war effort to its knees, then switched to a new and horrifying tactic devised by Twentieth Air Force's commanding general Curtis LeMay: low-level drops of incendiary bombs which set off firestorms in the target cities (easy, given how many of the buildings were constructed of quite flammable wood, bamboo, and rice-paper) and reduced most of them to ashes, killing hundreds of thousands in holocausts which exceeded the horrors of Coventry, Hamburg, and Dresden by several orders of magnitude.

The kamikaze madness, as could almost be expected, had spread to what was left of the Imperial Navy as well. On April 6, the opening day of the kamikaze assault, two submarines, the *Hackleback* and the *Threadfish*, reported to the Fifth Fleet that a group of Japanese warships had left the Inland Sea and were passing through the Bungo Strait to the East China Sea. The dispatch included the information that the lead ship in the formation was a big one; the last battleship the Japanese had left to them, and the greatest of them all.

The *Yamato*, once the pride of the Imperial Fleet, flagship of Admiral Yamamoto at Midway, and which had fired her great 18.1-inch guns in anger for the first time at Samar only five and a half months ago, was

The crew of the USS *Hancock* carries out the grim task of burying their ship-mates at sea; they were victims of the kamikaze assault at Okinawa, April 1945. National Archives 80-G-328574.

accompanied by the light cruiser *Yahagi* and a screening force of eight destroyers which now constituted the "Second Fleet," or "Special Surface Attack Force." They were loaded with the last 2,500 tons of fuel oil available in Japan — enough for a one-way mission, which this certainly was. Under the command of Admiral Seichi Ito, the ten ships of this "fleet," with no air support to back it up, were to challenge the Fifth Fleet, which then numbered some 1,500 surface units including 40 aircraft carriers of various classes and types, 18 battleships, and 200 destroyers. This mission was to proceed to Okinawa, where they would beach themselves on the reef and bombard both the invasion forces and the American fleet. When their ammunition was depleted, the ships were to be scuttled and the crews to join Lieutenant General Mitsuru Ushijima's forces to fight to the last man.

The tiny naval force had no chance of accomplishing anything whatsoever. The mission was an insane, suicidal *Götterdamerüng*, and when the two American subs spotted them the mission was hopelessly compromised.

The next morning, Mitscher dispatched three carrier groups to proceed to intercept position. Forty planes launched and fanned out in a search over the East China Sea. A Hellcat from the *Essex* sighted the *Yamato* and her escorts passing through the Van Diemen Strait and from that point on the superbattleship was doomed. As the force attempted evasive action, Ito watched as the planes gathered into a large pack on the horizon, and a little past 1230 hours they peeled off for the first attack. The dreadnought put up heavy antiaircraft fire but it was badly coordinated, and Helldiver and Avenger bombers swept down upon the massive target. Two bombs struck the *Yamato* and a torpedo opened a hole in her port side. The *Yahagi* also was hit hard, taking a dozen bomb and seven torpedo hits and becoming a charnel house both above- and belowdecks before she began to settle. Four of the destroyers were sent under, although their destruction was purely incidental compared to the main target of Mitscher's planes.

Initially the *Yamato*, despite a portside list, was making good speed and was zig-zagging to attempt to evade the air attacks. But for two hours, the great ship was hammered by successive waves of bombers and torpedo planes in what was a repeat of the battleship slaughter of 1941 which sank the *HMS Prince Of Wales* and *HMS Repulse*. The *Essex*'s planes were joined by those from the *Enterprise, Belleau Wood, Intrepid* and later the *Yorktown*. More bombs fell on the *Yamato*, compromising her antiaircraft defenses, and the portside list exposed part of her belly on the opposite side where she was relatively unprotected. The *Yorktown*'s Avengers pounced on her starboard side, sending in torpedoes set for shallow depths.

Two hours of sustained attack had put eleven bombs and sixteen torpedoes into the doomed *Yamato*. Her superstructure and main deck spaces were a shambled ruin, her guns demolished, and over a thousand men were trapped belowdecks as the ship flooded. Now, internal explosions began to wrack the great ship and she shuddered visibly in her death throes. Then, slowly at first, the last battleship of the Imperial Navy heeled dangerously to starboard. Shells rolling loose on the decks in the ammunition rooms exploded, adding to the damage, and the *Yamato* capsized and sank to the bottom of the East China Sea at 1423 hours, leaving only the smoke columns of her fires in her wake and taking 2,500 of her crew down with her, including Admiral Ito. The Americans had lost ten planes. The remaining four destroyers, all crippled and no longer capable of action of any sort, managed to escape or were allowed to escape because they simply no longer mattered.

It was the last action of the Imperial Japanese Navy, a force which entered the modern age under the legendary Heihachiro Togo and had become a formidable instrument under Isoroku Yamamoto. In only three

The end of an era: the superbattleship *Yamato*, sacrificed for a suicide mission, explodes as she sinks 250 miles north of Okinawa 6 April 1945. Her doom came upon the wings of over 900 aircraft launched against her by Task Force 58. National Archives 80-G-413914.

years, it had been utterly destroyed, overwhelmed by the very war machine Yamamoto feared would rise up to crush Japan and in its last actions had been effectively sacrificed to no effect. What few ships remained were a motley collection of wrecks and cripples languishing in the drydocks, or half-completed ships marooned on the slips, or ships which would never sail again for lack of fuel, ammunition, or crews to man them. In effect, they were little more than scrap metal rusting away in their ports.

The Imperial Japanese Navy had ceased to exist.

CHAPTER 12

Hiroshima

Between mid–June and early August of 1945, the Japanese nation was being pounded into rubble. Sporadic kamikaze attacks on the mighty American armada did nothing to relieve the pressure on Japan. Her navy was no more; the few remaining warships marooned in port, including two aircraft carriers, were destroyed in air raids on July 24 and 28 by Halsey's carrier task forces. Her air force no longer controlled the skies. Virtually every conquest gained in the triumphal years between 1931 and 1942 had been retaken by the Allies in only two and a half years. American armies now occupied Okinawa and Iwo Jima and from there and bases at Saipan and Tinian, launched wing after wing of B-29 bombers which unloaded deadly cargoes of high explosive and incendiary every day. And what they missed, carrier based fighters and bombers and the heavy guns of Halsey's battleships hit. Every major city had been reduced to rubble and some even to burnt out no-man's lands. The planes ranged at will over the skies of Japan, and the Third Fleet had cut all lines of communication to the outside world. The War Council and the generals still talked of death with honor and retribution. The people, as always, endured.

For the men of the United States Navy, however, there was no sense of triumph, because the mighty war machine which had propelled Americans 3,000 miles across the Pacific was now gearing up for the final push. Operation Olympic, the invasion of the southern Home Island of Kyushu, was slated for November of that year, and 190,000 men were scheduled to go ashore, under heavy fire and a new rain of kamikaze attacks, and establish the first beachhead in the conquest of Japan itself. The men who had been through the horrors of Pelileu and Saipan and Leyte, who had just faced hell at Iwo and Okinawa, were preparing themselves, as best they could, for ten times that horror at Kyushu and later, in March of 1946, Honshu — Operation Coronet. Planners were estimating casualties of as many as 69,000 just in the effort to establish the Kyushu beachhead, and the figure was almost certainly a conservative one. Troops from the war in Europe were being reassigned and allocated to the reserves for the pending

Death of a navy: Third Fleet planes bomb and sink the remaining warships of the Imperial Combined Fleet, including empty aircraft carriers, in their home port at Kure, Japan, 24-28 July 1945. National Archives 80-G-30-9660.

invasion. No one was yet calculating how many would fall in fighting to conquer the whole of Japan. Navy men considered this and wondered how many of them would not live to see the day Japan finally surrendered.

The Japanese themselves were preparing for a last-ditch defense of their homeland. Command was being divided, as was the island into five defensive districts. Nearly 10,000 planes—rebuilds of damaged aircraft or those assembled from the last stocks of prefabricated components—had been pulled off the inventories, hidden in camouflaged bunkers and were still available for kamikaze attacks on the American fleet, and the last reserves of aviation fuel had been hoarded specifically for that purpose. There were still two million men under arms available to throw the invaders back into the sea. Preparations were being made to arm the people with any weapon available—even bamboo spears.

Fourteen years earlier, the Japanese Army had invaded Manchuria and soon afterward embarked upon a campaign of conquest and devastation across China which ultimately expanded into a World War. Now the devastation which Imperial forces had visited upon others had come back upon the nation a hundredfold. Now, Japan geared up to face the onslaught of invaders. And in the Imperial Palace, Emperor Hirohito, desiring peace, was powerless to call a halt to the hostilities. The war party was still firmly in power, and even the Cabinet ministers he had appointed for the express purpose of finding a peaceful end to the war were advocating a fight to the end.

By May 20, 1945, Tokyo had been removed from the list of major industrial targets because the city had been utterly devastated by the LeMay fire raids. Indeed, the initial campaign Curtis LeMay had planned to run for three months had ended in only six weeks because the Twentieth Air Force had run out of targets. For the remaining industrial capacity, the situation was bleak. Steel production was down to only a third of the annual quota, as was aircraft production. Japan was running out of aluminum, iron, coal and oil. The railways had been utterly smashed, and the naval blockade was preventing even coastal transport from operating. The home-based assembly shops upon which so much of the Nation's industry was dependent were obliterated in the fire raids, which was one of the objectives of LeMay's campaign, and in itself was causing production to grind to a halt. The factories were all smashed and destroyed and the brutal reality was that total national collapse was a mere question of time. Courtiers in the Privy Council were already beginning to fear the possibility of a revolution. The death of Franklin Roosevelt on April 12 had not slowed the American advance by so much as a single day or an inch. And on May 8, Nazi Germany had surrendered unconditionally after the suicide of Adolf Hitler seven days before in his Berlin bunker headquarters. Japan was now totally alone and, bushido aside, the certainty of military defeat was looming over the horizon, closing in on them inexorably with each passing day.

Baron Kantoro Suzuki, a 78 year old retired Admiral and the new Prime Minister as of mid–April, publicly renewed the determination of the nation to fight to the very end. In secret, however, he and the other cabinet ministers were charged with finding a face-saving out, a means to end the war and somehow avoid the ignominy of surrender. Most importantly, their priority was to preserve the institution of the Emperor. Peace feelers were sent indirectly to the Allies through the Swiss consulate while simultaneous efforts to secure Soviet mediation were pursued. Contrary to the terms of the Axis pact, the Tojo government had signed a non-aggression treaty with the Soviet Union back in 1941 and had remained neutral in regards to the Nazi-Soviet war. That treaty had now expired and Josef Stalin, desiring a share in the spoils of victory in the Pacific, had already agreed to enter the war on the Allied side imminent to the planned

American invasion of the Home Islands. As a result, he was certainly not inclined to renew the neutrality pact. But he had his foreign minister, Vyacheslav Molotov, entertain the Japanese negotiators until he had sufficient forces transferred to the Far East, after which point all negotiations would be terminated and a formal declaration of war would be issued.

On April 25, the new American president, Harry S Truman, was at last fully informed of what had been the single greatest secret of the entire war — the development project of a wholly new type of superweapon, an atomic bomb. The news was presented to him by Secretary of War Henry Stimson and General Leslie Groves as the first session of the new United Nations organization was convening in San Francisco. Consideration of the proper employment of the bomb was conducted concurrently with the final planning for Operation Olympic. Following the collapse of Nazi Germany, Truman took the knowledge of this new superweapon to the Potsdam conference of the allied leaders in July, while the components for the weapon itself were being delivered to Tinian Island by the cruiser USS *Indianapolis*, a ship whose mission was crossed by fate — for after successfully delivering her precious cargo, she would be torpedoed by the submarine I-58. Because of the secrecy attending her voyage and the ship sinking with no time to get off an SOS, only 316 of the ship's crew of 1,000 would survive the disaster.

While Truman, Stalin, and Churchill were meeting in Germany, the Japanese negotiators were becoming increasingly aware that their efforts of a rapprochement with the Soviet Union were all but doomed. And in Tokyo, the government and the nationalists were becoming increasingly alarmed by the cant of the United States Congress and press demanding that "Hirohito must go" and placing on the head of the Emperor the sole responsibility for every atrocity committed in the war. Increasingly, Japanese leaders perceived that their enemies would settle for nothing less than the utter humiliation of the nation, and with each passing day it seemed the only course left was to choose death before dishonor, even if it meant death for the entire nation. In this environment, the conditions were just ripe for a single blunder to bring forth disaster. Indeed, it was yet one more of the savage ironies of this particular war that had begun with a terrible diplomatic blunder that its end would be determined by another. On July 26, the allied leaders had issued the joint statement which became known as the Potsdam Proclamation. Its direct object was a call for the immediate and unconditional surrender of Japan, stating explicitly that the failure to do so would result in "prompt and utter destruction." Since no reference whatsoever was made regarding the possible future status of the

Emperor, Admiral Suzuki issued what he took to be a statement of "no comment." But the word he used was *mokusatsu*. Translated from the Japanese, it meant to "kill something with silence" or to "treat it with contempt." Under such grave circumstances it was the single most dreadful response imaginable. The Allies took Suzuki's statement as an outright rejection.

But almost no one could have even remotely conceived what was coming next.

In the early dawn hours of August 6, a very small force of B-29 bombers took off from Tinian and set course for Japan. Leading the formation was the *Enola Gay*, piloted by Colonel Paul Tibbets. He and the other crews of the 509th Composite Group were headed for the port city of Hiroshima, which had largely escaped the bombings visited upon other cities. The residents thought themselves lucky — and safe. Rather, they had been reserved for something "special."

Perfect weather reigned that morning. The people were about their morning business, heading for the offices and the schools and the defense plants. A cautionary air raid siren blew, and people saw a lone B-29 over their heads. But since the B-29s seemed to use Hiroshima as a navigational point for the raids on other cities, there was no alarm among the populace of the city which had once been home port for the Combined Fleet and the home of Isoroku Yamamoto, who had foreseen the downfall of his nation but could never, in his deepest, darkest nightmares, have foreseen this day.

At exactly 8:15 a.m. local time, the plane released a single object, then went into a diving turn and veered away from the city at high speed. People watched as the object dropped to within 2,000 feet above the headquarters compound of the Second Imperial Army.

Then, the fireball blossomed forth.

When the blast wave from *Little Boy*, a uranium-collider type atomic bomb, swept over the city from which the Hawaii Operation had been conceived and launched five years ago, the war had finally come full circle. In its wake, 70,000 lay dead or dying in what was a vast, blackened wasteland where only moments before a city had existed. Weeks later, people would still be dying from radiation sickness, a whole new element added to the equation of war. Years later, people would still be suffering and dying from radiation induced cancers and their children would and do live to this day under the shadow of that fatal mushroom.

Three days later, *Fat Man*, the world's second plutonium bomb after the *Trinity* test-device detonated at Alamorgodo, New Mexico, obliterated the city of Nagasaki, which was only a hundred or so miles north of

Nagasaki, 9 August 1945. Five days later, Japan would announce it will surrender. National Archives 308-N-43888.

the bay in which the rehearsals for the Pearl Harbor attack had been staged every day for months, entertaining the fisher-folk of Kagoshima with what they had come to call the Navy's "flying circus." The two bombs which had wreaked such terrifying devastation and had opened the door to the potential annihilation of all mankind had been the end-result of the most expensive and complex scientific enterprise ever undertaken up to that time and initiated originally in response to the possibility of a Nazi atomic bomb. President Franklin Roosevelt, who was first warned of this terrifying threat in the form of a letter from physicists Albert Einstein and Leo Szilard, had spent two years in the effort to win financing for the American nuclear endeavor and was finally able to sign the order authorizing the Manhattan Project on December 6, 1941—just one day before the attack on Pearl Harbor.

Full circle.

Two days after Hiroshima was destroyed, the Soviet Union dropped all pretense at negotiation and declared war upon Japan, sending forty Red Army divisions across the Manchurian border on signal. The Japanese troops could not stop the swarm of tanks and soldiers upon their positions and were easily swept into headlong retreat. Hours after Nagasaki's destruction, the War Council convened in emergency session in an air-raid bunker under Tokyo's Obunko Library to determine the nation's future. Foreign Minister Mamoru Shigemitsu argued immediately that Japan now had no choice but to surrender. The nation could not endure the hardship of the war any longer, and it was now obvious that the United States could effortlessly destroy their entire country and its people and there was absolutely nothing their military could do to prevent it. The War Minister, General Korechika Anami, rejected even the suggestion of surrender outright, urging that even in the face of annihilation, the nation had to fight to the very end.

In effect, the War Minister was now calling for an act of national suicide. And with the council deadlocked and the life or death of Japan now literally hanging in the balance, Admiral Suzuki turned and asked the Emperor to decide the issue.

Admiral Suzuki's request was as complete a violation of the Imperial constitution as well as national tradition as was conceivable. For centuries, the Emperor had been little more than a figurehead, a symbol of the nation and its living link with the gods but with no actual power in the rulership of the country. The Imperial authority was instead based upon extraordinarily subtle and complex concepts connected with his divinity. His role was to give assent to the ruling council, not direct it — though because every Japanese owed personal loyalty to the Emperor, he could express his feeling upon an issue and thus motivate, in a limited fashion, the course of decisionmaking. Such subtle and unspoken influence had caused the extension of diplomatic efforts to find a genuine solution to the crisis between the United States and Japan before the outbreak of the war. For the Emperor to respond to Admiral Suzuki's request, however, would be an equally gross violation of tradition, constitution, and decorum, but Hirohito seized the opportunity offered to him to save his people from destruction, the only one he would ever get.

The room fell silent when he spoke. "I cannot bear to see my innocent people suffer any longer." To carry on the war, he went on to say, would amount to an utterly futile prolongation of cruelty and bloodshed. And so, to avert this, he would accept the terms of the Potsdam Proclamation. Japan would surrender.

The Truman administration decided to clarify the status of the Emperor to facilitate the political solution to the war, stating that the Emperor "would be subject to the Supreme Commander of the Allied powers." Controversy arose in the Imperial cabinet as to what this statement meant until it was quickly rationalized that the Emperor had always "been subject" to the authority of the Shogunate in ancient times and later to the Diet after the Meiji Restoration, and that in like context the Emperor's position would clearly continue to exist.

On August 14 the Domei News Agency told the Japanese people to expect a formal Imperial announcement which would be broadcast the next day over the NHK radio network. From Pearl Harbor, Fleet Admiral Nimitz issued a formal Peace Warning to all U.S. Pacific forces and ordered them to stand down from further offensive operations—though to remain in a state of defensive alert in case of kamikaze attacks by die-hard fanatics refusing to believe that the war was over. The precaution was prudent; even as the announcement of the surrender went forth, a Judy bomber made a run on the *HMS Implacable* of Vice Admiral Rawlings' Royal Navy Task Group. The Judy was followed by a flight of kamikaze planes, but instead of pressing the attack, the pilots obeyed the Emperor's order to cease hostilities. After circling in formation for a few minutes, they all dove and crashed themselves into the sea within the sights of the *Implacable*'s antiaircraft gunners. The preparations for Operation Olympic were immediately suspended. Word of the Japanese surrender spread like wildfire throughout the Pacific. William Halsey, aboard the flagship *Missouri*, threw off his cap and cheered aloud. He recalled the airstrike mission launched from Marc Mitscher's carriers, but ordered Combat Air Patrols to remain aloft to "investigate and shoot down all snoopers ... but in a friendly sort of way."

That night, the Emperor recorded his statement in a specially set up studio in the Imperial Palace, finally getting the recording to his satisfaction on the third take, and the wax discs were locked up in the wall safe of the court chamberlain Yohiro Tokugawa, a 17th generation descendent of the dynastic shogun, Ieyasu. It proved a wise precaution, because during the night a group of Imperial Army officers led by Major Keni Hatanaka stormed the palace grounds, seeking to seize the Emperor to persuade him to rescind the surrender, to destroy the recordings, and to execute the members of the Cabinet who comprised the peace faction. Admiral Suzuki was spirited away from the Prime Minister's residence minutes before another band of conspirators set it afire. Forged orders bearing the seal of General Takeshi Mori, who had been shot and decapitated by the conspirators, were sent to Eastern Army headquarters calling for troops to occupy the palace. But as dawn arose on the 15th, the coup had clearly failed. Eastern Army command refused to obey the forged orders and sent not a single man to aid Hatanaka. The Emperor was safe from the conspirators as were the discs. Hatanaka and four of his band promptly killed themselves. General Anami, a sympathizer but not a participant, took the whole blame for the Army's failure to win the war upon himself and subsequently committed seppuku. His was only the first of a wave of ritual suicides which swept through the ranks of the decimated Imperial military establishment. They could not face the shame of having lost the war — the first war to be lost by the Empire in 2,500 years — and they would not suffer themselves to live in a Japan which would now be humbled and powerless, ruled by *gaijin*. A second incipient rebellion led by Imperial Navy Captain Ammyo Kosono, who attempted to seize control of the airstrip at Astugi, collapsed when Prince Takematsu, the brother of the Emperor, led troops to put it down. Kosono was dragged off in a straitjacket, a raving madman.

At 11 a.m. on August 15, 1945 (August 14th in the United States), known in the Imperial calendar as the 20th year of Showa, millions of Japanese prostrated themselves before their radios as, for the first time in history, the people heard the voice of their God-Emperor. In a thin, reedy monotone, speaking in a somewhat archaic formal dialect, they listened as the Emperor declared that "the military situation can no longer take a favorable turn."

"Moreover," the voice continued, "the Enemy has begun to employ a new and inhuman bomb, the power of which to do damage is indeed incalculable, taking a toll of many innocent lives. To continue the war under these circumstances would not only lead to the annihilation of Our Nation, but to the destruction of human civilization as well." As the broadcast came to a close, the Emperor admonished that in order to pave the way for a grand peace for future generations, they would now have to endure the unendurable.

The morning of the 15th, Nimitz finally received formal orders from Ernest King terminating the war. The Congress appointed Douglas MacArthur the Supreme Commander of the Allied Powers, and charged him to receive the surrender of the Imperial government and subsequently to act as military governor of Japan. On his shoulders would lie the great twin tasks of rebuilding the devastated nation and the transformation of its society from militaristic feudalism to modern democracy — on the American model, naturally.

The day after the Imperial broadcast, Vice Admiral Matome Ugaki, onetime chief staff officer to the late Isoroku Yamamoto, was unable to accept the Emperor's plea for peace and acceptance of the surrender terms to the Allies, and resolved to lead a final kamikaze attack upon the ships of the American fleet at Okinawa. Issuing orders to the 701st Air Group, Ugaki proceeded to their base at Oita to personally take command of the mission. When he arrived, he found not three but eleven planes and their pilots waiting to follow him to the death.

En route, a message was received from Ugaki's command ship. In his statement, the admiral maintained that he alone was to blame for failure in the effort "to defend the homeland and to destroy the arrogant enemy. I am going to make an attack at Okinawa where my men have fallen like cherry blossoms. There, I will crash into and destroy the conceited enemy in the true spirit of bushido, with the firm conviction and faith in the eternity of Imperial Japan."

Four planes were compelled to turn back due to mechanical difficulties, but the remaining seven pressed on. At 1924 hours a last message was received that Ugaki's plane was diving upon a target and that the other six were going in after him.

That was the last that was ever heard of Matome Ugaki. His final fate remains a mystery to this day, because no American or British unit reported any sort of attack or even any sign of Japanese aircraft that evening.

In 1907, a 22 year old Ensign William Halsey, sailing with Teddy Roosevelt's Great White Fleet on its worldwide cruise announcing the arrival of the United States to the ranks of world powers, caught his first sight of Fuji, the sacred Imperial mountain. Thirty-eight years later, he was now riding again into Tokyo Bay aboard his flagship as the first occupation troops debarked by plane at Yokosuka on August 28. Fleet Admiral Nimitz flew out to Tokyo and established himself aboard the *South Dakota*. Originally, the surrender was to be signed on land, and this caused some resentment on Nimitz's part, which he was none too hesitant to voice since he saw it as an insult to the Navy which had carried the burden of conquering the Pacific Ocean. In the end, Navy Secretary James Forrestal solved the problem by proposing to President Truman that the instruments of surrender should be signed aboard the ship named for his own home state and that it was altogether appropriate for Admiral Nimitz to sign the documents for the United States as Commander-in-Chief of the Pacific Fleet. Truman readily concurred. The surrender would be received on the quarterdeck of the *Missouri* on September 2, 1945.

For the ceremony, William Halsey had the American flag that Commodore Matthew Perry had flown aboard the USS *Susquehanna* 92 years ago shipped out to him from the U.S. Naval Academy Museum, where it was proudly displayed above the table upon which the instruments of surrender were to be signed. It was an overcast day as Allied generals boarded the Third Fleet flagship, followed by Nimitz and MacArthur, whose flags flew side by side on the mainmast. Lastly, there came the Japanese delegation led by Foreign Minister Shigemitsu and General Yoshijiro Umezu, representing the Imperial General Staff. Officers, enlisted seamen and Marines crowded every inch of space of the *Missouri*'s aft upper works to witness the day they had all ached for and many thought they would never live to see.

MacArthur opened the ceremonies with a dignified address and then invited Shigemitsu and Umezu to sign the documents on behalf of the Empire of Japan. Next to sign was General Joseph Wainwright, frail and emaciated after three and a half years in a Japanese POW camp. He had endured brutal treatment and starvation and had been reunited with his former commanding officer only the previous night. After him came General Sir Arthur Percival, who had been forced to surrender at Singapore. Only then did MacArthur sign on behalf of the Allied powers, followed by Nimitz for the United States and each delegate in turn for his own nation.

With the signings complete, the 70 year old Supreme Commander addressed the assembled crowd on what was now the "temple of peace," as one of the Japanese delegates had poetically called the *Missouri*'s quarterdeck:

> The issues, involving divergent ideals and ideologies, have been determined on the battlefields of the world and hence are not for our discussion or debate. Nor is it for us here to meet, representing as we do a majority of the people of the Earth, in a spirit of distrust, malice, or hatred. But rather it is for us, both victors and vanquished, to serve, committing all our peoples unreservedly to faithful compliance with the understandings they are here formally to assume. It is my earnest hope, and indeed the hope of all

mankind, that from this solemn occasion a better world shall emerge out of the blood and carnage of the past. A world dedicated to the dignity of man and the fulfillment of his most cherished wish for freedom, tolerance, and justice. Let us pray that peace be now restored to the world, and that God will preserve it always. These proceedings are closed.

Almost as if on cue, at 0925 the sun broke through the clouds and shined down upon the *Missouri*. And upon that moment, accompanied by a low rumble, a formation of B-29 Superfortresses overflew the fleet. Followed by another and another and another. Wave after wave of aircraft, B-29s, Mustangs, Lightnings, Hellcats, Thunderbolts, Hellcats, Helldivers, Avengers, and Corsairs—1,900 planes in all—filled the skies above Tokyo Bay saluting not just victory but peace. With the surrender concluded, Shigemitsu and Umezu were saluted as dignitaries of a future ally and not treated as vanquished prisoners.

The war was over.

Opposite top: General of the Army, Douglas MacArthur, signs the peace treaty ending the Second World War on the quarterdeck of the USS *Missouri*, 2 September 1945. National Archives 80-G-348366. *Bottom*: The Third Fleet in Tokyo Bay, 2 September 1945. The 1,900 planes carried aboard the fleet's 50 aircraft carriers fly over the flagship *Missouri* immediately after the treaty is signed. National Archives 80-G-421130.

CHAPTER 13

Aftermath

"These proceedings are closed."

And with those words, it was over. A hideous war which had cost nearly four and a half million lives was ended. And the casualty count of the Pacific War was only a small fraction of the total number of dead around the globe. World War II, in all its totality, destroyed 55,000,000 lives, had destroyed organized civilization across two continents, and was marked by the opening of doorways into the darkest of old evils and the stark terror of a new one.

The atomic bomb completely changed the equation of warfare from that point forward. Used primarily to finally bring the Japanese to the surrender table, the Bomb was also America's "Big Stick," which President Harry Truman was quite eager to wield to keep the Soviet Union at bay. At the Potsdam meeting in which the surrender proclamation was announced, Truman had let slip to Josef Stalin the existence of the new superweapon. Quite to the disappointment and certain consternation of Truman and his entourage, Stalin merely replied coolly that he hoped it would be "put to good use" and betrayed no more emotion than the most subtle of poker players. Once back in Moscow, Stalin proceeded quickly to assemble a specialized unit of physicists and engineers, placed them in the charge of the dreaded head of the Soviet secret police, Lavrentri Beria, and ordered them to go forward with a crash program to produce a Soviet atomic bomb. Helping in the effort were Soviet moles lodged deep in the hierarchy of Los Alamos who duly passed along detailed technical information, though no one should underestimate the capabilities of Soviet nuclear physicists and engineers or discount the fact that in science, there are no secrets. The Soviet Union would eventually have cracked the secret of the atomic bomb for themselves, but the work of spies like Klaus Füchs helped them to speed up the development of their project — so much so that the Soviets exploded their bomb in 1949, only a scant four years since Hiroshima and up to ten years before any Western expert believed it possible.

By the time of that event, a new Cold War had already been in force. In Europe, the Soviet Union had proceeded to carve out of the destroyed continent its sphere of influence, as per their understanding of the Yalta Accords of early 1945, in which the Allies divided up the continent amongst them. The effort to rebuild a shattered Europe became a sharp clash of ideologies and, inevitability, war machines for the next fifty years. But despite the new military face-off which characterized the most intractable political struggle ever known, neither side would send armies pell-mell across the frontier. The Bomb had changed the equation. A bomb now equaled an army, and it could erase it or a city in less than a second. The United States used its then-pitiful but ever growing stock of atomic bombs to ward off the threat of Soviet divisions swarming across the West, until the Soviets ultimately had their own stockpile and both settled into an arms race which extended the Bomb's range globally with jet-powered intercontinental bombers and global-range ballistic missiles. In the end, the American-Soviet arms race bankrupted the one nation almost completely and nearly bankrupted the eventual winner.

But neither superpower would risk all-out nuclear war. For all the sabre-rattling and global military maneuverings which would ensue in the threatening years of the Cold War, neither side moved to take that last step to full-scale war, because it was too easy for an American or Russian to see Hiroshima in his nightmares and envision Washington, Moscow, New York, Leningrad, Chicago, and Kiev as radioactive ruins. The advent of hydrogen weapons, bringing the power of nuclear fusion within man's reach — and also that of the total destruction of human civilization as well — led to a circumspection which world powers had never exercised in all of human history and yet now exercised with the greatest of care. Caught in the middle were the civilians, billions of them, who would for three generations be born, come of age, and live under the shadow of annihilation.

Europe, whose cities would be rebuilt within a decade through the Marshall Plan, would remain firmly gripped in a vise between East and West for the next forty-five years. But in the Pacific Ocean, the United States was preeminent. Douglas MacArthur, the Supreme Commander of the Allied Powers, headquartered himself in Tokyo's American Hotel, a building designed in the 1920s by Frank Lloyd Wright, as the *de-facto* Shogun, and from his palace he would proceed to remake Japan from top to bottom.

When, in a speech before the public given on January 1, 1946, Emperor Hirohito definitively disavowed his own divinity, he heralded the beginning of a New Japan. While an army of construction engineers, designers, machinists, and laborers proceeded to rebuild the devastated cities, MacArthur's political officers proceeded to remake the social and political fabric of the land. A new constitution — drafted on the American model — formed the framework for a new, democratic and pacifist government. Women were given the vote and new laws were written ending many of the barriers between them and employment in the professions and other fields closed to them. Labor unions were legalized and organized, under the theory that a strong trade-union movement would further foster democracy and also check the power of the *zaibatsu*, the entrenched industrial combines which had dominated Japan's prewar and wartime economies in ways that even the most powerful Trusts of America's Gilded Age never could in the United States. Finally, as an ultimate signal of the Empire's total Westernization, the game of baseball — which had been considerably popular before the Kodo-dominated regime outlawed it — was reestablished and quickly became Japan's national passion. Indeed, with their inherent capacity for adaptation, the Japanese embraced the changes which were imposed over a gradual period of six years. By the time the calendar rolled around to the year 1951, Japan had been transformed more completely and profoundly than even the greatest dreams of Emperor Meiji aspired to. She had been modernized, democratized, pacified, and as far as was possible in an Oriental nation, thoroughly Americanized. Japan became an economic powerhouse and a bastion of Western ideology in what, on the Mainland, became a largely Communist Asia. The forces of Mao Tse-Tung, finally triumphing in a long civil war on the Chinese mainland, would claim rule of the Middle Kingdom, which soon became a Soviet ally, though that alliance would eventually prove not a long-lasting one. Japan would be a forward base in prosecuting a minor war, or as was to become the pleasant misnomer, "police action," against Soviet-backed forces in Korea, another Asian nation wracked by civil war which would be bloodily concluded in a standoff which persists to the present day, while the French would soon find themselves in a losing fight to retain their Far Eastern empire, as Indochina was lost in a war with the independence movement in Vietnam, which split between American and Soviet lines. While the American-backed forces created the independent nation of South Vietnam, Ho Chi Minh would seat himself in Hanoi as President of the Communist Democratic Republic of North Vietnam, setting the stage for America's most problematic war.

Before World War II, half of Asia was ruled by the old European colonial empires, Britain, France, and Holland. One goal of Japan's war leadership was to drive the Europeans out of Asia. Indirectly, they succeeded in that aim. By the end of World War II, those empires had been broken in the fight to destroy the Axis. Starting in 1948 when Britain finally granted India her independence, ending a century of the Raj, and in a movement which accelerated when France was forced to withdraw from Vietnam, they began leaving en masse. The old colonies gradually became independent states of their own. Britain hung on a little longer through the socioeconomic and cultural alliance of the Commonwealth of Nations, essentially an aggregation of her now independent and semi-independent dominions in Asia, Africa, and the Pacific, but for all intents and purposes the sun was finally setting at last on the British Empire. Gradually, Asia became a mirror for the Cold War, dividing between Communist and Western regimes. But while a large part of the East turned Red, the Pacific Ocean became literally an American lake.

The United States Navy, the only fully intact fleet left at the end of World War II, ruled the waves to an extent which not even the British Royal Navy enjoyed at the Empire's zenith. The massive war machine which had destroyed a navy in four years spread out to cover all the world's oceans, patrolling the sea lanes and projecting power far beyond the primitive geopolitics of colonial empire as a prime instrument of global superpower. Over the course of the next twenty-five years, the size of the navy would shrink to less than a third of the warfleet which had filled Tokyo Bay on the day of the Japanese surrender, but as jet planes evolved and missiles gradually became the primary strike weapons of warships, signaling the final death-knell of Big Gun power, the U.S. Navy while gradually shrinking in numbers became a far more deadly instrument. The bulwark of that instrument remained the aircraft carrier, though it too would evolve with the advent of jet fighters, bombers, reconnaissance and electronic warfare aircraft. It was not very many years before the venerable *Essex*-class flattops became outmoded. Their service lives were extended when a number of them underwent gradual modernization with new electronics and hangar facilities, and had built on them angled-decks, enabling the ships to land and launch aircraft simultaneously. The *Essexes* would continue as front-line combat platforms through the fifties, serving again as combat base ships during the Korean War. So too would the numerous jeep carriers which could still launch Corsairs on ground-strike missions. But the days of the prop-engined strike aircraft were numbered as more air forces and navies adopted jets, and as they became bigger, the old World War II veterans were also gradually reaching the end of the line. The *Midway*-class vessels, the first of which was launched after the end of the war, set the pattern for the future. Aircraft carrier development accelerated. In 1953, the first of the supercarriers, the USS *Forrestal*, was launched. She and her sisters *Saratoga*, *Ranger*, and *Independence* were

55,000 ton monsters each measuring over 900 feet long, almost dwarfing what not so long ago were among the most powerful and largest airstrike platforms ever built. They were only the first of the new supercarriers which rule the oceans the way the battleship did less than a century ago. The *Forrestals* were soon followed by the 59,000 ton *Kitty Hawk* (named, appropriately enough, for the North Carolina plain where Wilbur and Orville Wright made the world's first powered flight) and her sisters *Constellation* (continuing a venerable name in naval history), *America* and *John F. Kennedy*, named for the recently assassinated president who wielded the Navy to masterful effect in the blockade of Cuba during the tension-filled days of the Missile Crisis in October 1962, when the world teetered on the brink of the nuclear abyss, and who himself had been a PT-boat commander during the Guadalcanal campaign.

But as these new monster vessels of a more modern, technologically advanced navy — whose ships carried locked up within their hulls more firepower than all the navies of the Second World War combined — increasingly took their place upon the oceans, the World War II navy gradually began to disappear, as was inevitable, naturally. The old *Essexes* were decommissioned one by one. Some were modified to carry a full complement of helicopters and became, for a time, antisubmarine aircraft carriers and thus continued in service for a few more years. But as new destroyers, assault ships and cruisers all capable of boarding their own antisubmarine helicopters came into service, the CVS became redundant in the U.S. Navy. By the 1980s, all but Marc Mitscher's old flagship, the *Lexington*, then the fleet training carrier, wound up in the ever growing mothball fleet; ships partially demilitarized but sealed and cared for in naval yards in a condition to be reactivated if needed. In reality though, they were on the first step of their journey to the breaking yards, to be cut up and turned into razor blades eventually. Some of the cruisers, destroyers, and diesel-electric submarines displaced by more modern nuclear-powered craft would end up being sold to the navies of lesser powers, where they would enjoy an additional twenty years of service life. Some very few would become floating museums, preserved for posterity in various cities across the country to keep alive the heritage of World War II.

Most, though, were simply broken up for scrap. Some vessels of the World War II navy were already long gone, having been sacrificed in the early atomic tests in the Pacific. Among them were several of the Pearl Harbor battleships and the veteran flattop *Saratoga*, assembled in a motley target fleet consisting of battleships hopelessly obsolete at war's end, captured Axis ships including what was left of Japan's Imperial Navy that had been seized as war prizes, and ships too damaged to be worth the

Operation Crossroads, July 1946. Veteran Pacific Fleet warships, including battleships and the aircraft carrier *Saratoga*, are sacrificed to the cause of atomic science. National Archives 80-G-396229.

expense of reconstruction. Petitions to preserve the venerable carrier were too few and too late, and in 1946, in Test Baker at Bikini Atoll, she would have her bottom ripped out while being lofted the length of her hull by the 20-kiloton blast which achieved at last what the Japanese couldn't: sending her beneath the waves.

In 1956, the end came at last for the *Enterprise*. The last surviving sister of the *Yorktown*-class and one of the few vessels which had lasted through the whole of World War II, she had battle-stars for every major campaign and her name had written a legacy of honor and glory in battle in the best traditions of the service. She never boarded aircraft again after her post-kamikaze refit and was finally stricken from the Navy list and earmarked for scrap. Upon hearing of this, the retired Fighting Admiral, William Halsey, energetically began a petition and fundraising drive to save his one-time flagship and symbol of the navy he had helped lead to the most conclusive victory in history as a monument. Halsey and his committee fought for the *Big-E* with all the vigor he once expended against his Japanese enemies. But the effort proved inadequate and untimely, and in the end the ship which Tokyo Rose had declared sunk eight times between 1942 and 1945 would finally be scrapped in 1958.

However, even as the *Big-E* was consigned to oblivion, the Navy was building the prototype atomic-powered aircraft carrier. Nuclear propulsion had already been introduced into the U.S. Navy in the forms of the submarines *Nautilus, Seawolf, Triton,* the three boats of the *Skate*-class, and the world's first nuclear-powered surface warship, the missile cruiser *Long Beach,* which had gone into commissioned service early in 1960. This vessel, however, would be the world's largest surface combat vessel. State-of-the-art and capable of carrying slightly more than 100 strike aircraft, marginally more than any of the *Kitty Hawks,* she was finally commissioned into fleet service in 1961 and this revolutionary flattop was given a name appropriate for her and under which she continues to serve to this day: *Enterprise.*

The U.S. Navy ended up entering the Space Age when the former Navy man and then–President Kennedy committed the United States to the goal of landing a man on the moon before the end of the 1960s. The space program developed at an accelerated pace and its engineers designed space capsules for a splashdown landing in the ocean and at-sea recovery. It would be in this most complex and evolutionarily significant endeavor of the human species that some of the last vessels of the World War II fleet would participate as rescue craft. War machines would now embark on a mission of science and peace. In this pursuit, some of the remaining commissioned *Essex*-class flattops found their last measure of glory; *Lexington, Wasp, Intrepid, Ticonderoga,* and *Hornet* were among those vessels which plucked space capsules and astronauts from the Pacific and Atlantic oceans. Of them all, the *Hornet* would enjoy the singular honor of retrieving the three astronauts of the *Apollo 11* mission, two of whom — Neal Armstrong and Buzz Aldrin — became the first humans to walk the surface of another world.

At the time of writing, it is now 1999, on the cusp of a new millennium. The ranks of surviving veterans of the greatest and bloodiest war in human history are steadily thinning as age claims more and more of them every year. As living memory fades, furious efforts are being undertaken to preserve the heritage of the war as much as possible. But despite the effort of historians, preservationists, and archival researchers (especially those committed to preserving the legacy of the Jewish Holocaust), the Second World War, like most wars, is beginning to disappear from human consciousness. Indeed, people today seem to have no time for history as the pace of change grows ever quicker. Yet the world we live in now is the direct legacy of that war. It was the war which affirmed the principle of democracy over that of fascist militarism and yet split the world right down the middle into two irreconcilably opposed ideologies that faced off against one another in a Cold War which always threatened to heat up into the

Final War. The Cold War has come into vogue for popular historical interest, now that we're no longer in immediate danger of nuclear annihilation and there is no Soviet Union. But the collective psyche of that world split between two nuclear superpowers was an outgrowth of World War II, and national characters were forged in the furnace of that war which still shape their worldviews to the present day. For decades, as an example, the United States determined that it would never suffer a "nuclear Pearl Harbor" and predicated its military policies upon the trauma of that event of December 7 — and hence piled up over 25,000 nuclear weapons in a continuing military buildup which ultimately cost trillions of dollars, while the Soviet Union broke itself in the effort to ensure they would never be invaded again. Germany, for a long time a divided nation by the NATO and Warsaw Pact nations, is now trying to reconcile itself to its Nazi past.

It is a truism that the first casualty of war is truth. Often, truth is also the first casualty of both victory and defeat. The winning side always writes the history, and for decades afterward, it was the popular belief that the Japanese were among the unmitigated villains of World War II. It is true that the Imperial military committed terrible atrocities upon their victims. There is no whitewashing horrors such as the Rape of Nanking and the brutal treatment meted out to war prisoners. Hideki Tojo and others of the Japanese war leadership long ago went to the scaffold for war crimes, but attitudes die hard. Americans who were inured with the image of the "evil, treacherous Jap" would find it impossible to view Pearl Harbor without that hatred rising right back to the surface in a millisecond. But lost in that view was any sense that, from the Japanese point of view, a pre-emptive strike was the militarily correct thing to do. Also lost was the fact that Japan did not intend to launch their attack without the formal announcement of war as laid down in international law, something which Emperor Hirohito was most insistent upon in the weeks leading up to the attack. It was certainly not the intention of Kichisaburo Nomura to deceive the United States and in such a consumingly treacherous fashion, but he was counted as a scoundrel for years afterward and his nation a criminal one by millions of ordinary Americans, who lived and in many ways still do live in a very black-and-white world of good and evil. The notion that only an aggressor nation strikes first is a charmingly naive one which fails to take into account that governments are composed of human beings who make decisions on the same basis that any human makes any decision — that it seemed, at the time, the right thing to do — and that a government will undertake any action it deems necessary to the national survival at any time it sees fit, no matter the consequences. Our own government and press in the present day never find any difficulty in justifying any sort of aggressive military action as preempting the aggression of a potentially dangerous enemy. And also forgotten in the collective American consciousness for decades was the knowledge that it, the Home of the Free, incarcerated several thousand citizens of Japanese descent in internment camps for the sole reason that they were ethnic Japanese. Only now has any sort of responsibility been acknowledged for this most egregious betrayal of the freedoms and principles upon which the United States is based and which it was ostensibly fighting for in World War II.

For forty years, it was an unchallenged fact that the United States was subjected to a deliberately unprovoked surprise attack which caught our military and political leadership totally unawares, in an act of spectacular treachery coming as it did during the course of peace negotiations. However, starting in 1980, several comprehensively researched books began coming out which indicated that knowledge of the possibility of a Japanese attack was known to Roosevelt, his advisers, and the Pentagon but that such was not forwarded to either Husband Kimmel or Walter Short, who both took the full blame for allowing the base to be attacked and suffered the destruction of their careers as a result. To be certain, both Kimmel and Short made several critical decisions which lined the fleet and the air force up just perfectly as targets for Chuichi Nagumo's raiders. But had they been given much clearer warnings than they had received, they would have had a chance to disperse their forces and would have been alert for the strike force as it came in, and the war might have ended right there and then. Some books on the subject have gone as far as accusing Franklin Roosevelt of deliberately concealing his knowledge of a planned Japanese assault so as to have a perfect excuse to bring the United States into war, but eyewitness accounts have testified to the President being in a state of livid anger for days that half of Pearl's air force was caught and destroyed on the ground, and it is taking things a stretch to suggest that the President and George Marshall would countenance the destruction of their primary striking power in the Pacific for a wholly political reason at the expense of their capacity to wage any sort of war at all. Other books have researched the extent to which Britain's wartime Prime Minister Winston Churchill and his advisers — particularly those connected with Bletchley Park's decryption effort — knew of Japanese plans, under the theory that Churchill said nothing of a pending Japanese attack since the event would bring the United States into war against the Axis. But just as the imperative to guard the secret of Magic was so paramount to American military leaders that they would not reveal the extent of their intelligence to outsiders even in the military, it is certain that the British would have guarded the secret of Bletchley Park to the death, especially as its capacity to crack the German Enigma codes was vital to the nation's very survival. Furthermore, a war against Japan was as likely to cause the United States to turn away from concerns with Europe to fight the new enemy as it was to bring them in to the fight against Nazi Germany, so as a gamble for Churchill to take it would have been a potentially suicidal one for Britain. As it was, Adolf Hitler's insanity in declaring war against the United States solved that problem, and the Axis powers were crushed.

For the Japanese people, the war means one thing more than anything else — Hiroshima. They are the only nation to this day which has ever suffered a nuclear attack, and it is impossible for them to contain the horror of it within their consciousness. The Hiroshima Dome, the most famous ruin in history, is the centerpiece of the Peace Park, where at 8:15 a.m. every August 6 a gong sounds out, its mournful toll echoing over a city come to silence. But in the intervening decades, that silence has extended to cover the remaining history of the war, and their nation's responsibility for the aggressions and atrocities she committed in the pursuit of that war. The Japanese do not speak of the war because they have invested a great amount of emotional capital and national pride in being a peaceful nation, whose constitution (written by MacArthur's staff) outlaws war and a military establishment beyond that of a national self-defense force. There have been from time to time nationalists and traditionalists who have argued for Japan to reclaim her place as a great power, but they conveniently forget what happened the last time they tried to achieve that status through war. They also argue with great bellicosity that Japan has nothing to apologize for from the 1930s or '40s. Even they will not speak of the war for one major reason: Japan was defeated. The very concept of defeat — or more to the point, of surrender — is anathema to the Japanese national psyche, which was why only the atomic bomb finally brought about their capitulation. Even then, as the Emperor recorded the text of his surrender announcement, the word "surrender" was never uttered. From that point forward, a great silence regarding the war fell upon the nation and has persisted to this day. It is not substantively taught in history classes. In many ways, this attitude is quite understandable. Defeat carries a powerful and enduring stigma. Americans got a taste of that in the wake of Vietnam, whose ghosts we have yet to fully exorcise. For all that, the knowledge of their defeat, and of the crimes of their aggressions, does persist at a subliminal level, transformed into the nation's decades-long posture of pacifism and diplomacy. But slowly, some voices are heard advocating the need for the nation to reconcile itself with the past. They feel that only through this will Japan finally move on unencumbered into a brighter future, the one intended by Emperor Meiji a century past.

The World War II navy is long gone now. The last surviving vessels to see commissioned service from that time were the four *Iowa*-class battleships, the last ones in all the world. They were reactivated from time to time through the Cold War years, updated in their electronics and eventually fitted with cruise missiles, ostensibly as a more economical alternative to building new missile ships but, in reality, as a bow to those admirals and political leaders who still, even after all this time, believed in the Big Gun. In their subsequent deployments, the *Iowa*, *New Jersey*, *Missouri*, and *Wisconsin* would indeed fire against ground targets in Korea, Vietnam, and Lebanon. They would employ missiles against Libya and Iraq. But a 1989 fatal explosion in the number two turret of the *Iowa*, caused by improperly packed charges in the breech of one of the 16-inch guns, signaled the end at long last of the battleship. The *Iowas* are all decommissioned now and it is certain that they have all seen their last cruises. The *New Jersey* has been earmarked for preservation, while the fates of *Iowa* and *Wisconsin* have yet to be determined. Presently, the *Missouri* is permanently moored at Pearl Harbor, not far from where still lays the wreck of the USS *Arizona*. Long a monument herself, visitors can view the first casualty of the Pacific War from the enclosed observation deck which straddles her. To this day, eerily, every five minutes a drop of her remaining oil in the bunker tanks will bubble up to the surface, a signal to the world from those of her crew who are still manning their battlestations.

Other ships from that period can be found in various port cities around the United States; they are the centerpieces of dockside monumental parks. Some are *Fletcher*-class destroyers and *Balao*-class fleet submarines. Others are the most impressive monuments of any navy, battleships. The *Alabama* can be found in Mobile Bay, while her sister ship *Massachusetts* has long held the place of honor in Fall River harbor. USS *North Carolina* has also long hosted tourists over the years. And, last but certainly not least, there are the few surviving flattops, and all of them veterans of Task Force 58: the *Intrepid*, the *Yorktown*, the *Hornet*, and appropriately, Marc Mitscher's flagship, the Blue Ghost herself, USS *Lexington*, which recently took her place dockside in Corpus Christi, Texas. They are among the last reminders of a war long past and fading more and more from memory.

Other reminders of that war remain dotted on various islands scattered all over the Pacific: long-abandoned airfields where weeds are breaking through the tarmac; concrete pillboxes within which rusted guns still aim outward to face modern invaders— vacation tourist; rusted-out and decaying plane-wrecks, shipwrecks, guns, and tanks, left forgotten on the beaches and in the jungles which returned with a vengeance once the war was over.

And there are the wrecks—hundreds of vessels which litter sixteen million square miles of ocean bottom. No battlefield so totally claims and keeps its dead as an ocean. Tourists who visit Truk Island can go on dives in the bay and see the sunken ships which lay there, destroyed by Marc Mitscher's airmen decades ago and which now are coral reefs, repositories of new sea life. Similar sights are to be found at Eniwetok, Yap, Palau, Saipan, Rota, and Guam, among dozens of other such places. And, there's also Guadalcanal. The single most bitterly contested island of World War II was, fifty years later, the site of an oceanographic expedition mounted by the world's premier undersea explorer, Dr. Robert Ballard, whose greatest claim to fame was his discovery of the *Titanic* in 1985. With his team from Woods Hole Oceanographic Institute, Dr. Ballard proceeded to make a thorough exploration of Ironbottom Sound, cataloging and filming the wrecks, collecting every scientific detail from each vessel to be gleaned while experimenting with undersea search techniques, advanced models of robot submersibles and undersea television scanners, and on the whole advancing his quest to discover and identify as many of these ocean gravesites as possible for posterity. And as impressive as the Ironbottom Sound expedition was, it would be topped by a far greater exploration, which also served as a platform for healing old wounds.

In May of 1998, Ballard and the Woods Hole team would set out aboard the Institute's flagship *M/V Laney Chouest* on one of their most difficult expeditions ever, a quest for the long lost wrecks of Midway, the battle which changed the course of the war. Also on board were some of the last surviving veterans of that battle, grey old men in their late eighties and divided now only by language: *Yorktown* aerial mechanic Bill Surgi, Midway airman Harry Ferrier, *Kaga* pilot Haruo Yoshino and *Hiryu* airman Taisuke Maruyama, who participated in the second attack against the *Yorktown*. They were invited to accompany Dr. Ballard to be on hand when—if—the wrecks of the *Yorktown* and the flattops of Chuichi Nagumo's First Carrier Strike Force were discovered. It would be a difficult search, 16,000 feet down and 9,000 square miles of ocean bottom to comb through, and making it all the harder the fact that no precise coordinates existed for any of the Japanese vessels, particularly where they left the surface. As it was, Maruyama and Yoshino would never glimpse their one-time base ships ever again. But the central prize of Ballard's quest appeared on the monitors in the *Laney Chouest*'s plot room in the morning hours of May 19. Laying upright, listing slightly in the mud, and excepting for the torpedo damage almost perfectly intact, was the USS *Yorktown*, her paint still firmly adhering to the hull and preserving her from the corrosive forces of the deep ocean. Her antiaircraft guns were still in their sponsons and aimed upward, almost as if the ship was still on red alert and ready for action even after fifty-six years. During the expedition, the two American and two Japanese veterans, along with many of the *Laney Chouest*'s crew, gathered on the foredeck to toss a memorial wreath into the ocean and offered a ceremony for the dead of both sides. There were no longer any enemies, just people united in their honoring of those united in death decades ago.

A year later, on the opposite side of the Pacific, another oceanographic expedition set forth to explore and recover artifacts from the wreck of the greatest battleship ever built, the *Yamato*. Sponsored by RMS Titanic Inc., the French research and recovery company Aqua Plus, and Japan's Asahi TV network, the expedition left Sasebo, Japan, and proceeded to the wreck site 250 miles northwest of Okinawa on August 25th, during the Japanese season of Obon — a time of commemoration of one's ancestors. The exploration flotilla consisted of the *M/V Ocean Voyager* and a U.S. Seventh Fleet assault ship which, appropriately, is a namesake of one of the carriers which participated in *Yamato*'s destruction, the USS *Belleau Wood*. The two vessels arrived over the battlewagon's gravesite and proceeded to bring to the surface a number of relics, including the ship's bell. The entire expedition also represented a special memorial honoring the 4,250 men who went down with the supership and five of her escorts. The artifacts recovered are earmarked for display in the Maritime Museum at Kure, the port where the *Yamato* and her sister *Musashi* were built.

A half-century has passed since the end of the war against Japan. The various archipelagos over which warfleets battled one another are independent micro-nations and the island battlefields are vacation spots. Midway, where the power of the Imperial Japanese Navy was turned back, was designated a wildlife refuge in 1988 and given back to her ancestral residents, the goony birds and terns which nested there for thousands of years. Excepting those relics of battles long past, there is virtually no hint that a war ever took place. And as the last veterans age and die, the memory of that war recesses further and further into the mists of time.

It was a war which fundamentally altered the character of naval warfare, created the United States as a superpower, and changed the course of history in ways no one living today can conceive. It was a clash between two disparate cultures which are still divided at some level to this day. Neither may ever fully understand the another, but both took a step in that direction across the abyss of war and forged a common bond in tragedy and in an effort to build something better from the ashes of that war. The armies and navies of both sides were composed of professionals and also of ordinary men who did extraordinary things, the least of which was to carry on through horrors that would blast the souls of most men. Many are forever joined in the brotherhood of death, and their descendants share one thing in common, a determination that such a horror will never happen again. Never again. The great ocean is today what Vasco de Balboa named it when he first discovered it in 1510.

Pacific.

Chronology of Events

8 July 1853 — The United States Navy's Japan Expedition, commanded by Commodore Matthew Calbraith Perry flying his flag aboard the steam-frigate USS *Susquehannah*, arrives in Edo (Tokyo) Bay. Securing a meeting with the Prince of Izu, Commodore Perry delivers a letter from President Millard Fillmore announcing the intent of the United States to establish trading relations.

February 1854 — Commodore Perry returns to Japan, this time with a larger 34-ship fleet. The Treaty Of Kanagawa is negotiated, ending two centuries of Japanese isolation from the rest of the world.

25 June 1863 — The American steamship *Pembroke* is attacked by warships under the commission of the Prince of Choshu, a rebel, antiwestern member of the Shogunate. News of the incident reaches American consul Robert S. Pryun.

10 July 1863 — The USS *Wyoming* enters the Shimonoseki Strait and destroys the three ship "fleet" of Prince Choshu, in retaliation for the *Pembroke* incident.

1867 — The Tokugawa Shogunate is overthrown in the War of the Restoration, which places the forward-thinking, pro–Western Emperor Meiji on the throne. The Meiji Reforms include the adoption of a Western-style constitutional monarchy (though the Emperor retains his status as a Living God), with an elective parliament (the Diet) and lays the foundations for industrialization and the building of a modern, professional army and navy.

1893 — Mercenaries led by Sanford Dole overthrow the native Hawaiian monarchy in the hopes of adding the archipelago to American domains as the nation's first Pacific territory.

1896 — Captain Albert Thayer Mahan publishes *The Influence of Sea Power Upon History*.

18 February 1898 — The USS *Maine* explodes while she is visiting Havana harbor. Alledged by Americans jingoists to be the result of a mine, it triggers the Spanish-American War.

1 May 1898 — Commodore George Dewey attacks Manila. With the conquest of Cuba, Spain soon surrenders to the United States, which assumes control over Cuba, the Philppines, and Guam. Later that year, the United States annexes Hawaii.

Heihachiro Togo, the "Japanese Nelson," rises to prominence in the

Imperial Admiralty during the brief Sino-Japanese War, which ends in Japanese victory.

1899— The United States annexes Wake Island.

April 1900— John Holland develops the world's first practical gasoline-electric submarine.

1901— Theodore Roosevelt becomes President upon the assassination of William McKinley at the hands of anarchist Leon Czolgosz. Under his administration, Roosevelt will oversee the building of a modern Steel Navy and the Panama Canal, the engineering marvel of the age.

17 December 1903— Orville and Wilbur Wright make the world's first sustained powered flight in a heavier-than-air craft at Kill Devil Hills, *North Carolina*.

4 February 1904— Beginning of the Russo-Japanese War with a suprise Japanese naval attack on Port Arthur in Manchuria. Seven months later, Heihachiro Togo leads the Imperial Fleet to a conclusive victory over the Russian Baltic Fleet at the Battle of Tsushima. The war will end with a treaty negotiated by Theodore Roosevelt, for which he will be awarded the 1905 Nobel Peace Prize.

1905— Construction begins on facilities for Pearl Harbor on the Hawaiian island of Oahu.
   Physicist Albert Einstein publishes his famous Energy Equation, $E=mc^2$, used in the development of atomic energy.

16 December 1907— The Great White Fleet, under Admiral Robley D. Evans, begins its worldwide cruise. The mission, an exhibition of American naval power and technology, announces to the world the entry of the United States to the ranks of modern world powers. The impact of the cruise however is blunted when Britain launches *HMS Dreadnought*, a vessel which will set the standard for battleship design.

18 October 1908— The Great White Fleet anchors in Tokyo Bay. Admiral Evans is treated to a reception hosted by the Emperor Meiji himelf and Admiral Togo. Among the junior officers present are Ensigns William Halsey, Ernest King, Raymond Spruance, and Chester W. Nimitz.

14 November 1910— Eugene Ely successfully pilots a Curtiss Flyer off of a hastily constructed wooden deck aboard the armored cruiser USS *Birmingham*.

18 January 1911— In a related experiment, Eugene Ely succeeds in landing his Curtiss upon a specially erected wooden platform on the stern of the armored cruiser USS *Pennsylvania*. The biplane is brought to a halt by snagging a hook upon steel arrestor cables stretched across the deck. One hour later, Ely flies his craft off the *Pennsylvania*. Though nobody knows it at the moment, these experiments— the first such aviation feats in all the world — have just heralded the eventual doom of the battleship and the advent of the aircraft carrier. Increasingly, the Navy will experiment with seaplanes and develop a naval aviation program.

6 April 1917— The United States formally declares war on Germany following the revelation of the Zimmerman Note, in which Germany offers support for a Mexican reconquest of the southwestern United States. America's entry into the Great War decisively tips the balance of power against Germany, and she is forced to sue for an armistice on 11 November 1918.

28 July 1919—Germany is forced to sign the punitive Versailles Treaty, which accords sole blame for the Great War upon the defeated nation and her allies, strips her of her navy, her air force, all her overseas colonies, her industrial heartlands in the Saar and Ruhr valleys, and imposes harsh, financially ruinous reparations payments. Japan, having fought on the Allied side, gains Germany's former Pacific possessions of the Caroline, Marshall, and Mariana islands.

1920—American strategic planners formulate the first version of War Plan Orange, which conceives a long naval campaign (spearheaded by battleships) through the Central Pacific against Japan.

Japan builds the *Hosho*, the world's first purpose-designed aircraft carrier.

21 July 1921—U.S. Army Air Service General William Mitchell demonstrates the potential efficacy of aircraft against surface ships with an experiment in which bombers sink the ex–German battleship *Ostfriesland* at anchor off the Virginia Capes. The demonstration is sufficent to prompt the Navy to proceed with the project to convert the collier ship USS *Jupiter* into its first aircraft carrier, which is recommissioned as the USS *Langley*.

Isoroku Yamamoto, a Japanese naval academy exchange student, studies engineering at Harvard University, during which time he also tours the industrial heartland of America. He also develops a fascination for aviation and its possibilities.

6 February 1922—The Washington Naval Disarmament Treaty is ratified by the Five Powers.

1926—Crown Prince Hirohito mounts the Chrysanthemum Throne as Japan's new emperor.

1927—Isoroku Yamamoto becomes the first captain of the newly commissioned aircraft carrier *Akagi*. He is the most air-minded of Japan's young naval officer corps.

24 October 1929—Black Monday hits the New York Stock Exchange as the Dow tumbles 500 points. In one day, the market loses $16 billion in value. This triggers the worldwide Great Depression.

18 September 1931—An explosion on the railroad tracks outside Mukden gives the commanding generals of the Japanese Imperial Kwangtung Army, acting increasingly independently of the civilian government in Tokyo, all the excuse they need to launch a new Sino-Japanese War. The outbreak of fighting adds to the forces pushing Japan further toward fascism.

30 March 1932—The Japanese puppet Republic of Manchukuo is proclaimed in the Manchurian capital of Darien. The Kwangtung Army place deposed Chinese emperor Pu Yi on the throne as Head of State.

April 1932—Pressured by increasing political unrest, which includes a wave of assassinations carried out by the Cherry Blossom Society, Emperor Hirohito is advised by Prince Saionji to invite Admiral Makoto Saito to form a new government. It is the first of Japan's military governments.

November 1932— Franklin Delano Roosevelt is elected 32nd President of the United States on a platform of economic recovery.

May 1933— Adolf Hitler is appointed Chancellor of the Reich by the dying President Hindenburg. Hitler's Nazi party has steadily risen to power in Germany on a platform of economic recovery, national resurgence, anti–Semitism and anti–Bolshevism.

1934— A study to revise War Plan Orange reveals the extent to which America has allowed her military forces to wither into near-impotence in the years following the end of the Great War. Franklin Roosevelt pushes for the construction of 26 new warships, including the *Yorktown*-class aircraft carriers, to bring the Navy up to minimum treaty standards. Alarmed by American weakness in a time of rising international tension, Congress authorizes funding for 100 new warships and a thousand aircraft.

26 February 1936— Emperor Hirohito appoints Prince Hiroto Koki as Prime Minister in a futile attempt to rein in the militarists, but the power of the military bureaucracy has become strong enough to dictate government policy no matter who is in office.

1 June 1937— Prince Fumimaro Konoye, the pro-military advocate of the "Greater East Asia Co-Prosperity Sphere" concept of Japanese hegemony in Asia, serves his first term as Prime Minister.

1 July 1937— An incident at the historic Marco Polo bridge in Peking formally touches off the second Sino-Japanese War. The campaign, referred to as a "war of chastisement," now expands into a Napoleonic drive to secure the conquest of all China.

September 1937— Franklin Roosevelt, in a speech in Chicago, calls for an international effort to quarantine Japan. With isolationist sentiment still holding sway over more than half the American population, the speech falls on deaf ears.

12 December 1937— The gunboat USS *Panay*, one of the vessels evacuating refugees from the Rape of Nanking, is bombed and sunk on the Yangtze River. This triggers the first public outrage in America against Japanese actions.

March 1938— Admiral Harry Yarnell conducts Fleet Problem XIX, an exercise involving a mock attack on the U.S. Pacific Fleet base at Pearl Harbor, which is launched at dawn on a Sunday morning. The squadrons sweep over the base and theoretically destroy every capital ship in anchorage.

July 1939— Admiral Isoroku Yamamoto becomes the new Commander-in-Chief of the Imperial Combined Fleet. Under him, the service becomes a true bluewater fleet with aviation as its chief striking component.

1 September 1939— Wehrmacht troops invade Poland. Forty eight hours later, Britain and France declare war on Nazi Germany. Poland falls to the Nazi advance inside of six weeks.

11 September 1939— Franklin Roosevelt sends a letter to First Sea Lord Winston Churchill urging him to "keep in touch with me personally." It is the beginning of the historic partnership between the two wartime leaders.

27 September 1939— Germany, Italy, and Japan sign the Tripartite Pact, binding the three fascist powers into an Axis partnership. Imperial Navy officers privately forsee disaster for Japan with the pact.

26 October 1939— Franklin Roosevelt wins approval from Congress for a "cash-and-carry" amendment to the 1937 Neutrality Act to allow the sale of war muntions to Britain and France.

November 1939— Franklin Roosevelt sets up a Uranium Advisory Committee in response to a letter from physicists Albert Einstein and Leo Szilard warning of the grave potential of Nazi research on atomic weapons.

7 January 1940— Isoroku Yamamoto begins his early conception of a surprise attack against the U.S. Pacific Fleet base at Pearl Harbor.

April 1940— The bulk of the U.S. Pacific fleet is transferred to permanent anchorage at Pearl Harbor.

May 1940— Nazi forces invade France. Winston Churchill is invited by King George VI to assume the office of Prime Minister.

June 1940— France falls. The collaborationist Vichy government will allow Japan to occupy French Indochina. The Battle of Britain is about to begin.

26 July 1940— Prince Konoye returns for another term as Prime Minister. That same day, Franklin Roosevelt announces an embargo on aviation fuel, rubber, scrap iron, and steel exports to Japan.

4 November 1940— Franklin Roosevelt defeats Republican Wendell Wilke to win an unprecedented third term in office.

11 November 1940— British carrier strike forces successfully attack the Italian naval base at Taranto on the Mediterranean, sinking three battleships and bottling up the harbor.

29 December 1940— In a radio fireside chat, Franklin Roosevelt first announces to the American public the Lend Lease concept. Lend Lease is a response to the looming bankruptcy of Britain, severely pressured by the expense of maintaining its war effort against Nazi Germany.

6 January 1941— Franklin Roosevelt declares the United States to be the Arsenal of Democracy.

1 February 1941— Husband E. Kimmel is commissioned the new Commander-in-Chief of the U.S. Pacific Fleet.

12 February 1941— Kichisaburo Nomura, known for his pro–American sympathies, is received in Washington as the new Japanese ambassador.

12 March 1941— The Lend Lease Bill is signed into law by Franklin Roosevelt. Fifty obsolecent destroyers are immediately transferred to the British Royal Navy for convoy protection duty.

27 March 1941— The ABC1 War Plan, incorporating the Europe First strategic concept, is formally adopted. This is decided because of the danger of Nazi control of the Atlantic sea lanes and the possibility of Nazi atomic weapons development.

The Operation Magic codebreaking project is organized, combining Army and Navy signal intelligence programs into a coordinated decryption effort to crack Japanese ciphers, particularly the Purple diplomatic code.

10 April 1941 — With initial planning for the Pearl Harbor attack completed, the Combined Fleet is reorganized.

13 April 1941 — Despite the terms of the Tripartite Pact, Japan concludes a Neutrality Pact with the Soviet Union, pledging not to join the Axis in any war against Russia.

15 April 1941 — Lend Lease supplies are shipped to China.

28 April 1941 — The Pacific Fleet battleships *New Mexico*, *Mississippi*, *Idaho*, and *Texas* along with the carrier *Yorktown* and escort destroyers are transferred to the Atlantic.

27 May 1941 — Franklin Roosevelt declares an "unlimited state of national emergency" and will proceed to freeze the assets of Germany and Italy in the United States.

28 July 1941 — Japanese assets are frozen, and Franklin Roosevelt announces an embargo on all oil shipments to Japan. The shutoff of oil begins to adversely affect the Japanese industrial and war machines within weeks.

6 September 1941 — At a cabinet meeting, Emperor Hirohito reads aloud a haiku verse: "All the seas everywhere are brothers to one another/Why then do the winds and the waves of strife rage so violently over the world?" It is a subtle hint from the throne to find a diplomatic solution to the growing crisis with America.

13 October 1941 — By this date, a steady and surreptitious ferrying of B-17 bomber aircraft to the Philippines has increased the strength of Douglas MacArthur's air force to 227 planes. The force is also supplied with over six million gallons of gasoline.

16 October 1941 — After failing in his efforts to secure a personal summit with the American president, Prince Konoye is forced to resign. General Hideki Tojo, the War Minister and veteran of China, becomes the new Prime Minister.

3 November 1941 — Under a blunt threat from Isoroku Yamamoto to resign from the Imperial Navy, the General Staff finally grants full approval for Operational Plan Z. Vice Admiral Chuichi Nagumo is placed in command of the First Air Fleet (a.k.a. the First Carrier Strike Force).

5 November 1941 — The ships of the First Air Fleet, minus the *Ryuho* and her escorts, slip out of their various ports and proceed under complete radio silence to a rendezvous in the Tankan Bay in the northern Kurile Islands.

7 November 1941 — Congress repeals sections of the 1937 Neutrality Act, permitting the arming of American cargo vessels and direct transport of war materiél to belligerents.

26 November 1941 — With no progress in negotiations, the First Air Fleet is ordered to weigh anchor and begin its voyage eastward. Ambassadors Nomura and Saburo Kurusu continue talks, unaware of the attack mission.

27 November 1941 — General George C. Marshall in Washington formally issues a war warning to Admiral Kimmel and General Walter C. Short, commander of the Hawaii Army Department.

28 November 1941 — The carrier USS *Enterprise*, under Rear Admiral William F. Halsey, is dispatched to Wake Island to deliver Wildcat fighters to reinforce the island's air defenses.

2 December 1941 — The British Admiralty dispatches Force Z, centered upon the battleships *Prince of Wales* and *Repulse*, to Singapore.

3 December 1941 — The First Air Fleet achieves rendezvous with its refueling ships at the turning point for its last leg on the voyage to Hawaii. Chuichi Nagumo receives a fleet signal from Isoroku Yamamoto ordering him to proceed to the target.

5 December 1941 — The carrier *Lexington*, under Rear Admiral J.H. Newland, is dispatched to deliver Wildcat fighters to Midway Island.

6 December 1941 — Franklin Roosevelt makes a final appeal to Emperor Hirohito to help preserve the peace. That same day, Roosevelt signs authourization for Project S-2, the American atomic weapons research effort.

7 December 1941 — The United States Pacific Fleet is crippled and effectively neutralized by the attack of the First Air Fleet on Pearl Harbor, but the base itself — repair docks, machine shops, and vast stores of aviation fuel and oil — is left intact. The same day, Japanese forces hit Midway, Wake, Guam, Singapore, Rangoon, Hong Kong, Shanghai, Siam, and the Philippines. An attack on Clark Field in Luzon wipes out most of Douglas MacArthur's air force on the ground.

8 December 1941 — Franklin Roosevelt, making his famous Day of Infamy speech, calls for Congress to declare war on Japan. He gets it with only one dissenting vote.

10 December 1941 — The *Prince of Wales* and *Repulse* are sunk by Japanese carrier planes in the South China Sea. Guam falls to the Japanese. Japanese troops land on Luzon while carrier planes bomb Cavite Naval Yard in Manila Bay.

11 December 1941 — Nazi Germany and Italy declare war on the United States. World War II has now begun in earnest. That same day, an initial Japanese invasion assault on Wake Island is thrown off the beaches by the U.S. Marine defenders.

17 December 1941 — Husband Kimmel and Walter Short are formally relieved of their commands.

22 December 1941 — Wake Island falls to a second invasion assault backed by the carriers *Hiryu* and *Soryu*, detached from the First Air Fleet.

23 December 1941 — The Japanese bomb Rangoon.

24 December 1941—Luzon is overrun. Douglas MacArthur withdraws his army to Bataan.

25 December 1941—Hong Kong falls.

26 December 1941—Manila is declared an open city.

27 December 1941—Chester W. Nimitz formally assumes command of the United States Pacific Fleet. With no battleship available to serve as flagship, he hoists his flag aboard the submarine USS *Growler*.

1 January 1942—The Atlantic Charter, cornerstone of the United Nations Pact, is signed by the representatives of 26 nations in Washington D.C., forming a global alliance to combat the Axis.

2 January 1942—Manila and Cavite are occupied.

3 January 1942—The ABDA (American, British, Dutch, Australian) Command is formed. It is the first attempt to weld together a multinational battleforce under a unified command. Sir Archibald Wavell is overall commander, while the naval force is placed initially under the command of U.S. Asiatic Fleet commander Thomas Hart.

11 January 1942—The carrier *Saratoga* is torpedoed south of Hawaii, sending her to the repair dock.

13 January 1942—Bataan is besieged.

23 January 1942—ABDA naval forces attack Japanese shipping off Balikpapan, Borneo.

24 January 1942—Rabaul falls.

25–27 January 1942—The carriers *Enterprise* and *Yorktown*, under William F. Halsey, raid Japanese bases in the Caroline and Marshall islands.

1 February 1942—The carriers *Enterprise* and *Hornet* raid Japanese bases in the Gilbert and Marshall islands. The raids are little more than harassment, but provide vital combat training for American carrier pilots without risking a major fleet engagement.

4 February 1942—Japanese aircraft inflict major damage upon an ABDA cruiser-destroyer force, halving the fleet's overall striking power.

15 February 1942—The British are forced to surrender Singapore.

20 February 1942—The carrier *Lexington* beats off an air attack 350 miles ENE of Rabaul. Lieutenant Edward "Butch" O'Hare shoots down five planes, becoming the Navy's first air ace.

24 February 1942—The *Enterprise* raids Wake Island.

27 February 1942—The ABDA fleet suffers a major defeat in the Battle of the Java Sea. Dutch admiral Karel Doorman, then in command, is killed in action. The surviving ships are steadily hunted down and destroyed. The fall of Borneo is mere weeks away.

4 March 1942—The *Enterprise* raids Marcus Island.

11 March 1942—Under direct orders of the President, Douglas MacArthur is evacuated by PT boat to Australia along with his family and staff officers. Major General Joseph Wainwright assumes command of the U.S. Philippine Army.

24 March 1942—The Netherlands East Indies are conquered, barring final mopping-up operations.

1 April 1942—American and Filipino troops on Bataan are forced to go on quarter-rations. All supplies are rapidly being exhausted.

2 April 1942—The carrier *Hornet,* boarding sixteen land-based B-25 Mitchell medium bomber aircraft of Lieutenant Colonel James Doolittle's special volunteer group, departs San Francisco. The *Hornet* will rendezvous with the *Enterprise* and her escorts at sea on the 13th.

5 April 1942—The First Air Fleet hits Ceylon in a surprise raid. Four days later, Chuichi Nagumo catches the carrier *HMS Hermes* unawares and sinks her, along with two destroyers and two tankers. Nagumo's victorious campaign breaks British naval power in the Indian Ocean.

9 April 1942—Bataan falls. In the largest mass-capitulation of American forces in history, 75,000 troops surrender to the Japanese. Joseph Wainwright continues to hold out on Corregidor Island, which keeps the harbor of Manila bottled up.

18 April 1942—The *Hornet* launches Colonel Doolittle's squadron 750 miles east of the Japanese home island of Honshu. The planes arrive over Tokyo two hours later and bomb the capital, as well as targets in Kobe, Nagoya, and Yokohama. The damage wrought is light but the shock to Japanese morale is devastating.

26 April 1942—Isoroku Yamamoto formally proposes an operation to invade and occupy the island of Midway to hopefully end the war by breaking American naval power in the Pacific.

May 1942—HYPO, the U.S. Navy's decryption team based at Pearl Harbor under Commander Joseph Rochefort, finally succeed in cracking JN25, the top Japanese naval cipher. The first dividend of this intelligence coup is knowledge of a planned Japanese invasion assault aimed at Port Moresby, New Guinea. Chester Nimitz dispatches the *Lexington* and *Yorktown* task forces to intercept.

3 May 1942—In a pre-invasion sortie against Dutch Harbor in the Aleutians, Warrant Officer Tadayoshi Koga is forced down on Akutan Island, but is killed when his plane flips while trying to land on marshy turf. Five weeks later, the U.S. Navy salvages his virtually intact A6M Zeke fighter and sends it to San Diego.

6 May 1942—General Joseph Wainwright surrenders Corregidor. The Japanese force Wainwright to go on the radio and order the immediate end of all remaining resistance.

7–8 May 1942—The Battle of the Coral Sea takes place—the first ever carrier engagement. The Japanese lose light carrier *Shoho,* while Japanese carrier planes hit the *Lexington* and *Yorktown,* damaging both ships. American planes heavily damage the *Shokaku* and virtually annihilate the *Zuikaku*'s entire strike wing. The *Lexington* later explodes and sinks and the *Yorktown* is forced to withdraw, but without carrier support the Japanese invasion force aborts its mission. Not only has the United States won a clear strategic victory, but the two heavy Japanese carriers will now be unavailable for the Midway Operation.

18 May 1942—The last organized resistance in the Philippines on the island of Panay ends as American and Filipino troops surrender. Many of their number succeed in deserting to the jungles to join the Filipino guerrilla forces, who will continue to fight on for the next 30 months.

20 May 1942—Swallowing the bait of a false message transmitted in clear from Midway Island on the insistence of Joseph Rochefort, HYPO decrypts a JN25 intercept which reads: "AF is short of fresh water"—confirming Midway to be the next enemy objective.

25 May 1942—The Aleutians Invasion Force, spearheaded by the light carriers *Ryujo* and *Junyo*, depart from the northern Honshu port of Ominato.

26 May 1942—Task Force 16 arrives in Pearl Harbor. The *Yorktown* pulls into dock the next day. The Midway Invasion Force departs from bases in Guam and Saipan.

28 May 1942—The opposing battlefleets depart their ports for the historic confrontation at Midway, the Combined Fleet from the Inland Sea and Task Force 16 from Pearl Harbor. The *Yorktown*, with repair crews still on board, will depart later that day.

1 June 1942—A formation of Japanese submarines finally arrive on station to take up picket duty off Hawaii, but their delay in departure from the base at Kwajelin due to a typhoon means that they are already too late to observe the movements of the Pacific Fleet.

2 June 1942—Task Forces 16 and 17 arrive at Point Luck, 300 miles NE of Midway, and await the arrival of the First Carrier Strike Force, Yamamoto's spearhead.

3 June 1942—The carriers *Ryujo* and *Junyo* commence raiding Dutch Harbor.

4 June 1942—The Battle of Midway begins. In the first day's fighting, American planes destroy the four flattops of the First Carrier Strike Force, while Japanese planes damage the *Yorktown* badly enough to force the crew to abandon ship. Without carrier support, any invasion of Midway is untenable. Facing the reality of the disaster, Isoroku Yamamoto is forced to cancel the Midway Operation.

5 June 1942—The second day of the Battle of Midway is inconclusive. American planes strike and heavily damage the cruisers *Mikuma* and *Mogami*. Ensign George Gay, lone survivor of Torpedo Squadron 8, is rescued by a Navy PBY flying boat. The *Yorktown* is still afloat and a salvage crew scrambles to board her and rig the carrier for towing back to Pearl Harbor.

6 June 1942—American carrier planes strike the crippled and retreating *Mikuma* and *Mogami*, sinking the one and sending the other to the drydock for an entire year. The Japanese submarine *I-168* torpedoes the damaged *Yorktown*.

She will sink the next morning. Up in the Aleutians, bombing raids against Dutch Harbor continue, and Japanese troops land on Attu and Kiska, but without the occupation of Midway or further support of the Combined Fleet, which now cannot do so, the Aleutians invasion is doomed to eventual failure. Midway is the first total defeat suffered by the Imperial Navy since 1592, and Combined Fleet operations are actually paralyzed for an entire month.

11 June 1942— The carrier *Wasp*, accompanied by a battleship, a heavy cruiser, and eight destroyers, passes through the Panama Canal to join the Pacific Fleet. For the first time since 7 December 1941, the balance of power in the Pacific is roughly equal.

25 June 1942— In Washington, Ernest King confers with George Marshall on a plan for an amphibious invasion of the Solomon Islands for a target date of 1 August.

3 July 1942— Japanese troops land on Guadalcanal Island from nearby Tulagi and begin construction of an airstrip. Ernest King orders the immediate implementation of Operation Watchtower to capture Guadalcanal.

14 July 1942— Isoroku Yamamoto reorganizes the Combined Fleet, creating a new force designated the Eighth Fleet under Vice Admiral Guinichi Mikawa to support operations in the Solomons.

16 July 1942— Buildup of materiél and forces for the coming Guadalcanal operation proceeds. Simultaneously, the Japanese make preparations for a second invasion attempt against New Guinea.

20 July 1942— Task Forces 11, 16, and 18 assemble at Fiji for Operation Watchtower.

22 July 1942— Japanese troops land at Buna and Gona, and begin advancing slowly toward Port Moresby.

31 July 1942— The Operation Watchtower invasion force departs Fiji.

5 August 1942— The superbattleship *Musashi*, sister of the *Yamato*, is commissioned into fleet service. That same day, a third reinforcement convoy lands at Buna.

7 August 1942— Guadalcanal is invaded by the 1st Marine Division. Within two days the Marines capture the airstrip and invade nearby Tulagi and Florida Islands to consolidate their position. Accompanying the Marines are the first unit of Seabee construction workers.

9 August 1942— Guinichi Mikawa's Eighth Fleet, under cover of darkness, enters Savo Bay to attack the Allied cruisers and destroyers guarding the invasion beachhead. He sinks five cruisers (one Australian), but withdraws before completing his mission out of fear of airstrikes after dawn. For five days the Marines and Seabees on Guadalcanal are left totally alone when Kelly Turner pulls his transports away. They complete the airstrip but prepare for a last-ditch stand.

11 August 1942— Isoroku Yamamoto redeploys the Combined Fleet to Truk Island to better support operations in New Guinea and at Guadalcanal.

15 August 1942—Four Navy transports loaded with aviation fuel, ammunition, and supplies arrives to reinforce the Marines. Henderson Field is completed and fully operational five days after this delivery.

18 August 1942—The first run of Rear Admiral Raizo Tanaka's Tokyo Express convoy runs is made. Six destroyers carrying the Ichiki Detatchment, 900 men in the first load, are landed at Taivu Point.

20 August 1942—The escort carrier *Long Island* ferrys 31 attack planes of the 23rd Marine Air Group to Guadalcanal, the first planes to be stationed at Henderson Field.

21 August 1942—Without waiting for the rest of his unit to be landed, Colonel Kiyano Ichiki marches his men right toward the Marine entrenchments at Alligator Creek and are slaughtered to the last man.

22 August 1942—Army P-40 fighter planes are delivered to Henderson Field, adding to the growing "Cactus Air Force."

24 August 1942—In the Battle of the Eastern Solomons, planes from the *Saratoga* sink the Japanese light carrier *Ryujo*. The *Enterprise* is damaged in the fight and put temporarily out of action.

27 August 1942—The Japanese continue landing reinforcements at Milne Bay, New Guinea, but are contained by Australian defenders. Nine more P-40 fighters are delivered to Henderson Field.

28 August 1942—The new fast-battleship USS *Washington* passes through the Panama Canal on her way to Guadalcanal.

29 August 1942—The initial units of the Kawaguchi Detachment are landed at Guadalcanal along with the remaining troops of the late Colonel Ichiki's unit — 2,200 in all. In New Guinea, the Japanese are forced to withdraw from Milne Bay.

31 August 1942—The *Saratoga* is torpedoed and put out of action by the Japanese submarine *I-26*. The carrier balance is beginning to shift toward Japan's favor again.

3 September 1942—The Tokyo Express convoys begin to encounter increasing aerial resistance. In the meantime, the United States copies the Japanese strategy, using destroyers to ferry in supplies and reinforcements.

8 September 1942—Despite having breached the Gap in the Owen Stanley mountain range, the Japanese Imperial Seventeenth Army is unable to push through to Port Moresby. The order is given to terminate the operation, and the surviving troops fall back to Buna.

The Tokyo Express runs have reinforced Major General Kiyotaki Kawaguchi's force to 6,000-man strength. On the way out, the destroyers shell Tulagi.

13 September 1942—General Kawaguchi begins his offensive on Guadalcanal. At the Battle of Bloody Ridge, however, he runs into well fortified Marine positions on high ground, and is repulsed with heavy losses. The retreat is disorderly.

15 September 1942— The carrier *Wasp* is sunk in a torpedo attack which also damages the fast battleship *North Carolina* and the destroyer *O'Brien*. But this does not prevent the landing of additional reinforcements for General Alexander Vandegrift on Guadalcanal. By September 20, his force has grown to a strength of 19,000 men. Within 15 days, the Marines expand their defensive perimeter.

6 October 1942— Alexander Vandegrift lays plans for an offensive on Japanese positions on the Matanikau River, but heavy rains two days later bog down all operations. In the succeeding weeks, Vandegrift will employ a strategy of probing attacks on the Japanese line to inflict casualties rather than direct assault.

9 October 1942— Japanese forces on Guadalcanal have grown to a strength of 21,000 men. Harukichi Hyakutake, commanding general of the Seventeenth Imperial Army, arrives to personally assume command of operations. But that same day, Admiral Kelly Turner's convoys deliver an additional 2,800 reinforcements to Alexander Vandegrift.

11 October 1942— A U.S. Navy cruiser-destroyer force attempts to ambush the Tokyo Express, which is accompanied this run by a cruiser-destroyer force under Admiral Aritomo Goto. In the resulting Battle off Cape Esperance, the Japanese lose one crusier and two destroyers. Admiral Goto is killed in the action. It is the first American victory in a night battle, but the Tokyo Express succeeds in landing additional reinforcements for Harukichi Hyakutake.

12 October 1942— Kelly Turner's convoy lands troops of the Americal Division the morning after the Battle off Cape Esperance, countering the Japanese reinforcement landing. The American garrison on Guadalcanal is now up to 23,000 man strength.

16 October 1942— Both the *Zuikaku* and the *Enterprise* return to active combat duty in the Solomons.

18 October 1942— Vice Admrial Robert Ghormley is relieved of command of the South Pacific Force, judged by Chester Nimitz to be too pessimistic and hands-off in his leadership to be retained. William Halsey, recovered from the shingles attack which beached him before Midway, replaces him. Morale among the personnel in the Solomons area rises precipitously at the news. Halsey's first move is to replace Jack Fletcher with Admirals Thomas Kinkaid and George Murray in carrier command. The command reshuffle is timely, since the campaign for Guadalcanal is about to enter the critical phase.

20 October 1942— The *Shokaku* returns to active service, joined by the light carriers *Hiyo* (which will suffer machinery problems and be replaced by the *Zuiho*) and *Junyo*. Chuichi Nagumo, partially rehabilitated from disgrace, is placed in command as Isoroku Yamamoto plans a new sea offensive.

23 October 1942— Harukichi Hyakutake attempts multiple assaults upon the Marine defensive perimeter's southern line, but unit coordination breaks down and his forces are bloodily repulsed by Marine Lieutenant Colonel Meritt Edson's troops. Once again, the Japanese attempted to attack a fortified position on a ridge. Hyakutake is forced to retreat the next day with heavy casualties.

24 October 1942—The *Enterprise* and *Hornet* are sortied to seek out and intercept a Japanese carrier task force known to be operating in the area of the
Santa Cruz islands. While off Lunga Point at Guadalcanal, a Japanese cruiser-
destroyer force shelling the Marine positions is beaten off by air attacks from
squadrons based on Henderson Field and airfields on Espiritu Santo.

26 October 1942—The Battle of Santa Cruz begins when the American and Japanese task forces literally blunder upon one another. In the savage mélée which
follows, both *Enterprise* and *Hornet* are damaged, with the latter reduced to
a burning wreck which is abandoned and later scuttled by the Japanese when
she is judged unsalvageable. The *Zuiho* and *Shokaku* are both damaged, the
latter so badly that she is out of action for an entire year, and the Japanese
suffer a huge loss of attack planes in the engagement. The reinforcement convoy accompanying Chuichi Nagumo's task force is forced to retreat.

1 November 1942—General Vandegrift's Marines finally launch a direct assault
against the Japanese line on the Matanikau River, backed by offshore bombardment, land artillery, and tactical air support. The weakened Japanese formations are steadily pushed back from their line. Marine assaults upon
Japanese positions at Kokumbona and Point Cruz force the entire enemy
front into a westward retreat across the island.

8 November 1942—The Tokyo Express lands reinforcements for the Japanese units
at Koli Point, but a combined Army and Marine force accomplishes an
amphibious end-run around them. That same day, a reinforcement convoy
escorted by the *Enterprise*, two battleships, eight cruisers and twenty-three
destroyers sets sail from New Caledonia.

9 November 1942—Isoroku Yamamoto decides to commit all his avaialble forces
into a determined offensive to retake Guadalcanal and sorties Nobutake
Kondo's Second Fleet, including a troop convoy, from Truk for an action
scheduled for the 12th and 13th. His decision will lead to the terminal battle
for Guadalcanal. Two days later, the Japanese launch an air assault from
Rabaul against Henderson Field.

12 November 1942—Alexander Vandegrift pulls his Marines back to defensive
positions, having received word of the expected Japanese counteroffensive.
    Near midnight, American and Japanese surface forces clash in Ironbot-
tom Sound. In the resulting battle, the USS *Atlanta* along with four destroyers are sunk, three cruisers and two destroyers are damaged, and Admirals
Norman Scott and Daniel Callaghan are killed. The Japanese suffer severe
damage to the battleship *Hiei* and the loss of one destroyer in the engagement. Hiroaki Abe, the Japanese admiral, pulls out on the eve of seeming
victory, leaving the Americans on the island unmolested.

13 November 1942—The crippled battleship *Hiei*, trailing behind her task force,
is caught repeatedly by Marine aircraft and planes from the *Enterprise* and
subjected to shuttle bombing. The ship is so heavily damaged that Admiral
Abe decides to scuttle her. He will later be dismissed from command under
a cloud of disgrace.
    The USS *Juneau*, a light cruiser, is torpedoed and sunk by a Japanese

submarine. Among the dead are all five Sullivan brothers of Waterloo, Iowa, the worst such loss to a single family in the entire war.

Guinichi Mikawa takes four cruisers into Ironbottom Sound to shell Henderson Field, but the ordnance employed isn't heavy enough to inflict any real damage. The Seabees have the field operational by morning.

14 November 1942— Throughout the day, Raizo Tanaka's eleven transport convoy is subjected to shuttle bombing attacks from the *Enterprise* and squadrons from Henderson Field. Nobutake Kondo's reluctance to commit his carrier airpower leaves Tanaka with no protection whatsoever. Only four burning transports manage to make it all the way to Guadalcanal and must beach on the Tassafaronga landing zone.

Nobutake Kondo leads a formation of one battleship, four cruisers and four destroyers to accomplish the mission Hiroaki Abe and Guinichi Mikawa both failed at. Waiting for him in Ironbottom Sound is Rear Admiral Willis Lee with the modern, fast battleships Washington and *South Dakota*, accompanied by four destroyers. Lee's battlewagons, with radar-directed 16-inch guns, destroy Kondo's flagship *Kirishima* and the light cruiser *Sendai*. Kondo withdraws, leaving Lee in firm possession of Ironbottom Sound.

30 November 1942— Eight Japanese destroyers clash with an American crusier-destroyer force off Tassafaronga Point trying to run the blockade and reinforce Harukichi Hyakutake. Though the American force suffers heavier losses, the Japanese force lacks the firepower to prevail and is forced to break off. It is the last Japanese naval challenge in the Guadalcanal sector.

December 1942— Japanese strength on Guadalcanal reaches its zenith, 30,000 men. They will consolidate defensive positions in the interior of the island, but starvation, disease, and lack of resupply bleeds their strength away, while the American garrison on Guadalcanal continues to grow ever stronger.

On New Guinea, Lieutenant General Robert Eichelberger is put in charge of the Allied effort to drive the Japanese from New Guinea. Gona falls to Australian troops on the 9th. Buna is retaken on the 22nd.

31 December 1942— Prime Minister Hideki Tojo makes the decision to abandon the "Island of Death," conceeding the Empire's defeat in the campaign for Guadalcanal.

The United States Navy commissions the flattop USS *Essex* into fleet service. She is the lead vessel in a 26-ship class of new-design aircraft carriers ordered in 1939. The same day she leaves port on her shakedown trials, her sister ship USS *Yorktown* is launched.

4 January 1943— Imperial General Headquarters, Tokyo, issues the official order to evacuate Guadalcanal.

8 February 1943— The last Japanese troops are evacuated from Guadalcanal.

17 February 1943— The new carrier USS *Lexington* is commissioned into fleet service.

18 February 1943— U.S. Navy cruisers begin shelling Japanese positions on Attu Island.

28 February 1943— The Japanese land 7,000 troops at Lae to reinforce their holdings on New Guinea.

4 March 1943— U.S. Army Air Force squadrons attack a Japanese convoy bound
for Lae. In the resulting Battle of the Bismarck Sea, 350 attack planes succeed
in wiping out the entire convoy for the loss of only 21 planes.

26 March 1943— Two cruisers and four destroyers under Rear Admiral Charles
McMorris beat off a stronger Japanese force of four cruisers, four destroyers
and a transport off the Komandorski Islands in the Aleutians Theater. It will
be the last ever daylight surface battle not involving aircraft or submarines.

3 April 1943— Isoroku Yamamoto flies out to Rabaul to confer with General
Hitoshi Immamura on a strategy for Operation I-GO, an air campaign
intended to reverse the tide of battle on New Guinea.

7 April 1943— The weather finally permits Hitoshi Immamura to launch his
squadrons against Allied positions on New Guinea and the Solomons. The
bulwark for the operation is provided by Eleventh Air Fleet planes augmented
by the squadrons from the carriers *Zuikaku*, *Hiyo*, *Junyo*, and *Zuiho*, which
were reassigned to Rabaul. Although the pilots report massive damage
inflicted upon Allied shipping and ground positions, they only manage to
sink a transport, a destroyer, and a corvette.

15 April 1943— The new USS *Yorktown* is commissioned into fleet serivce.
     William Halsey and Douglas MacArthur begin three days of intensive
conferencing on plans for an invasion of the islands surrounding Rabaul, to
be designated Operation Cartwheel.

16 April 1943— HYPO decodes a JN25 intercept which contains the entire itinerary of Isoroku Yamamoto's inspection tour of the Outer Defense Perimeter,
including a flight to the island of Bougainville.

18 April 1943— P-38 Lightning fighters of the 339th Fighter Squadron intercept
two Betty bombers carrying Isoroku Yamamoto and his staff officers. Both
are shot down over Buin, Bougainville. Admiral Matome Ugaki survives but
Admiral Yamamoto himself is killed. The day is the first anniversary of the
Doolittle Raid.

22 April 1943— Admiral Minechi Koga is named the new Commander-in-Chief
of the Imperial Combined Fleet. Upon his return to Truk, he will reorganize
his forces to create a new Mobile Fleet, a detatched force which can be scrambled for action as needed. Limited resources, however, will severely restrict
its operations. Based at Truk, it ends up serving more as a standing deterrent force than an active combat force.

25 April 1943— A U.S. Navy amphibious task force under Thomas Kinkaid departs
San Francisco, following a troop convoy on its way to Attu to commence the
operation to expel the Japanese from North American soil. Accompanying
the force are the rebuilt battleships *Nevada* and *Pennsylvania* and the escort
carrier *Nassau*.

11 May 1943— Thomas Kinkaid's invasion force arrives off Holtz Bay, Attu. The
battleships *Pennsylvania*, *Nevada*, and *Idaho* commence shelling the port prior
to landing 11,000 troops.

19 May 1943—Colonel Yasugo Yamakazi withdraws his men to the cul-de-sac of Chichagcof Harbor and digs in. Though outnumbered five-to-one, he has a good defensive position and the semifrozen mud will force Allied troops to come forth on foot.

   The battleship *Musashi* and escorts detached from the Mobile Fleet are scrambled in a hasty mission to relieve the Japanese garrison on Attu, but Imperial General Headquarters aborts the mission, unable to justify the expenditure in fuel oil for the risk. The ships anchor in Tokyo Bay and are soon sent back to Truk.

20 May 1943—The Joint Chiefs of Staff in Washington outline a plan for the defeat of Japan, involving thrusts up the Gilbert and Marshall islands, the Bismarck Archipelago, and in Burma.

26 May 1943—Japanese submarines manage to slip past Charles McMorris' blockade to begin a covert evacuation of troops from Kiska Island. The besieged Japanese on Attu have been left to their fate.

29 May 1943—Yasugo Yamakazi's remaining troops make a doomed banzai charge on American positions. The last 500 commit mass suicide with grenades at the foot of Engineer Hill.

12 June 1943—Addressing the Diet (parliament), Prime Minister Hideki Tojo is forced to admit the Empire's defeat at Guadalcanal, the Aleutians, in the Solomons and Bismarck Sea sectors, and also to losses in China and Burma. It is the first open admission that the war is beginning to go badly for Japan.

20 June 1943—Having completed all preparations, the convoys for Operation Cartwheel begin sailing for their first objectives, Woodark Island, Kirwina Island, Rendova and Munda, New Georgia.

23 June 1943—Cartwheel landings are made on Woodark and Kirwina. A cruiser-destroyer squadron is detatched to shell Japanese positions on Shortland Island.

25 June 1943—Vice Admiral Charles Lockwood, the new commander of Pacific submarine forces, orders a full review of the Navy's submarine torpedoes to analyze their poor performance in action, and institutes a new program of training and strategic planning.

2 July 1943—The main Operation Cartwheel invasion force lands at Rendova, quickly capturing Viru Harbor. Once establishing artillery positions, troops of the U.S. 37th and 43rd divisions ferry across to land on Munda.

   On Munda, Major General Nabor Sasaki adopts the American tactics used on Guadalcanal; setting up reinforced pillbox strongpoints and an innner ring of camouflaged machine gun positions on high ridges with overlapping fields of fire. Sasaki is outnumbered three-to-one, but his defense inflicts heavy casualties before Munda is overrun, an effort which takes five weeks.

5 July 1943—The Japanese set up a new Tokyo Express operation to try to resupply their garrisons on New Georgia. One convoy of eight destroyers is intercepted by Third Fleet cruisers and destroyers in the Kula Gulf.

13 July 1943— At Kolombangara, another Japanese reinforcement convoy is inter-cepted. The cruiser Jintsu is sunk, while the Allied naval force suffers dam-age to all three of its cruisers and the loss of one destroyer.

20 July 1943— The Joint Chiefs issue formal orders to commence the planning for Operation Galvanic, the invasion of the Gilbert Islands.

30 July 1943— U.S. forces secure Rendova.

5 August 1943— Nabor Sasaki and his surviving troops pull back to Kolomban-gara Island and again set up the same layered defensive positions as they employed on Munda. With the garrison already on the island, Sasaki has 10,000 troops to fight the Allies with.

8 August 1943— An attempted Japanese air assault against Allied positions on New Georgia results in the loss in one day of 350 aircraft for only 93 American planes. The next day, Japanese troops are driven out of their positions and pursued into the interior of the island.

11 August 1943— At the urging of Chester Nimitz at Pearl Harbor, William Halsey, Third Fleet commander, decides to mirror the tactics of Thomas Kinkaid in the Aleutians and adopts a strategy of bypassing Japanese strongholds in favor of taking surrounding islands and cutting off the sea and air lanes, completely isolating the Japanese on their bastions and leaving them to starve.

15 August 1943— American and Canadian troops finally land on Kiska, only to find the island completely deserted save for three half-starved dogs.

16 August 1943— The Third Fleet lands invasion forces on lightly defended Vella Lavella island, just ahead of Kolombangara. The island is large enough to accommodate a Marine air group, and Seabee construction gangs immedi-ately set to work building the airstrip, even though Japanese resistance con-tinues through the next six weeks. Within two weeks, the Americans have complete control over the Slot.

17 August 1943— Fifth Air Force bombers hit the Japanese airfield of Wewak on New Guinea, destroying 200 planes on the ground, nearly their whole air strength on the island.

25 August 1943— Organized resistance on New Georgia ends.

George Marshall, attending the Quebec Conference with President Roosevelt, sends a recommendation to William Halsey and Douglas MacArthur that Rabaul be bypassed by occupying New Britain and New Ire-land.

30 August, 1943— Throughout the spring and summer months, the U.S. Pacific Fleet has grown considerably, not only by the steady return of ships from repair or reconstruction, but by the addition of six aircraft carriers, two new-design fast battleships, two cruisers, and twenty destroyers. The fleet is now already double its prewar strength. More ships are building and will join the fleet by 1944, again doubling its size.

The influx of ships necessitates the creation of the new Fifth Fleet, under the command of Vice Admiral Raymond Spruance. The growth in carrier strength results in a new mode of strategic thinking to most efficently employ them in operations. The Fast Carrier Task Force concept is formulated, based upon using carrier airpower as the main offensive force.

1 September 1943—The first experiment in fast carrier tactics is conducted with a raid on Marcus Island by Charles Pownall's Task Force 15.

A second fast carrier unit, Task Force 11, under Willis Lee and Arthur Radford, conducts a similar raid on Baker Island, additionally landing a force of Marines to occupy it. Baker, east of the Gilberts, completes an encircling operation in which Phoenix and Ellice islands were also invested.

4 September 1943—Douglas MacArthur leads the 41st U.S. and 9th Australian divisions in landings east of Lae. By the next day, MacArthur has established a siege line, encircling the port completely, and begins to wear down the remaining Japanese garrison.

17 September 1943—Task Force 15 arrives to conduct another experimental fast carrier raid at Tarawa, the main objective of the coming Gilberts invasion. But command and procedural botchups result in the failure to conduct complete photoreconnaisance of the Japanese pillbox positions.

22 September 1943—Salamaua is taken by Allied forces. That same day, Australian troops land on the Huon Peninsula despite heavy Japanese resistance.

25 September 1943—Lae falls to Douglas MacArthur.

5 October 1943—With the timetable for Galvanic winding down, Chester Nimitz decides upon one more fast carrier experiment. Task Force 14, under Alfred Montgomery and this time divided into two "crusing groups" of unequal size, arrives at Wake Island. Zeke fighters are scrambled, but are heavily outnumbered and shot down. The action is the first definitive combat test of the new F6F Hellcat fighter, developed from test data on the Zeke fighter salvaged from Akutan Island the previous year. Airstrikes and offshore bombardment leave the Japanese base in flames.

25 October 1943—Off Cape St. George, six American destroyers intercept six Japanese destroyers carrying reinforcements for the garrison on Bougainville, sinking three of them and forcing the other three to retreat.

26 October 1943—The Mobile Fleet, having scrambled to relieve Wake Island, returns to Truk after finding nothing to intercept. The fleet has scrambled after each fast carrier raid and always for no purpose. The Wake attack, however, causes them to strip away all their air defenses around Eniwetok and Tarawa to cover an anticipated invasion of Rabaul.

27 October 1943—Unable to simply bypass Bougainville, William Halsey's Third Fleet commences an invasion effort, landing a diversionary attack on Choiseul Island to mask the main assault. Simultaneously, the 8,000 men of the New Zealand 8th Brigade are landed on nearby Mono and Stirling in the Treasury Islands. The diversion works and the New Zealanders are left free to build their airstrips for the main invasion.

1 November 1943—The main invasion force for Bougainville lands at Cape Torokina and Empress Augusta Bay. Shelling of Buin and Buka has diverted Japanese defenders from the beachheads, allowing the troops to land unmolested. During the landings, carrier strikes are conducted against Buin and Buka.

2 November 1943—Third Fleet cruisers under A.S. Merill beat off an attempted attack on the Empress Augusta beachhead by a Japanese cruiser-destroyer squadron.

3 November 1943—Ten cruisers and twelve destroyers are detatched from the Mobile Fleet and sortie from Truk to reinforce Rabaul. Their transit is spotted by Navy reconnaisance aircraft the next day. William Halsey is forced to detach the *Saratoga* and the light carrier *Independence*, along with a hastily assembled destroyer screen, to hit Simpson Harbor.

5 November 1943—The *Saratoga* and *Independence* launch a 96 plane strike force to hit the ships at Rabaul, backed by planes from the Fifth Air Force. The raid knocks down 25 planes and damages ten warships in the harbor. Dock facilities are also heavily hit.

8 November 1943—In response to a call for reinforcements, the carriers *Essex*, *Bunker Hill*, and CVL *Monterey* detached from the Fifth Fleet rendezvous with William Halsey's Third Fleet. With five carriers at his disposal, Admiral Halsey decides to put an end to the threat of Rabaul for good.

11 November 1943—The *Essex*, *Bunker Hill*, *Saratoga*, *Independence* and *Monterey* arrive offshore of Rabaul and launch five waves of attack planes throughout the day. The strikes devastate Simpson Harbor, sink a cruiser, and decimate Japanese air forces on Rabaul.

13 November 1943—The Operation Galvanic invasion force departs Efate Island on its way to Tarawa and Makin, the two main islands in the Gilberts.

14 November 1943—Allied strength on Bougainville is now up to 34,000 men. The 40,000 Japanese defenders are scattered all over the island and on the surrounding islands and cannot concentrate their force.

18 November 1943—Task Force 50 commences initial airstrikes on Tarawa and Makin, backed by massive offshore bombardment.

20 November 1943—The initial Galvanic landings take place as the 2nd Marine Division storms Beito, while Kelly Turner lands Major General Ralph Smith's 27th Division on Makin. The Marines find themselves up against hardened pillboxes missed by the photoreconnaisance mission back in September. After nine hours of fighting, only 1,500 Marines have managed to push 100 feet inland.

The CVL *Independence* is torpedoed in a counterattack by Japanese Betty bombers, putting her out of action for six months. Upon receiving the reports from Tarawa, Chester Nimitz issues a direct order to Raymond Spruance to shift his carriers to full offensive operations.

21 November 1943—Task Force 50 launches heavy air attacks against Major Keiji Shibasaki's positions. Marines finally manage to reach the pillboxes, pour gasoline into the ventilation shafts, and toss grenades down afterward.

22 November 1943—The Marines finally capture the airstrip on Beito, Tarawa. Makin falls the same day. One thousand Marines were killed, while 97 percent of the Japanese garrison were slaughtered.

24 November 1943— The escort carrier *Liscombe Bay* is torpedoed and sunk with heavy loss of life, including Rear Admiral Henry Mullinix, Captain Issac Wiltsic, and Pearl Harbor hero Dorie Miller, the first black man to win the Navy Cross.

25 November 1943— The Japanese defenders on Bougainville attempt their first counterattack, but by this date, Allied defense perimeters are too well established and enforced. The assault is beaten off with heavy casualties.

Japanese night bombers attempt an after-dark attack on the Fifth Fleet. A flight of specially rigged night fighters launched from the *Enterprise* intercepts them. The bombers are shot down, but so is Commander Edward "Butch" O'Hare.

3 December 1943— At the Cairo Conference, it is decided that William Halsey and Douglas MacArthur will continue their two-pronged offensive up the Central Pacific toward the general direction of Formosa and the Philippines.

Chester Nimitz has the Japanese bunkers on Tarawa reconstructed on an outlying Hawaiian island for bombardment tests and orders a thorough review of the conduct of Operation Galvanic and related operations leading up to it. The review takes place concurrently with the planning for Operation Flintlock, the invasion of Kwajelin.

4 December 1943— Task Force 50 conducts major airstrikes against Wotje and Kwajelin. The raiders claim 55 planes and six transports while damaging two more and two cruisers. The *Lexington* takes a torpedo hit.

10 December 1943— Seabees complete the airstrip at Empress Augusta Bay on Bougainville. Allied forces have all the shore positions in their possession. With the fall of Buin and Buka, the Japanese garrison is bottled up in the interior of Bougainville.

15 December 1943— William Halsey lands the 112th Cavalry on Arawe, New Britain.

25 December 1943— The carriers *Bunker Hill* and *Monterey*, under Rear Admiral Frederick Sherman, launch airstrikes against Kaeving, New Ireland.

26 December 1943— William Halsey lands the 1st Marine Division at Cape Gloucester, New Britain. Their objective is the airfield.

29 December 1943— After three days of heavy fighting, the Marines seize the airfield and have Cape Gloucester secured. With this accomplished, Rabaul is neutralized. Its 135,000 man garrison are effectively prisoners of war.

The Seventh Air Force raids Majuro, Roi, Taroa, Wotje, and Kwajelin in initial softening-up for Operation Flintlock.

4 January 1944— The *Bunker Hill* and *Monterey* raid Kaeving, New Ireland, a second time.

5 January 1944— American and Australian forces link up at Kelanok, rendering the Japanese position on New Guinea untenable.

7 January 1944— Fast carrier Task Force 58 is officially activated under the command of Vice Admiral Marc Mitscher. The unit is built around a force of twelve aircraft carriers, eight fast battleships, six cruisers and thirty-six destroyers.

28 January 1944—Task Force 58, accompanied by Kelly Turner's invasion fleet, weighs anchor for the Marshall Islands.

31 January 1944—Operation Flintlock begins with the landing of 55,000 troops on the islands of Kwajelin, Roi-Namur, and Majuro. Majuro falls by 0955 hours that day.

5 February 1944—Kwajelin secured.

7 February 1944—With the successful conclusion to Flintlock, Raymond Spruance draws plans for an offensive strike mission against the main Japanese naval base on Truk Island.

11 February 1944—Minechi Koga decides to relocate the Combined Fleet away from Truk due to the increasing difficulty in keeping the base properly supplied, in large part a result of massively improved performances by American submarines against Japanese shipping.

17 February 1944—The carriers of Task Force 58 commence launching airstrikes against Truk Island. By the time the sun sets, 200,000 tons of merchant shipping, two cruisers and three destroyers are at the bottom of the lagoon, 225 attack planes are destroyed on the ground (with 50 shot down), and the base itself is left in flames.

Kelly Turner's amphibious invasion force, accompanied by three of Task Force 58's carriers detatched for cover, commences landings on Eniwetok.

19 February 1944—Eniwetok and Engebi are secured. These islands along with Majuro and Kwajelin will become major fleet and air bases for the United States.

21 February 1944—Prime Minister Hideki Tojo ends the deadlock in the Empire's military command by sacking Chuichi Nagumo as Navy Chief of Staff and appointing himself the Army chief and placing a puppet officer in Nagumo's former post. Following this, Minechi Koga and the Imperial General Staff develop Operational Order 73, designating a new Inner Defense Line anchored on the island of Saipan in the Mariana Islands.

22 February 1944—Task Force 58, steaming for the Mariana Islands, faces an attempted attack by Japanese squadrons which is beaten off with heavy losses by the task force's combat air patrol.

24 February 1944—Task Force 58 launches massive air raids against the Mariana islands of Saipan, Tinian, Rota, and Guam. The force has now grown to a strength of 15 carriers, 8 battleships, 21 cruisers, and 69 destroyers; the total of 112 ships including submarines is in itself larger than the whole Pacific Fleet of 1941.

26 February 1944—By this date, the United States Navy has commissioned into service eight new fleet carriers, nine light carriers, and 43 escort carriers, boarding a total of 1,777 aircraft. Japan in this time has only added three fleet carriers, four light carriers, and four escort carriers boarding 419 aircraft. Japan is losing the battle for production in all areas.

30 March 1944—Task Force 58 attacks the new Combined Fleet bases at Yap, Palau, and Ulithi islands. The squadrons roar over the installations unopposed and destroy 150 aircraft on the ground and 36 ships at anchorage.

31 March 1944— Minechi Koga, flying out to Davao in the Philippines to establish his new fleet headquarters, is lost in a storm and soon presumed dead. A briefcase, with the details of Order 73, washes ashore at Cebu and is picked up by Filipino guerrillas and soon relayed to Chester Nimitz at Pearl Harbor.

Vice Admiral Soemu Toyoda, the new Commander-in-Chief of the Imperial Combined Fleet, formulates Operation A-GO, a plan to lure the U.S. Navy within range of their major island bases in the Marianas and use combined land- and carrier-based airpower to destroy the enemy fleet. Toyoda reorganizes his forces to form the First Mobile Fleet, placing Admiral Jisaburo Ozawa in command.

Prime Minister Tojo officially announces to the Japanese people that the war is going badly for the Empire.

21 April 1944— Task Force 58 conducts airstrike missions against Hollandia and Wakde on the northern portion of New Guinea. Invasion troops are landed on Hollandia the next day and on Wadke on May 19.

23 April 1944— Senior military planners inside the U.S. War Department determine that victory in the Pacific war can only be accomplished by an invasion of Japan itself.

29 April 1944— Task Force 58 returns to Truk for a second raiding mission. In two days, the squadrons destroy an additional 100 aircraft and all remaining fuel supplies, eliminating the base as a strategic asset.

6 June 1944— American strategic planners settle on a date for Operation Olympic, the invasion of Japan: 1 October 1945.

Operation Forager commences when Task Force 58 departs Majuro for the first invasion objective, Saipan. Combined with Kelly Turner's invasion transports, the force headed for the island comprises an armada of 535 ships, with over 900 aircraft boarded on the fleet's fifteen flattops. It is the largest fleet ever assembled in history.

11 June 1944— Task Force 58 closes to attack range of Saipan and launches a first wave of air raids over Saipan, Tinian, Guam, and Rota islands, destroying 150 planes on the ground.

12 June 1944— Seven Task Force 58 carriers, dispatched by Fifth Fleet commander Raymond Spruance, launch raids on Iwo and Chichi Jima in the Bonin Islands, destroying 350 planes on the ground.

13 June 1944— Jisaburo Ozawa's First Mobile Fleet finally departs its base at Tawi Tawi for Saipan. Ozawa has a 70 ship fleet centered on nine aircraft carriers with 423 planes. He does not know that the land-based airpower he is counting on has already been destroyed.

15 June 1944— Twenty thousand Marines swarm ashore on Saipan and begin pressing inland towards the Aslito airstrip. General Yoshitsugu Saito, having misjudged the location of the expected landing zone, attempts to charge to the beaches, and 75 percent of his force are rendered casualties by airstrikes and offshore destroyer bombardment.

16 June 1944— Yoshitsugo Saito withdraws his surviving troops to prepared bunkers on Mount Tapotchau to await relief from the First Mobile Fleet.

Fifth Fleet picket submarines observe the movement of the First Mobile Fleet through the San Bernadino Strait in Philippine waters.

18 June 1944— The submarine USS *Cavalla* begins shadowing the First Mobile Fleet as it nears Guam. Task Force 58 makes radar contact for the first time with Ozawa's force the same day.

19 June 1944— The Great Marianas Turkey Shoot takes place as the Combat Air Patrols and antiaircraft defenses of Task Force 58 destroy 346 of Ozawa's planes. Fifth Fleet submarines, including the *Cavalla*, torpedo and sink the fleet carriers *Shokaku* and *Taiho*, the newly commissioned flagship of Admiral Ozawa.

20 June 1944— Finally unleashed by Raymond Spruance, Task Force 58 launches an attack at extreme range against the First Mobile Fleet. The squadrons sink the carrier *Hiyo*, inflict heavy damage on the flattops *Zuikaku*, *Junyo*, *Ryuho* and *Chiyoda*, a battleship, and a cruiser, and destroy an additional 65 Japanese planes. The American attack force returns after dark and is recovered when Admiral Marc Mitscher orders all his ships to turn their lights on.

25 June 1944— At a meeting of the War Council, Emperor Hirohito hears from his generals that the Outer Defense Line is no longer viable and that all remaining military power in the Pacific must be relocated to islands closer to Japan.

1 July 1944— Yoshitsugo Saito and his officers commit seppuku after exhorting their troops to resist to the last man. Admiral Chuichi Nagumo, posted to the island in command of a "fleet" of supply barges and coastal gunboats, shoots himself in his bunker.

Seabee construction gangs begin preparing the Aslito runways to accommodate the new long-range Boeing B-29 heavy bombers, which will be able to reach Japan from the Marianas.

The Japanese Fifteenth Army in Burma is driven into retreat before the advance of the British Fourteenth Army under Lieutenant General William Slim.

9 July 1944— The last resistance on Saipan is crushed. Nearly the entire 27,000 man garrison is killed in action, at a cost of 3,200 American dead. Additionally, thousands of Japanese civilians commit suicide.

18 July 1944— Following the Saipan disaster, Hideki Tojo is forced to resign from his governmental and military offices. General Kaniaki Kosio becomes the new Prime Minister. Soemu Toyoda gives the new government his blunt assesment that the Combined Fleet will not survive the year.

20 July 1944— American landings on Guam commence.

24 July 1944— Tinian Island is invaded by United States Marines.

26 July 1944— At a strategic conference held at Pearl Harbor and attended by President Franklin Roosevelt, Chester Nimitz, and Douglas MacArthur, MacArthur successfully makes his case for an invasion of the Philippines instead of Formosa.

27 July 1944— Seabees begin rebuilding and expanding the airfield on Tinian.

29 July 1944—Marine regiments capture Orote Airfield on Guam.

1 August 1944—All remaining Japanese resistance on Tinian is crushed.

4 August 1944—U.S. Army and Marine divisions link up on Guam, cutting the island in two.

5 August 1944—Task Force 58 carriers and battleships hit Iwo and Chichi Jima in a second round of raids, destroying shore facilities and many aircraft.

10 August 1944—Organized resistance on Guam ends, though mopping up will continue until the end of the war. Guam will become the third and largest of the new B-29 bases.

15 August 1944—By this date, American submarines have sunk 245,000 tons of enemy merchant shipping for the month. The American submarine campaign is beginning to strangle Japan's ocean lifeline.

18 August 1944—The submarine USS *Rasher* sinks the escort carrier *Taiyo* off Luzon, the twelfth flattop lost in action by the Imperial Navy since the beginning of the war. Japanese carrier strength is now down to less than 50 percent.

22 August 1944—The Japanese commence abandonment of Ulithi Island in the western Carolines.

8 September 1944—The Joint Chiefs in Washington formally approve Douglas MacArthur's plan for the invasion of the Philippines, scheduled for 20 December 1944.

Chester Nimitz executes a rotation of the commands in his Pacific forces. William Halsey replaces Raymond Spruance in command of the redesignated Third Fleet.

9 September 1944—Task Force 38 launches a series of raids against airfields at Leyte, Luzon, Mindanao, Yap, Palau, and Ulithi.

12 September 1944—William Halsey radios Chester Nimitz in Pearl Harbor, reporting that Japanese airpower in the Philippines sector is virtually extinct and that the archipelago itself is wide open to attack. He urges abandonment of the coming Pelileu invasion in favor of an all-out effort against Leyte for October. Because preparation for Pelileu is too far advanced, Halsey's first recommendation is rejected but his second to advance D-Day on Leyte by two months is approved.

At an Allied conference in Canada, Franklin Roosevelt and Winston Churchill concur that the balance of the Allied effort can now be shifted against Japan, now that Nazi Germany is losing the war in Europe.

15 September 1944—Pelileu is invaded by U.S. Marine forces. A bloodbath ensues as Marines face fanatical defenders dug into mountainous terrain.

21 September 1944—Task Force 38 launches another series of airstrikes on Luzon.

22 September 1944—Ulithi falls without a shot to a U.S. Marine regiment. The atoll is ideal for a major fleet anchorage. Seabees commence construction of dock facilities almost at once.

23 September 1944—Seabees finish refurbishing the airstrip on Pelileu, which is immediately pressed into service for air support against the Japanese garrison.

30 September 1944—American and Filipino guerrillas mobilize to support the coming invasion.

1 October 1944—The "Happy Time" for American submarines in the Pacific begins. By the end of the month's campaign, the boats will claim 328,000 tons of Japanese shipping, with 185,000 tons being destroyed by American planes. The only reason for diminishing sinkings afterward is due to the submarines literally running out of targets.

4 October 1944—Task Force 38 completes replenishment and rest at Ulithi. Two days afterward, the force commences a ten day raiding campaign against targets in the Philippines, Formosa, the Ryukyu and Bonin islands.

11 October 1944—Admiral Soemu Toyoda and senior military planners develop the Sho strategic operational portfolio, a series of defense plans for the three expected targets of American invasion. Sho-1 is activated when the Philippines are definitely identified as the next American objective. The plan will involve last-ditch defenses on the ground combined with a two-pronged battleship offensive on the landing zone, and kamikaze suicide plane attacks on the enemy fleet. The remaining operational carriers of the First Mobile Fleet, almost completely without aircraft, are to be sacrificed as decoys to draw the American fleet away from the beachheads.

14 October 1944—Task Force 38 completes a three-day attack upon airbases on Formosa, destroying 280 planes and breaking Japanese airpower in the area. The force then puts about and returns to rendezvous with the rest of the Third and Seventh Fleets marshalling for the invasion of Leyte.

15 October 1944—The Japanese garrison on Pelileu is exterminated, barring a few scattered holdouts who will continue fighting until November.

17 October 1944—The three task forces of the First Mobile Fleet set out from their bases to be on station to intercept the American invasion forces, on a mission which is already doomed to failure even before it has begun.

20 October 1944—General Douglas MacArthur finally returns to the Philippines, commencing his crusade of liberation by landing on Leyte with Lieutenant General Walter Krueger's Sixth Army. In 24 hours, 200,000 troops will pour ashore on Leyte.

23 October 1944—The heavily outmatched First Mobile Fleet task forces are finally entering Philippine waters. The two battleship forces under admirals Soiji Nishimura, Kiyode Shima, and Takeo Kurita thread their way through the Sibuyan Sea while Jisaburo Ozawa's six flattops, with a total of 116 planes, take station off Cape Engaño NE of Luzon.

24 October 1944—The three-day Battle of Leyte Gulf commences, involving scattered action all over the Philippines sector. By the time it is finished, the Empire's naval power is broken, with the Japanese losing four aircraft carriers (including the *Zuikaku*, last of the surviving Pearl Harbor raiders), three battleships, ten cruisers, seventeen destroyers, and 89 planes shot down. The

Americans lose one light carrier, two escort carriers (one to the second kamikaze attack of the war), and three destroyers. Several of the rebuilt battleships from Pearl Harbor participated in a night action, the last ever battleship duel. Although the decoy portion of the Sho-1 plan did work as anticipated, drawing away William Halsey's Third Fleet, it made absolutely no difference to the final outcome.

27 October 1944— The kamikaze campaign against the American fleet begins in earnest, inflicting damage upon the carriers *Essex, Intrepid,* and *Hancock,* and the CVL *Cabot.*

11 November 1944— The Imperial Navy hastily commissions the new aircraft carrier *Shinano* into service, a 69,000 ton heavily armored monster converted on the slipway from the third *Yamato*-class battleship under construction.

24 November 1944— The first B-29 missions against Japan launch from Saipan.

27 November 1944— The submarine USS *Archerfish* catches the carrier *Shinano* in the Inland Sea on her shakedown cruise and sinks her with a full spread of torpedoes.

8 December 1944— Naval and Army Air Force planes begin a 72 day bombing campaign against Iwo Jima. The planes will be joined by Third and Seventh Fleet cruisers and destroyers rotating in and out providing offshore bombardment.

15 December 1944— Douglas MacArthur's forces land on Mindoro Island, the last stepping stone to Luzon. That same day, 53 kamikaze planes are transferred to the island and attack the landing ships, sinking two LSTs.

18 December 1944— The newly commissioned carrier *Unyru,* passing through the Shimonoseki Strait (where the USS *Wyoming* fought the Japanese 81 years earlier) is torpedoed and sunk by the submarine USS *Redfish.* The *Unryu,* like the *Shinano,* was carrying Okha manned flying bombs on board when she was caught and destroyed.

20 December 1944— The Imperial General Staff inform the Japanese garrisons on Leyte that they can expect no further reinforcement or resupply. They will begin running out of food and ammunition within two weeks.

31 December 1944— Task Force 38 departs Ulithi, after replenishment, for a renewed series of airstrikes on Okinawa, Formosa, and the Philippines to reduce the kamikaze menace.

6 January 1945— The Third and Seventh Fleets enter Lingayen Gulf for the invasion of the main Philippine island of Luzon. They are met by a renewed wave of kamikaze assault planes and manned suicide torpedoes.

9 January 1945— Douglas MacArthur's forces land on Luzon. The Sixth Army debarks 100,000 troops on the Lingayen beaches in one day. Manila is 100 miles from the landing zone.

13 January 1945— Kamikaze attacks have inflicted a cost of four ships sunk, thirty-nine damaged with a casualty count of 738 dead and 1,400 wounded in the course of the Philippines campaign to date.

21 January 1945 — Task Force 38 hits Japanese airbases on Okinawa and Formosa, destroying 100 aircraft on the ground.

22 January 1945 — American air raids are conducted against the fortress on Corregidor Island.

26 January 1945 — Raymond Spruance is rotated back in command of the redesignated Fifth Fleet.

27 January 1945 — U.S. amphibious forces depart Pearl Harbor. Destination: Iwo Jima.

28 January 1945 — Mindoro falls.

29 January 1945 — Amphibious landings are made at Subic Bay, north of Bataan.

31 January 1945 — The U.S. 11th Airborne Division is landed at the south entrance to Manila Bay.

3 February 1945 — The U.S. Sixth Army is at the gates of Manila. The attack is launched three days later, with the Japanese garrison putting up stiff resistance. Army troops liberate the POW camps holding 4,000 starved survivors of the Bataan Death March.

9 February 1945 — Task Force 58 departs Ulithi for air raids against Tokyo and Okinawa to suppress enemy air forces prior to the planned Iwo Jima landings.

14 February 1945 — Fifth Fleet PT boats enter Manila Bay as initial landings are made on the peninsula of Bataan.

15 February 1945 — The main U.S. landings on Bataan's southern end complete the encirclement of Manila.

16 February 1945 — The 4,000 man Japanese garrison on Corregidor Island is slaughtered in a surprise attack with paratroopers and amphibious assault. Corregidor's capture nails shut the only possible escape route for the Japanese in Manila.

     Battleships of the Fifth Fleet commence shore bombardment on Iwo Jima.

19 February 1945 — Thirty thousand Marines swarm ashore on Iwo Jima, 800 miles south of the Japanese home islands. The 22,000 man Japanese garrison retreats to the interior of the eight square mile island, fighting behind hardened pillboxes and in caves.

21 February 1945 — The kamikazes reappear, crashing into the *Saratoga* and sinking the escort carrier *Bismarck Sea*.

23 February 1945 — U.S. Marines raise the Stars and Stripes on Mount Suribachi. Effective control is secured at the landing zones and the main airfield.

25 February 1945 — Following a review by 20th Air Force commander Curtis LeMay of the largely ineffectual bombing campaign against Japan to date, the first Fire Raid is conducted, with 334 B-29s coming in low and unloading incendiary ordnance. Sixteen square miles of the capital city of Tokyo are reduced to burned wasteland in the strike.

1 March 1945—Fifth Fleet aircraft commence initial softening-up raids in the Ryukyus preparatory to the Okinawa invasion.

3 March 1945—Manila falls. The last scattered resistance on Corregidor is ended. The capture of the Philippines cuts Japan off from all resources in the East Indies.

9 March 1945—Another Tokyo fire raid, involving 279 B-29s and 1,700 tons of ordnance, results in a firestorm which kills 84,000 civilians.

19 March 1945—A combined conventional and kamikaze air attack against Task Force 58 results in heavy damage to the carriers *Yorktown*, *Wasp*, *Enterprise*, and *Franklin*. The latter ship suffers chain-reaction explosions which she survives with a seven hour firefighting effort, but at a cost of 830 dead and 300 wounded. The *Franklin* is put out of action for the rest of the war.

21 March 1945—Over 150 fighters from the flattops *Hornet*, *Bennington*, *Wasp*, and *Belleau Wood* intercept and shoot down a squadron of Japanese Betty bombers carrying Okha manned flying bombs.

1 April 1945—The invasion of Okinawa commences, with 60,000 U.S. troops landing unopposed on the beaches. The Japanese garrison have withdrawn to prepared defensive bunkers to await the assault forces, a strategy which insures a very bloody fight for the island.

3 April 1945—The Soviet Union announces it will not renew the Neutrality Pact signed between it and Japan in April 1941. They have already agreed, at the Yalta Conference, to enter the war on the Allied side concurrent with the invasion of Japan.

4 April 1945—The Imperial Cabinet resigns. Baron Kantoro Suzuki, a retired admiral, is made the new Prime Minister in mid–April, and his government is charged in secret with the task of finding a means to effect an armistice with the Allies.

6 April 1945—The kamikazes join the battle for Okinawa. In the first attack against the Fifth Fleet, a massive formation of 355 planes manages to push its way past the CAP screen over the fleet, next encountering the antiaircraft defenses. Twenty-two planes manage to survive to crash into various ships and sink the destroyers *Bush*, *Calhoun*, and *Emmons*.

The "Special Attack Fleet" of Admiral Seichi Ito, consisting of the super-battleship *Yamato* accompanied by the light cruiser *Yahagi* and eight destroyers, is sent to Okinawa on its own kamikaze mission to challenge the 1,500-ship U.S. Fifth Fleet. Its passage through the Bungo Strait is observed by American submarines.

7 April 1945—Task Force 58 planes hit the "Special Attack Fleet" with 900 aircraft over two hours and sink the cruiser *Yahagi*, four destroyers, and the *Yamato* in the East China Sea. Though four of the destroyers manage to return to home waters, it is the finish of the Imperial Japanese Navy.

12 April 1945—Over 150 kamikaze planes are shot down by the guns and planes of the Fifth Fleet, though one Okha flying bomb gets through to sink a destroyer. Increasingly, kamikaze attacks will target the picket destroyers providing early radar warning for the U.S. fleet.

13 April 1945— President Franklin D. Roosevelt dies of a brain hemorrhage in Warm Springs, Georgia. Harry S Truman succeeds Roosevelt as the 33rd President of the United States.

19 April 1945— The Fifth Fleet provides intensive offshore bombardment and tactical air support for a new push against stubborn Japanese resistance on Okinawa.

23 April 1945— Remaining Japanese resistance on Palawan and Cebu in the Philippines is crushed.

24 April 1945— The U.S. Navy begins clamping down a total blockade on all Japanese ports. Since before the Iwo Jima landings, American submarines have been operating intensively off home waters in combination with commerce-raiding sorties by carrier task forces and mine-barrages from B-29s to completely close down the sea lanes leading into Japan. Nagoya becomes the first port to totally cease operations.

25 April 1945— President Harry Truman is finally informed by Secretary of War Henry L. Stimson and General Leslie Groves of the Manhattan Project, the American atomic weapons effort, and that two designs have been developed, with one scheduled to be test detonated in New Mexico in July.

3 May 1945— The kamikazes have their best day against the Fifth Fleet, sinking 17 destroyers. The destroyer *Aaron Ward* suffers hits by ten suicide planes before nightfall, but manages to remain afloat.

8 May 1945— Nazi Germany surrenders to the United Nations following the suicide of Adolf Hitler on April 30 and subsequent Soviet capture of the Nazi capital of Berlin. Japan is now totally alone against the Allied forces. U.S. troops in Europe are rotated home for leave, but earmarked as replacement reserves for the invasion of Japan.

10 May 1945— U.S. Army troops reach the outskirts of the Okinawan capital of Naha.

11 May 1945— Two kamikaze planes hit Marc Mitscher's flagship, the USS *Bunker Hill*. Fires on board kill 396 of her crew and render the flattop unoperational. She is put out of action for the rest of the war.

14 May 1945— A lone kamikaze plane crashes into the forward deck of the USS *Enterprise*, forcing her withdrawal from the theater of operations for a major overhaul. The *Enterprise* has been away from the United States for over 500 days, having participated in every major action in the Pacific from Pearl Harbor onward.

16 May 1945— Japanese troops continuing to resist in scattered pockets outside the Philippine capital of Manila are hit with over 300 tons of napalm. The use of napalm largely breaks remaining Japanese resistance in the Philippines.

17 May 1945— Japan's last capital ship at sea, the cruiser *Haguro*, is sunk by British destroyers in the Strait of Malacca.

20 May 1945— Japanese divisions are withdrawn from China to reinforce the defense of the Home Islands.

25 May 1945— U.S. strategic planners schedule Operation Olympic, the invasion of the Japanese southern home island of Kyushu, for November 1. Logistical preparations commence shortly thereafter. Operation Coronet, the invasion of the main home island of Honshu, is tentatively scheduled for May of 1946.

27 May 1945— The port of Tokyo is closed. The same day, William Halsey is rotated back in command of the redesignated Third Fleet.

28 May 1945— The Japanese launch their final kamikaze assault against the Third Fleet. For the loss of 150 planes they manage to sink only one destroyer.

30 May 1945— The Okinawan capital of Naha is in U.S. hands, except for the airfield which is taken seven days later. The remaining Japanese on Okinawa will end up trapped in the Oroku Peninsula.

17 June 1945— Japanese garrison commander General Mitsuru Ushiijima commits seppuku after ordering his surviving forces to fight to the last man. U.S. Army troops breach the Japanese defensive line at Oroku.

18 June 1945— Japan's major cities are crossed off the 20th Air Force's industrial targets list, having been almost completely burned out. The B-29s begin hitting the secondary cities.

20 June 1945— For the first time in the war, over 1,000 Japanese soldiers surrender on Okinawa rather than fight on suicidially. Okinawan civilians also begin surrendering once they are convinced that they will not be abused or massacred by U.S. troops.

22 June 1945— Okinawa finally falls. In the 81 day fight for the island, only 7,800 of the 118,000 man Japanese garrison were taken alive. American casualties total 36,480 wounded and 12,520 dead. At sea, the U.S. Navy suffered the loss of 34 ships sunk, 368 ships damaged, and 4,900 personnel killed. In the kamikaze assaults, the Japanese lost 7,800 attack planes.

9 July 1945— The Third Fleet, with Sir Bernard Rawlings' British Far East Group attatched (designated Task Force 31), arrives in Japanese home waters. Three days later, Third Fleet planes commence bombings on the airfields and remaining industrial installations in and around Tokyo.

12 July 1945— The Japanese government begins sending peace-feelers toward the Soviet Union in the hopes of their mediation with the Allied powers. The Soviet government ignores the Japanese contact.

14 July 1945— For the first time, the Japanese Home Islands are shelled by Third Fleet battleships, hitting the port of Kamamishi.

16 July 1945— The first plutonium-based atomic bomb, *Trinity*, is successfully test-detonated at Alamogordo, New Mexico. The blast yield measures out at equivalent to 20,000 tons of TNT. The design for *Trinity*, based on the principle of implosion to achieve critical mass, will be the pattern for future atomic weapons.

21 July 1945— U.S. radio broadcasts call for Japan to surrender or be destroyed.

24 July 1945— In a four day campaign, Task Force 38 and Task Force 31 planes hit the Japanese naval base at Kure, sinking most of Japan's remaining warships marooned in port, including two aircraft carriers (with three damaged beyond repair) and the last four battleships. That same day, President Harry Truman formally signs the order authorizing the atomic bombing of Japan.

25 July 1945— Through mediators in Switzerland, the Japanese leadership informs the Allies that they are willing to accept terms for armistice but not unconditional surrender. The Imperial General Staff divides the Home Islands into five defensive districts under independent command. They have 9,000 kamikaze planes still held in reserve. Civilians are drilled to fight with bamboo spears, and preparations are made for a last-ditch defense against the expected American invasion.

 The cruiser USS *Indianapolis* pulls into the anchorage at Tinian Island to deliver the components of *Little Boy*, a uranium gun-type atomic bomb, to the 509th Composite Group. She pulls out the same day, under radio silence and continuing conditions of secrecy — meaning her sailing plan has not been filed with CINCPAC.

26 July 1945— The Big Three issue the Potsdam Proclamation, calling for Japan to unconditionally surrender or face "prompt and utter destruction." In response, Prime Minster Suzuki, meaning to issue a statement of "no comment," makes the unfortunate response of *mokusatsu*, which means to "kill with silence" or "treat with contempt." This is taken as an outright rejection of the surrender demand.

27 July 1945— Japan's cities are leaflet-bombed. The leaflets warn of coming air raids, pointing out to the people that their military can no longer protect them, and urge surrender.

28 July 1945— The destroyer USS *Callaghan* is the last ship sunk by kamikaze aircraft.

29 July 1945— Third Fleet warships shell naval and air bases on Honshu.

30 July 1945— The cruiser USS *Indianapolis* is torpedoed by the Japanese submarine I-58 and sinks before an SOS can be transmitted. Because of the secrecy attending her mission, it is three days before the ship is posted missing. Only 316 of her 1,000 man crew survive to be rescued.

3 August 1945— The naval and air blockade of Japan is now complete, totally cutting off the nation from the rest of the world.

6 August 1945— The B-29 *Enola Gay* drops *Little Boy* on the Japanese port city of Hiroshima. Detonating 2,000 feet above ground zero with a blast-yield of 21 kilotons, the bomb immediately kills 70,000 people. Burns, injuries, and radiation sickness will claim an additional 30,000 through the week. Within a year, up to 54 percent of the civilian population succumbs to radiation-induced diseases.

8 August 1945— The Soviet Union declares war on Japan. Forty divisions of the Red Army swarm across the Manchurian border, routing Japanese troops all along the front line.

9 August 1945— The B-29 *Bock's Car* drops *Fat Man*, a *Trinity*-class atomic bomb, on the city of Nagasaki. Dropped off-target, the hills surrounding the district where the bomb explodes screens the force of the blast (17.5 kilotons), and only 30,000 persons are killed outright, but civilian deaths will again reach the 54 percent level within a year. The atomic bomb proves to be the most compact and efficent killing machine ever invented.

Hours after Nagasaki's destruction, the War Council meets in emergency session in an air raid bunker under the Obunko Library in Tokyo. In an unprecedented move, Emperor Hirohito himself directs that Japan must surrender to the Allies, according to the demand of the Potsdam Proclamation.

13 August 1945 — Japanese cables transmitted through Switzerland to American Secretary of State James F. Byrnes offer the Empire's surrender but ask for the preservation of the Emperor's status. Secretary Byrnes replies that the Emperor would be "subject to" the Supreme Commander of the Allied Powers.

14 August 1945 — After reassuring themselves that Secretary Byrnes' response does not call for the abolition of the Imperial institution, the Japanese leadership communicate that they will surrender unconditionally to the Allied powers. At Pearl Harbor, Chester Nimitz issues an order suspending all further offensive operations. Preparations for Operation Olympic are immediately suspended.

15 August 1945 — Despite an attempted coup d'état by fanatical Imperial Army officers, the Emperor's formal broadcast (recorded the night before) announcing Japan's surrender to the Allies goes out over the NHK Radio Network. It is the first time ever that the people have heard the voice of the Living God. General Korechika Anami, the War Minister, commits seppuku, blaming himself for the Empire's defeat. It is the first of a wave of suicides among the officer corps.

Ernest King issues formal orders to Chester Nimitz at Pearl Harbor terminating the war. Operation Olympic is cancelled. Congress appoints Douglas MacArthur as Supreme Commander for the Allied Powers. He will rule Japan during the occupation as the de facto shogun.

16 August 1945 — Unable to accept the surrender of the Empire, Vice Admiral Matome Ugaki leads a final kamikaze sortie of eleven planes, all volunteer pilots, out to Okinawa. His last radio message stated that he was about to crash into a warship, but no Allied naval units report any Japanese planes in their skies. Ugaki's fate remains a mystery to this day.

28 August 1945 — The Third Fleet enters Tokyo Bay, and the first occupation troops are landed at Yokohama.

2 September 1945 — The instruments of surrender are signed aboard the Third Fleet flagship USS *Missouri*. Peace with Japan ends the Second World War.

15 September 1945 — The USS *Enterprise* returns to the Pacific to ferry American troops home from the Pacific. She will be decommissioned from active service following this mission.

U.S. Navy minesweepers commence the task of clearing the sea lanes of the thousands of mines filling the China Seas and Japanese home waters.

November 1945 — The USS *Midway*, lead ship in a new class of aircraft carrier ordered in 1943 and incorporating a fully armored flight deck and large enough to board an air group of 120 planes, is launched. The remaining six vessels of the *Essex*-class building program are cancelled.

1 January 1946— Emperor Hirohito goes on radio to publicly disavow the traditional Imperial concept of the Emperor as the Living God. It is the signal heralding the building of a new, modern Japan. Douglas MacArthur's staff begin work on a new, American-style constitution — which includes granting women the vote. In addition, MacArthur orders the institution of land reform, the fosterage of the trade union movement, and the breaking of the power of the *zaibatsu*, the entrenched industrial combines which backed the previous fascist regime.

1 July 1946— The carrier *Saratoga*, along with a number of veteran battleships and Axis vessels, are assembled at Bikini Atoll for the Operation Crossroads atomic tests. The *Saratoga* is sunk in the second blast, Test Shot Baker, 25 days later.

4 July 1946— Fulfilling the pledge made by Franklin Roosevelt, the Philippines are granted full independence from the United States. Even then, there are still Japanese soldiers fighting on as guerrillas, unaware that the war is over, as there are on scattered islands all over the Pacific. Some will still be in the jungles 40 years later.

1948— The British withdraw from India, ending a century of the Raj. It is the beginning of the end of the British Empire.

1949— Communist forces under Mao Tse Tung defeat Chiang Kai-Shek and his Nationalist government, proclaiming the establishment of the People's Republic of China. The Nationalists withdraw to Formosa, which remains separated from China to this day.

August 1949— The Soviet Union explodes its first atomic bomb. The United States and the Soviet Union, having already clashed with an attempted blockade of the western zone of Berlin, begin a Cold War and arms race which will last for the next fifty years.

June 1950— Communist North Korean forces invade South Korea, beating South Korean and American forces down into a small perimeter at Pusan. President Harry Truman gains U.N sanction against the Soviet Union for backing the invasion and authorizes military action to rescue South Korea. The war, into which Communist China will intervene, will finally end with a cease-fire concluded in 1953 and a stalemate at the 38th parallel which is still in force.

1951— The occupation of Japan officially ends. The country is thoroughly rebuilt, modernized, democratized, and pacified. In the succeeding years, she will become one of the world's leading economic powers.

1953— Both the United States and the Soviet Union explode hydrogen bombs, introducing thermonuclear weaponry to the world's arsenals.

1956— The French are finally driven from Vietnam following the victory of the Vietnamese Peoples' Army at Dien Bhen Phu. The Democratic Republic of

Vietnam is proclaimed in Hanoi under the leadership of Ho Chi Minh, but the United States only recognizes the Republic of Vietnam based in Saigon under the leadership of Bao Dai. President Dwight D. Eisenhower will soon send U.S. military advisers to South Vietnam, beginning America's involvement in what is already a decade-old civil war.

The USS *Enterprise* is officially stricken from the Navy list and condemned to eventual scrapping. William Halsey begins a petition drive to preserve his one-time flagship as a floating monument. The effort will prove too little and too late, and the Big E will be scrapped in 1958.

1961— The brand new, nuclear-powered supercarrier USS *Enterprise* is commissioned into fleet service. She was building on the slipways even as her namesake was being scrapped. The *Enterprise* continues in service to this day, having undergone a full modernization in 1998.

24 July 1969— The USS *Hornet*, still in fleet service, recovers the Apollo 11 space capsule with astronauts Neil Armstrong, Buzz Aldrin (the first two humans to walk on the moon), and Michael Collins, in the Pacific Ocean. *Essex*-class carriers have been involved in at-sea recovery of space capsules since Project Mercury in 1961.

1983— The USS *Bunker Hill*, last of the *Essex*-class ships in active fleet service, is decommissioned. Only the *Lexington* remains, serving as the fleet training carrier. Having become completely outmoded, the remaining *Essex*es will all be scrapped, barring the *Intrepid, Yorktown, Lexington,* and *Hornet,* which eventually become museum ships.

19 May 1998— An expedition led by Dr. Robert Ballard (discoverer of the *Titanic*) and including American and Japanese veterans of the Battle of Midway as passengers, locates the wreck of the USS *Yorktown,* lying upright on the ocean bottom in 16,000 feet of water 330 miles northeast of the island of Midway.

25 August 1999— A French oceanographic expedition accompanied by the modern assault ship USS *Belleau Wood* recovers artifacts from the wreck of the superbattleship *Yamato,* lying at the bottom of the East China Sea 250 miles northwest of Okinawa. The items, including the ship's bell, are intended for display at the Maritime Museum at Kure, Japan, the port where the *Yamato* and her sister *Musashi* were built.

Annotated Bibliography

For further reading on the Second World War in the Pacific:

Adcock, Al. *Escort Carriers in Action: Warships No. 9*. Carrollton, Texas: Squadron/Signal Publications, 1996.

    One of a series of guidebooks published by Squadron/Signal, a hobbyists' source for information on warplanes, warships, uniforms, and various military subjects. Includes comprehensive photographs, deck plans and profile drawings, detail drawings, and historical-technical text.

Ballard, Robert D., and Rick Archbold. *The Lost Ships of Guadalcanal*. Toronto: Madison Press Books, 1993.

    Dr. Robert Ballard's book detailing his 1992 expedition to explore the wrecks of Allied and Japanese warships located on the floor of Ironbottom Sound, meshed with a detailed history of the Guadalcanal Campaign of 1942. Illustrated with both period and expedition photographs, maps, and paintings by artist Ken Marschall. Excellent as both a text of history and scientific adventure.

_____ and _____. *Return to Midway*. Washington D.C.: National Geographic Society, and Toronto: Madison Press Books, 1999.

    Dr. Robert Ballard's excellent book, lavishly illustrated with period and expedition photos, maps, and paintings by artist Ken Marschall, detailing both the history of the Battle of Midway and the oceanographer's 1998 expedition to the battle site to search for the wrecks of the aircraft carriers sunk on June 4 and 6, 1942, culminating in the successful discovery of the *USS Yorktown*.

Barker, A.J. *Pearl Harbor: Ballantine's Illustrated History of World War II. Battle Book n. 10*. New York: Ballantine Books, 1969.

    British military historian A.J. Barker's detailed examination of the Pearl Harbor attack of December 7, 1941, with particular focus on the political and diplomatic machinations between the United States and Japan and a comprehensive description of the Japanese strategy and its successful tactical execution as well as its overall strategic failure.

Castillo, John. *The Pacific War 1941–1945*. New York: William Morrow, 1981.

    John Castillo's book is the definitive one-volume history of the Second World War in the Pacific Theatre, detailing the war on all fronts from China-Burma-India to Australia, from Manchuria to Midway, from the South Pacific

to the Arctic. Details all ground, aerial, and naval combat actions throughout the course of the war.

Dunnigan, James F. and Albert A. Nofi. *Victory at Sea: World War II in the Pacific*.
New York: William Morrow, 1995.
   The authors of *Dirty Little Secrets* present a one-volume analysis of the
Pacific War. Includes detailed breakdowns of campaigns, balance of forces,
ships, planes, analyses of logistics, war production, information warfare and
technology, and political and diplomatic intrigues. Also provided are cap-
sule-biographies of the significant figures of the war, a detailed chronologue
of the war, and speculative analyses regarding the outcome of battleship duels,
the possible defeat of Japan even following an American defeat at Midway,
and the course and outcome of the never-executed invasion of the Home
Islands. Can be read in sequence or randomly. A treasure-trove of handy
facts, tables, and historical research. Very highly recommended.

Ireland, Bernard. *Jane's Naval History of World War II*. New York and London:
HarperCollins, 1998.
   From the publishers of the definitive guides to military hardware and
the world's warfleets. Focuses upon ships, weapons, technology, and the strategy and tactics employed by the Allies in both the Atlantic and Pacific.

Jablonski, Edward. *Airwar* (two volumes). Garden City, N.Y.: Doubleday, 1971.
   Incorporates four histories of the war in the air 1941–45: *Outraged Skies*,
Wings of Fire, *Terror From The Sky*, and *Tragic Victories*, and published as a
Book Club two-volume set. Covers both the war against Nazi Germany over
Europe, Africa and the Middle East and the war against Japan over the Pacific
and China.

Jane's Fighting Ships of World War II. Crescent Books, a division of Random House
Value Publishing Inc., 1998.
   Reprint volume of the original material from the 1942–46 editions of
Jane's Fighting Ships, the internationally recognized guidebook to the world's
warfleets.

Jones, James. *World War II*. New York: Ballantine Books, 1975.
   The author of *From Here to Eternity* tells the story of World War II from
the point of view of the soldier, offering a first-person perspective. Lavishly
illustrated with combat art. Jones' narrative develops its particular angle on
the evolution of a soldier.

Marshall, Ian. *Armored Ships*. Charlottesville, VA: Howell Press, 1997.
   Valuable more as an art book, featuring author Ian Marshall's superb
watercolors of battleships and armored cruisers but includes accompanying
historical text which is concise and well-presented. Warships from 1880 to
1945 featured.

Mason, R.H.P., and J.G. Caiger. *A History of Japan*, revised edition. Rutland, Vt.,
and Tokyo: Charles E. Tuttle, 1997.
   A handy pocket-sized one-volume overview of Japanese history.

Miller, Nathan. *The U.S. Navy: An Illustrated History*. New York: American Heritage Publishing Co., and Annapolis: Naval Institute Press, 1977.

The American Heritage history of the United States Navy, with photos, engravings, and period paintings. Revolutionary War to Vietnam.

Naval History. Annapolis: United States Naval Institute.
Bimonthly publication by the Naval Institute on naval combat history, strategy, and biographical articles of famous sea commanders in American history.

Potter, E.B. *The Naval Academy Illustrated History of the United States Navy*. New York: Thomas Y. Crowell, 1971.
Essentially the same comprehensive history of the United States Navy from the Revolutionary War to Vietnam, but with considerably more detail than the American Heritage/Naval Institute Press volume.

Reynolds, Clark G. *The Fast Carriers: The Forging of an Air Navy*. New York: McGraw-Hill, 1968. Revised edition, Annapolis: Naval Institute Press, 1992.
Detailed and complex history of the evolution of carrier warfare and the fast carrier task force concept during the Pacific War, incorporating biographical details of the air admirals, discussion of battle and theatre tactics, and offering criticisms of certain officers where appropriate. Includes maps, statistics, and organizational tables of U.S. Navy carrier task forces campaign-by-campaign.

Sea Classics. Canoga Park, CA: Challenge Publications.
Monthly publication of historical and contemporary articles on ships of the United States Navy and foreign navies, with periodic special edition issues. Also covers warship preservation efforts.

Smith, Michael C. *Essex Class Carriers in Action: Warships No. 10*. Carrollton, Texas: Squadron/Signal Publications, 1997.
Another volume in the Squadron/Signal military hardware guidebook series. Includes combat history, plan- and deck-views, colorplates of camouflage patterns, and detail drawings of weapons, planes, and radar systems mounted by *Essex*-class carriers.

Steinberg, Rafael, and the editors of Time/Life Books. *World War II: Island Fighting*. Alexandria, VA: Time/Life Books, 1978.
Volume in Time/Life's World War II book series detailing the Guadalcanal and Solomons campaigns.

Sulzberger, C.L. *The American Heritage Picture History of World War II*. New York: American Heritage/Bonanza Books, 1966.
Another of American Heritage's illustrated histories, this one focusing on the Second World War. A fine coffee-table edition with enough detail to be engaging.

Taylor, A.J.P. (Editor-in-Chief) *The Illustrated History of the World Wars*. New York: Galahad Books, 1978.
One-volume history of World Wars I and II, illustrated with photographs, maps, and charts as well as period propaganda art. Includes tables on casualties and monetary expenses of both conflicts. Special section devoted to Battle of Midway.

Terzibaschitch, Stefan. *Battleships of the U.S. Navy in World War II*. New York: Bonanza Books, 1977.

    Comprehensive guide to the operational battleships serving in the U.S. Navy during World War II, illustrated with photographs and plan-view drawings.

Zilch, Arthur, and the editors of Time/Life Books. *World War II: The Rising Sun*. Alexandria, VA: Time/Life Books, 1978.

    Volume in Time/Life's World War II series focusing upon the opening phase of the Pacific War and Japan's early march of conquest across East Asia and the Western and Southern Pacific.

Index